Cambridge Studies in Social Anthropology

NO. 7

CONTEXTS OF KINSHIP:
AN ESSAY IN THE FAMILY SOCIOLOGY OF
THE GONJA OF NORTHERN GHANA

Cambridge Studies in Social Anthropology

General Editors

M. FORTES, E. R. LEACH, J. R. GOODY, S. J. TAMBIAH

CONTEXTS OF KINSHIP

An Essay in the Family Sociology of
the Gonja of Northern Ghana

ESTHER N. GOODY

Fellow of New Hall, Cambridge

CAMBRIDGE
AT THE UNIVERSITY PRESS
1973

Published by the Syndics of the Cambridge University Press
Bentley House, 200 Euston Road, London NW1 2DB
American Branch: 32 East 57th Street, New York, N.Y. 10022

© Cambridge University Press 1973

Library of Congress Catalogue Card Number: 72–78892

ISBN: 0 521 08583 7

Printed in Great Britain by
C. Tinling & Co. Ltd., London and Prescot

Contents

Tables

Illustrations

ix

Preface

This book is the result of fieldwork I carried out in central Gonja from July 1956 to March 1957 and again from July to December 1957. Since that time, I have worked in eastern Gonja (Kpembe, April to September 1964) and in western Gonja (Bole, July to October 1965). In addition some time was spent at the administrative capital in Damongo. The observations made and numerical material collected in other regions of Gonja broadly confirm the data presented here, and for a few key problems extracts of this later material are given in the Appendices. Otherwise I have tried to restrict the present study to central Gonja where language, population density, and some aspects of the economy produce a particular set of background conditions only partially shared by other regions.

This study of central Gonja kinship was first written up as a doctoral dissertation for the University of Cambridge. But until I had been able to work in other parts of the Gonja state I felt that its publication would be premature. Although very little material from these later field trips actually appears here, it provides boundaries to the analysis of central Gonja which would otherwise have been lacking. The original thesis has now been extensively rewritten using in particular a deepened understanding of the relational idioms, but keeping to the field data from central Gonja.

I am indebted to others for many kinds of assistance in the planning, fieldwork and analysis which have led to this volume. The introduction to modern sociology provided by the seminars of Everett Wilson and Alvin Gouldner at Antioch College set me off on the systematic search for 'social facts'. As a graduate student in the Department of Social Anthropology at the University of Cambridge, I found that while the subject matter had shifted to small-scale societies, the concern with an interaction between social, psychological and cultural levels of analysis was still important, and for me more accessible. I must thank the members of the social anthropology research seminar[1] who have

[1] I am particularly grateful for Edmund Leach's persistent incredulity that Gonja men should be willing to support elderly female kin, for I had come to take this as self-evident.

Preface

listened patiently, and commented pertinently on various versions of much of what follows. These thanks are due in a very special way to Professor Fortes, whose writings on the Tallensi and the Ashanti have been a constant source of ideas, questions, and comparative material. Indeed the work of Professor Fortes and of my husband, Jack Goody, provides such a fundamental basis, both conceptual and ethnographic, for any study of northern Ghana that I am sure that I have often 'borrowed' from them without acknowledgement. I am delighted to be able to take this opportunity to express my debt to them both.

Assistance of a different kind made possible the fieldwork in northern Ghana. The first period of research, on which this study is mainly based, was financed by the Ford Foundation's Foreign Area Training Fellowship programme which generously allowed me both an initial period in the field and a return trip the following year. The Bartle Frere Fund of the University of Cambridge also made a grant towards this first research. Later periods of field work were sponsored by the Wenner-Gren Foundation of New York, and by a grant from the Child Development Research Unit of the University of Ghana. Equally vital support came from the hospitality of Jim and Catherine Panton, and the engineers of the Gonja Development Corporation, and from Father Vachon and Father Herity of the White Fathers' Mission in Damongo, whose welcome never failed, whatever the hour.

I have not space to thank individually all those whose interest and patience made fieldwork in central Gonja so rewarding. My field assistants, Adamu Dari, Kofi Mahama, James Salifu, and in particular Mahama Katangi, deserve special mention, as do my closest friends among the women of all three social estates, Bumunana, the Damba Yiri Wuritche, the Supini Wuritche, Grunshi and Adisa. The Busunu Akurma, Nyiwuledji, the KabiasiWura and the MankpaWura gave particularly freely of their time. Many are no longer living, and others will never see this book, yet without them it would never have been possible.

Cambridge   E. N. G.
2 January 1972

xii

For Ted and Mary Newcomb

Symbols used in the text

△   indicates living male

▲   indicates dead male

○   indicates living female

●   indicates dead female

⊘   indicates male or female

⊘—⊘   indicates full siblings

⊘ ⊘   indicates half-siblings

⊘ʔ⊘   indicates classificatory siblings ('siblings')

○=△   indicates marriage

○≠△   indicates divorce

△≠≠   indicates multiple divorce

△≈○   indicates lover (*jipo*) relationship

⊘ ⋰ ⊘   indicates fostering relationship

Village name in parentheses – (Mankpa) – indicates village of father or village with which person is identified.

1

Problems

This is a study of domestic organization in what was once an important state in West Africa. Indeed, the state of Gonja is still the centre of the world (elsewhere is 'wilderness') to most of its people, even though it has been included first in the British Protectorate of the Northern Territories of the Gold Coast (1897), and subsequently in the independent state of Ghana (1957).

Many of the peoples of northern Ghana, and of West Africa as a whole, have a social organization based upon unilineal descent groups. Such groups tend to operate in the political as well as the kinship domain. In Gonja descent groups are of little importance, but despite their absence it has proved impossible to study the patterns of kinship and marriage without also examining some aspects of the political organization. One of the problems of the study, then, is to trace the interrelationships between political and domestic institutions, and to try and understand the working of a largely 'bilateral' system.

This problem could be examined at the level of the state as a whole. But there is considerable variation within the extensive area covered by the Gonja state (now, in 1971, the administrative districts of Eastern and Western Gonja), and I have chosen to examine the material collected in three divisions in the central area of Gonja, even though subsequently I have worked in the east and the west. I shall therefore be particularly concerned with this more local level, concerned with the interplay between activities and obligations based on neighbourhood (contiguity) and those determined by kinship ties, which because of the nature of marriage and child-rearing tend to be widely dispersed.

The limitation of the material to that from central Gonja has another reason. The data are essentially ethnographic. I am concerned with describing the norms, what people see as the correct behaviour, and the patterns of action, what people in fact do. It is important to analyse as much of the relevant material of this kind as possible within the inevitable restrictions of space and continuity. Once the record for central Gonja is available, then the variations in other areas can be described and the differences considered in relation to historical, economic and other factors. If the record were a combined one from the start, then later comparative analysis within Gonja would not be possible.

The central problems, however, lie in the realm of the sociology of the family. How does a stratified political system allow marriages between virtually all categories of citizen – Muslims, diviners, people of the Earth shrine, blacksmiths, slaves, and chiefs of all degrees? And what are some of the consequences of such a situation? How is this related to a tradition which has long permitted many young people to seek their own spouses through courtship? Or to the high frequency of divorce and what I have called 'terminal separation'? Is the common practice of sending children to be reared by their parents' kin primarily a response to economic constraints, or a function of the short duration of many marriages? Is it related to political factors, or best understood as an aspect of the kinship system? And finally, what kinds of obligations between kin emerge as central in a largely bilateral system like that of Gonja? And how are such obligations sanctioned when these kin are dispersed, often separated by many miles and living in different political divisions? Problems of this sort grow out of the data, but at the same time relate to a number of issues in the contemporary sociology of the family.

At certain points during the course of the study of the roles and norms that are the basis of marriage and kinship, a different mode of analysis is used. At one level of abstraction any system of relationships between those in core roles (husband and wife, parent and child, sibling and sibling) can be examined in similar structural terms. Yet there are also cultural differences between societies that have direct bearing on behaviour but are not simply a matter of different rules nor of the social groupings within which they function. Such differences have to do with the very meaning given to social relationships, and with the ways in which people are believed to influence one another. There are four modes or idioms of relationship which are the stuff of everyday life in Gonja. Without an understanding of these a formal analysis of roles and behavioural regularities cannot be complete. The first of these relational idioms is the complex of greeting and begging behaviour, which is the basis of the respect and deference that are the fundamental characteristic of a child's relationship with his parents. The same idiom is employed in establishing a wide range of relationships in which one person seeks help or a favour of some kind from another, in return for which respectful support and deference are offered. It operates at the political as well as the domestic level.

The sharing of cooked food is a second idiom for expressing a close, dependable relationship; beliefs in mystical poisons render the accept-

2

ance of cooked food dangerous. Therefore when it is offered, not only is nurturance expressed, but trust invited. A number of ceremonies, both in the course of the annual cycle and at key points in the individual life cycle, turn around the sending of cooked food between all the compounds of a village. Here again, as with the greeting idiom, a mode of expressing close relations within the family also operates in a wider political context. In both contexts, these idioms have manipulative as well as expressive aspects.

The two remaining relational idioms are less benign. The ability to control mystical forces and direct these against enemies is associated by the Gonja with the power to change shape, and to fly through the night, as well as the hunger for human souls which we term witchcraft. All powerful and important men are thought to be witches, in part because it is believed that one element in the achievement of positions of power is fighting by means of witchcraft. Women are, however, more feared as witches than men, for they are thought to attack those who annoy them through witchcraft poisons put in the food they cook. Thus relations with men in positions of authority, and with all women, are potentially dangerous. Individual motivation is as complex in Gonja as elsewhere, and those who possess the power to harm may always do so for their own private ends as well as for more public purposes.

Finally, it is not only relations between humans that are of importance. The several forms of supernatural forces to which men are subject are partially controlled with the help of diviners, shrines and various propitiatory acts. When these forces are thrown out of balance a state of mystical danger exists which threatens a man, his dependants and all his activities. The mystical dangers inherent in contact with shrines are not greatly feared, though where community shrines are involved they are more serious, and annual purificatory rites are the rule. Of greater personal concern is mystical danger associated with the breaking of norms governing close relationships. One class of such norms limits sexual intercourse in relation to childbirth, while the other, the most serious of all, specifies obligations to kin. Thus all activities, but especially those involving kin, carry with them the threat of precipitating a state of mystical danger. In normal everyday life this is guarded against in a number of simple ways. But care is necessary, particularly where moral obligations are involved. In this sense the moral community includes the conjugal family, the community, and kin wherever they are living.

The links between political and domestic institutions occur at several levels then: in terms of the domestic groups which live together,

3

co-operate in various ways and are subject to the single jurisdiction of the compound head; in terms of citizenship through one's father in a social estate and a specific territorial division of the kingdom; in terms of the individual's links with kin of both parents which provide particular ties with a set of relatives and the entire villages in which they live; and finally in terms of the idioms of behaviour through which relations are established, interpreted and maintained both within the domestic sphere and with the wider political community.

Before it is possible to see how these links between the domestic and political spheres work in practice, it is necessary to look separately at the institutions concerned. In the remaining two chapters of this first section the political and economic context of life in central Gonja is described, detailed consideration being given to the organization of the village and structure of the compound. Section two examines several aspects of marriage, since this institution is fundamental to the establishment of domestic groups and to their development. In section three, I discuss the delegation of some aspects of parenthood when children are sent to be reared by kin, and relate this practice to the strong ties which continue to bind kin however far apart they live. Finally, section four examines patterns of residence in space and through time, and seeks to relate these to both the political context and to the form taken by authority in the kin group.

2

The historical, political and economic setting

The brief sketch of the historical, economic and political background which follows is essential for an understanding of the status system of central Gonja. All of these factors together provide the setting for an examination of domestic life.

Formerly Gonja was an important state, the northern neighbour of the Ashanti, one of a cluster of savannah states in the Voltaic area. Today the old kingdom of Gonja forms two administrative districts in modern Ghana whose independence was celebrated in 1957 while I was working there. The districts of East and West Gonja extend across the breadth of northern Ghana, from the Black Volta on the west where the river marks the border with the Ivory Coast, to the River Oti in the east just inside the boundary with Togo. Immediately above the eighth parallel the Black Volta swings east and flows across the country before dropping south to the Atlantic; this eastern course marks Gonja's southern boundary (Map I). The area of the administrative districts of Western and Eastern Gonja covers a total of 14,469 square miles, about the area covered by the Gonja kingdom in the late nineteenth century. In 1948 the population was 80,112, with an overall density of 5.5 per square mile. By the time of the 1960 census the reported population had increased by a dramatic 48%, and stood at 118,229, with a density of 8.2 persons per square mile.[1]

Before independence the Gonja people had experienced some fifty years of British colonial rule, with the associated taxes, labour levies, district officers' attempts at adjudication and intermittent efforts to codify and reorient political institutions. On the whole many Gonja traditions and institutions escaped relatively lightly from these attentions because of the remoteness of most villages and the sparse population; undoubtedly the most profound impact was made by the outlawing of the use of force except by the colonial power. I am not

[1] A large proportion of this increase is accounted for by migration into Gonja of LoDagaa in the west and Konkomba in the east. Comparison of the census figures for 1948 and 1960 for the three central Gonja divisional capitals studied shows increases of between 9% and 20%. Even these figures are difficult to interpret, however, as two of these towns have moved, and the third has been augmented by people of more remote villages who wished to live on a road.

5

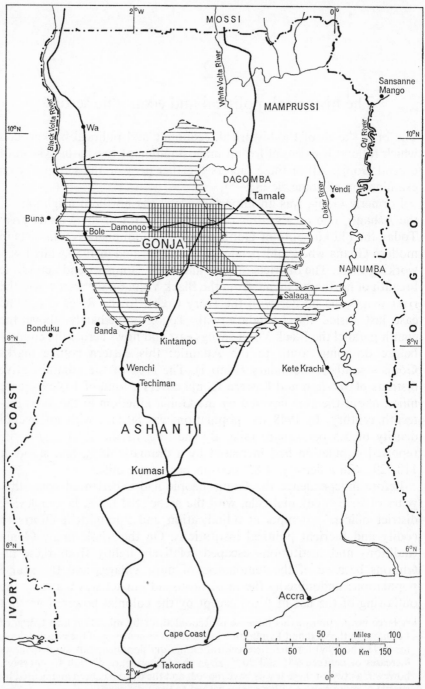

Map I. Ghana, showing the State of Gonja. Cross-hatching indicates the area of central Gonja in which fieldwork was carried out.

aiming to reconstruct the past but to analyse life in Gonja as I found it in 1956 and 1957; nevertheless, it is necessary to include a sketch of the past as it is seen by the Gonja, since this has such importance in their present way of looking at the world.

THE GONJA PAST

The Gonja kingdom was situated at the point where forest met savannah and where the trade routes from Hausaland in the north-east and 'Mande' in the north-west reached the hinterland of Ashanti, rich in kola and in gold.

It seems to have been the strategic position of this area for trade which led to its conquest and unification. Gonja traditions place the origin of the kingdom in the seventeenth century, when a band of Mande horsemen ended a period of wandering by conquering and settling the land between the three rivers. According to the legends, they came on horseback, armed with spears. With the help of a certain Mallam called Fati Morukpe the invaders easily subdued the autoch-thons who opposed them on foot, armed only with bows and arrows. Although the conquest is usually described as though there had been only a single battle, there are subsidiary traditions which indicate that it must have taken place over a much longer period. For instance, there is a spot at the junction of the Black and White Volta rivers where the canoe of ManWura is said to have sunk in an earlier campaign. Man-Wura's son, NdeWura Jakpa, is usually credited with the creation of the kingdom. Yet he is variously said to have come into Gonja from the north-east, from the south, and from the south-west. All accounts agree, however, that Jakpa was responsible for the foundation of the political system, with its semi-autonomous territorial divisions. Tradition holds that Jakpa divided the new land among his sons, sending one to rule each of the important towns with its subordinate villages. It is these units which are designated as divisions (see Map II). Jakpa himself continued to lead the horsemen in new campaigns, and it was during the conquest of Kawlaw in the south-east corner of the kingdom that he was fatally wounded. He was carried back to Buipe, where his youngest son was chief, and it is there he died and was buried.

Jakpa's title was NdeWura, 'chief of the towns'. His pre-eminent position rested, almost certainly, on his generalship of the armies. With his death, and the pacification of the country, the question of routinizing the succession arose. The position of paramount chief was in fact institutionalized in the office of YagbumWura, 'chief of the great

7

company'. This paramountcy was held in turn by the 'sons' of Jakpa, and subsequently by the descendants of these 'sons' in the male line. Since the sons had been sent to rule the outposts of the kingdom, this meant that the paramount came from each of the territorial divisions in turn, but always from among the descendants of the invading horsemen, the Gbanya.

Nyanga, the former capital of the Gonja kingdom, had but few villages under it. Their chiefs were the councillors (*begbampo*) of the paramount. The capital, situated as it was off the major trade routes, was always considered remote. The usual explanation given for a divisional chief refusing his turn to become the paramount (a decision which might cause his division to be permanently dropped from among those eligible) is that he did not wish to leave his native division in order to 'sit in the bush' (*tchena kapunto*). For aside from the right to one tusk of each elephant killed anywhere in the kingdom, and the right to marry twin girls, the paramount had few tangible perquisites. On the other hand, divisional chiefs whose land was crossed by trade routes could count on considerable profit, both from direct levies placed on caravans passing through their territory, and from the sale of food, beer and services to the wayfarers.

The conquerors settled among their subjects, intermarried freely with them, and both became incorporated in the new political system. The peoples found living in each locality were recognized as owning the earth and still today provide the Earth priests (*tindaana, kasawalewura*). While the authority of these ritual office-holders is less than that of their counterparts in the stateless societies to the north (e.g. among the Tallensi and LoDagaa), it is still recognized in ritual matters concerning the earth.

THE SOCIAL ESTATES

Past history has resulted in a political and status system, many features of which persist today. The major social categories consist of the ruling estate (*Gbanya, ewuribi*), Muslims (*karamo*) and commoners (*nyemasi*).

The ruling estate consists of the primary segments of the dynasty which are localized in each of the divisions. It is the members of these segments that fill the major chiefships, for which there is still intense competition. But only in the division of his father is a man eligible for a major chiefship; and it is from one of these first rank chiefships that a man is promoted to the chiefship of the division itself. And in the same way it is from among the divisional chiefs that the paramount is appointed.

8

Some of the divisions have no rights in the succession to the para-mountcy. There are at present only five divisional chiefs who are considered eligible for the office of YagbumWura. In the remaining eleven divisions the members of the ruling estate still consider them-selves to be descendants of NdeWura Jakpa, and still hold chiefships on the same basis as the Gbanya in the eligible divisions.[2] However, in these terminal divisions, the divisional chiefship is the highest post to which a man may aspire.

Each of the divisions is ruled from its own capital. Here the divisional chief lives and holds court; within the territory of each division are villages governed by minor Gbanya chiefs, appointed by, and respons-ible to, the divisional head.

In addition to the dynastic segments, each division contains groups of Muslims, some strangers, and many commoners, into which have been incorporated those of slave descent, formerly a numerous category. As I have noted, the commoners continue to provide the Earth priest, although his role is generally very limited. Also important among the specifically commoner offices are those of shrine priest (*kagbirwura*), holder-of-the-sacrificial-knife (*kupo*), and war leader (*mbongwura*). Perhaps because the bulk of the fighting men were inevitably drawn from the commoner element, in time of crisis they were led by a commoner holding the hereditary office of MbongWura.[3] The war leader sometimes also held the office of executioner for the divisional chief under whom he served, carrying out the sentence passed on witches and others with whom the community had resolved to do away.

The chief of each division is advised by councillors from among such commoner office-holders. Also in attendance at the capital, either permanently or occasionally, are the commoners who hold either village chiefships or chiefly titles by virtue of their maternal links with the ruling estate. These offices, Sister's Son chiefships, are reserved for the children of women of the ruling estate (*etche pibi*). Commoner office holders of either sort are often the most trusted of advisers because they cannot themselves aspire to first rank chiefship, and hence have more to gain from maintaining the power of a friendly chief than from destroying him.

The Muslim estate is represented in most divisions by an Imam

---

[2] The exact number of divisions of the kingdom has clearly varied over time.

[3] This title is probably based on the Gbanyito word for their Ashanti enemies to the south, the Mbong. War leaders were sometimes refugee Ashanti gunmen, and those who were not no doubt modelled their craft on the powerful and much feared Mbong, who fought with guns while the Gbanya depended upon horses and spears.

(*Limam*) who is usually selected from a patronymic group known as the Sakpare, who are descendants of Fati Morukpe, the companion of the founding hero, NdeWura Jakpa. In addition there are several other groups of Muslims, of the sort referred to as clans in much of the literature, the members of which claim different origins, some Mande, some Hausa, others from Bornu and Songhai. From among these other groups is appointed the divisional spokesman (*dogte*),[4] who is the equivalent of the Ashanti *okyeame*, or linguist.

To a Gonja, the designation *karamo* (Muslim) means a person of one of the Muslim clans, and thus by definition someone who prays to God. Despite the descent connotations of the term, there are converts to Islam. They seem to belong mainly to two categories, ex-slaves and members of the ruling estate. A large proportion of those who were slaves, or whose fathers were slaves, have adopted the Muslim religion. By so doing they have gained membership of a fellowship, 'those who pray', as well as access to spiritual support. Further, many Muslim men wear a characteristic long gown, and some Muslim women a loose veil, not covering the face, but trailing down over the shoulders. Such distinctive dress identifies one as a Muslim, and for the ex-slaves provides a visible sign of status in the community. It is very doubtful whether most of those professing Islam are aware of the universalistic creed that all men are brothers, though the particular application of this, that as Muslims they receive a measure of respect and status in the community, does not escape them. It is possible for such a convert to become a Muslim priest (*mallam*), though the few who did so lived apart from the main Muslim sections of town and were distinguished in other subtle ways.

The other main source of converts is the ruling estate. In both eastern and western Gonja several of the chiefs openly prayed before taking office, and some at least continue to do so privately. There is still, however, an insistence on the rule that a chief ought not publicly to profess Islam, and in particular that he should not enter the mosque. In central Gonja the chiefs do not pray, but remain aloof from the Muslim religion in their personal lives, while calling on Mallams for the ritual services which they traditionally render.

INTERACTION BETWEEN ESTATES

The social estates appear always to have been distinguished not only by

[4] In the eastern Gonja division of Kpembe the spokesman is a Sakpare, known by the title of *NsauWura*.

10

their traditions but also by their political and religious roles. In pre-colonial times as now, however, interaction between members of the estates was varied and continuous, despite the linguistic situation. The Gbanya and most Muslims speak *Gbanyito*, a dialect of the Guang sub-group of the Kwa languages. Among the autochthons there are peoples speaking some fourteen dialects of the Mossi, Grusi, Gurma and Senufo sub-groups of the Gur languages and a few who are also Guang speakers.[5]

Gbanyito is the court language throughout Gonja. Members of the ruling estate from all corners of the kingdom can speak together, as well as to their councillors, both Muslim and commoner. Their original Mande tongue was possibly abandoned for this Guang dialect when the horsemen took local wives during their sojourn to the south of Gonja, before the establishment of the kingdom. Today the sharing of the Gbanyito tongue, like the sharing of their descent from NdeWura Jakpa, is a symbol of the common origin of the ruling group. It is a critical factor in the ease with which members of this estate move from one part of the kingdom to another, and makes possible the effective circulation of the office of paramount among the different divisions.

In central Gonja some of the commoner groups apparently also spoke Guang dialects. At the present time these dialects have virtually disappeared. All the inhabitants now speak Gbanyito, which means that it is the language of the domestic group as well as of the court. In the major divisions of the east and west of the country this is not the case. Rulers and Muslims are there bilingual, or more often multi-lingual, as are many commoners. Such a facility with several languages follows naturally upon a situation where, as in Gonja, marriage continues to be very common between members of groups speaking different languages.

As I have remarked in describing the Muslim estate, conversion is not uncommon and is often tied to marriage. A commoner bride automatically becomes a Muslim at her marriage, and she may with almost equal ease become a backslider on divorce. In religious affiliation, as with linguistic matters, intermarriage is important. Members of all groups can marry each other and do so with great frequency. This situation certainly existed in the past too. Slave women were regularly taken as wives by all three groups. Although women of the ruling and Muslim estates were discouraged, and even actively prevented, from marrying men of ex-slave status, they did have affairs with them. But so regularly did marriage between the main estates take place that

[5] See Westermann and Bryan (1952); Manoukian (1952); and J. Goody (1954 and 1963). See also Appendix I.

11

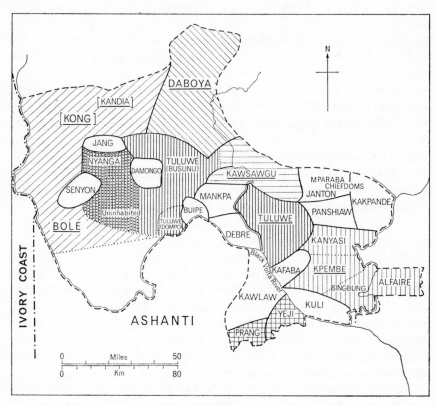

Map II. The divisions of Gonja. Hatching indicates divisions eligible for paramountcy. Cross-hatching shows other areas included in the Gonja administrative district in 1957. Names underlined are divisions that can succeed to
paramountcy (1956). Names in square brackets are dissolved divisions.

among the kin of most people are to be found members of two and often of all three groups. This is unequivocally true in the divisional capitals, and reaches its limiting conditions in the more remote villages where some commoner families may lack such inter-group ties.

In the religious field there is much interaction between the groups, especially in the major political ceremonies. But even at other times, in central Gonja at any rate, there is little to distinguish the religious behaviour of commoner and ruling estates. Both seek the services of Muslims for aspects of naming ceremonies, funerals and certain sacrifices, at least in those towns where there are Muslims available. All persons of whatever estate are constrained to abide by the ritual edicts of the commoners who hold the local offices associated with the Earth, or with a major shrine (*kagbir*). Thus none should fire the bush or gather the new crop of shea nuts until the Earth priest announces that the time is right, and initiates the activity himself. A similar kind of inter-relationship holds for the political system.

THE LOCAL POLITICAL SYSTEM

The advent of the colonial powers, Britain in the west and Germany in the east, at the end of the nineteenth century, brought far-reaching consequences for the kingdom of Gonja. Though it had been partly conquered before by Ashanti troops, and in any case was not a highly centralized organization at the national level, the imposition of colonial over-rule meant inclusion in a more extensive empire, and a consequent loss of authority by the ruling estate.

The British forces arriving in central and western Gonja were greeted as liberators, since they freed the population from the armies of the Mande invader Samori. In eastern Gonja their presence was seen as a counter to the strength of the Germans at Kratchi and of the Dagomba who had been called in by the Kanyasi segment of the ruling estate when it rebelled against exclusion from office.[6]

Liberation was followed by control, with first military officers and then civilians being established at Bole in the west and Salaga in the east. After the initial conquest, central Gonja was relatively isolated from contact with the agents of the colonial government, although their existence soon put limits on the use of force, by Gonjas as well as by

[6] See J. A. Braimah and J. R. Goody, *Salaga: The Struggle for Power* (1968), for a detailed description of conditions in eastern Gonja at this time, as seen by the Kanyasi segment of the ruling estate, by British and German colonial officials, and through the writings of a Muslim scholar.

their enemies. At the same time, chiefs themselves became agents of the government, having to provide carriers for supplies, recruits for the army, labour for roads and telegraph, and later on children for schools.

Despite these disruptions the indigenous political system of the former kingdom of Gonja continued to operate under the colonial over-rule in a modified way, both at the divisional and the national levels. Within the ruling estate chiefly office was subject to strong competition, as in earlier times, but greater limits were placed on the resolution of conflicts by force. At the divisional level, with only occasional interference from the District Commissioners, the traditional rotational system of succession to office continued in force. This works in the following way: the number of secondary dynastic segments of the ruling estate within a division varies between two and three. If the present chief of a division is of segment A, then his successor should come from either segment B or C. This is expressed on one level by the rule that a man may not succeed directly to a chiefship held by his father. In eastern Gonja this prohibition is further reinforced by the rule that the sons of a divisional chief may not hold any office while *either* parent is still living.

While he is in office a divisional chief may try to bestow on the men of his own dynastic segment the titles and minor chiefships which fall vacant. But in theory the offices within a division ought to go to the Gbanya of all dynastic segments in order of seniority, that is, first in terms of generation and secondly of age. Any divisional chief who regularly passes over senior men of other segments in favour of junior members of his own in awarding vacant chiefships risks loss of support. And although a Gbanya chief could not traditionally be deposed but had the right to retain his office until he died, there was no way of keeping disaffected elements from hastening his death. In pre-colonial times discontent occasionally took the form of armed rebellion by segments of the ruling estate which felt slighted in the distribution of office. Divisional chiefs know they are dependent on the continuing support of the other segments, and indeed this was even more true when control of the commoner population was a matter of maintaining armed superiority.

Within each division the titles and chiefships are roughly ranked in order of importance. Although a man often succeeds first to a title associated with an abandoned village rather than to a village chiefship, in time he is promoted. As holders of the senior offices die, or are themselves advanced, he will move up in the hierarchy. When this involves succession to a village chiefship, he must usually leave the capital and

14

make his home in the village over which he has been appointed to rule. Later, if he succeeds to the chiefship of a larger village or to the divisional skin, he will have to move again.[7] If the division is among those eligible for succession to the paramountcy, he may eventually become Yagbum-Wura and move, with his close kin and wives, to the national capital.

Because of this pattern of chiefs moving in and out of the smaller villages, there are enclaves of members of the ruling estate in most villages in the division. They include those attached to the present chief, and those kinsmen of the previous chiefs who have preferred to remain. However, the divisional capital serves as the headquarters for all of the dynastic segments. Men who have not yet succeeded to office come back when they judge that their turn is near. And almost all those junior chiefs who hold titles to which no village is attached live in the capital, where they spend their time greeting one another and the divisional chief, discussing divisional affairs, and hearing such cases as come before the court.

In addition to the titles and village chiefships held by men of the ruling estate, a few of the senior women may hold women's chiefships. These are the *ewuritches*. They have no formal duties except the preparation of the cooked rice for the annual Damba ceremony, but they lead the other women of the ruling estate in greeting the divisional chief on important occasions. *Ewuritches* always appear to live in the divisional capital, usually either in their own compound, or in a section of a brother's compound. The similarity between these female chiefs and the queen mothers of Ashanti is only superficial. The Gonja office carries no responsibility for advising the divisional chief, nor any right to nominate office holders. However a divisional chief tends to appoint older women whose judgement he trusts and he may consult them, especially about domestic ritual and 'women's affairs'.

Citizenship for a commoner is more closely bound up with the particular villages of his mother and father. Unless his people hold one of the divisional councillorships, his citizenship in the division will be mediated through his identification with one or both of his parents' villages. Nevertheless, divisional citizenship is meaningful for commoners from the outlying villages. It impinges most directly in the person of the resident Gbanya chief. The chief takes an active role in daily economic and social life, in addition to his duties in settling disputes, mediating between the villagers and dealing with threats of either political or mystical nature. Such an incoming chief usually has kin in the village already, and will very likely take a wife there, as well as arranging one

[7] The skin pillow (*kawal puti*) is the throne and symbol of chiefship in Gonja.

15

or more marriages between his children and the inhabitants of the village. While the formalities of respect are observed, ostentatiously so on public occasions, the villagers tend to treat their chief as someone very like themselves, who happens to have added powers and responsibilities.

Once or twice a year the outlying villages are formally brought into a special relationship with the central political authorities. At Jentigi (the new-year fire festival) they may be asked to contribute to a token tribute, and at Damba (the celebration of the circumcision of the prophet) they attend the dancing and feasting which marks the affirmation of fealty to the divisional chief. Occasionally they may be asked to provide food and shelter for a visiting dignitary of the ruling estate. And when a new chief is appointed to rule in their village, they send a representative to the installation ceremony, to signify their acceptance of the candidate.

All villages have their commoner office holders, whether Earth priest, shrine priest, or designated elders, positions which tend to be vested in a local kin group, usually in the agnatic line. A commoner whose family holds such an office has rights of residence and farming, and rights to office as well. Like the members of the ruling group, a commoner holds dual citizenship, in the village and division of his father, and also in his mother's home village and division.

Muslim offices, the named Imamships, also pass in the paternal line, with the important proviso that an aspirant must have satisfied the electors as to his Koranic scholarship. In fact, there are very few such offices, only one in each of the divisional capitals where there are still resident Muslims. The large trading centres like Salaga had several mosques, and learned Mallams were often associated with these. However, there has never been a hierarchy of Muslim judges in Gonja as is found in some of the states of Northern Nigeria. Litigation went through the chief's court and followed local traditions rather than the Koran. There is, however, scope for individual achievement among the Muslims. A man who pursues his Koranic studies, perhaps with several masters in different towns, can win a reputation for his learning; he will be consulted by those in trouble, and often receives pupils in his turn. Such a man will be referred to as Mallam. While a Muslim convert could never succeed to the named Limamships[8] he can win for himself the title of 'learned man'.

The distribution of members of the Muslim estate within the division is more limited than for the other two groups, for they tend to be concentrated in the capital, together with a handful of other villages. Not

[8] The Imams are known locally as Limams.

16

every estate, then, is represented in every village. There is at least one town, Larabanga, which is regarded as being composed entirely of members of the Muslim estate. And there are in every division villages which have no resident Gbanya chief. While there are villages which lack official representatives of the Muslim and ruling estates, none but Larabanga is without a commoner element. But many villages, and all of the divisional capitals, consist of local segments of each estate. As will become clear in the course of the discussion of local organization and residence, even those villages which appear to be most homogeneous contain individual members of the other estates.

Such was the local political system at the time of independence of Ghana in 1957. At that time Government Agents replaced District Commissioners; earlier, in 1944, the seat of the paramount had been moved from Nyanga to Damongo, a divisional capital nearer the centre of the country. And the advent of parliamentary elections in 1951 soon led to the introduction of national politics on the local level. But despite all these changes, it was in terms of the indigenous political system that the inhabitants of central Gonja acted in most continuing social contexts.

THE ECONOMY TODAY

In former times the social estates had different economic roles, even though all were dependent eventually upon the primary productive processes. Members of the ruling estate descended with their horses upon acephalous neighbours and took home human booty whose labour provided them with a standard of living above subsistence level. Taxes on trade provided a further source of revenue, while goods and services from subordinate groups added to their income and way of life.

Muslim groups were more active than others in trade and many merchants in the towns became wealthy by comparison with their fellow citizens. Others were sustained by the religious services they provided to the 'pagans' as well as to the faithful. Indeed, the obligations of the chiefs to be generous to their Muslims is a constant theme of the annual celebrations, and the large calabash of porridge prominently displayed during funeral prayers is always sent after the Mallams as they leave.

Commoners were more locally oriented, more tied to the land. But even they might achieve some differentiation through craft production or slave ownership.

After the British conquest the strategic position of Gonja in long-distance trade changed with the shift of the significant boundary northwards to the international frontier with Upper Volta, with the advent

B   17

of motor transport and with the spread of European goods. Taxes on trade now became the prerogative of the colonial administration.

With the disappearance of slavery and the falling off in craft production, even commoners became more equal. Indeed, members of all three estates were forced to rely on agriculture to a much greater extent than in the pre-colonial era. At the time I worked there, some fifty years after the imposition of colonial over-rule, the effects of modern education and national politics had yet to appear in central Gonja on more than a peripheral level. By and large the impact of economic differentiation on social life was slight. Nearly everyone depended on cultivation of the land by the hoe and the limited technology was associated with a limited difference in styles of life.

The first result of modern changes in the polity and economy was thus a decrease in even the existing differentiation. Ultimate political power was taken from the chief by the District Commissioners; one major source of livelihood, raiding for booty, dried up with the establishment of the colonial truce. And, except in certain fields, the bulk of the trade passed into the hands of strangers, the Yoruba, the Europeans, even merchants from southern Ghana.

Although the long-distance trading caravans no longer pass through Gonja, and the old markets are deserted, the economy is no more self-contained than in the eighteenth and nineteenth centuries. Now it is manufactured goods from the south and across the seas which are the object of aspirations and the spur to have a cash income of at least a few pounds. There are few jobs in the north, however, either for the unskilled or those with some schooling behind them. The major alternatives are labouring work on roads or the occasional construction project, independent trading, or travel to seek employment in the south.[9] It is still mostly Muslims who take up the challenge of trade, limited as this is.

Unlike many of the more densely populated areas of West Africa, there is in central Gonja no market week, with a market held in each of several settlements on a regular day. When a man has farm produce to sell, or a woman has more peppers or vegetables than she needs, someone, usually a child, is sent to carry this surplus around the village calling out the price that is being asked. Itinerant traders stop in the smaller villages at irregular intervals with a variety of wares, mostly of European manufacture: torch batteries, padlocks, bicycle parts,

[9] At the time of field work in central Gonja neither the co-operative farms nor the Worker's Brigade farms of Nkrumah's period had been instituted. These provided some opportunity for cash cropping and unskilled labour respectively.

patent medicines, and Manchester cloth. In the larger villages their stalls are always a feature of the central clearing. In this same clearing one or two women are often to be seen in the early morning selling gruel or fried yams. But at no time is there more than sporadic activity, and this area cannot be called a market-place without doing violence to the usual meaning of that term.

There are today a few large permanent markets. Some of these – at Bole, Damongo, and Salaga – lie within the kingdom, while those at Tamale, Wa and Kintampo, although they are outside its borders, are much used by the people of north-eastern, north-western, and southern Gonja, respectively. It is through one of these permanent markets that any large surplus of yams, grain or shea butter is most likely to be disposed of. These markets are also the source of the goods of the itinerant traders, and to one of them will go the person who wishes to select an important purchase, a bicycle or iron cooking pot, from as large a stock as possible.

These regional centres also offer a window on the consumer society which southern Ghana has begun to adopt from the West. Local branches of the large international trading companies are very modest by urban standards, but compared to the itinerant trader's stall they offer what must seem an incredible range of goods. More frequented by those of modest means are the stores of Lebanese traders, some of whom have been established in Tamale, the administrative centre of northern Ghana, for many years. Their stock falls between that of the individual trader and the international commercial company, but is more than adequate for the needs, and resources, of most Gonja visitors, which are limited by the nature of their agricultural production. This economy I describe in some detail as it is of central importance, not only to the question of stratification, but also to the organization of the domestic group.

THE AGRICULTURAL ECONOMY

Gonja agriculture is based on the hoe cultivation of yams (*Dioscorea* sp.), millet (*Pennisetum spicatum*), guinea corn (*Sorghum vulgare*), maize (*Zea mays*), and cassava (*Manihot utilissima*). The soil is generally poor, and varies greatly in depth within small areas. Where the underlying laterite reaches the surface, bald spots punctuate the more general tangle in this land of orchard bush. At the end of the rains, the grass reaches over six feet where there is sufficient soil. But following the annual firing of the bush only a desolate wasteland remains, stretching

19

as far as the eye can see with the hardier trees, blackened and leafless, standing stark against the sky.

The rainy season (*kicherso*) usually extends from April through October, often with a relatively dry spell during the months of June and July. The south of Gonja falls within the belt where annual mean rainfall is between forty and fifty inches, while the northern half of the state receives an average of less than forty inches (Boateng, 1959: 33). As the dry season (*kitarso*) proceeds, water grows increasingly scarce and following a year of light rains drought is a serious problem in some of the villages.

Although virtually all men, whatever their skills or office, are also farmers, the population is sufficiently small for there to be land for all who wish to cultivate. This is possible because men expect to make their farms at some distance from the village. They may be as close as a mile, or as far away as five or six miles. Very occasionally the midden behind the house is planted with a few tobacco plants; otherwise there are no compound farms at all. Although this might appear to be inevitable where settlements take the form of nucleated villages, in fact the Dagomba, who also live in such villages, regularly grow maize as well as tobacco on compound farms (Akenhead, 1957).

A field is used for about four years and then left fallow. Preference is given to clearing a previously uncultivated stretch of bush, or one in which the trees and shrubs have grown to a height of ten or fifteen feet; a rough guess would put this period of regeneration at fifteen to twenty years.

The early yams mature in late June or early July and from then until December pounded yams (*kapol*) form the staple food for the large evening meal. With the grain harvest in December and January, porridge (*kude*) replaces yams as the main food until the following June. There is no real hungry period in the agricultural year, though the first supplies of both yams and grain are welcomed, for they herald times of relative plenty as well as a change of diet. The central food prepared for all ritual occasions is porridge, though rice forms the basis of the ceremonial of the annual Damba ceremony.

Farming is men's work. Women are required to help with the planting and harvesting of grains, and to carry seed yams to new fields. They are also expected to assist in carrying produce from the farm to the village, though the men bring the bulk of domestic provisions home in the evening when they return from the farm. But women are seen as contributing unskilled labour. It is true that each married woman cultivates peppers and vegetables among her husband's yam mounds, but this is

20

'women's work', not proper farming. "Women do not farm" (*etche ba man doa*), the Gonja insist.

All men set traps for small animals on their farms, and they hunt for larger game – antelope chiefly, but occasionally wild boar and buffalo – if they own a gun or can borrow one. A few who have their own guns and a knowledge of the hunting 'medicines' consider themselves as mainly hunters (*ekpampo*). But even they do most of their hunting during the dry season when farm work is light and when movement is easier through the burned-over countryside.

Most men also join in the communal fishing drives which take place at the end of the rains when streams are at their height. Before the drives, individuals build fish dams and set traps on the section of the nearby streams which they 'own' or to which they have obtained rights for that year. Temporary rights must be procured from the commoners in whom permanent ownership is vested, and 'rent' for fishing rights takes the form of a portion of the catch.

SPECIALIST OCCUPATIONS

In some of the villages there are resident blacksmiths who ply their trade in addition to farming. Sometimes they belong to a named patronymic group of blacksmiths, others may be strangers of Ashanti or Hausa origin, or they may be Gonja who have learned to make (or repair) hoes, cutlasses and bullets. However, all blacksmiths, even of the traditional smiths' groups, are free to marry as they please, and they take wives from any of the three estates.

There are many different kinds of drum, each with its characteristic shape and function. Any man may play those used for entertainment, and there is probably no village in Gonja without its own drummers for dancing and the rhythmic games that people enjoy so much. Other drums have more specialized functions: the Bintiri led into battle; the Ntympani, which are modelled on the Ashanti 'talking drums', recite the titles and exploits of past chiefs twice a week in the divisional capitals; the Kontunkuri was the guardian of the history of the kingdom, played only at the national capital; somewhat similar are the Mbontokurbi drums found only in the central Gonja divisions of Kawsawgu and Debre, which also recite ancient traditions. The hourglass drum, which praise-singers use to accompany their eulogies, is really a Hausa instrument and does not appear in central Gonja, though praise-singers attend divisional chiefs on important occasions in the eastern and western divisions. Like the other specialists, the men who are adepts of

21

each of these drums also farm. But like the others, they take pride in their skill and tend to be identified as drummers. Whether or not a particular sort of drum is played only by members of one kin group varies in different divisions. Usually this is not so; rather it is a matter of the current player taking as an apprentice a youth who shows talent. Those who play dance drums pick up the skill by watching others and by fooling around.

Other specialists include diviners of several different types, weavers, and nowadays a few carpenters. Of this list, only diviners are found in every village. Certain towns are known as centres of weaving and dyeing, though one may find a single loom set up under a shady tree in any village. All old women used to spin thread in their spare time, and this would be sent to one of the dyeing centres, either to be woven there or else brought back if there was a weaver in the town. The Gonja sometimes describe themselves as 'people with cloth' in distinction to the recently immigrant LoDagaa and Konkomba peoples. Neither divining nor weaving is restricted to particular kin groups, but there is a pattern of learning from one's kin which results in concentrations of weavers in a few families (especially in Daboya in the north). Divining is both a skill and a matter of 'divine' guidance; not just anyone can decide to take it up. It usually seems to be those with a relative who was known for his divining skills who pursue the work successfully. There is one kin group who are known throughout Gonja for their particular form of divination. These are the *lejipo* who are settled in a few towns (especially Manful, Mankuma, Busunu and Kito) and occasionally travel to others in order to hold seances. Only members of this kin group can communicate with the spirits in this manner.

Aside from spinning cotton thread, which until recently was the universal occupation of old ladies, there are no crafts specifically reserved for women, except pottery, and even this is practised by few. Some women practise as healers, midwives, and use certain forms of divination. Those who do so keep quiet about their skills and tend to restrict their activities to family and close friends. As often seems to be the case in other cultures, older women who are known to be expert with medicines, or to 'see' what others cannot, risk being labelled as witches. In Gonja even now, this label is too dangerous to justify the small income these skills might bring.

EDUCATION AND NEW JOB OPPORTUNITIES

In the beginning the establishment of schools in a thinly populated area like central Gonja presented enormous problems. Of the three divisional capitals in which I worked, only one, Busunu, had even a primary school. There had been one in Buipe for a few years, but this was abandoned. Indeed, in 1956–7 there was only one primary school in the entire area covered by these three central Gonja divisions. It was to the middle school at Damongo, the new capital and administrative centre, that most boys found their way if they were able to continue their education.[10]

It is perhaps not surprising, then, to find that in 1956 the number of men from central Gonja who had received the equivalent of even a middle school education was very small. At that time, however, a middle school training was sufficient as a basis for teaching and work in administrative offices in the north. Thus there were several teachers, a few primary school headmasters, and a few policemen, clerks and secretaries who had entered the modern sector of employment through the possession of literate skills.

Of those without education, a few young men spend some time working in the south. However, there is not the regular seasonal movement of agricultural labour for the cocoa farms during the dry season which has become the pattern among the acephalous peoples in the north of Ghana and the Mossi of Upper Volta. This is at least in part due to the negative view of farming which is shared by the ruling and Muslim elements, and which seems to have also influenced the commoner peoples to some extent. This attitude seems responsible for the failure of the Gonja farmers to take up the opportunity offered by the growing market for foodstuffs in the south. Instead it is largely the immigrant LoDagaa and Konkomba peoples who supply the lorry-loads of yams which head for Kumasi and the coast as the roads again become passable at the end of the rains. Every farmer, however, hopes to have some surplus at the end of the season to sell as a source of the cash which is increasingly necessary for even everyday needs. The main items which must be bought are printed cloth, metal bowls, iron pots, guns, hoes and axes, salt, matches and, increasingly popular, kerosene lamps and fuel. A traditional import which remains

[10] It is only fair to point out that primary schools were opened in both Mankpa and Buipe when these towns moved onto the new road (see chapter 3) and the number in central Gonja, as elsewhere in northern Ghana, increased dramatically after independence as part of a determined government effort to achieve universal primary education. However the situation I have described is that which had existed during the childhood and adolescence of the adults I knew, and which continued throughout the period of fieldwork in central Gonja.

of central social and ritual importance is the kola nut, which grows profusely in the forests of Ashanti, but not in the north.

It is inevitable that the need for cash will increase. In 1956–7 the lack of opportunity for employment was recognized as a problem by the younger men, but had not yet been openly acknowledged by their elders. Farming for subsistence was the accepted way of life of the majority of the members of all three estates. There is of course still some differentiation. Especially outside central Gonja, some chiefs have made themselves rich on 'gifts'; so too have some politicians, who tend to come from the ruling estate.

Travel outside of Gonja for trade is still almost entirely a Muslim pattern. Some take advantage of the fellowship their faith allows them to claim with co-religionists elsewhere in the north, in southern Ghana and indeed throughout the western Sudan. Some young men of the ruling estate also travel about, trading or seeking temporary employment. Men of the commoner estate, while they may travel for hunting or trading, seem less inclined to venture beyond the borders of Gonja.

These occupational differences between and within estates inevitably entail some differences in resources. Wealth is most easily judged by ownership of cattle, except in the few well-watered areas where tse-tse flies make the keeping of livestock impossible. The building of concrete, zinc-roofed houses, a favoured form of investment in the south, had not yet been taken up in central Gonja.

Only the most senior chiefs have more than a few beasts, and on the whole wealth is not nowadays a criterion by which the three estates may be distinguished in this poor central area. While important chiefs always have some cattle, so also do representatives of the other two groups. This is hardly surprising, as only those chiefs who actually rule over a village or a division receive more than very occasional perquisites of office from their subjects. Even for acting chiefs, these are of limited value: one hind leg from any large animal killed on his land by a stranger, and in the past the services of the young men of the town in clearing and weeding his farms. In addition, any man in a position of influence or power may receive gifts from those seeking his help. Such 'greeting gifts' tend to flow towards the divisional chief, but usually consist of small amounts, kola nuts and drink, except where important issues are at stake. In addition, some senior chiefs receive a monthly payment from local taxes in compensation for the loss of other revenues.

It is to a closer examination of the internal organization of the division and its villages that the next chapter turns. For it is at this level that the political and domestic domains intersect.

3

Three divisions of central Gonja and their villages

The three social estates are recognized throughout the kingdom, although the particular groups and offices which constitute each estate vary from one part to another. A second major dimension is the organization of the state into territorial divisions. For all three estates it is true to say that one is a citizen of a division first, and only then of the Gonja state. Together, estate and divisional citizenship provide a matrix in which the individual is anchored, and in terms of which he places others. But at this level it is a matrix with a very wide mesh. In this chapter, I want to consider in some detail three cells within it, those represented by the three divisions of Buipe, Mankpa and Busunu.

Viewed at close range each cell is itself structured in both social and spatial terms. Physically a division consists of the capital and its subordinate villages. Typically each village has its own special character based perhaps on the language of its people, or on a particular skill, the presence of shrines, a unique natural feature or some historical event. The totality of these attributes of the constituent villages and the capital give the division itself a unique quality and its role in the kingdom as a whole.

These two levels of organization, the division and the village, have their primary significance in the political domain. Their relevance for the individual lies in citizenship, eligibility to office, and relationships of various kinds to authority: the very stuff of political organization.

The main problems with which this study is concerned, however, lie in the domain of domestic relations. They have to do with the ways in which individuals depend on one another in the pursuit of daily economic tasks, for companionship, and in times of crisis. The processes to be understood are those by which such relations are sustained or broken, and through which new patterns of relationship are formed. The arena in which these relations and processes are central is the internal system, "the domestic field of social relations viewed from within" (Fortes, 1958: 2). In so far as this has a spatial focus, it is the cluster of rooms which comprise the household.

The compound, containing one or more households, mediates between domestic relations and those of the politico-jural domain.

25

There are a number of occasions, in both the individual and the cosmic cycle, when residents of the compound participate collectively in rituals and celebrations of several kinds. Every compound has a recognized head who has duties with respect to the village chief, but who also has rights and obligations with respect to those living in his compound. In a sense the compound head faces both inward towards the domestic domain, and outward towards the community and the wider politico-jural domain.

These physical units provide relatively fixed points of reference around which much of an individual's behaviour is organized. At no level do the physical units correspond neatly to descent groups, or to ordered segments of any kin-based group. Yet a great many of the relationships with which this study is concerned are defined in terms of kinship, and the two central processes, marrying and the fostering of children, are processes for generating and organizing kinship relations. In analysing these relationships and processes, the physical units constantly recur as important to the actors in orienting their behaviour and in choosing appropriate courses of action. There is a halo effect which endows the compound and village in which one grew up, or from which a parent came, with a quasi-kinship status. The Gonja often speak, for instance, of the importance of one's 'mother's place'. This village is often equated with one's mother's kinsfolk, one's 'mother's people', when literally this is far from accurate. Thus, before turning to the consideration of kinship institutions, it has seemed important to explore these physical foci of orientation, as a basis for later examining the interaction between the two.

THE DIVISION

The various divisions of the state of Gonja have recognized boundaries usually marked by streams and occasionally by well-worn paths. Within these boundaries the divisional chief has rights in the meat of large animals killed, and his permission must be obtained before a non-Gonja may hunt on the land. In the days before a colonial administration was established, that is before the beginning of the present century, it was the divisional chief who had the right to tax traders and caravans passing through his territory. Such disputes as could not be settled by the kin of those concerned, nor conclusively resolved by the chief of the village in which they occurred, might reach his court at the divisional capital; very occasionally a dispute would be taken on appeal to the court of the paramount at Nyanga. It is the divisional chief who selects

26

among the candidates for vacant Gbanya titles and chiefships, although the system of succession does not give him full latitude.[1] The chiefs of all the subordinate villages are required to attend the annual Damba festival in the divisional capital, at which time they pay homage to the divisional chief, acknowledging his authority over them and thus over their villages.

While these are the attributes which formally define a division, the Gonja think of it primarily in terms of the constituent villages. These are relatively permanent, not only geographically but also with respect to their grouping into units of political administration, that is, the divisions. Permanent is used here in a relative sense, as villages occasionally are deserted as the result of war, drought or flood, or some catastrophe which renders the site mystically uninhabitable. There is also a tendency for villages to creep over the ground with the passage of time as new compounds are built and others abandoned. The distance involved here is of the order of no more than a few hundred yards, however, and such movement is of quite a different order from that found in societies where shifting cultivation requires the abandoning of villages as well as fields every few years.

With respect to the inclusion of villages within the sphere of political influence of a given division some reservation must also be made, although it seems likely that such fluidity as is apparent here has been aggravated by the superimposition of administrative districts for the purpose of the colonial government. Divisional chiefs do speak of having had jurisdiction over villages now under the control of neighbouring divisions. These are always villages located on their borders, and it is possible that there has always been a certain amount of competition for control of such marginal villages, the edge in the quarrel going to the more powerful chief. At a given point in time, however, there is seldom any doubt as to the alignment of villages under the various divisions, for this is determined by the occupant of the village chiefship: initially by the divisional chief who appointed him or recognized his succession, and the divisional capital in which he was enrobed, and annually by the divisional chief to whom he tenders his fealty at the Damba festival.

Among the villages, the capital is by far the most closely identified with the division as a whole. Indeed, it is not uncommon in speaking

---

[1] The form of the installation ceremony makes explicit the fact that representatives of the other two estates must also approve these appointments. The pressures which they may bring to bear are informal and in fact, short of open rebellion, there is little that can be done to coerce a divisional chief who is determined in his choice.

with a stranger to use the name of the capital rather than that of a small village with which it is assumed he will not be familiar. For through the capital are mediated the political dealings of the smaller villages with the outside world. Succession to office for members of the ruling estate must be legitimated by establishing rights in the division of a man's father, not rights to the chiefships of particular villages. These rights are expressed by the maintenance of a compound in the divisional capital, although in a few divisions each of the dynastic segments is localized in a separate village, and the capital rotates with the segment in office.

Muslim offices tend also to emphasize the importance of the capital village, for if there is only one mosque in the division it is here that it is built. Thus the divisional Limam's religious duties require his residence in the capital as does his role of spiritual adviser to the divisional chief.

While the villages of most divisions form a territorially compact unit, this is not always the case. The divisions of central Gonja in particular, control villages which are situated within the boundaries of their neighbours. There are three such villages attached to the division of Buipe: Gbãso and Frufruso are surrounded by Busunu land, and Katangi is within the boundaries of Kawsawgu. The village of Jembito is attached to Mankpa, although it is separated from it by Buipe division and is surrounded by villages belonging to still a third, Tuluwe. The village of Gurupe is administered by Busunu, although it occupies land belonging to the division of Bole.

BUIPE DIVISION

None of the three central Gonja divisions in which I worked was among those which in turn supplies the paramount, the YagbumWura. However, each has an important position in the constitution of the kingdom. Buipe has a unique status, for in many ways it balances the power of the paramountcy. When a YagbumWura dies, it is the BuipeWura who must be officially informed by the sending of the sandals, smock, staff and horse of the dead ruler. He then dispatches the senior commoner chief of Buipe division, the KagbapeWura, to enrobe the new paramount at the national capital. Thereafter neither the KagbapeWura nor the BuipeWura may see the reigning YagbumWura. During the British colonial administration, when these two chiefs were summoned to attend the same meeting, a curtain was hung between them lest this prohibition be violated. The YagbumWura's Limam is also attached to Buipe division, and usually lives in Buipe when not at the capital.

28

The BuipeWura himself is an extremely important chief whose identification with the grave of the founder of the kingdom, NdeWura Jakpa, gives him power to settle disputes between the heads of other divisions. It is believed that if he complains, even to himself, about the disrespect of another chief, his annoyance will bring a state of mystical danger; the spirit of Jakpa will hear and be angered. Buipe is also the most important of the central Gonja towns which serve as sanctuaries for fugitives from other divisions or from the capital. None may pursue them here. Because Buipe is a town of peace, there is no office of war leader attached to the division.

The selection of a new BuipeWura is confirmed by the senior Mallam of the Kante family in Buipe, who also enrobes the new chief. The MiserassiWura, who tends the grave (*miseri*) of NdeWura Jakpa, is a Muslim of the Jebaagte group. Together with the Sakpare, who traditionally supply the Limam to the paramount, these form the three distinct Muslim elements in Buipe.

The division of Buipe includes only a few villages, and these are scattered. The commoner population of the villages lying around the capital is mainly Mpre and Dompo, though Morno, a crossing point for the Volta River, has many ferrymen (*nterapo*). There has clearly been a large slave element over the centuries, but the absence of descent groups with exclusive criteria of recruitment has facilitated their assimilation. There remain today in central Gonja no slave villages or slave sections of villages as separate elements in the social fabric. The commoner groups in and around Buipe have either lost their language (Mpre, Nterapo) or speak a Guang dialect very close to Gbanyito (Dompo). There is thus a single language spoken by members of all estates in this division.

Buipe is atypical in the pattern of chiefship. Of the four subordinate villages which had resident chiefs during the period of fieldwork, none had a chief of the ruling estate. In Morno the chief was a member of the ferryfolk. The other three village chiefs were men whose mothers came from the Buipe ruling estate, that is, they held chiefships of the second rank, Sister's Son chiefships. These were the JapaWura at Kolonso, and the chiefs of Katangi and Frufruso. The senior office holders of the ruling estate all lived in Buipe itself.

In 1956 when I first went to Buipe it could be reached only by Land Rover during the rainy season. According to our census it was then a town of 363 people, despite the fact that the divisional chief, his immediate family, and a few followers, had moved to a new site on the Volta. A major highway was under construction, designed to link the

29

north and the south of Ghana after the creation of the Volta lake by the new dam, and the road was to cross the river by bridge at that point. The government wanted Buipe to move on to the road both for ease of administration and as a source of services to the heavy flow of traffic expected. When we arrived in the old town, however, there was little sign of an impending move. Most of the elders, particularly the Muslims, were strongly opposed to leaving the shrines and monuments which were their trust. Dire calamity was predicted, not only for the towns-people, but for the whole state, if the old town were to be abandoned. Yet nine years later, when we again made our way along the track to Old Buipe, only a few families remained among the ruined compounds. While the move to New Buipe was no doubt hastened by the arguments and assistance of the government, it follows a well-established pattern of the movement of towns which have become isolated to join new lines of communication.

A comparison of the census figures for Buipe in 1948 with those for New Buipe in 1960 shows an increase from 348 to 426, or about 18%. However, in 1960 many were still in Old Buipe (not listed) and there were an unknown number of construction labourers included in the figures for New Buipe, so such a comparison is extremely difficult to interpret.

BUSUNU SUB-DIVISION

The division, or more correctly the sub-division, of Busunu contrasts with Buipe in many respects. The chiefs of both Tuluwe and Busunu maintain that originally the two formed a single administrative unit, and that, even today, the TuluWura 'owns' Busunu. However, in practice, the BusunuWura is as autonomous as other divisional chiefs: he holds Damba in his own capital, enrobes the Gbanya chiefs whom he appoints to fill vacancies, and is himself enrobed by one of the Busunu commoner elders without reference to the TuluWura.

In direct contrast to Buipe, Busunu is a warriors' town. The Gbanya who first settled there were accompanied by the war leaders of Tuluwe division, and they have retained possession of the war shrines. Busunu people are often described as the warriors of the paramount and, unlike the other divisions, their Damba ritual centres around the war shrines. The families which provide the war leaders are Gonja com-moners (*gbanyamasi*) and not fugitive Akan as in several of the other divisions.

There are no Muslim offices attached to the divisional court, and

30

indeed no Muslim kin groups established in the capital, although a few individuals of the Muslim estate have settled there, either as traders or on the basis of maternal ties. Nor is there an official spokesman at the BusunuWura's court. One of the senior commoner councillors performs the duties which usually fall to the divisional spokesman.

The pattern of circulating succession of office among dynastic segments of the ruling estate is fully worked out in Busunu, which has four major village chiefships, as well as a number of titles associated with villages that have now disappeared. Further, Busunu chiefs tend to live in the villages to which they have been appointed, returning to the capital only occasionally, except at Damba time. The commoner population around the capital, in the neighbouring hamlet of Moape, and in the villages of Langanteri and Baka (Kadendilimpe), are Hanga and speak a dialect of the Mole-Dagbane sub-group of the Gur languages. Those in the much larger villages of Gurupe and Murugu to the west speak dialects of Grusi. Members of the ruling group must be multilingual, although most commoners speak at least some Gbanyito.

Busunu today stands on the site of the old village of Damba Yiri. The move from the previous position, several miles to the south, was made at the beginning of the century. Damba Yiri was on a well-travelled trade route between Yendi and Bole, and the people there were profiting from the sale of food and beer to the travellers. It was this, I was told, which led the Busunu chief to decide to amalgamate the two towns. The court, with the chief and his councillors, settled in Damba Yiri, which henceforth was known as Busunu.

The figure for population given in the 1948 census for Busunu and the hamlet of Moape is 748. By 1960 this had grown to 934, an increase of 20%. This is in line with general trends of population increase for sub-Saharan Africa, but much below the 48% increase between the two censuses for Gonja as a whole. This again underlines the continuing thinness of population in the central Gonja area.

MANKPA DIVISION

The three secondary dynastic segments of the ruling estate in Mankpa also claim descent from one of the sons of NdeWura Jakpa. The divisional chief, the MankpaWura, is not among those eligible for the Yagbum skin, but is recognized as the second in importance of the royal councillors of the paramountcy. The capital, also known as Mankpa, is the home of two of the three segments of the ruling estate.

31

The GbampeWura, probable successor to the MankpaWura as divisional chief, has settled with the few remaining members of the third
segment in another village, Kabalipe, on the Sorri river. There is no
KabalipeWura but the MankpaWura has delegated a kinsman to act
as his representative there.

The part of central Gonja in which Mankpa lies appears to be particularly vulnerable to drought. The old town of Bute, whose commoners
used to speak Mpre, has a number of wells hollowed out of the laterite
which collect the surface water during the rainy season and hold it for
use during the long dry spell. Bute was also the site of large three-storey
houses, the last of which was still visible in 1969. The people now live
in compounds which are clusters of single rooms, as elsewhere in
central Gonja, because, they say, the old multi-storey houses are no
longer necessary for defence against the Ashanti, so that people do not
want to take the trouble to build them.

Bute is the home of a famous shrine and is under the authority of
the shrine priest, the Bute KagbirWura, rather than of a Gbanya chief.
Also from Bute comes the senior Earth priest of the division, who lives
in the town of Mankpa and serves as a councillor at the divisional
court. The other major town under Mankpa is Jembito, many miles
away, south-west of Buipe. This too is a shrine town, and has a Kagbir-
Wura instead of a chief as its senior official. At the present time the
Jembito shrine is more widely consulted than that at Bute, with people
coming from considerable distances to seek its aid. Unlike the grave of
Jakpa at Buipe, the Bute and Jembito shrines are not associated with
the invading Gbanya, but belong to the commoners. Only the elders of
the priestly families can communicate with the spirits of the shrines and
secure their help for supplicants. A popular and powerful shrine is a
source of prestige and prosperity for its custodians. In certain contexts
such shrines act as an alternative to the authority of the ruling Gbanya.
Oaths are sworn on them as sanctions against adultery, theft and
witchcraft, in a way which parallels the resort to the chief's secular
authority. Especially on the occasion of the annual shrine festival, the
shrine priest holds court in a way very similar to a chief, with many
followers in attendance. He receives gifts from supplicants and, through
the shrine, adjudicates differences between human beings and supernatural forces.

There are today no Muslim officials attached to the Mankpa court,
aside from the divisional spokesman. Nor were there any Muslims
settled in Mankpa when I lived there. If a funeral or naming ceremony
requires the services of a Mallam, one must be brought in from a

neighbouring division. It is said that there used to be Muslims at the court, but that long ago the Limam was grossly insulted by the Mankpa-Wura. He left, taking all his kinsmen with him, and swearing that thereafter the Mankpa people would never be able to have the services of resident Muslims.[2] Rulers and commoners alike now speak Gbanyito in Mankpa and its villages.

When I was there in 1957, Mankpa lay about twelve miles off the new road along the main track to the capital of Debre division. It was only possible to drive along this route during the dry season, and the people of Mankpa and the villages beyond were attempting (unsuccessfully) to have it improved so that lorries could reach them. The MankpaWura was no more successful in his efforts to get a permanent water supply for his capital, despite very severe hardships. With a population of 144, according to the 1948 census (it was almost exactly the same when I was there in 1957), the authorities clearly did not feel the expenditure justified. The drought was particularly severe in the dry season of 1957, and most of the people of Mankpa left to join relatives in other communities not so far from a water source; some went to Bute, some to Buipe and some to Kabalipe.

During the drought of 1957 the MankpaWura remained in the capital, but in 1965 he and his court had moved permanently to Kabalipe on the new motor road to the south, and only a few people remained on the old site. The 1960 census does not list Kabalipe among the villages in the Northern Region. Mankpa is shown as having a population of 159, an increase of a modest 9%. As Kabalipe must have contained well over one hundred people at this time and as it is directly on the main road, it is hardly likely to have been overlooked. It was almost certainly recorded as Mankpa since the divisional chief and his court were living there.

The position of Buipe, Busunu and Mankpa relative to each other and to the other divisions in the Gonja state appears on Map II (p. 12). On Map III the approximate boundaries of the divisions are indicated as well as the positions of their villages, including those now deserted. This map also shows the rivers and the modern motor roads. In the interest of clarity I have omitted the extensive network of paths between villages, some of which follow the old trade routes. Because of the

[2] It proved quite impossible to establish the date of the Muslims' departure. One cannot but wonder whether it coincided with the decline of the central Gonja trade route, for this area is so sparsely populated that there would have been little opportunity for the Muslims to pursue their traditional work of trading and writing prayers once the caravans ceased to pass that way.

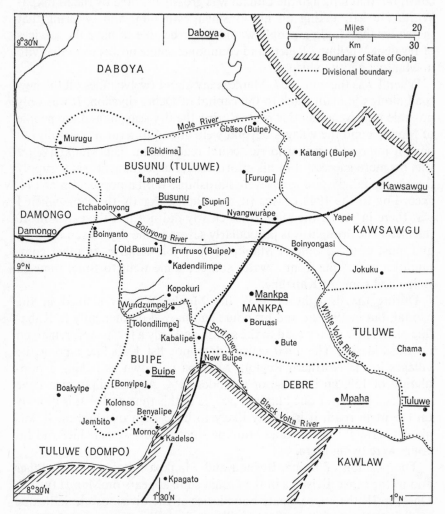

Map III. Central Gonja. Parentheses indicate the allegiance of a village outside the divisional boundary. Square brackets indicate the site of a former village. Underlining indicates divisional capitals. Names of divisions are in capital letters.

dispersion of close kin and the patterns of residence and of marriage, people move constantly between villages within and between divisions. Inevitably, therefore, reference will often be made to villages other than those in which fieldwork was done. It is intended that Map III should help the reader to trace the spatial correlates of the institutions and relationships whose description follows.

THE VILLAGE AND ITS SECTIONS

It is difficult to convey the intensity of feeling which surrounds one's natal village. In a vast and for the most part empty sea of scrub and grass, the villages are like islands, promising food and drink, shelter and companionship, and above all a haven from the animals and spirits of the wilderness. But one's own village is more than this. It is for each man the point of reference with respect to which his map of the world is constructed. The fact that travel is constant between these islands only emphasizes the importance of the home village, and the man or woman who is away on a visit eagerly questions each traveller for news from home.

The first indication that a village is nearby is the appearance of farms and of farm tracks leading off from the main path. The scrub shows gaps where old farms are only partly overgrown; pawpaw and cassava often remain to testify to their former use. The path may cross a stream, or in the dry season a stream bed, where the banks are worn smooth by the feet of women and children from the village who come here to fetch water or to do their washing. And finally, above the grass and brush can be seen one or two tall trees, silk cotton or baobab, which mark the site of the village itself.

Then suddenly the path leads into the open space surrounding the village, an area kept clear by the grazing of goats and cattle and annually cleaned again to guard the houses from dry season grass fires. From the outside can be seen only the backs of the thatch-covered mud rooms and behind them sprawling heaps of rubbish spotted with the stalks of discarded grain which has perversely germinated. Among the refuse chickens and guinea fowl hunt for grain and grubs, avoiding the pits from which earth has been dug for the building of new rooms.

The path stops abruptly here and the stranger must pick his own way through the maze of rooms. Within the village there are cleared areas – around a resting bench, under a shade tree, an open stretch where traders have set up their temporary stalls or where the hollow square of the village dancing ground is placed, and yet another in front

35

of the chief's council hall (*lembu*). But around these open spaces the huts, some square or oblong, others round, appear to be scattered arbitrarily over the ground. Occasionally a mat of woven grass stretches between two rooms to enclose a bathing place, but otherwise one may pass freely among them. They do not form neat units or compounds, as is the case in Dagomba country to the east where the rooms of one extended family are bounded by a high mud wall which allows access only through the reception room of the compound head. Nor do these central Gonja rooms share a single flat roof as is the case in the predominantly Vagala and Safalba villages in the west of the state. Rather, each hut consists of a single room – very occasionally partitioned into two – and stands free among several others.

The villagers themselves, however, distinguish between different sections of the village in various ways. On one level the village is differentiated into sections (*kawutchu*, pl. *nwutchu*) which reflect the alignment of groups within the village. The distinguishing term for a section may be descriptive or designatory. The chief's section is universally referred to as *ewurkpa*; others may be known by the name of a senior man, living or dead, or by some characteristic landmark – a shade tree for instance.

In some villages the sections are spatially distinct, separated by a few hundred yards of grass and the inevitable refuse heaps. In others they are less so, being but clusters of rooms demarcated from each other only by alleyways which are recognizable both by the fact that they are used as paths by those who have no business inside the section, and because the adjacent rooms all present blank rear walls to the path, the doors opening inwards to the courtyards of the compounds. In the dry season all the earth within the village itself is beaten smooth and hard by the constant comings and goings of people, goats and cattle. Thus the area surrounding the rooms is indistinguishable in appearance from the paths referred to above, and these are not immediately apparent to the stranger. Such *de facto* boundaries of the groups of rooms which form compounds are flexible and exist only in use. If a new room is added on the outskirts, the path becomes the space behind it. Thus each compound, and by extension each section, consists of the space occupied and enclosed by the constituent rooms. Boundaries are not otherwise defined and no land outside is considered to belong to the section.

Although in any village local segments of estates may be, and usually are, concentrated in different sections, the division of a village into sections cannot be regarded as a direct function of the division of the people of Gonja into three social estates. For all villages are internally subdivided, even when they are homogeneous from the estate point of view. Rather, the divisions within any given village reflect the lines of opposition which are locally relevant.

A few examples may make this clearer. In the central Gonja village of Jembito the two sections represent a differentiation within the commoner estate, apparently based on a group of autochthons on the one hand and on the other an immigrant commoner group. In Mankpa, the sections were three in number. In two of these live each of two dynastic segments of the ruling estate with their kin. The third is the section of the JipoWura, the senior Sister's Son chief of the division, and it is within this section that the senior Earth priest, also a commoner, has built his rooms. The Muslim estate in Mankpa is only represented by two families of spokesmen who are attached to one of the Gbanya sections. Thus, the village is laid out neither on the basis of the internal divisions within a single estate, nor on the basis of the assignment of a sepeate section to members of each (see Figure 1).

The town of Busunu is larger than either of the other two divisional

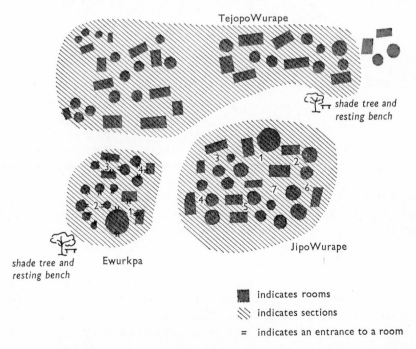

Fig. 1   Village of Mankpa showing compounds and sections. Courtyards are numbered in selected compounds.

capitals studied. It is also more complex. Leaving aside the predominantly commoner hamlet of Moape some 500 yards to the east, Busunu consists of four main sections: Ewurkpa, TandaWurape, the Earth priests' section (Tindanape) and the place of the chief of the Youngmen (KaiyeribiWurape). It is important to stress here that, although these sections are characterized as belonging to an estate, or a segment of an estate, they are by no means solely tenanted by members of one estate alone. For example, the following table (3-1) shows the distribution of the residents of two adjacent sections in the village of

Table 3-1. *Residence of adults in two Busunu sections: percentage of adult men and women who belong to each estate*

		Estate:			
Section:		Ruling	Commoner	Both	
Ewurkpa					
	men	7	12	19	
		37%	63%	100%	
	women	10	27	37	
		27%	73%	100%	N=56
TandaWurape					
	men	4	37	41	
		10%	90%	100%	
	women	7	34	41	
		17%	83%	100%	N=82

Busunu by their estate affiliation. One, Ewurkpa, is that in which the chief of Busunu lives with his wives, several of his adult 'children' and several kinsmen of the previous chief. In the second section, Tanda-Wurape, lives the senior of the Sister's Son chiefs, the TandaWura, and many of his kinsmen, as well as the distantly related members of several other compounds. Even in the chief's section only slightly over one-third of the men (37%) are of the ruling estate, the remainder being commoners. In TandaWurape there is an even higher proportion of commoners among the residents, 90%; here too are found a few representatives of the ruling estate, four men, or 10% of the adult males living there.

We shall later examine the specific mechanisms which result in this dispersal of the members of each estate.

This reservation as to the actual composition of a section holds also for those which are less obviously distinct. The village of Buipe is an example and illustrates yet another form of internal differentiation (see Figure 2). Buipe differs from both Mankpa and Busunu in that about one-third of the population is Muslim by patrifiliation. Among the remainder are represented the two dynastic segments from which the chief of the division of Buipe is taken in turn, and also people of the various commoner groups found in this area. There are many possible ways in which such a heterogeneous population might group itself spatially, but the people of Buipe see the village as being divided roughly into two, and these sections are referred to as Limampe (the place of the Limam) after the senior Muslim functionary, and Ewurkpa (the place of the chief).

It is characteristic of sections that although there may be one man recognized as senior (as is the village chief in his section) there is no

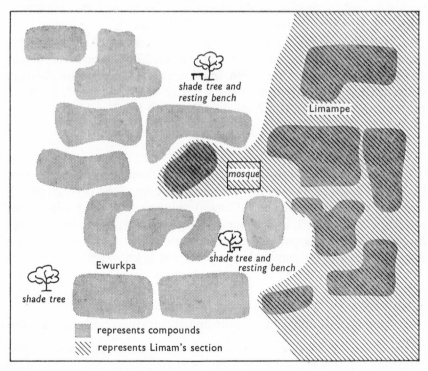

Fig. 2   Village of Buipe showing compounds and sections.

necessity for this. For instance, there are several offices vested in the Muslims of Buipe. One is the Kante Mallamship, the holder of which is the senior officiant in those annual performances which assure the well-being of the town and division, and is also the spiritual adviser to the Buipe chief. But also resident in Buipe is the Limam, whose duty it is to preside over the installation of a new paramount ruler of the Gonja state. Each of these men recognizes the other as supreme in his own sphere, but neither would agree that the other was senior to him, a point perhaps borne out by the insistence of each that he was the elder.

It is evident from the description of the sections of these villages that their organization may take various forms depending on the actual constitution of the population of the village involved. It must be emphasized that the internal constitution of each section is not based on agnatic kin groups, in spite of the fact that they are often differentiated in terms of estates which are themselves agnatically defined.

The second point which requires emphasis is that these sections are physically distinct units, yet they emerge in opposition to each other only in certain contexts and do not form a continuous basis for differentiation in daily activities. In showing a stranger around Busunu a local man is quite likely to say, "Over there is the chief's section, this is the part of the Tindaana's people and there, on that side of the dancing ground, is the place of the Sister's Son chief." But to one who knows the village, directions are given more specific reference in ordinary conversation: "Oh, he lives in the old war leader's house", or "You must mean the resting bench by the silk cotton tree."

THE COMPOUND

To the village folk, however, the most significant units are the compounds (*bilangta*, sing. *langto*). The term for compound is based on the word for the central courtyard (*langto*) around which the rooms of the residents are grouped, and common usage includes the courtyard, the rooms, and their occupants. Whereas a section does not necessarily have a recognized head, a *langto* always does, and is known by his name or title. A map of a village in which each compound was designated by name would also provide a list of the main office holders and senior men.[3]

Compounds are thus named units and these names provide the main

---

[3] It might first be necessary to decode the list of compound names. A few may still be known by the name of the previous elder, or by a reference to some aspect of the head's character or reputation.

40

points of reference within the village. A compound may be known by the title or office held by the compound head, or by his personal name if the head holds no office; sometimes a descriptive phrase is used. This senior, or head man, in each compound is known as the *langwura* (literally, 'chief of the compound'), although *wura* in this usage is descriptive, an honorific term that does not designate an office formally incorporated within the political system. The suffix *-wura*[4] is often used to mean 'leader', or one who is superior in a given context, or again, of someone who has rights over an article, activity or resource. Thus, people speak of one who has introduced a particular dance, or who performs it especially well, as the *katchawura*, 'chief of the dance'. Similarly the man who is farming a given plot of land is the 'farm owner' (*kadɔwura*), and the woman who owns a mortar the *kipiniwura*.

The absence of a term for section head is the more significant when composite terms are so readily coined. As this suggests, there is no leadership or representative role associated with village sections. Relations between the chief and compound heads are direct and not mediated through a section head.

The compound head represents those who live with him in dealings with the village chief, who in turn communicates with his subjects, in the first instance, through the head of their compound. This is most clearly seen in patterns of greeting. A stranger goes first to the room of a kinsman or friend, who takes him to greet the compound head. The head of the compound must then take the stranger to greet the village chief. In this way the stranger is temporarily given a place in the community and introduced as 'belonging' to one of the compounds. This is one of the several ways in which greeting may be used as a mode of establishing a relationship or in pressing for a favour.

GREETING AS A RELATIONAL IDIOM

There are three general functions attached to 'greeting' (*choro*, noun form *katchoro*) in Gonja. First, it is used to open a sequence of communicative acts between two persons, irrespective of their positions. Second, it is a means of defining, and affirming, both identity and

---

[4] The suffix *-wura* will occur frequently in the following pages, both in its formal meaning as titleholder, chief, and with the informal connotation of 'one who holds rights' (of whatever sort). When it is used in the former sense it will appear capitalized, otherwise it will be written with a small 'w'. There are a few instances of people who have been named for title holders. When this occurs the proper name will have only the initial capital, i.e. a man named after the MankpaWura would be Mankpawura.

rank. And third, because the standard forms of greeting contain an element of deference which is status-enhancing, greeting becomes a mode of entering upon, or manipulating, a relationship in order to achieve a specific result.

How to greet, when to greet, and whom to greet are among the very first lessons to be mastered in Gonja. Forms of salutation are readily grasped, as is the etiquette of taking a small gift when greeting an important person, and of receiving kola nuts or a chicken in return. Less readily understood is the fact that both gift and return gift are *katchoro* ('greetings/thanks'), as are the verbal formulae that accompany them. And only gradually does one become aware of the other contexts and implications of the greeting idiom.

GREETING AS VERBAL BEHAVIOUR: SALUTATIONS AND THANKS

The verbal salutations exchanged so freely are highly formalized and carry a largely phatic content (see Malinowski, 1927: 313–16). They fall into a number of classes which may be collectively termed topical salutations, as they reflect particular circumstances like weather, time of day, enquiries after health, and so on. All may be answered simply by "all right" (*awɔ*, literally 'cool') or "well" (*alanfia*, 'healthy'). One of these topical salutations, "greetings for work" (*ansa ni kushung*) has the added meaning of "thank you", for which the phrase "I greet (you)" or "I greet you very well" (*me tchoro, me tchoro fo ga!*) may also be used.

ABASEMENT GESTURES AND THE APPROACH PATTERN: THE PHYSICAL DIMENSION OF GREETING AND THE RANKING FUNCTION

Even the briefest discussion of topical salutation, however, immediately leads beyond the realms of phatic communication. Within the domestic family and close proximate kin, the tendering of respect is of central importance and takes the form of obligatory morning and evening greetings that combine salutations with the abasement gestures marking the approach of junior to senior.

Every morning and evening children (even as adults) must greet parents and grandparents, wives must greet husband, his brothers and his parents. In each case the junior goes to the senior, crouches by the open door of his room, offers the appropriate salutation, receives any instructions for the day, and slips quietly away. This greeting is not simply empty form; it conveys respect of junior to senior, and it expresses subordinate/superordinate status relations. The junior comes *to* his senior; *he* crouches, *he* initiates the greeting rite and may receive instructions, ask a favour, or report some occurrence. This is an example, in its simplest form, of the ranking function of greeting. That is, the institutionalization of greeting ritual in such a way that its participants act out their respective and unequal statuses. And the combination of obligation to greet with institutionalized deference reinforces this ranking effect.

Daily greetings are only obligatory within the compound and between close kin. But twice weekly, on Monday and Friday, the sub-chiefs and elders must greet the town chief in the morning and again in the evening. This is a formal occasion: the chiefs assemble outside and are then led by the spokesman into the council hall where they sit down in order of precedence. When all are settled, they remove their hats and prostrate themselves before the chief, lying on their left sides, left arms extended, greeting with one voice. The chief responds through his spokesman and the elders and sub-chiefs return to a sitting position. Now the business of the morning can begin. Here again, obligation to greet and institutionalized deference have the effect of expressing status differences between the town, divisional or paramount chief and his sub-chiefs on the one hand, and among the sub-chiefs themselves, seated as they are in order of precedence, on the other. In greeting the town chief, the sub-chiefs literally present their respect, and thus express their subordination.

However, the ranking function of greeting is not restricted to relations within the family and between officeholders. Daily life in the village constantly provides further examples. When two people meet on a path, the junior stoops, knees slightly bent, and offers a short greeting to which the other briefly replies before both pass on. A woman returning from the waterside with a heavy calabash on her head may make a verbal greeting only, if it is a young or unimportant man she passes. But should she meet her husband, or a chief, a woman will remove her burden and crouch beside it until he has gone on. Similarly, a young man passing an elder, even at a distance, bends low before continuing on his way. Two elders meeting will both bend slightly while exchanging the customary phrases. Only children are exempt from this reflex act, as though they were invisible.

It would be a mistake if, in emphasizing the ranking aspect of such behaviour, one were to imply that greetings convey no further information. Anyone coming from afar is subjected to a barrage of questions regarding his maternal and paternal kin, his wife and children, the people of his town, and of the towns he has passed through on the way. The visitor answers "all right" or "well" after each query. But having made the required responses, when the greeting routine is over, real information is exchanged concerning common kin and friends. Both ranking and information are combined when the stranger is taken by his compound head into the presence of the town chief. Both by his visit to the chief and by the form of his initial greeting, the stranger expresses his deference. And the chief responds with the same questions as did the host, and receives appropriate answers.

GREETING TITLES: THE PLACING FUNCTION OF GREETING

There is yet another way in which verbal greetings convey information. For the form of address accompanying a greeting varies with the status of the person spoken to. The use of kin terms constitutes one form of 'placing', by putting the person so addressed in a specific category such as 'father' or 'grandfather'. This is the form used in addressing a stranger about whom nothing whatsoever is known, while among intimates kin terms may be used with morning and evening greetings. But for that vast area of social space lying between intimates and strangers, the placing function is fulfilled not by assimilation to a kinship status, but by identifying a person's estate affiliation, and often rank, local origin and occupation. This information is conveyed by greeting titles (*adilibi*), which follow the first phrase of a salutation. Thus, when a Gonja greets "Good morning", it is in the form of "Good morning, child of the Jembito Earth priest's people" or "Good morning, woman of the court Muslims." Every adult is placed by such a greeting title.

Both men and women are greeted by titles appropriate to their paternal kin, so I have designated those people who have a common greeting title as a patronymic group. The following outline summarizes the different principles stressed by the pattern of greeting titles for each estate, for not only do the actual terms differ, but the way in which they are assigned varies as well.[5]

1. RULING ESTATE
(i) *Hierarchy is a dominant principle in greeting titles of the ruling group*
   Only the ruling group is internally stratified beyond the designation of

[5] These principles were derived from an analysis of the greeting titles of Muslim and commoner groups from all parts of Gonja, in addition to the *adilibi* of the ruling estate.

44

single office holder and 'the rest'. In the ruling group, the hierarchical principle separates office holders from those without office, both among men and women. Among office holders, both men and women can be ranked for relative seniority. There are two entirely separate series of titles, one for men and one for women.

(ii) *Spatial unity is the other dominant principle in greeting titles of the ruling estate*

The greeting titles of the ruling group scarcely distinguish spatial origin at all. Non-office-holding men have different greetings in the centre, west and east of the country, but these variations are not fully observed, i.e. a member of the ruling group from eastern Gonja will be addressed by western terms for non-office-holding royal while he is in the west. It is essentially a dialect difference. Otherwise the same greetings and titles are used for members of the ruling estate throughout Gonja.

2. MUSLIM ESTATE
(i) *Equality is a basic principle among Muslim groups*

With a single exception, Muslim patronymic groups do not recognize hierarchy. This exception is the holder of the office of Limam, that is, the official head of all Muslims in the community.

(ii) *Spatial origin is another primary principle of Muslim greetings*

Muslim greeting titles almost always lump men and women together, and refer not to the sex or status of the one greeted, but to the group of origin. Nearly all these groups have a spatial referent outside Gonja (indeed outside Ghana); Hausa, Bornu, the Ivory Coast, Haute Volta are all represented.

3. COMMONER ESTATE
(i) *Commoner greeting titles allow weak distinctions by rank and sometimes by sex*

Some commoner groups differentiate greeting titles by sex, but many do not. Many commoner greetings utilize the principle of hierarchy in designating a single office holder and differentiating him from other members of the group. This office holder may be a shrine priest, an Earth priest, or a war leader. Occasionally assistants to shrine priests have special greetings, but when this happens they are the single office holders in their own kin group.

(ii) *Local reference is the major principle of commoner greeting titles, and this is often expressed by their association with Earth shrine parishes*

Most villages include members of two or even three commoner patronymic groups, and equally, members of a single group are rarely confined to one village. Yet the distribution of a given commoner greeting title is usually limited to several adjacent communities, or to communities known to be linked by migration. People think of a given commoner greeting title as pertaining to the people of the Earth shrine of village 'X' or to those who speak a single dialect, and they almost certainly represent autochthonous enclaves. There appear to be certain greetings which are Dompo, and others which are Mpre, Hanga or Tampluma. This is clearer from the women's greetings than the men's. Even where men of two villages have different greetings, their women often share a single form. In any case the spatial referents of commoner greetings are interlocking, adjacent, and within Gonja. They are thus different as one moves across the country. Those of eastern Gonja are little known in the west and vice versa.

(iii) *Some occupational groups have distinctive greeting titles, but they are not endogamous, and are usually not localized*
The exception to the emphasis on locality among commoners are those greeting titles that have an occupational rather than a spatial referent. Certain forms of divination are known and practised within families, each of which has greetings indicating their particular skill. In the same way, barbers are greeted as *ase*, as are some blacksmiths (others are *langsamo*) and ferrymen who 'have the spear', associated with the Mande conquerers, are *yitcha*. Akan who came to act as warriors for the Gonja are *anyaado*.

Thus greeting titles have placing functions and may also have ranking functions. But it must be remembered that, by placing a man or woman in the commoner estate, the greeting title also ranks them below members of the ruling estate in political contexts, though not necessarily in the day-to-day life of the village. And anyone addressed by a greeting title of the commoner or ruling estate is assumed not to be of the Muslim faith and, in the view of the Muslims, to be of a lower ritual condition. Placing in Gonja involves contextual ranking.

All aspects of Gonja greetings to which I have referred are included in the referents of the word *choro*, to greet or thank. Greeting titles, patronymically determined terms of address, are also considered a part of greetings, as indicated by the fact that a man can equally well ask a stranger, "How do they greet you?" (*nsum ba choro fo?*) or "How do they title you?" (*nsum ba dila fo?*). In either case the answer will be in terms of the appropriate greeting title (*kadilibi*).

Verbal greetings are compounded of greeting titles and topical salutations, and they are usually accompanied by physical gestures, and sometimes by gifts. It is by means of all these elements that greetings serve to open channels of communication and lay the basis for further interaction. While at first the words used in the salutation seem the most significant aspect of greeting, in fact they convey little information compared to that contained in the greeting title that accompanies them. And non-verbal behaviour, in the form of approach patterns, deferential gestures and the giving of gifts, further define the status of both parties. These are the building blocks of Gonja greeting idiom. They lay the basis for interaction between members of a heterogeneous society. But they also serve as the means by which changes of status are recognized (as in *rites de passage*) and as one of the primary means by which political influence is affirmed and manipulated. Finally, by making possible the initiation of relationships between non-kin, formalized greeting is a way of obtaining favours that are paid for in a currency of respect and deference.

THE MANIPULATIVE ASPECTS OF GREETING

The definition of status conveyed by a greeting title is determined at birth by the patronymic group of the father, and remains fixed throughout a person's lifetime, unless a man should succeed to office. However, relative changes of status do occur with the major *rites de passage* of birth, marriage and death, and these are the occasions for reciprocal acts of greeting. As a class, these acts of greeting associated with *rites de passage* serve to place individuals in new roles. Apart from the content of the role itself, they do not imply or enforce status differences. Shifts in domestic and kinship roles have no important effects on the hierarchy of the political domain, and greetings in the course of associated *rites de passage* tend to be reciprocated, so that in the end the account is even. First others greet the novice, then the novice returns their greetings. Obligations to kin and neighbours are acknowledged and thanks given. These latter observances, although called 'greetings' by Gonja, could equally well be termed 'thanks for greetings'. And as already noted, there is a sense in which *choro* means 'thanks'. Neither party has deferred to the other, and no status imbalance exists.

Prestations are a pervasive element in the complex of greeting behaviour. For instance, there are situations in which a visit or a gift are equivalent; if it is not convenient to make a visit, the sending of a gift, which is also referred to as *katchoro*, will do equally well. Even when the two are combined, as in the case of a man bringing some kola nuts on coming to greet, the gift is often referred to as the greeting: *fo ba katchoro nde* ("here is your greeting") is the verbal formula which accompanies the handing over of kola nuts or a bottle of gin.[6]

---

[6] The *Gbanyito* word for kola nut is *kapushi* and it is entirely consistent with the composite nature of the greeting idiom that in daily parlance *kapushi* is often used to mean 'money'. Thus if a man says he greeted the chief or an elder with *kapushi*, it is impossible to know whether he actually gave kola nuts, or whether he is

GREETING AND THE AFFIRMATION OF HIERARCHY

In the political sphere, regular greeting has two main functions which follow from the reaffirmation of status differences, that is, from ranking. In the first place, by regularly greeting the town, divisional, or paramount chief on Fridays and Mondays, elders and sub-chiefs demonstrate their acceptance of his authority, and do so in a way which publicly provides him with a following. This is obvious at the higher levels of the state hierarchy, when the paramount's council hall is crowded with richly robed men who prostrate themselves before the elevated platform on which the YagbumWura sits on his skins of office. But it is equally, indeed perhaps more, important for the lowly village chief whose daily life is so close to that of his subjects, and who is often linked to them by ties of kinship and marriage, as well as of neighbourhood. For him the public performance of greeting ritual on Mondays and Fridays is an occasion when he is clearly set apart from his followers as the recipient of their respect and deference. And on this day the whole village sees the homage of their elders to the chief. He is seen to be respected and to have a following. A similar, but far more spectacular, expression of this public homage occurs at the annual Damba ceremony when all the minor chiefs assemble in the capital and, under the direction of the spokesman, prostrate themselves three times in the dust in front of the divisional chief and a crowd of onlookers.

Given the central importance of greeting in defining the relations between superior and subordinates in the political realm, it is not surprising to find that greeting and more specifically 'greeting to beg' (*choro n' kule*) has a prominent place in the suit for a vacant chiefship. The Gonja insist that they do not buy chiefship like some other Ghanaian peoples, a practice which they despise. There is considerable evidence to suggest that formerly this was true in the sense that greeting to beg for chiefship was done, not with money, but with gifts of bush meat, kola nuts, drink, and perhaps an embroidered gown or a horse. Nowadays a gift of money is presented by each candidate to the divisional chief, though the sums involved are small in comparison with those which

---

obliquely referring to a money gift. Similarly when a person says he 'greeted' someone (*choro*), it is impossible to tell whether a visit and verbal greeting is meant, or whether he is referring to the sending of a gift (of whatever sort), or to both together. Uchendu's analysis (1964) of 'kola hospitality' among the Igbo suggests that in this acephalous system such a dual meaning is not assigned to the giving of kola nuts.

pass elsewhere in the country. The Gonja view is that a would-be chief must greet with money in order that his superior will take his candidacy seriously as well as to show respect. A man who does not respect the divisional chief by greeting properly as a candidate is thought unlikely to do so when an office holder himself. So 'greet' he must.

There is no return of these cash gifts to the unsuccessful candidates, nor is this demanded. The divisional chief remains the political superior, and to alienate him would be unwise. He has, after all, control over other offices and may grant other favours. Rather, what seems to be happening is that cash 'greetings' are left to 'gather interest' as unredeemed debts. In this way the two men are bound in a relationship of mutual self-interest. The office-seeker has shown his loyalty and he hopes eventually to be rewarded. The chief in turn has received tangible proof of the willingness of a subject to recognize and defer to his authority, and stands to benefit by retaining this loyalty with some form of reward. The request for preferment has been properly made and ought to be honoured, if not now, then later. It is an investment in the future benevolence of the divisional chief. Next time he may be more obliging – but only if he is persuaded of the loyalty of his supplicant, that is, if the debt of respect stands in his favour.

Greeting rituals then are institutionalized at every level of the political system, as well as in the domestic domain within the compound and between close kin. Within the family the junior greets and defers to the senior: child to parent, younger sibling to older, and all to the compound head. Greetings in the course of *rites de passage* are first given between more distant kin and between compound heads, and then reciprocated. Here the account is squared and no status imbalance results. When the same relational idiom is used in a political context, the 'greetings' flow all in one direction, from junior to senior, thus expressing the hierarchical nature of the relationship. At the same time, the fact that the political superior remains in receipt of deference and gifts for which he has made no tangible return means that there is an outstanding debt in the subordinate's favour.

GREETINGS AS GIFTS: RECIPROCITY AND RESPECT DEBTS

Such a formulation ought not to appear strained if we take seriously Mauss's assertion (in *The Gift*, 1925) that a prestation establishes an obligation, only satisfied by a return gift. Even in its non-material form, greeting is a gift, a gift of respect and deference, both valuables of great worth in Gonja eyes. Seen in this way, it is no longer confusing to find that the Gonja use the verb 'to greet' to cover not only visiting and verbal exchanges, but also the offering of gifts.

In the view of both donor and recipient, greetings establish a debt based on the proffering of respect. The obligations incurred are diffuse and may cover the right to protection and justice at the chief's court. But quite specific claims can also be pressed through the idiom of begging by greeting. One who wishes to learn a skill, such as drumming or divining, does not seek out an expert and ask him how much lessons will cost. Rather, a would-be apprentice sets up a pattern of greeting his selected teacher, morning and evening, and on some of his visits may bring with him a few kola nuts, a bottle of local gin or, if he is a hunter, some bush meat. Only after some time, during which these greetings have been regularly made, will the supplicant venture to state his request. In order to beg successfully a man must greet assiduously, for favours cannot be expected of strangers. Courtship, discussed in the next chapter, is another example of the use of greetings to initiate a new relationship and to secure favours, ultimately the hand of the bride.

THE INTERNAL ORGANIZATION OF THE COMPOUND

All adults in the compound ought to greet the compound head in the same way as his children, that is in the early morning and in the evening. In this way he keeps in touch with their affairs. He will be informed of any illness, births or betrothals, and his permission will be asked if a trip is contemplated. Through regular greetings the residents also show their respect and deference to the compound head, and their dependence on him. It is on the basis of this relationship, built on a kinship tie of some kind, but not a mechanical 'reflex' of kinship, that the rights and obligations existing between residents and the head of their compound come to be seen as binding.

However, both the heterogeneity of the relationships within a compound and the mobility of households over time, tend to weaken the control of the compound head over the residents of larger compounds. For compounds vary widely in size, and with increasing size the relationship between residents is inevitably more distant. The compound head and adult residents are often separated by one or two genealogical steps. Both men and women live in compounds where their relationship to the head is traced through kin of either sex. This pattern holds for each of the three estates, for it arises from the domestic institutions which they share.

The mixed composition of many compounds is reflected in the lack of a clear internal structure. Like the other units into which the village may be divided, the compound is variable in its physical layout. Some stand out immediately to the eye, while others appear to merge into one another. Of several adjacent courtyards, two may belong to a single compound while a third and fourth each form a separate one. Village architecture in central Gonja depends entirely on spaces and paths, and on the positioning of doorways and fireplaces, for the definition of boundaries. While this allows maximum flexibility to the participants, it can also present acute problems of analysis for the observer.

At first sight the square and round rooms within a compound seem quite arbitrarily placed. Yet a closer look will show that each room is related to the others near it by the way its single doorway opens on to the courtyard, and by the position of the fireplaces. In the diagram of the Mankpa sections and compounds (Figure 1), the chief's compound, Ewurkpa, contains four inner courtyards. The rooms opening on the first of these are the MankpaWura's own sleeping and private reception rooms. On to the large central courtyard open the rooms of his several wives, each with its own fireplace. The third contains the rooms of a 'son' of the chief, and of his wife. Finally, the fourth courtyard belongs to the MankpaWura's elderly mother; several of the unmarried youths of the compound sleep in an empty room next to hers. There is thus a courtyard for each of three adjacent generations, and one for the wives of the chief.

Most compounds are not so clearly laid out. That of the JipoWura contains seven inner courtyards, in which live the JipoWura and his wives (1); the household of a mother's sister's son of the JipoWura (2); the households of two sons of JipoWura's dead father's brother (3); three households of JipoWura's sons (by different mothers) (4 and 7); households belonging to sons of the JipoWura's dead brother (5); and two households of the Mankpa Earth priest, a cross-cousin of the compound head (6). Several of these households have dependants who do not appear on the schematic genealogy in Figure 3. Also omitted are the youths and young men who, not yet married, have no households of their own.

There seems to be a paradox here. In the context of village organization the compound is viewed (as it were from outside) as a functional entity. It is referred to by the name of the compound head who acts in public on behalf of those who live with him. Yet from within, the compound consists of a number of adults, related more or less directly to the household head, but often only distantly to each other. What

51

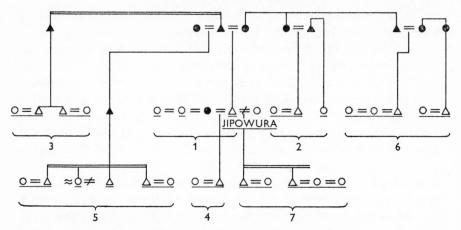

Fig. 3   Schematic genealogy showing relationship of households to compound
head in the compound of a Sister's Son chief (the JipoWura) in Mankpa.
Those currently resident are underlined. The brackets indicate those
living in a single courtyard, and the numbers correspond to those of the
JipoWura's compound in Figure 1.

sort of interdependence exists within the compound? Under what conditions, and on what bases can such a heterogeneous group co-operate?

THE DOMESTIC ECONOMY: FOOD PRODUCTION,
PREPARATION AND CONSUMPTION

In order to analyse the social determinants of compound organization,
a brief discussion of the nature of the domestic economy is first necessary. The sexual division of labour is such that, broadly speaking, men
provide food and women prepare it. This gives rise to two co-operating
units, the farming group and the cooking group, which together tend to
correspond to the personnel of the conjugal family. Since this correspondence is not complete, however, I shall use the term household
to refer to that group of men and women, and the children dependent
on them, whose food is grown by a single farming group and prepared
by the members of a single cooking group. A compound may contain
from one to seven or more households; the mean number is between
2.3 and 3.7, see Table 10–3.

While adolescent youths each have a few rows of yams, it is usually
only married men who have their own fields of both yams and grain.
These each man cultivates separately with the help of his sons and
foster-sons. Where full brothers live in the same compound they often
farm together in the sense that one day they will work side by side in

the fields of one and the next day in those of the other. But each married man has his own fields and stores his produce in his own granaries located in them. When a man's sons marry they gradually take over the daily work of cultivating their father's crops in addition to their own, but separate granaries are retained for the produce of father and son. A grown son, however, farms for his father in the sense that he farms under his authority. The father is still considered the owner of the farm, and some food from the fields cultivated in his name goes to the members of his household.

At the end of the rains, in late November or early December, new fields must be cleared to replace those which are exhausted; at this time or later on, the yam mounds for the next year are prepared. In these heavy tasks a larger group co-operates, several farmers together with the youths who regularly assist them. This farm-clearing group is usually based on the compound, although it may include residents of two or more adjacent compounds and, occasionally, representatives of only two or three of the courtyards which comprise the total compound area. This group clears the farms of its members in order of seniority, beginning with that of the compound head. He in fact seldom participates, except on the first day when he decides on the boundaries of the new farms. In practice each man may use as much land as he can manage. The boundaries are only roughly indicated to provide a framework within which the clearing proceeds. On the day when a man's farm is being cleared, his wife must provide an evening meal for the labourers with ample pounded yams and a particularly rich soup.

Food preparation is based on the unit of the conjugal family, although not so closely as is production. A monogamous wife cooks every evening, while co-wives take turns, either day by day or in spells of three or four days. An unmarried girl does not 'cook' (*dang*). However great her actual share in the preparation of a meal, she is only said to have 'helped' (*e tche muto*). It is true that widowed or divorced women living with kin may cook, but they do so primarily in connection with their role as mothers. A woman with no children, or an elderly woman whose children are grown up, seldom cooks for herself.

The distribution of cooked food does not correspond to the production unit, nor to that of food preparation, nor yet to the farm-clearing group. It is wider than all of these. When the porridge and soup are ready, the cook 'cuts' (*e tchige kude*) as many portions as are necessary, placing each in a separate pan or calabash. The young children of the household are then sent to deliver them. Women, girls and young children eat together, in the same units as those on which the preparation of food is based. That is, if two co-wives take turns at cooking, they will eat from one pan, whoever has prepared the meal. However, not infrequently co-wives refuse to do this and each takes her food into her own room to share with her children; in spite of this they are always described as eating from one pan.

Another portion is always sent to the compound head. This is done by every woman who prepares food grown on a farm of which he supervised the clearing. It may be that there are two men from a single compound and farm-clearing group, both of whom are considered senior men (*benumu*); in this case both will be sent a dish of porridge by the wives of members of the farm-clearing group. Next, a large portion is cut and sent to 'the young men' (*mberantia*), a general term used in this case to refer to the married men who clear farms together, and to the youths who help them.

So far the distribution and consumption of cooked food follows the lines of the farm-clearing group, senior men eating alone and the other men consuming together the food sent by the wives of each. The cooking group sets the limits of the consumption unit for women and children. However, most of the actual divisions of cooked food I recorded included one or more additional portions to be sent to a kinsman resident in another compound. Where obligations of this type exist, they tend to be regular and not casual. Those who are most often supported in this way, the mother or father of either husband or wife, or occasionally a parent's sibling, must be sent food every time a main meal is cooked, a practice that is carefully adhered to. Such obligations represent a regular lien on the resources of the conjugal family. A man is also responsible for the support of an unmarried sister or daughter who lives in his compound, and his wife must send her food whenever she cooks. If such a woman has young children with her, she may prefer to do her own cooking, in which case she will be brought yams and grain from the farm as is a wife. In this situation, wife and sister may either exchange cooked food, or the wife may send a portion only occasionally. Unless there is a regular exchange a woman does not send cooked food to a married brother with whom she is staying.

IMMEDIATE AUTHORITY: THE ECONOMIC, JURAL AND RITUAL
AUTHORITY OF THE COMPOUND HEAD

The compound head has direct rights to the labour of youths and adult males who co-operate in the heavy work of farm-clearing. This is most clearly demonstrated by the fact that his fields are cleared first. After this it is usually his own sons and foster-sons who plant, weed and supervise the harvest, but he may require other men in the farm-clearing group to help them. He need do no farming himself, although many compound heads go regularly to the farm and supervise or even join in the day-to-day work. The correlate of his right to labour is that in case of need any of the men of the farm-clearing group may take produce from his farm either for food or for sale. However, just as the compound head seldom calls upon their labour save to clear the land, so they rarely make use of this privilege. Whether or not a farmer claims to 'own' the produce of the compound head's farm in this way depends on the context of the discussion. But when claimed, ownership is justified by the fact that they made the farm for him (*anyi dɔ n'sa mu* – 'we farm and give him').

It is the compound head who decides when the annual clearing shall begin, and in choosing his own site he determines where many of the other farms in the group will lie. While there is no necessity for men in the same compound to farm adjacent fields – some do and others do not – many men appreciate the companionship this gives. And for the sons of the compound head, who are responsible for his crops in addition to their own, proximity has the added advantage of decreasing the distance travelled between tasks.

Within the compound the head must agree to the sites of new rooms, although I know of no instance when this was in dispute. When soil and water have been brought and the building is about to begin, the compound head is often called to supervise the process of lining out the walls so that they are straight. The same group of married men and youths co-operates in the building of a new room as in the clearing of new farms. Where the group is very large, the older men who are acknowledged to be more skilful do the actual constructing of the walls, and all the youths help in the mixing and carrying of the swish. The other senior men may drop in from time to time, to gossip and comment, but many take no other part.

The formal authority of the compound head is limited to those who are also his junior kinsmen, but in practice his word carries great weight and he assumes responsibility for the peaceful functioning of his compound. When quarrelling becomes loud enough to draw his attention, a message from him, or a reproving word delivered in person, usually restores at least outward peace. Minor disputes within the compound are brought before him if those immediately senior to the combatants are unable to work out a solution. Children's quarrels

are most often settled by the parents or their siblings, but when disagreements occur between adults of near-equal status, it is apt to be
difficult to resolve them without resort to one recognized as senior to
both.[7] Disputes between residents of two different compounds may
first be heard by one of the compound heads. If no agreement is reached
at this level an appeal will be made, first to senior kinsmen of both
those concerned, and finally to the village chief.

Disputes may be settled in one of two fashions: either the parties
concerned may be brought to an agreement by skilful questioning and
long discussion, or those consulted may decide upon what they feel is
an equitable solution and force its acceptance. When the latter pattern
is followed, enforcement is usually secured by pressure from senior kin.
The elders lend their weight to attempts to reach a settlement 'in the
room', both to avoid the discussion of disputes in public and because
'room cases' can more easily be treated according to the norms of a
particular estate. Thus, there are legal precepts in the Koran and its
commentaries which Muslims ought to follow, but which are not
always accepted by the other estates. Commoner elders have a very
substantial pride in the ways of their own people; further, each occasion
on which it is necessary to accept the authority of the chiefs is a reminder of their subordinate status. The members of the ruling estate
itself can hardly wish to expose their internal disagreements to public
comment. As this suggests, cases which do reach the chief's court tend
to be the more serious ones, and those between members of the different
estates. This reluctance to resort to the public court adds to the authority
of the compound head.

When arbitration by the compound head fails, then a different quality
of authority is brought to bear by referring the matter to the village
chief. This office represents the sanctions of the external system. The
hearing of a case before the assembled elders of the village brings it to
the attention of the whole community and the weight of public opinion
becomes a force for securing compliance with the verdict. And behind
this is the implied threat of force, for the chief has the right to con-
fiscate property, to banish wrongdoers from his village and division
and, in cases of homicide and witchcraft, the divisional chief formerly
had the power to impose the death penalty.

In stating that the authority of the compound head is formally of a
limited nature, I refer to the fact that he has behind him only the

---

[7] The Gonja find it hard to think of any two people as precisely equal; if there
exists no other status difference a discrepancy in ages always gives stature to the
elder individual.

sanctions inherent in co-residence, that is, the threatened withdrawal of co-operation and companionship, the sharing of farm surplus in time of hardship, and the provision of assistance in trouble. This I have characterized as immediate authority. However, a dissident resident can leave the compound and live elsewhere. If the compound head is also the senior kinsman in whom final authority over the resident is vested, his position is much stronger. However, mobility is common and can be justified on a number of grounds, so withdrawal from the compound is still an alternative, even where immediate and final authority coincide in the same figure.

The last of the areas in which a compound head exercises a measure of authority is that of ritual. When life-crisis rituals related to birth, marriage and death are performed by the residents of his compound, he is said to be in charge, although frequently he appears to play no part at all. The significant roles in such rituals are determined by kinship; where the compound head is closely involved on this account he may take a prominent part. Otherwise he is merely informed and a portion of the ceremonial meal is sent to him. If it is a minor ritual he may or may not attend. Neither in rites performed by compound residents for the purpose of supplicating dead parents (*nyina*), nor in those rites directed to their personal shrines (*akalibi*), is the compound head involved except as determined by particular kinship ties.

But there is another category of ceremony, determined by the Muslim calendar, which is celebrated on a community-wide basis. At Jentigi, the new-year fire festival (Arabic, *'Ashūrā*), at Dongi, the festival of the 'Great Sacrifice' (Arabic, *al-'īd al-kabir*), and at Damba, the prophet's circumcision (Arabic, *Rabī 'al Awwal*), the compound head performs rites and is sent portions of the ceremonial meal on behalf of those in his compound. Thus at Damba, when cooked rice is prepared with the meat from the cow that was sacrificed by the chief on behalf of the whole village, a portion is sent to the head of each compound. By accepting this food the compound head affirms his participation in the sacrifice and ensures that the benefits which it secures will also descend on him and those resident in his compound.[8] At Jentigi the compound head sets out bowls of food for the ancestors, and it is said that all the dead (*bubuni*) associated with the compound will come and partake. However, the dead are no more tied to a single spot than are the living. The SupiniWuritche of Busunu explained that when her mother's sister's son, Amati, in whose compound she was

[8] This interpretation is less abstract than it may appear. It is simply the meaning given to the sharing of ceremonial food.

living, set out food for the ancestors at Jentigi, both their mothers would eat of it there. Amati's father, on the other hand, would eat in the compound of his oldest son (Amati's half-brother), who had succeeded him in the office of war leader, while her own father, who had been chief of Busunu, would come for his portion to the compound of the current chief, his sister's son. Amati, then, set out food for the ancestors on behalf of those in his compound, but only for those of their forbears to whom no one could claim a more direct relationship.

This discussion has concentrated on those aspects of a compound head's authority which are a function of joint residence. In fact the picture is made more complex by the interaction of kinship roles with the obligations of contiguity. Distant or putative kin may live in courtyards loosely attached to a compound and yet not participate in the work of farm clearing. Where this is so, they do not join in the commensal group based on this co-operative unit. Even where the relationship is fairly close this separateness occasionally exists. Such a situation is usually an index of an impending division into two compounds. That is, co-operation breaks down some time before the two functionally independent units are physically separated. More extensive co-operative groups may also be found when compounds headed by office holders of any of the three estates form the focus for co-operative ties with dependants in other compounds. Both of these situations are exceptions to the general pattern, however. Usually the compound and the personnel of the farm-clearing group are co-extensive.

It should be stressed that the selection of farm-clearing as central among the activities determined by compound residence is mine, and is not made explicit by the Gonja. It is, however, one which fits closely with compound composition, and which reflects, through eating groups, the alignments within and also between domestic groups.

There are quite explicit ideas about the position of a compound head as well. This is the way that the JipoWura, a Sister's Son chief and head of a large Mankpa compound (see Figure 3) defined his rights and obligations with respect to those living with him:

I have to pay any fines levied against the people in my compound. I won't take any money from them; if I did they would run away. And if they run away they will be hungry and have no one to protect them. If their farms spoil, or the food on them is finished, I have to find them food. Again if I don't they will run away. If any of the boys want money to court a girl and marry her, I will help him find it. Not if he wishes to make love to a woman for nothing, though. Then I will not give him any. If they make money from working on the new road they will take out some for food and bring the rest to me. I will keep it for them. If they want money to buy a cloth or to marry then I give it to them.

I place this account at the end of the discussion of the position of the compound head because it is highly idealized, and holds in full only for those residents of the JipoWura's compound over whom he is also in a position of authority by virtue of kinship status. However, it expresses very well the pattern of authority which results when the rights and duties of close kinship overlap with those based on co-residence. And in this idealized form it serves as a charter for claims which can be made in a situation of crisis by all compound residents when close kin are not at hand.

THE HOUSEHOLD AND THE ROOM

The household is a group of individuals all of whom are directly related to each other by ties of kinship or affinity. This is the unit which co-operates daily in economic activities and whose women form a single cooking unit. The members of a household commonly occupy adjacent rooms opening on a single courtyard. Where there are several households, those less immediately related to the compound head may share a single large courtyard set slightly apart. What they have in common here is not genealogical proximity to one another, but genealogical distance from the compound head.

The smallest unit of residence is the room. Every married adult expects to have his or her own room, and thus this unit does not, as might be expected, coincide with the conjugal family. In fact there is no complex of rooms which necessarily does so. The household most often comprises a man and his wife or wives and their children, it is true. But it may also include one or more foster children, or a pair of brothers and their wives and children. Or a household may consist only of a widow or a divorcée and her children and foster children. In this last instance we are again dealing with an example of the overlapping of two levels of differentiation. For a woman and her young children share a single room, and in the case of an unmarried woman, the room and the household may coincide. This coincidence of the minimal social unit, that of a woman and her children, with the minimal physical unit is not fortuitous. Spatial mobility in Gonja is high, and so is the incidence of divorce. The relative autonomy of an adult woman as indicated by the occupation of a separate room with its own cooking places corresponds to her freedom of movement and to the fact that it is the group thus fed and housed which is the mobile unit. For when a woman leaves the compound of a recently deceased husband (an obligatory move), or when she goes from the compound of a father or brother to a new husband, her young children go with her, as do at least some of her adolescent and pre-adolescent daughters.

The growing independence of adolescent youths is similarly represented by claiming the right to occupy a separate room, apart from that previously shared with a father or older brother. And the same theme is echoed again in the ceremony establishing a wife in her own room on the completion of the period of several months during which she is regarded as a bride but still a stranger. Indeed, the very large round room (*lembu*) in which every village chief receives strangers, holds court hearings, and in which the esoteric portions of public ceremonies are conducted, may also be seen in this light. That is, it serves to separate his role as a chief *vis-à-vis* the community as a whole, from the positions he simultaneously occupies as head of a household and of a compound.

The purpose of this chapter has been to outline the framework of Gonja domestic life. Within the broad context provided by divisional citizenship and estate affiliation, one's home village and the villages of both parents form the main points of orientation. Indeed, villages have a multiple reality: they are the epitome of social life in contrast to the wilderness that surrounds them; they are the constituent elements in the political system, for a division is thought of in terms of the villages it controls; and one's village people are one's neighbours and, at the same time, one's kin.

In looking at the internal structure of the village several levels emerge, each based on a characteristic principle of differentiation. There is no single principle operating, such as genealogical relationship, actual or putative. In the division of the village into sections, the determining factor is the way in which the various estates, or segments of estates, are aligned. The grouping of households into compounds represents the way in which the kin of senior men are localized at a given time. Households are basically conjugal families, modified in many cases by the vicissitudes of marriage – divorce and widowhood – and by the addition of personnel whose presence is based on the sibling bond.

The central Gonja villages on which this study is based are all remote from urban centres, and even from local markets. Their economies are based on subsistence agriculture in which all men participate, each being responsible for growing, trapping or hunting sufficient food for his dependants throughout the year. Domestic organization and domestic authority are firmly anchored in small-scale agricultural enterprise, and are dependent on the co-operation this requires.

The position of the compound head is based on the responsibilities he assumes for those who live with him, and on the services they render in exchange. As a compound head he also receives recognition as a village elder. If this status is not augmented by a title or office, it will be of an informal nature. Nevertheless, as a compound head a man must be informed of village affairs, and included in the ceremonial distribution of cooked food. The compound is thus at once the smallest physical unit in the political system, and the largest in the domestic sphere.

However, movement of people between these fixed points – household, compound, village and division – is frequent. It is to a consideration of the processes responsible for this fluidity that the next section of the study is devoted.

SECTION II
MARRIAGE

The extreme division between male and female spheres of interest and competence which is generally characteristic of West African societies holds for the Gonja as well. Men and women do not eat together, only rarely work side by side, and are most likely to spend their leisure with others of their own sex; in some fundamental way they are felt to be in opposition on most matters. Marriage provides a slender bridge across this gulf. It is also the institution which, as anthropologists from Tylor to Lévi-Strauss have pointed out, forces the potentially self-sufficient unit of parents and children to turn outward. Through marriage, strangers become intimates; and opposites are forced to join forces for the bearing and rearing of children. In the chapters of this section various aspects of contracting and establishing a marriage are examined, and the relationship between spouses considered in some detail. Two relational idioms which convey between them some of the emotional undertones of conjugal roles are briefly sketched. The final chapter treats of the manner in which Gonja marriages are dissolved, and we are left to conclude that the bridge is indeed a slender one; in fact the conjugal union is likely to be limited to the period of rearing a family.

Some of the important questions about Gonja marriage and divorce were not formulated in a way that led to the collection of numerical data until after the fieldwork in central Gonja had been completed. There is a small amount of such data available for the three divisions on which this study focuses. Where they are clear and important to the argument these figures have been placed in the text despite low numbers and in some cases arbitrary samples. Less satisfactory data have been relegated to the appendices, or omitted altogether.

Later it was possible to spend periods of several months in both eastern and western Gonja (in 1964 and 1965 respectively). Some additional material on marriage was collected in eastern Gonja, while a carefully planned study of divorce and re-marriage was carried out in Bole (western Gonja) and Daboya (north-central Gonja) in 1965. The findings of these later studies confirm very well my earlier impressions from central Gonja. There are however several minor differences among the divisions involved, in language, economy and in population density in particular, which make it impossible to present the data from the later studies as though they applied directly to the three divisions in central Gonja on which this analysis is based. Thus these data too have been placed in appendices to emphasize their separateness from the main argument. However, where the results of the later studies confirm points not directly supported in the central Gonja data, this fact is mentioned in the text.

The two main sources of numerical data on central Gonja are the census made of all residents in Old Buipe in September 1956, and the personal data sheet kept on adults in Busunu who came to us for medicine during the summer and fall of 1957. The Buipe census has the advantage of completeness, but lacks depth, while the Busunu Health sample contains more information, but the sample is self-selected and thus of doubtful general validity. A partial census was also made of Busunu (a considerably larger town than Buipe), but as this has the drawbacks of both the other groups of data without any compensating advantages, it has not been utilized in this phase of the analysis.

Where sufficient information was included, I have preferred to use the Buipe census, since the total sample it represents is more dependable as a basis for generalization. Where the census does not contain sufficient detail, the Busunu Health sample has been used.

4

Courtship and patterns of marriage: open connubium

The analysis of marriage begins in this chapter with the consideration of three related questions: How are spouses chosen? What are the norms relating to marriage and to permitted and prohibited sexual relations? And, what are the actual patterns of marriage with respect to social and spatial boundaries?

Or to put it even more generally, how do people come to marry as they do, and what are the patterns that result?

COURTSHIP

Courtship (*katcholta*) is a major adolescent pastime, and its chief characteristic is the exchange of gifts by youths and young men for favours from their sweethearts.

Certain dances, particularly *sumpa*, and a host of clapping and skipping games are much enjoyed by girls from an early age. During festivals or on moonlight nights, the play will draw an audience of youths who enjoy the singing and rhythm, but who also come to look over the participants. Even in small villages where they have all grown up together, the exhilaration of dancing and being the centre of attention lends a new attraction to the girls. And there is always the possibility of a visitor from another village.

When he has found someone who catches his fancy, a boy will make an opportunity to give her a small gift, perhaps only a penny at first. If she is not too shy this present provides the occasion for an exchange of words. With repeated tokens of his interest, a girl gains confidence and the two may begin to tease each other (*ba pol*, 'they play'). If she continues to accept his gifts, now more substantial (perhaps a shilling or two, a towel, or a head scarf), the boy will understand that she is willing to sleep with him. Then *ba ji kajipo*, 'they are lovers'. If a girl accepts the gifts but refuses her favours, the boy has no recourse except to complain loudly that she is fickle. His friends may take heed and be more cautious. Or they may hope to be more fortunate.

The importance of courting gifts is indicated by the distinction

65

between the lover relationship[1] and rape. Rape (*purma*) is sexual intercourse after the woman has refused to accept any courting gifts. In other words, failure to give a gift, or the insistence on intercourse when a gift is refused, is equivalent to taking by force. The proffering of a gift, however small, gives the woman a chance to indicate whether she wishes to enter into an intimate relationship or not. It is morally wrong to force her.

The level of concern about rape is indicated by the dramatization of the threat it poses during the distribution of meat on the final day of the Damba ceremonies. The distribution is made before a large crowd who have converged on the capital for the main political occasion of the year. After the homage of the subordinate office holders to the divisional chief, and the presentation of porridge and soup by the royal women, the senior spokesman offers portions of the Damba sacrifice to representatives of each of the elements which go to make up the state: first the major groups within the division are named – the Sister's Son chiefs, the senior commoners, the *ewuritches* (female chiefs), the Muslims. Then each of the other major political divisions is called, one by one, and any bystander who is a citizen of that division may come and claim the meat as it is held aloft. Finally, shares are announced for three special categories: for the witches (*begbe*), the thieves (*bayur po*) and the rapists (*purpo*). Raucous laughter and jocular summonses among the young men accompany the spokesman's call for representatives of these last three categories. But there is always someone ready to swagger out and claim the compromising portions.

It would seem that these three sorts of anti-social behaviour have something in common which requires recognition at the time of the formal statement of correct political relationships. All three involve violation of the rights of others. But while witch, thief or rapist may be caught and convicted in a chief's court, their crimes are committed secretly and often go unpunished. The offer of portions of the Damba sacrifice is a warning to the participants that these threats exist (indeed they are increased by the assemblage of people from far and near) and at the same time also seeks to pacify the culprits, since they may escape undetected. In a sense they are being bought off, lest their activities disrupt the orderly nature of the occasion.

---

[1] The word for lover (*jipo*) has explicitly sexual overtones when used of the relationship of a man and a woman. Perhaps because these are always understood, the term is often used in a joking way between two friends of the opposite sex, and very frequently between joking partners.

There is a special relevance to the concern with rape during Damba. This has to do with the attendance of men from other villages and of strangers from further afield who may find the local women attractive. For there is a sense in which the enticement of one's womenfolk, even if it is done according to the rules, is considered to be like forceable abduction. In a society like Gonja, where virilocal marriage is the norm, a woman who marries a man from another division must follow him and leave her own people. In pre-colonial days, when three major trade routes passed through the kingdom, it is clear that these two aspects of rape were likely to be combined: strangers travelling through may have attempted to seduce the Gonja women, and even to persuade them to follow the caravan. By seeing rape placed publicly in the same category of anti-social acts as witchcraft and theft, strangers present at Damba are given notice that their association with Gonja women must at least follow the rules of courtship, and be based on a properly established relationship in which the woman indicates her consent by accepting gifts.

The period of late adolescence and early adulthood, when courtship is particularly engrossing, coincides with the time when, in addition to helping his father, a young man is establishing his own farm. When a number of youths had had good harvests, they used to celebrate with a courting feast. They would arrange to bring yams from their farms and meat from their traps, to take to their lovers on the same day. The girls then prepared a large meal of soup and pounded yam for the evening. Quite late, about the time when others were ready to retire for the night, the couples would gather to eat. The food was served in two large portions, one for the girls, and the other for the youths, for although it is not forbidden in Gonja for men and women to eat together, this seldom happens. When the meal was finished, the couples slipped away, two by two, for the night.

Such courting feasts no longer occur, perhaps because gifts of money and manufactured goods have become more important than yams in winning a girl's approval. Their relevance for understanding courtship lies in part in the opportunity they provided for youths to demonstrate skills as farmers and hunters, while giving the girls a chance to show how well they could cook. In addition, of course, the feast itself was an occasion much enjoyed by both sexes (at least so far as an informant's delight in recalling them can be taken as evidence). In the courting feast the lover relationship was given a semi-public recognition. However, by placing the roles of cook and provider of food firmly in a group context, these affairs were, in Gonja eyes, clearly distinguished from marriage. For it is the exchange of sexual and domestic services in a domestic setting that is the main criterion of a conjugal relationship in central Gonja.

Not all courtship leads to marriage, and the lover relationship is enjoyed for its own sake. Indeed, girls seek to postpone marriage as long as possible and young men seem to prefer a period of freedom from the cares and responsibilities of family life before they settle down. 'They roam about' (*ba ji kalembo*) it is said. This may mean a period spent working in the south, or prolonged visits to kin in other villages. That this practice is a long-established one is indicated by the stories told by older men about their youthful travels. Wherever they find themselves, such youths look over the girls and may establish a lover relationship. Two young men who worked for us in 1956–7 had two and three *jipo* respectively during this period, but both remained unmarried.

Nor are all lovers inexperienced adolescents who have never known the responsibilities of marriage. The social recognition of the lover relationship fits very well into the Gonja situation where older men and women must establish new conjugal unions on divorce or the death of a spouse. A mature courting couple may continue as lovers for some time, each living with their own kin, while the woman visits the man at night. Or if they come from different towns, the woman may come to live with her lover on a trial basis for a few months before they decide whether or not to marry. The delay in the final decision is most likely to be due to the woman's concern to see how she gets on with the other women in the new household, and, if she has children with her, how they are treated.

The exchange of gifts for sexual favours during courtship must be seen in the context of the greeting/begging idiom which we have noted as one of the major modes of relationship in Gonja social intercourse. As in several other spheres, the presentation of a small gift or verbal greeting (both *katchoro*), especially when repeated over time, serves to lay the basis for a relationship between two people who otherwise might have no claims on one another.

This interpretation of courting gifts is supported by the way the Gonja themselves interpret them. For in discussing courting one is told that the suitor will give small things – farm produce, salt, meat, kola nuts, or a few shillings – to both the girl and her mother, and may also give a few shillings, yams, meat, beer or kola, to her father or mother's brother. No distinction is made in conversation between the occasional gifts to her parents and gifts to the girl herself, which in fact are a preliminary and accompaniment to a *jipo* relationship. Indeed in a sense the parents are also being courted, since their approval is necessary if the courtship is eventually to end in marriage.

The greeting of the parents offers a recognized way in which the suitor may introduce himself and seek to win approval, by showing that he is prepared to be respectful, as befits a son-in-law, and is not 'going behind their backs'. Because of shyness a youth may ask a kinsman to present his greeting gifts to the parents. But he must also at some point come himself and greet the girl's parents, so that they can see him. Here the formalities of the standard greeting allow for interaction with a minimum of personal exposure.

The early phases of courtship involve the giving of small gifts in return, eventually, for sexual favours. At this stage, either cessation of courting gifts or denial of physical intimacy ends the relationship. There is no clear point at which this early phase ends. Not infrequently a girl accepts courting gifts, and attentions, from more than one young man, though to enter into more than one sexual relationship at a time is strongly disapproved of. There may also be several suitors greeting her parents in hopes of obtaining preference for themselves. When this happens, the mother ought to put aside anything she receives until the choice between suitors is made, and then return the gifts of those who were unsuccessful. Small amounts are not returned, but any substantial gift, cloth or a lump sum of money, would be.

When courtship continues to the point at which there is an understanding between the pair that they wish to marry, the suitor may be making larger gifts to both the girl and her parents: to the girl herself cloth, hair ties, powder, and perhaps larger amounts of money which she saves towards the purchase of pans and if possible a *kubba* (wooden cupboard or box); and to the parents, greetings of several shillings or even a few pounds. When the man feels he is ready to bring the new wife into his home, he finds a kinswoman who goes with one or two followers to fix the time for the sending of the marriage kola, and the subsequent removal of the bride. If at this stage the bride changes her mind and wishes to refuse the match, her parents are likely to try to persuade her, on the grounds that she has encouraged the suitor to expect that she would agree, and has accepted his gifts. How insistent they will be depends on their own attitude to the suitor, and how urgently they want to see their daughter married.

When a man is ready to marry a woman, he sends kinsmen with kola nuts and twelve shillings to her parents to ask for her. The girl should be summoned and asked three times whether or not she wishes to marry this man. If the marriage has been arranged by her parents, she may not know the suitor. Theoretically a girl in this position is free to refuse her consent, but it is clearly very difficult for a young girl to oppose her parents in this way, and she probably rarely does so. When the bride has agreed, the kola nuts are distributed among those present, who take a bite to signify their own approval; even absent family members should receive a portion of a nut. The twelve shillings is also divided among the kinsfolk of the girl and acceptance of even a penny indicates that the person has witnessed the agreement to marry.

Once the kola has been sent and accepted, the couple are considered to be married. If a bride at this stage refuses to go to her husband's house she will be very firmly persuaded indeed. One strong-willed girl in Buipe spent several nights in a tree on the outskirts of the town in an attempt to avoid joining her husband. Her kin were adamant that she had accepted his gifts and attentions, and had agreed to the marriage when the kola was sent. Now she was his wife and he had a right to bring her to his house. In this particular case the bride slipped on to a lorry and reached Kumasi where she joined her older brother. However her kin in Buipe sent a messenger to insist that she return home. Here the relatives of both spouses were agreed that the husband had a right to a period during which the girl could get used to being a wife. If she ultimately insisted that she could not remain, she would not be prevented from leaving. In a somewhat similar case in eastern Gonja, the bride kicked and screamed all the way to the husband's compound and then ran back to her own room. So determined was she that after a hectic few days of persuasion and negotiation, she was allowed to return home 'unmarried' and the husband was persuaded that he would be happier with someone else. Both these girls were particularly independent. Many more go reluctantly, but silently, to the responsibilities of marriage after the relative freedom of the courting period.[2]

While a marriage in which the husband unsuccessfully tried to bring his wife to his own home might conceivably mean the return of courting gifts, I know of no such instance. Once the couple have set up house together, return is not demanded. In one extreme case, an older woman left her husband of a few months after being ostentatiously courted. Public opinion held that, while she had obviously only married for the gifts, there was nothing the husband could do without looking foolish.

Courting gifts, then, are instrumental in initiating the lover relationship, and in persuading the girl and her parents to agree to its conversion into a marriage. Their acceptance, if it is followed by the acceptance of

[2] See also the discussion of Ashetu's first marriage, in chapter 9.

the marriage kola, is seen as entitling the husband to have his wife live with him for at least a trial period. As I show later, this in turn implies an exchange of sexual and domestic services between the spouses. But neither courting gifts nor marriage kola signify the transfer of prescriptive or permanent rights over the wife.

Why should there be such an emphasis on courting gifts if they are not recoverable and do not secure any lasting rights? Part of the answer lies in the pervasiveness of the greeting idiom in social intercourse in Gonja. The presentation of small gifts is the normal way of establishing a new relationship or of seeking a favour. Courting involves both these things and fits naturally into the greeting idiom.

However, the emphasis on courting gifts has wider implications which have to do with the balance between marriages which are arranged in the first instance by kin, and those which are initiated by the pair themselves. It also appears to be related to open connubium, the pattern of marriages between estates and across village and divisional boundaries. This is because courtship facilities marriages between those who have no previous kinship ties or neighbourhood links, and whose parents are unknown to one another.

ARRANGED MARRIAGES

Some marriages, however, are arranged, and this has certainly always been the case. In the Busunu sample, 28% of the recorded marriages had been first planned by the parents. While these marriages include first and later unions, it is recognized that a girl who agrees reluctantly to a first marriage arranged by her parents should be allowed to choose a subsequent husband herself. The data from other parts of Gonja show much the same pattern. While there are variations between regions and among estates,[3] between 10% and 40% of first marriages are arranged by parents (see Appendix II). Most arranged marriages are between kinsfolk; they are intended to redefine ties that time and sometimes distance have threatened. A few are expressions of gratitude or friendship, and sometimes senior chiefs who have many wives, and thus

[3] The present study cannot treat regional variation in any detail, at least so far as causal factors are concerned. However the data suggest that first marriages are more often arranged in western Gonja than in the east. This pattern appears both in a survey of men's marriages, and in a quite separate study of marriages of women. In eastern and western Gonja commoner men are least likely to have marriages arranged for them, Muslims most likely. Unfortunately comparable data are not available for central Gonja, but the pattern is almost certainly similar.

many daughters, may arrange marriages to cement their links with other office holders, or to reward a faithful follower.

The one case I came across where a chief had made use of the marriages of his daughters and dependants in this way is of interest because of its unusual nature. This man had succeeded to his divisional skin irregularly. As a sister's son of the previous incumbent he was strictly speaking ineligible. But he was his uncle's favourite, and on his death-bed the old chief threatened to bring terrible misfortune on the town if his wishes for the succession of his nephew were not followed. When I knew him, the nephew was himself a very old man, who during his long rule had had many wives and children, even for a divisional chief.[4] Over the years he had married his daughters and grand-daughters to the paramount and to several divisional chiefs, as well as giving wives to many of the senior men of his own division. His avowed purpose was to secure respect, for as he said ruefully, "I have given daughters to all the important chiefs in Gonja, what more can a man do to ensure that people will greet him?"[5] His unusually large resources enabled him to arrange many more marriages than most men. The fact that such alliances do not generally figure prominently in marriage arrangements is probably a function of the autonomy of the political divisions and the simplicity of economic relations. In any case they are unusual.

Girls who have been promised as brides by their parents are not supposed to have lovers before marriage. While there is no particular concern with the virginity of such a bride (and indeed there is no term for a virgin other than *sunguru*, which simply means 'young unmarried girl'), parents do not like to see a daughter establish a lover relationship when she has been promised to someone else. The risk that she will try to avoid the arranged marriage is too great. The usual solution to the problem is to see that a promised bride goes to her husband as soon as she is physically mature. In this situation the daughter is likely to try to hide the fact that her menstrual periods have begun by washing the cloths at the house of a friend. However, once the friend's mother notices, then the secret is out and freedom at an end.

There is no doubt that the authority of the parents has been undermined by the changes which have followed the penetration of first colonial and then national administration into northern Ghana. This has affected their ability to insist that their children go through with marriages which they have arranged, and it has also limited the effec-

[4] Sixty-four and 153 respectively, so he claimed.
[5] To greet his father-in-law regularly and respectfully is a husband's duty. Flagrant neglect will probably lose him his wife.

tiveness of the parental veto on a lover who is considered unsuitable as a spouse. There is no very satisfactory way of measuring how substantial this change may have been, but nevertheless there are a number of factors which suggest that courtship has long been institutionalized. One such index is the existence of the term *katcholta*, and its use by elderly informants to describe their own early experiences. For example, one woman of 55 told of how at her first marriage she had to be reminded to weep when her bridegroom's people came to take her to his house. He had courted her and they had been lovers, and she was so delighted that her parents had agreed to their marriage that she forgot the customary forms.[6]

The now-abandoned courting feasts also show that young men and women of earlier times were directly concerned with the selection of a marriage partner. If all, or even most, first marriages had been arranged, then it is scarcely likely that such public courting would have been tolerated.

CONSTRAINTS ON SEX AND MARRIAGE

Attitudes about incest and adultery with wives of close kin are not codified in the sense that they appear to have been in Ashanti (Rattray, 1929). None of these acts constitutes a formal crime against the state, against ancestors or against shrines associated with divisional government. Not surprisingly in such an ethnically mixed population, there is some variation in beliefs about the relative seriousness of breaches of sexual norms, though virtual unanimity on the norms themselves.

There is no word in Gbanyito which means specifically 'sexual intercourse with a close kinswoman'. The word which is used (*katcheji*, 'to eat a woman') covers any sexual relationship which ought not to occur for moral (as opposed to pragmatic) reasons. For a man to sleep with his mother is *katcheji*, but so also is intercourse between two unrelated people whose parents have, even briefly, been lovers; the same term is applied to sexual relations between a man and his brother's wife, or, indeed, between a man and any married woman. In the absence of bounded kin groups, prohibitions on sexual relations (as with marriage prohibitions) must be based on particularistic relationships.

Members of all three estates concur in classifying sexual relations

---

[6] A bride must weep to show her reluctance at leaving home, and her dependence on her natal kin (see also chapter 5). In this case my friend said that her father's sister pinched her sharply to make her cry when she had been ready to go off without protesting.

within the nuclear family as *katcheji*. There is also agreement that
parents' full and half-siblings, parents' own parents, and ego's own
maternal and paternal half-siblings are "like your own father and mother
and the child of your mother's stomach", that is, to sleep with them is
also *katcheji*. All groups include the daughter of the mother's full or
maternal half-sister in the same category, and all but the Muslims include
the father's full or half-brother's daughter as well. All three estates also
agree that for a man to sleep with the wife of a parent or parent's sibling,
the wife of a sibling, or with a spouse's sibling, or the wife of a child is
much more serious than simple adultery, though both are termed
katcheji. The extension of the prohibition on sexual intercourse with
kin outside the nuclear family is fairly easy to establish, since it is cross-
cut by the preference for cross-cousin marriage. Full and half-siblings
fall clearly within the prohibited category, and cross-cousins outside of
it. First degree parallel cousins are marginal; you cannot marry them,
and should not sleep with them, but the same degree of concern is not
expressed over a breach as in the case of full and half-siblings. Residence
probably affects attitudes here, though this is only an impression. The
extension of the prohibition on sexual intercourse with affines is less
precise, and very much wider, since it includes not only kin of present
wives or relatives' wives (incestuous adultery), but kin of lovers, divorced
wives and widows, as well as the children of these women by other
husbands. This last group often includes women not currently married,
and is thus clearly an expression of concern over confusion of relationships within the kindred, rather than of concern with violating the
rights of a current husband as in simple adultery.

Perhaps an example will make this clearer. When Pantu, a youth of
18, met a girl he had known as a child, he was much attracted and began
to send her small gifts and to pay her the attentions which initiate a
courtship. Almost immediately his elder brother summoned him,
together with a younger brother and a son of their father's paternal
half-sister, to his village (some twenty miles away) to discuss an important matter. The council concerned Pantu's new girl friend, whom he
and the other lads were cautioned never to sleep with. For the girl's
mother had come to the senior brother, much upset, and confessed
that she and their father had briefly been lovers. The affair had ended
some time before and there had been no child, but it would be dangerous
if any of the 'children' of the couple should subsequently become lovers.
Two points are worth noting in this example. The first is that the
prohibition was on sexual relations, and not simply a matter of the
inability to marry; it applied not only to the children of the older

couple, but also to siblings' children. And secondly, the prohibition was subject to supernatural sanctions, and was not simply a matter of embarrassment to those concerned. Had the mother said nothing it is unlikely that others would have known of her earlier affair with Pantu's father, for they never lived together in the same compound. That she did speak was due to her concern for her daughter's safety. My informant (Pantu himself) thought that, once the mother died, it might be possible to court the girl again, but he was clearly uneasy at the suggestion.

While there is general agreement on the sorts of relationship which are a bar to sexual intercourse (and hence to marriage), there is less unanimity on the consequences of violating these rules. Three types of sanction were mentioned; the distinction stressed the difference between violations about which nothing could be done, and those for which it was possible to do something to restore the *status quo ante*.

All forms of incest within the nuclear family are felt to be abhorrent, though that between father and daughter is least so. People differed in the relative opprobrium they attached to mother–son and sibling incest. In both cases those involved would become 'worthless people' (*esa jigge*, 'spoiled people'). As such they would be the subject of gossip and ridicule, and would probably be shamed into running away from the town where their behaviour was known. If misfortune should strike the community soon after, the Earth priest might interpret this as due to the incestuous act of either a mother and son, or a brother and sister, and he could drive the culprits away or demand a purificatory sacrifice. But generally it was considered that shame would be the most severe punishment. Indeed it was said that shame can kill such people, though mystical trouble (*mbusu*) mediated by the ancestors may also cause the death of the guilty.

Where incestuous adultery occurs between very close kin (child's wife; parent's wife; sibling's wife), the consequences are of the same order: the earth may be polluted, and require expulsion or reparation; the ancestors may kill those concerned; the wrongdoers may be driven by shame to flee or commit suicide. The ruling and commoner estates appear more concerned with violations involving a sibling's wife ("you would surely die, it is the same as sleeping with your own sister"), while Muslim informants emphasized equally the danger from incestuous affairs with wives of the parental and filial generations. Indeed, Muslims ought to take care never to be alone in a room with a kinsman's wife, lest suspicion be aroused.

Only in the case of incestuous adultery with classificatory kinsmen's wives is the matter likely to be taken to court. Then a man may try to recover damages for adultery, though this is usually settled within the kin group as a 'room case' (*ebuto ba kamaliga*). Where nuclear kin and close affines are concerned there is no actionable case (*kamaliga min'tɔ*). But when a man sleeps with a relative's wife they must perform certain rituals to 'remove the trouble' (*ler mbusu*) in order that they can continue to greet one another. Even after the rituals a man who has slept with his 'brother's' wife may not greet the 'brother' if he is ill, eat food from the same bowl with him, or inherit his property (*kapute*). And if a man who has performed the purificatory ritual should again sleep with the woman, he will either die or become impotent. Where incest occurs between nuclear kin no ritual can be used to 'remove the trouble'. "We leave them to God."

For the Gonja, to have sexual relations with a close kinsman or kinswoman of a proximal generation is wrong. It brings great shame and may mean either voluntary or forced exile from the community. But to have sexual relations with a sibling or a sibling's spouse is considered extremely dangerous. If the affair involves a married woman (as in the case of a sibling's spouse) a breach of the husband's marital rights is also involved, and this requires both restitution and purification. These and other aspects of adultery are considered in a later chapter, but they are different, and separable, from the confusion of sexual and sibling relations which is for the Gonja the worst form of incest.

PROHIBITED AND PREFERRED MARRIAGES

The social estates do not themselves provide the basis for prescribed marriage arrangements; they are neither exogamous nor endogamous. Nor do any of the patronymic groups within the estates form discrete units with respect to marriages. Nevertheless, there is a preference on the part of men for marriage with kin. This is termed 'family marriage' (*kanang ta etche*; *fe kil kanang konle*); 'marriage to a consanguine', (*ko kurwe kil*); or marrying 'a wife within the room' (*ebuto betche*). The reason always given for preferring marriage to a kinswoman is that, should there be a divorce, the children will not be lost to the husband since the wife is also a relative. Men also say that they have more control over a related wife, since her parents will not take the wife's part against the husband if related to both. Women, on the other hand, say they prefer to marry into a different family (*kanang pwɔte*), as they have more freedom, and feel better able to prevail on an unrelated husband to agree to something against his will. However, 'family' is used in this context as it is in English.[7] The preference is for (or against) marriage with a relative, and not for a member of a bounded group of kin.

Within the designation 'relative' the Gonja distinguish certain relationships as providing a suitable basis for marriage, and others as rendering marriage impossible. None of the subgroups of any of the three estates in central Gonja permits marriage with a matrilateral parallel cousin. Only the Muslims allow patrilateral parallel cousin marriage, and even they make very few, usually between second cousins. All three estates allow marriage between both patrilateral and matrilateral cross-cousins, and under some circumstances these may be preferred unions. Again, nearly all cross-cousin marriages are between second cousins, or those even more distantly related. All cousins, both cross- and parallel-cousins, are referred to by the same terms as siblings. But to the Gonja, marrying a parallel cousin seems like "marrying your own mother's child", while to take the daughter of a father's sister or mother's brother as a wife is not so perceived.

While cross-cousin marriage is the only form of union between kin that is explicitly preferred, marriages do occur between people related in other ways. These are often sufficiently distant that the exact relationship is lost; the spouses know only that they stand as 'father'/'daughter', 'mother'/'son', 'mother's brother'/'sister's daughter' or 'grandparent'/'grandchild' to one another. Sometimes the genealogical relationship can be traced. Here, except for cross-cousins, the linking relative is at least three generations removed. There is no prohibition on marrying any particular category of classificatory kin. Of the 63 marriages recorded for the Busunu sample, 28 (44%) were between people who considered that they were related. Of these marriages between kin, only 8 (29%) were between 'cross-cousins'. Twelve per cent of the Busunu sample as a whole, then, had married a 'cross-cousin'.

If the proportion of marriages between kin seems high, it should be remembered that, in all but the larger Gonja villages, most people can fit nearly everyone into one kinship category or another. Because these are particularistic ties, rather than ties based on membership in descent groups, the more distant classificatory relationships do not affect daily activities. Indeed, I gave up the attempt to map the kinship links in Busunu when my first informant listed every adult in the village as kin, and then proceeded to group them all into the broad categories of 'grandparents', 'fathers', 'mothers', 'siblings', 'children' and 'grandchildren'.

[7] See chapter 9 for a discussion of these terms.

Given such a situation it may seem pointless to distinguish between kinship marriages and others. But kinship marriage is a concept of importance to the Gonja and for this reason must be given serious consideration. If the marriages reported in the Busunu sample as being between kin are interpreted as unions between people who may refer to one another by any of the possible classificatory kin terms, but who may or may not be able to trace a specific relationship, then the picture is a fair one. But to read these figures as applying to marriages of close kin would be misleading.

This is also true of 'cross-cousins' but to a lesser extent for two reasons. In the first place, cross and parallel cousins are not distinguished terminologically in daily parlance. Both are equated with ego's older or younger siblings. Thus, in order to know that he has married a 'cross-cousin' and not a 'sibling', ego must be aware that they are related through members of the parental generation of the opposite sex. Secondly, in those cases where a marriage between cross-cousins was also an arranged marriage, the link must have been known, and fairly close.

In a sense, it is easier in Gonja to marry a kinsman than someone with whom there is already an affinal link. A man may never marry his brother's widow, nor the woman whom his brother divorces; nor ought he to marry the ex-wife, or child of an ex-wife, of any close kinsman. In the same way, marriage to two sisters (e.g. the sororate) is forbidden, except for the YagbumWura who is expected to marry twin girls. The form of this prohibition most often met by the Gonja is the rule against a widow remarrying again into her husband's kindred. The widespread African institution of widow inheritance, where a kinsman of the dead husband assumes his conjugal rights and obligations, is thus not permitted in Gonja. Again the Muslims are a partial exception here, in that they are allowed to inherit the widow of a paternal half-brother, or a patrilateral cousin. To marry the widow of a 'sibling' related through the mother is considered to be mystically dangerous. Marriage to the widow of any member of the senior generation was likened by one Muslim informant to marrying one's mother. "That is very bad! You would not last a week!" he added. The prohibition on taking the wife of a member of the junior generation coincides with that which forbids any sort of inheritance from younger to older person. The only instance of widow inheritance recorded among Muslims was between patrilateral parallel first cousins.

The paramount and divisional chiefs used to take the widows of their immediate predecessors, and the custom was followed until the early years of the present century. However, with the coming of the British courts it lapsed, as the widows objected, insisting that they were not slaves to have their husbands chosen for them. However, in a system where office passes between dynastic segments (between territorial divisions in the case of the paramountcy) the old chief and the new one cannot be close kin. Where a successor is related to the previous chief, he is prohibited from marrying any of his wives.

Despite several attempts, it proved impossible to specify the limits within which marriage to an affine was prohibited. Given the classificatory nature of the kinship terminology, and the lack of detailed genealogical knowledge of most people, this is perhaps not surprising. In effect this is a prohibition on marrying twice into the same family (where the previous link is known). But it is a prohibition which vanishes with time. From the perspective of the children of a marriage their parents are kinsfolk, not affines. Parents' siblings cease to be in-laws and become 'fathers' and 'father's sisters', 'mothers' and 'mother's brothers', and their children are cousins, some of them cross-cousins – the most eligible of marriage partners.

CROSS-COUSIN MARRIAGE

Although the overall frequency of marriage to real and classificatory cross-cousins is low (12% in the Busunu Health sample), there is no doubt as to its normative significance. Cross-cousins may be descriptively designated as father's sister's children (*tana pibi*) or mother's brother's children (*wopa pibi*), and both are joking partners (*mitcherpo*). Perhaps more so with cross-cousins than with any other joking relations, one may 'play' (*pol*) in ways that involve mock aggression and sexual allusion. Often just the mention of a joking partner's name will bring a grin to the face of the speaker. Cross-cousins are born into a category which children are taught from infancy to delight in considering in sexual and conjugal terms. This fact itself probably accounts for part of the emphasis given in conversation to this form of marriage.

In addition, one aspect of the special relationship between a man and his sister's son (also discussed in chapter 8) is his obligation to find a wife for his nephew. At the Jentigi fire festival, both boys and girls ought to go and 'sweep' (*fege*) the compound of their mother's brother; this is a euphemism for the obligation to offer to perform some small service for him. And he should give them something in return. A boy may ask for a wife and, although his request may be turned aside with a quip at the time, it ought eventually to be met. By nominating a child, the time for finalizing the marriage is deferred, and the outcome of the offer left in doubt.

One young man who had been promised a mother's brother's daughter described it in this way:

I took several bundles of firewood to my mother's brother [his mother's maternal half-brother] in Kpogato last Jentigi [the fire festival]. He said I should have his daughter to marry. She is still a child. I will give her cloths at Damba and send things to my mother's brother. When she is grown, I will marry her if she agrees. But if she doesn't want me, I can't do anything nor can I ask for my things back because it is a family matter. If she marries someone else, I will not be angry. I will be pleased when she comes to my house. Now I call her father *wopa* [mother's brother] and his wife Adjira *niu* [mother]. When I marry their daughter I will call them *ma sha*.[8] But the girl may not agree, so I can't call them that now. So I call Abena *nsupotche* [younger sister] and not *etche* [wife].

Although it is the mother's brother's gift of a wife to his sister's son which the Gonja speaks about, the preferred and more frequent marriage is with a daughter of the father's sister. This seems to hold equally for all three estates, though there are too few cases in central Gonja to allow for a firm statement on this point. Why should marriage to the father's sister's daughter be more common? Looking again at accounts of the fire festival, we find that girls are reluctant to sweep their mother's brother's compounds lest they be seized and given as brides against their will. Again this is said in a humorous vein, as though the threat were a remote one. But again it expresses a real possibility. For the Gonja say it is a woman's brother and not her husband who has the right to pawn her child in order to pay a debt, or to sell it into slavery should this become necessary in time of famine. And while ordinarily it is a girl's parents who arrange, or agree to, her marriage, her mother's brother still has this final authority, should he choose to use it.

Marriage to a father's sister's daughter (when it is an arranged marriage and not simply a coincidence of courtship and kinship) is marriage to a girl over whom one's father has a residual right of bestowal. Since there is a reluctance to allow even cross-cousins to marry when the relationship is too close, such marriages are usually between second or third cousins. Thus it is formal kinship authority which is involved and not simply an understanding between full brother and sister that their children should marry.

But given such a clear normative preference for cross-cousin marriage,

---

[8] In fact the parents-in-law will never be 'called' *sha* for this is a term of reference. This is not clear in the text.

how is it that the overall incidence, even including classificatory cousins, is so low? In Gonja cross-cousin marriages are always considered dangerous as well as desirable. In a marriage between kin the inevitable disputes between spouses are liable to supernatural intervention. If the dead kinsfolk (*bubuni*) of the pair see that there is quarrelling or infidelity, they may chastise them, usually by sending illness to the children. Good behaviour is thus expected at all times, and the couple ought never to separate, though divorces do in fact occur.[9] In this, as in other contexts, it is women's ancestors and dead female kin who are most feared. It appears possible that the generalized anxiety which surrounds cross-cousin marriage may be focused on the ancestors of the wife, that is on the female element in the relationship. If so, this would (in the prevailing male view of affairs) render marriage to a mother's brother's daughter more dangerous than where the wife was related through one's father.

Marriages arranged by the parental generation are more likely to be between kin than to involve an unrelated couple. Also there is probably a tendency for marriages based initially on courtship to be more often between non-relatives. Marriages contracted by young men during the time they are 'roaming about' often fall into this category. However, kinsfolk court, and an arranged marriage may link an unrelated couple. Despite an explicit preference for marriage with a kinswoman, there is no simple formula: marriages are arranged between kin but courtship takes place between strangers.

PATTERNS OF MARRIAGE

THE INCIDENCE OF POLYGYNY

Polygyny is permitted to members of all three estates, but for Muslims the number of wives should not exceed four at any given time. That this is not a severe restriction for most Muslims is suggested by the fact that no one in Buipe had more than three wives at the time of the census. Table 4-1 gives the figures for current number of wives of those adult males in Buipe and Busunu who have ever been married.

[9] Compare Gluckman's account of Lozi marriages between kin. While known relatives of any kind ought not to marry, a distantly related pair occasionally insist on doing so against the wishes of the elders. When this happens kinship between them is considered to have come to an end, and they and their immediate kin adopt affinal terms. The elders place a special curse upon them so that they (alone of all Lozi couples) may not divorce. And their siblings' children and their children, who call one another 'sibling', may not marry (Gluckman 1950: 173–4).

Table 4-1. *Percentage of all married or once married men by number of wives*

	Number of wives per man:*							
	0	1	2	3	4	12	Total	men
Village:								
Buipe	12	48	9	2	—	—	71	
	17%	68%	12%	3%				100%
Busunu	13	88	18	4	2	1	126	
	10%	70%	14%	3%	2%	1%		100%
Both	25	136	27	6	2	1	197	
	13%	69%	14%	3%	1%	†		100%

†=less than 0.5%

Average number of wives per man in:		Proportion of all marriages which are polygynous in:	
	Buipe	1.01	Buipe	19%
	Busunu	1.24	Busunu	22%
	Both villages	1.16	Both villages	21%

Probably the most surprising feature of these data is the number of men who were unmarried: 17% of all adult men in Buipe, and 10% in Busunu. This group consists partially of young and middle-aged men whose wives have left them and have not yet been replaced, and partly of older men who will be unlikely to remarry now that their wives have either died or returned to their kin. In Buipe this group of unmarried men outnumbers those who are polygynously married. In Busunu the reverse is the case. This difference between the two villages is too small to be reliable.

In both villages, by far the largest proportion of the male population had only one wife at the time of the censuses: 68% in one case and 70% in the other. The proportions of those having two and three wives are substantially the same in both villages.

The incidence of polygyny is as low as it is for Africa (21% of all marriages are polygynous if the figure for the two communities are combined) partly because there is no inheritance of wives. Thus it is generally the case that only those men who are outstanding in some respect, either in holding an important chiefship, in being unusually

* Excluded from the table are four cripples, two in each village, three of whom are blind and the other so deformed by leprosy as to be unable to move about. These men are totally dependent on kin and have not been married since becoming disabled.

wealthy, or in possessing particularly powerful medicines (*aduru*), will have more than three wives at one time. The one man in Busunu who had twelve wives was the sub-divisional chief, and of the two who had four wives, one was the senior of the chiefs attendant on the Busunu-Wura and the other was the wealthiest man in the village.[10] Such men of high status are apt to be of middle age or older. They stand in direct contrast to those who have two and occasionally three wives. For these are usually young adults in the full vigour of manhood; men who by their own efforts can cultivate enough land to feed the large household resulting from polygyny, and who have the energy to satisfy and control more than one wife. Older men, those past 50, seldom have more than one wife, and many have none.

Table 4-2. *Number of current wives by estate of husband: Buipe*

	Number of wives:				Total married or once married men	
	0	1	2	3		
Estate of husband:						
Ruling	1 9%	7 64%	2 18%	1 9%	11	100%
Muslim	4 14%	20 71%	3 11%	1 4%	28	100%
Commoner	7 22%	21 66%	4 12%	0 —	32	100%
	12 17%	48 68%	9 12%	2 3%	N=71	100%

There is no pronounced difference in the incidence of plural marriages among men of different estates. In the Buipe data there is a very slight tendency perhaps for proportionately more men of the ruling estate to have two or more wives; no commoner had more than two wives. But this is based on very low numbers and should not be exaggerated. In Busunu, for instance, there were two commoners with four wives each. The highest proportion of men with no wife is in the commoner estate in Buipe, but the Busunu data do not show this difference. Wealthy

[10] I use as a convenient measure of wealth the number of cattle owned, for these serve as a repository of surplus wealth. This man owned thirteen cows while most men own none.

members of each estate, and those in positions of prestige and authority, always tend to have more wives than their less distinguished fellows.

PATTERNS OF MARRIAGE BETWEEN ESTATES

While all three of the villages studied contained both ruling and commoner elements, Buipe was alone in having a substantial Muslim population. Only in a community where all three estates are well-represented can the full range of possible marriages be expected. The analysis which follows will therefore concentrate on data from Buipe. The reader should keep in mind that in communities with less highly differentiated populations, marriages will be accordingly more limited in range.

In Buipe intermarriage between estates is frequent, as indicated by the figures in Table 4-3. It is clear that, as the Gonja themselves contend, there are no restrictions on intermarriage between any of the estates. However, certain trends are observable.

Table 4-3. *Estates of husband and wife in sixty-five current marriages in Buipe**

| | Husband's estate: | | | |
Wife's estate:	Ruling	Commoner	Muslim	All
Ruling	1	5	5	11
Commoner	8	12	14	34
Muslim	4	6	10	20
All	13	23	29	

N=65

There is a decided tendency for members of the ruling estate to marry either Muslims or commoners rather than one of their own number. The Gonja explain this by saying that "two chiefs cannot stay in the same house". That is, if both husband and wife are of the ruling estate

* The fact that commoner women outnumber those from the other estates, although among the men Muslims predominate, is due to the concentration of members of ruling and Muslim estates in Buipe itself. Thus women who marry in from neighbouring villages are mostly commoners. Similarly, ruling and Muslim women who marry out to these villages take mainly commoner husbands. These out-marrying women are not, of course, represented in this table.

they may be so concerned with their own status, and that of the dynastic segment to which they belong, that the competition between them disrupts the marriage. When Miama, a daughter of the previous Buipe chief, divorced the present BuipeWura, the failure of their marriage was laid to this cause.

From Table 4-3 it appears that Muslim men more frequently marry non-Muslims than do Muslim women. Half of the marriages of the latter are to Muslims, while only about one-third of the marriages of Muslim men are to women of the same estate. This imbalance is recognized by the people themselves, who explain it by referring to the food prohibitions enjoined by Islam. While a man may require that his wife learn to pray and prepare food in the prescribed fashion, a woman cannot demand that her husband refrain from eating meat which was not ritually killed. Thus, if she wishes to remain strict in her observances, a Muslim woman who has married a non-Muslim will often have to fast or prepare her own food separately. In fact Muslim women who marry pagans tend to lapse in piety. That many may be reluctant to risk this is suggested by the relatively high proportion who marry within the Muslim estate.

Table 4-3a. *Percentage of married women in each estate by estate of husband*

Wife's estate:	Husband's estate:			
	Ruling	Commoner	Muslim	N
Ruling	10	45	45	(11) = 100%
Commoner	24	35	41	(34) = 100%
Muslim	20	30	50	(20) = 100%

N=65

A rough index of the degree of marriage within the estates has been calculated for Buipe as a whole by dividing the total number of marriages by the number in which both partners were of the same estate. Table 4-4 presents this index and the information on which it is based. Approximately one-third (35%) of these sixty-five marriages were estate-endogamous: in the remaining two-thirds the partners came from different social estates.

Table 4-4. *Number of marriages within each estate*

Ruling   1
Commoner 12
Muslim   10
Total marriages within: 23
Total marriages: 65
23/65=35%

PATTERNS OF MARRIAGE IN SPACE

The degree of estate endogamy, and the extent to which all three of the Gonja estates are represented in mixed marriages in any given village, is in part a function of the composition of the population of that village and division. There are no territorial restrictions on marriage, either formally or in practice. But the choice of a partner is limited by a person's range of acquaintance. Because of the regular visiting between kin and the way in which young men 'roam about', this range spreads far beyond the boundaries of village or division. Nevertheless, there are more available (in the sense of known) mates in a person's own village and in the villages of his close kinsfolk.

Opinions are divided as to the merit of marrying in one's natal village as against 'marrying out'. Women on the whole concur in preferring the former: in the words of one woman of the ruling estate, "It is better to marry in your own village because if you get sick your kin are there to help you. If you marry in a different town who will care?" And men often agree with this view, for as Akurma, the commoner drummer of Busunu, said, "to marry in your own town is better because if anything happens to your kinsfolk you will know". This statement may be interpreted in two ways. In time of illness or trouble a man who has married and settled in his father's village will be on hand to give support. But also, if disputes occur, or issues of inheritance or succession arise, he will be present to defend his interests and to claim his due.

From the standpoint of the senior generation there are also arguments both for and against marriage at a distance. Parents fear that if their daughters marry in far-off villages they will come to visit less and less frequently until all contact is lost. On the other hand, where they have kin there already, marriage is seen as the best possible way to reinforce existing ties. And even where such bonds have not previously existed, to establish kinship connections outside one's own village is viewed as desirable: "To marry your children in a distant village is good because then you will have kin there."

From the husband's point of view, a frequently heard justification for seeking a wife from afar is that such a woman is less likely to return to her kin because of a quarrel. The adolescent son of the KagbaapeWura explained that "Buipe youths don't like to marry Buipe girls because they run away (back to their kin) too easily." And there is an element of familiarity about the girls with whom one has grown up which deprives courtship of much of its glamour, they say. On the other hand, a wife whose parents and close kin are living in the same village will not be constantly begging to visit them. Such visits are a source of anxiety to husbands who must shift for themselves during the absence of a wife, for not infrequently they initiate separation and divorce.

Although some women say that it does not matter whether one marries in one's own village or another, I have never heard a woman express a preference for marrying at a distance. What does seem clear is that a woman is more secure and has greater freedom of movement when she marries in her natal village. It is startling how accurately the differences in the interests of men and women are reflected in the responses to this single question. For not only is it the men who express concern to establish kinship ties outside their natal village, but, when picturing himself as the in-marrying stranger,[11] a man's concern is not over who will care for him in case of trouble, but rather over his responsibilities towards his distant kinsfolk.

The figures in Table 4-5 indicate the territorial dispersion of thirty-five current marriages of Buipe men whose fathers were also from Buipe. This is given both in terms of social units (the villages and divisions) and in terms of miles. About one-quarter were between partners whose natal village was the same, that is Buipe. In an identical percentage of marriages, the pair came from the same division, but from different villages within it. The remaining 48% were between spouses whose fathers were from different divisions. The importance of this last figure lies in the fact that the children of these marriages have certain citizenship rights in two political units. Through his father, a man is entitled to direct succession to such offices as fall to members of his estate and family, while through his mother he may succeed to chiefships and offices reserved for 'women's children' (*etche pibi*). Rights

[11] To characterize a man as 'an in-marrying stranger' is somewhat misleading. Since marriage is virilocal, a man who marries outside of his natal village will not be going to join his wife in her home but may either be living in avunculocal residence with other kin, or very rarely as the foster child of a chief. Thus he is usually among kin, but not among those to whom he considers himself most closely related.

Table 4-5. *Marriages of thirty-five men whose fathers were from Buipe by residence of wife's father and distance from Buipe**

	Buipe	Wife's father from: Other village in Buipe division	Other Division	
Number	9	9	17	N=35
Percentage	26%	26%	48%	100%
Average distance from Buipe in miles	0	14.7	43.0	

of daughters to women's chiefships are usually traced through their fathers only.

The figures for the distance in miles separating the natal villages of marriage partners are included to give a concrete referent to the various statements made about the 'considerable distances separating kin'. For it cannot be emphasized too strongly that what are fragile affinal ties in one generation become, for the next, bonds of kinship of life-long importance. And it is across distances of the order noted in the tables that such bonds are maintained, by the sending of children to be fostered and by continual visiting.

It is possible, of course, that the greater freedom of movement which followed the *Pax Britannica* has significantly influenced the pattern of marriage. Table 4-6 compares the distances separating the natal villages of the spouses in twenty-three past marriages with those of forty-six

* For the purposes of tabulation natal village was equated with father's village and it was assumed that both partners married from their father's village. An examination of residential histories reveals that many people do not grow up in, and hence do not marry from, their father's village. Unfortunately, information as to where each spouse was living at the time of marriage is available for too small a number of marriages to permit tabulation of this variable. The most regular deviations will be those instances in which a man or woman has grown up in the village of maternal kin and married there. In these cases, while the distance between the natal villages of the pair is accurate, it does not represent the distance between the villages in which they were reared and where they courted. Since most men eventually return to their father's home, however, this is less of a distortion than it might seem. In any case, our interest is not so much in the circumstances surrounding the selection of a marriage partner, as it is with conditions affecting the marriage and the offspring of the union. And here a measure of the distances separating the natal villages of the husband and wife is directly relevant.

current marriages.[12] It appears that, rather than increasing, the distance has slightly declined in the past twenty-five years. While the difference is too small to be significant, it seems likely that any lessening of the distance is due to the declining control of the older generation over the marriages of their children. For some at least of the marriages over long distances were arranged to renew bonds with maternal kin whom the mother has left far away at her own marriage. As was explained by a woman of the ruling estate, who had left her own kin in Daboya to marry in Bole, ninety-five miles away, "I tried to send my daughter back to marry in Daboya but she refused. Nowadays if you try to force children, they run off to the South and you never see them again. So I left it."

Table 4-6. *Average number of miles separating village of husband's father and village of wife's father for past and present marriages: Buipe**

	Past marriages	Current marriages
Number	23	46
Average distance in miles of natal villages of spouses' fathers	26.6	24.5

N=69

* See also Appendix II.

Territorial patterns of marriage do vary by estate, though the difference in average distance is not marked. In Table 4-7 marriages of men in each of the three estates are compared as to distance between the natal villages of the partners and the proportion of marriages within the village of Buipe itself. When all marriages are considered, the difference between averages for each estate is less than five miles. This crude average, however, masks another variable which reverses the position

[12] The current marriages are all those for whom the natal village of the fathers of both spouses was reliably ascertained. The past marriages are all the marriages of the parents of this group for which reliable information was available. Because the relevance of establishing the natal villages of parents' parents was not recognized at the time of the census, the number of past marriages on which there is sufficient information for this comparison is unfortunately small. The marriages of the parents of currently married adults are assumed to have occurred between twenty-five and sixty years previously.

Table 4-7. *Distances between spouses' natal villages in marriages of men of each estate: Buipe*

| | Estate: | | |
	Ruling	Commoner	Muslim
Number of marriages	32	21	32
Average distance in miles*	19.7	20.5	24.4
Number and % of marriages in Buipe	10 31%	5 24%	13 41%
Average distance in miles for other marriages*	30	25.6	43.2

N=85

* The first figure for average distance is based on all marriages tabulated. The second (in the last row of the table) is the average distance after marriages within Buipe have been excluded. This is included because of the different frequency with which men of each estate take their wives from Buipe itself, as reported in row 3 of the table.

of ruling and commoner groups. This is the extent to which men of each estate take wives from Buipe itself.

Commoners are least likely of all the estates to marry within the village of Buipe. Three-fourths of the wives of commoner men come from outside the village, but they do not on the average come from very far away. The villages around Buipe are almost entirely composed of commoners who are mainly Dompo concentrated in the villages of Benyalipe, Boatchipe and Kadelso. Morno, at the edge of the Volta, has a small population of ferryfolk (Ntere) and Tchakpotasi. Jembito and Kalonso are mainly Mpre. Since there is complete freedom of inter-marriage among the commoner groups themselves, these villages have Dompo or Mpre populations only in the sense that these people predominate, and that each village is characterized as 'belonging' to one or the other.

The pattern of Muslim marriages is very different. Forty per cent of the Muslim men married within the village of Buipe, and the remainder mostly from villages outside of the division. Many of their wives come from Larabanga, Bole, Salaga and Daboya, all distant villages with large Muslim populations. Some, of course, do come from nearby villages. But the overall picture is one of a dense network of kinship and affinal ties within Buipe itself, to which are added widely dispersed ties which cover the whole state of Gonja and, indeed, reach beyond its borders.

The pattern of the marriages of men of the ruling estate is intermediate between these two extremes. Like the commoners, their identification is primarily with the geographical area represented by the division of Buipe. Succession to the divisional chiefship sets them apart as a group, but at the same time ensures that their interests will always be closely bound up with those of the other inhabitants of the division. Territorial and divisional identification are perhaps greater in Buipe because it is not one of the eligible divisions from which the paramount chief is recruited. Yet the members of the ruling estate are very conscious of their kinship with other members of this estate in other divisions. "All Gbanya are kin" (*Ngbanya kike le basa konle*), they say, and in proof cite the fact that they are all descended from one or another of the sons of Jakpa. This dual identification is reflected in the pattern of marriage, with 30% of Gbanya marriages within Buipe but the remainder distributed between women from villages in Buipe division and women from distant towns. A daughter of the BuipeWura is married to one of the kinsmen of the chief of Bole. And the Buipe chief himself has married a 'daughter' of the BusunuWura. These unions do not represent particular, enduring and special relationships between the chiefs involved, but rather reflect the fact that they think of themselves as belonging to a single kin group which it is well to redefine by marriage. And while no one of these is ever likely to depend directly on the other for political advancement,[13] it is always well to have friends among those in authority.

OPEN CONNUBIUM

These data suggest certain general conclusions about the patterns characteristic of Gonja marriage. While polygyny is desired and practised by those who are wealthy or powerful enough to keep more than one wife, divorce and the return of widows to their kin mean that the incidence of polygyny in the population as a whole is relatively low for Africa. Intermarriage is freely practised between members of all three estates. There is a slight tendency for Muslim women to prefer men of

[13] As it happens, each of these three chiefs holds an office different in character. The Buipe chiefship is of great ritual importance in the Gonja constitution, and is an end in itself. Bole is one of the 'gates' to the paramountcy, as well as being one of the wealthiest and most important towns in Gonja. Busunu is not a divisional chiefship, but has come to operate in much the same way although there is no question of the BusunuWura succeeding to the paramountcy.

their own estate. The preference expressed by those of the ruling estate to seek spouses among either Muslims or commoners is supported by the figures. Marriages occur both within and between villages, and between the villages of different divisions. This frequently results in marriages in which the partners' natal villages are many miles apart. The exact pattern of diffusion of marriage ties varies for each estate. Among the residents of Buipe, marriages of the Muslim and ruling estates often extend far beyond the borders of Buipe division, although members of these two groups marry frequently within the village of Buipe itself. Commoners, on the other hand, are less likely to marry either within Buipe or at great distances, but tend to find their mates within the commoner villages of the Buipe and Tuluwe divisions. Members of the ruling estate also marry in the commoner villages, thus reinforcing political authority with kinship bonds.

This pattern of free marriage between estates and across village and divisional boundaries stands in complete contrast to that reported from the caste-based societies of the Indian sub-continent. There marriage across caste and sub-caste boundaries is prohibited, with important consequences for the kinds of social relationships prevailing between these units. The type of stratification usually contrasted with the caste system is that based on socio-economic class. Although also hierarchical, class-stratified societies lack religious sanctions against marriage between strata. Nevertheless, accounts of such societies repeatedly stress the dis-approval attached to marrying 'beneath one's class'. Conversely, the man or woman who is anxious to rise in the hierarchy is often described as 'marrying up'. Marriage in such systems is far from free, but rather subject to constraints derived from the need to maintain or improve social or economic status.

The situation described here for Buipe is very different. The major constraint seems to be a function of the proximity factor:[14] there must be *some* kind of contact between the partners, or their families, before a marriage is possible. Yet even this has surprisingly little effect on the dispersion of marriages. Because this pattern of open connubium seems central to many aspects of Gonja social structure, it is important to ask whether it is characteristic of the state as a whole. Studies in both eastern and western Gonja show the same pattern as that found in

[14] J. H. S. Bossard's original paper on 'Residential Propinquity as a Factor in Marriage Selection' (1932) led to a number of studies. These tend to confirm his original generalization that the proportion of marriages between members of a given sample decreases as the distance between the partners increases. They further showed that the relationship holds under a variety of different conditions.

Buipe. Both men and women of all three estates marry into the others. Many women have successive husbands from two or even three different estates, and men wives from each. This pattern is most characteristic of the divisional capitals where all the estates are well represented. It is less clear in remote villages in which there may be no, or few, members of Muslim or ruling groups. Spatial dispersion is also marked in western Gonja, but less so in the eastern division of Kpembe which in many respects functions as a virtually autonomous unit (see Appendix II). Open connubium, free and frequent marriage between communities and between social elements of the society, is a consistent pattern throughout Gonja.

Let us now reconsider the emphasis on courtship which characterizes adolescence in Gonja and initiates a substantial majority of all marriages, including first marriages. Boys are allowed to court girls who take their fancy both at home and when they are 'roaming about'. Indeed, they say they prefer girls from other villages, as they are too used to those with whom they have grown up. There is little stress on go-betweens or extended negotiations, perhaps because substantial amounts of capital are not involved. Courtship is rather a period during which the couple get to know one another, and if a youth has decided that he wishes to marry the girl, he seeks to persuade her parents of his respectful character and of his ability to make a good husband and dutiful son-in-law. Courtship, then, allows for the setting up of particularistic ties between individuals: between the youth and his girl friend, and between the suitor and his prospective parents-in-law. Courtship depends initially on the attraction between the young couple, and is not concerned with their respective status or citizenship. On the basis of this attraction, first the lover relationship and then (often but not always) marriage give more permanence to the association. As a lover relationship approaches marriage, the parents of first the girl and then the youth are drawn in through consultation and through requests for assistance in making the arrangements. At this stage they can, if they wish, exert very strong pressures against a marriage, though these are not always heeded. But courtship is above all an institution which leaves the initiative to the young people most concerned. Where this is so, and there are few formal constraints on choice imposed by social norms, an institutional bias towards open connubium is likely to be realized in practice. Why these facilitating conditions should occur is a separate question. The purpose of this chapter has been to document the pattern of open connubium, and to show that it is found together with a long-standing preference for the initiation of marriage by courtship, with which it is entirely consistent.

5

Establishing a marriage

For the Gonja, courting gifts are viewed as consumption goods and not as a form of bridewealth. They hold that they do not 'buy' their wives as, they claim, do the LoDagaa and the Grusi peoples of northern Ghana. But aside from their own view of things, two factors support this interpretation. On the one hand, while kinsmen are sometimes anxious about a possible suit for the return of courting gifts if a marriage has been particularly short-lived, no such cases came to my attention. But even more important, the transfer of gifts is not related to the validity of a marriage nor to the legitimacy of its issue. The one transaction which must occur in every case in order for a marriage to be recognized as legitimate is the presentation by the groom's representative of twelve kola nuts and twelve shillings, and this gift must be accepted by the kin of the bride.

Other rituals are almost always observed as well, though the forms used vary greatly from one couple to another. Most first marriages proceed along the following lines. A day is fixed by the bride's kin and the groom for escorting the bride to her new home. On this day a party of youths arrives and pretends to seize the bride, who should struggle and weep. Accompanied by two or three unmarried girl friends, she is taken to the groom's village and placed in the room of a senior woman in his compound. The bride remains secluded in the room (*e lure ebuto*, 'she enters the room') for seven days, during which time she does no work, but sits with her companions and is visited by her husband and his friends. During the period of seclusion an all-night dance is held for the young men of the village and shortly after dawn the bride is brought out to sit at the edge of the dancing ground. During the course of these seven days she is taken to her husband's farm and shown the boundaries as well as the portion where she may plant vegetables for making soup. When she finally emerges from the room (*e ler ebuto*), the new wife is taken round to greet all the compounds of the village, receiving a few pennies at each.

The initial seven-day seclusion of the bride is followed by a period of several weeks, or even months, during which she continues to share a room with one of the other women in the compound. Throughout this time she is referred to as 'the new wife' (*etche puper*) and in many ways is treated more like a guest than a member of the household. She has, for instance, no fireplace of her own and, although she helps the other women cook, she does not take her turn in the rota for cooking the major evening meal. This is a time of mutual trial and adjustment. When it becomes clear that the marriage is reasonably satisfactory, or when the new wife becomes pregnant, she is placed in a room of her own (which must not be a new one) and given a fireplace. Then, with the preparation and distribution of a ceremonial porridge, the bride is formally installed as a wife and member of the household.

When looked at from the standpoint of the husband's group, these three phases of the establishment of a Gonja marriage clearly correspond to van Gennep's periods of withdrawal, marginality, and re-incorporation. However, it is characteristic of Gonja society that the establishment of a marriage can be considered in a similar way when it is seen from the point of view of the kin of the wife; here too it is possible to observe these same stages by which their kinswoman is removed, secluded and returned to them in a new role. For a girl's first marriage must be initiated by a formalized reluctance on her part to leave her natal home. In spite of this she is forcibly removed by the groom's representatives to the compound of her husband. There she must remain until the end of the period of mutual trial is marked by her installation in her own room. Until this time she will not be granted permission to return to her natal village. But shortly after her assumption of full wifely status, a girl does visit her natal kin. And there, for the first time, she pursues on her own behalf those activities which are the concern of adult women. Specifically, she will prepare shea butter for her cooking, and make soap, "with which to wash my husband's clothes", as one young wife proudly put it.

Thus marriage not only marks the incorporation of a woman into the household and community of the husband, but, for the wife, her first marriage marks her assumption of adult status among her own kinsfolk. The importance of this recognition of a woman's dual role – that of wife in another household and of adult kinswoman in her natal community – lies in the claims which she may make in each of these roles for shelter, support, medicine and ritual assistance.

FORM AND FUNCTION IN GONJA MARRIAGE

Although it is possible to present an idealized outline of marriage rituals, at almost every stage there are alternative forms and exceptions which

Table 5-1. *Elements in Gonja marriage ritual: a girl's first marriage*

Variation appears to be based on:

Elements:	Estate			Region			Other factors
	R	M	C	E	C	W	
Seizure of bride	+	+	+	+	+	+	
Washing bride (*fer kijafo*)	—	+	—	+	+	+	
Tying *furu*	(+)	+	(+)	+	+	+	Muslim converts and well-to-do husbands
Procession with courting gifts	(+)	(+)	(+)	+	+	+	Only a well-to-do husband does this
Seclusion of bride: with groom	—	—	+	—	—	+	
Seclusion of bride: with older woman	+	—	—	+	+	+	
Seclusion of bride: with girl companions	—	+	—	+	+	+	
Killing of chicken for ancestors	+	—	—	+	+	+	
Sending chicken to bride's parents as 'placation' gift	+	?	—	+	—	—	
Gift of 500 kola to bride's kin	+	+	—	—	—	+	
Gift of lump sum to bride's parents	+	+	?	+	—	—	
Showing the husband's farm	+	+	+	?	+	?	
Dance for men of husband's village	+	+	+	?	+	+	
Greeting of compounds by new wife	+	+	+	+	+	+	
Preparation of ceremonial porridge by bride for distribution in village	+	?	+	—	+	—	
Placing bride in own room by husband's sister	+	?+	+	?—	+	—	
Finding water pot and fire stones by husband's sister	+	+	+	?—	+	—	
Formal permission for bride's first visit home	+	?+	+	?	+	?	

would lead many Gonja to dispute any such account. Some of these variations (which are set out in Table 5-1) are related to Islam, others to beliefs about the powers of the ancestors; some are regional in origin, while others seem to be a function of relative affluence.

All marriages are formalized by sending and accepting the marriage kola.[1] Additional variations occur where the marriage is not the bride's first, where the bride is very young or very old, where she holds a women's title or is active in trading (though these latter occur rarely in central Gonja).

While this list of the institutionalized elements in the rituals of marriage may seem a long one, it is probably incomplete, since there are so many possibilities for alternatives specific to ethnic and occupational subgroups. However, it draws on material from communities in eastern, central and western Gonja, and on marriages between members of all three estates, so that it is reasonably representative of the kinds of elements which comprise marriage ritual. Aside from the sending of the marriage kola, all of these elements are optional for some people, but either obligatory or at least highly desirable for others.

It seems best to view these different ceremonies and observances as an array of elements which are relatively independent of one another, but which are used in given combinations depending upon such factors as estate membership, locality, and relative affluence.

MUSLIM ELEMENTS

The two main Muslim elements are the 'washing of the bride' (*ba fer kijafo*) and the tying of *furu*. The first time that any woman, whatever her estate, marries a Muslim, she must be taught to pray and instructed in the rules concerning cleanliness and food. The washing of the bride marks the completion of her initiation into Islam, and thus her readiness to be a Muslim's wife. It is usually carried out in the bride's home, and should include the dyeing of her hands and feet with henna, as well as a ritual bathing by a senior Muslim woman. A woman is only 'washed' once; should she later marry a second Muslim husband, this rite is not repeated since she already 'knows how to pray'.

The tying of *furu* is essentially a religious ceremony; its core is the binding of a kola nut with cotton thread while verses from the Koran

---

[1] It is possible that some of the commoner groups do not send marriage kola among themselves, though it would be necessary for them to do so when contracting marriage with members of other estates. Until information is available on every one of these commoner groups, any statement about procedures followed by 'all Gonja' must of course be qualified.

97

are recited. The kola nut splits naturally into two halves, and the symbolism of binding these two parts together is recognized by the Gonja. The hope is that the Muslims' prayers will help to bind the couple together in the same firm fashion.

Those *furu* ceremonies which I witnessed were large public gatherings attended by all senior Muslims of the village, as well as by the kin of the bride and groom, though the couple themselves were not present. However, the tying of *furu* is not restricted to Muslims. Just as Mallams may be summoned to take an important part in naming rites, funerals and even in the offering of food to the dead, by those who do not themselves follow the Prophet, so their services are sometimes sought in solemnizing a marriage.

There are two aspects of the tying of *furu* which together appear to account for its adoption by non-Muslims. The first is the efficacy which is assigned to the performance of the ceremony itself. Where marriage tends to be unstable, as in central Gonja, a rite which invokes super-natural assistance in preserving a union has much to commend it, at least so far as the kin of the couple are concerned. Secondly, there is the element of display which is associated with *furu*. The gifts which the groom has made to the bride, together with such valuables and domestic utensils as she has been able to acquire herself with the help of kin, will be laid out in the courtyard where the tying ceremony takes place. Often, though not uniformly, they will first have been carried in procession through the town, to the accompaniment of drumming and dancing. Thus it is said that, while Muslims are obliged to perform this rite, a man who does not pray will only do so if he is rich.

COMMONER ELEMENTS

The Dompo people of south-central Gonja announce the completion of a marriage with the preparation by the bride herself of a special meal which is distributed to all the households of the village. A Dompo bride who marries in her natal village may remain in her parents' compound for a few years (until her first children are weaned) before joining her husband. The distribution of cooked food by the new wife emphasizes that whether or not she is living in the same compound she has taken on the obligation of a wife to feed her husband.

Further north, where Dompo and Mpre are mixed with Hanga peoples, great emphasis is placed on the installation of the new wife in a room of her own, with her own fire stones and water pot. The husband's sister ought to supervise the preparation of this room for the bride and it is her responsibility to find the stones for the new fireplace, and the large clay water pot which will stand at the back of the room. The importance of these for the marriage is indicated by the fact that if a man is determined to send his wife away for ever, he either breaks down her fireplace or smashes her water pot. Nothing, it is said, will then induce his wife to return to him. None of these commoner groups kills a fowl to inform the ancestors of the marriage. Such an act is ritually binding, and people fear that should the wife later commit adultery, she would die.

ELEMENTS CHARACTERISTIC OF THE RULING ESTATE

The only one of the elements of the marriage ritual which is especially characteristic of the ruling estate is the killing of the chicken on the morning after the new wife is brought to her husband's compound. Although for the remainder of the period of seclusion the bride stays with the older woman to whom she has been entrusted, the couple spend this first night together. At dawn the next morning a cock is killed by the senior kinsman of the groom, who informs the ancestors that their son has taken a new wife. He asks them to look after the couple, and to give them children. Later on food is made from the meat of the bird and given to the couple to eat.

It is easy to see why some of these elements are not found in all marriages: commoners show a greater concern with the wrath of their ancestors than do members of the ruling group; hence they dare not seal a marriage with a sacrifice lest the wife later prove unfaithful. Only Muslims need to ensure that their brides will be able to follow the injunctions of the Koran. Men with little to display will avoid ceremonies which draw attention to this fact. And elements which stress the incorporation of a wife in her husband's household will not be appropriate where the couple have in fact been living together for some time, or where they do not share the same compound at all. The Gonja in fact show little concern that every marriage should follow the same sequence of elements, though as we have seen estate and regional identification do place certain constraints on choice.

FORM AND FUNCTION

There is then no single pattern of elements for Gonja marriages. At the level of function, however, certain regularities appear:

(1) Courtship always means courting gifts and the gradual establishment of a relationship (usually including a sexual relationship) between the man and the woman. An arranged marriage tends to be either the consequence of a similar pattern of greeting and gift-giving from the husband to the bride's kin, or else an expression of gift-giving and respectful deference by the bride's kin to the groom.

(2) The involvement of the families of bride and groom is expressed in the sending and accepting of the marriage kola. The bride must at least appear to agree before the kola are accepted.

(3) At her first marriage a girl ought to display reluctance to leave her family.

(4) Removal of the bride to the groom's compound is followed by her seclusion for a period of time.

(5) In one or more different ways the bride is introduced to the household and community of her husband.

(6) In one or more different ways the bride is established as a wife with rights to domestic facilities, farm land, and to her husband's attentions over and against other wives.

Selection among the various possible elements is a matter of regional and estate affiliation, and in part of economic resources. But all marriages are formalized by the payment of twelve kola and twelve shillings. Marriage in Gonja is based on this common minimal factor. So long as this common minimal element serves as a constant in all marriages, the wide variation in the other elements does not appear a problem to those concerned.

The legitimation of marriage by a single common rite, which is in itself of neither economic nor ritual significance,[2] must be seen in the context of the ethnic and social heterogeneity of the Gonja state. Given the pattern of open connubium which is characteristic of the Gonja, marriage between people who belong to different social estates and come from different villages and divisions is a regular, not an exceptional occurrence. If each section of the community and each region insisted that to be valid a marriage had to follow their own forms and no others, open connubium would lead to constant problems of legitimacy. So long as the giving and receiving of marriage kola is recognized throughout the state as the formal criterion of marriage, this ambiguity is avoided and other elements of ritual may vary according to local custom and estate affiliation.

[2] The distribution of kola, a single cowrie shell, or nowadays a penny, is a common way of securing witnesses to a transaction. These tokens are called 'eyes' (*anishi*), and anyone who accepts one has the duty to testify to what he has witnessed if later asked to do so. The marriage kola are distributed in exactly this way among the bride's kin.

Establishing a marriage

In seeking to understand the factors involved in the establishment of a marriage, it is important to recognize that the families of bride and groom have very different points of view, though they share the hope that the marriage, when finally settled on, will be amicable and fertile. For the bride's people it is the right to give or withhold consent to their daughter's marriage that is the chief concern. They may wish to see her married to a kinsman, or to a friend and ally. Or they may simply wish to be sure that her husband is a man of good character, and one who will respect his parents-in-law. But her kin are anxious to have a prominent part in the decision. Norms of courtship throughout Gonja stress the showing of respect for both the girl and her parents by the repetition of gifts and minor services, and in this way emphasize the importance of the good will of the bride's parents. Exactly what is required to secure parental consent does vary slightly from one part of Gonja to another. This matters little, so long as the consent is properly given by the acceptance of marriage kola.

The husband's kin, on the other hand, have the problem of incorporating a stranger into their domestic life. Many of the variations noted in elements of marriage ritual relate to special ways of integrating the bride in her new surroundings. For example, there are the differences in whom she stays with during seclusion, and for how long; in who greets her and whom she later greets; and in whether at the end of the transitional period she cooks for all the other compounds, or her husband's kin prepare the ceremonial porridge on her behalf. In all these areas the choice of particular elements is a matter for the husband's people, since it is they who must incorporate the new bride.

The emphasis on courtship with its provision for winning the consent of the girl and her parents, and the recognition of a common minimal element (the marriage kola) as the formal criterion of marriage are both consistent with, and indeed facilitate, open connubium. They are both also concerned with the proper establishment of relationships between individuals, spouses and affines, rather than with the transfer of rights over women between descent groups. For in Gonja, marriage itself is based on a continuous exchange of services rather than on a ceremonially ratified package deal, where rights in a wife are permanently, or even provisionally, vested in a kin group in exchange for some form of capital asset, in turn renegotiable for wives. It is with the rights and services which characterize Gonja marriage that the following chapter is concerned.

6

The Conjugal Relationship

Far from being 'made in heaven', the distinctive feature of Gonja marriage is that it is a contractual tie which, made by man, can readily be broken. In this it is directly opposed to the bonds of kinship which are permanent in that they inhere in relationships established by birth. Those who are kin have no choice in the matter and cannot break off the tie. Failure to observe the duties of kinship may result in a reciprocal withholding or delay of some rights – a Gonja father is, for instance, less likely to agree to the marriage of a lazy son than of an industrious one – but the kinship bond is not broken as a consequence. A serious failure to meet the role expectations attendant on kinship indicates a flaw of character (da) and may materially affect a man's status with his peers. But it does not alter the fact of kinship. A similar failure to fulfil conjugal role expectations is much less personally damaging, but it is likely to end the relationship.

Marriages, then, are conditional on the continuing mutual respect and affection of the spouses. Perhaps because of this, feelings between husband and wife tend to be intense and personal, based in the first instance on affection rather than on obligation. Obligations exist within marriage but are not sufficient to maintain it. In Bimaka's words, "If my husband cries, I cry. If my brother (her full brother) Mallam Tiaru cries, I do not cry. But if I hear anyone speaking ill of my brother, I will fight them and abuse them. And a woman's tongue is strong." While her loyalty to her brother was fiercely protective, emotionally she felt far more closely identified with her husband.

Yet quarrels between husband and wife do occur, and they are accepted as inevitable in marriage, whereas they are seen as being a serious breach of decorum among kin. An incident one evening demonstrated this distinction very clearly. Dari and Hawa, a couple living in the compound behind mine, were sitting by the fire conversing when gradually their voices rose in argument. "Did you tell her?" "No, why should I tell her about it?" "But you knew I said I would ask her, why didn't you?", and so on in a crescendo followed by sudden silence. Enquiries the next day revealed that the dispute centred about a debt of 3d which a creditor of Dari's sister, Mina, had asked him to pay. He had put the woman off, saying that his sister was in another village, but that when she came back he would get the money from her. When his sister had come to greet him on her return the previous day, Dari was on the farm and his wife, Hawa, had said nothing to her about the matter. When her husband asked her that evening why she had not got the money from his sister, Hawa protested that she did not wish to quarrel with her sister-in-law. "Had I mentioned it", she explained, "Mina would have accused me of interfering in what was none of my business. For a wife to talk of money matters between her husband and his kin always brings trouble. I already had to pay one debt for Mina of 4*d* when the woman to whom she owed the money died and the kin asked about the debt. This time I want to know nothing about it." Dari himself was anxious to avoid taxing his sister with her debt, preferring to leave it to his wife to settle. But if there was to be a quarrel, better apparently that it be between him and his wife than with his sister.

Husband and wife ought, however, to treat one another with respect, as is indicated by the convention that they address each other reciprocally by the term for older sibling (*nda*). After the birth of children, the couple address one another teknonymously as 'father' (or 'mother') of their child.

The conjunction of these contradictory themes – respect and hostility, affection and the awareness of mutual obligations – can be resolved in different ways. One couple may be very reserved in public, while another may joke and pretend to quarrel. It is said of husbands and wives that they 'play' but this does not have the connotation of the rougher behaviour of joking partners who may hurl insults at each other with impunity. To insult one another in public, or to joke using sexual imagery, would be as unthinkable between spouses as it is expected of cross-cousins and members of alternate generations.

MARITAL RIGHTS AND DUTIES

The sexual division of labour in Gonja separates the major productive activities from services and is directly reflected in the role obligations of husband and wife. A man is responsible for providing his wife with food. And all wives are entitled to equal portions of foodstuffs, regardless of the number of children they must feed. But since each wife must in turn cook the large evening meal for the whole household, apparent inequalities tend to even out over time. It is also the husband's responsibility to provide a woman and her children with suitable shelter and a minimum of clothing. In addition to her rights to food and shelter, a wife has sole rights to the use of her husband's fields for planting condiments. In central Gonja this is cited as one of the key prerogatives of marriage, since although a man often supports a mother or sister, these kinswomen may not plant in his farm.

A wife's duties are essentially services: the preparation of food, washing of clothes, provision of firewood and water, the cleanliness of the compound and the care of children are her major tasks. However, once a woman's obligations in the household have been met, she is free to use her time as she wishes. By the rendering of shea butter to sell in the large markets, and by the local sale of gruel and fried cakes, each woman sets aside small amounts which are hers alone. Such money is generally spent on clothing, trinkets or household utensils.

These reciprocal rights of service and support persist in illness except under certain special circumstances. When a man's sickness is thought to have rendered him sexually impotent or sterile while leaving him otherwise healthy, it is assumed that his wives will seek to leave him. In this they are thought to be completely justified. The Gonja do not make any provision for the begetting of children in another man's name, so a woman whose husband cannot give her children must divorce him and marry another unless she wishes to remain childless. And to bear children is every woman's right. If, on the other hand, a woman does not conceive after several years of marriage, her husband is still bound to support her, for he can ensure that he will have children by taking additional wives. Should the husband die first, a portion of his goods is set aside for the use of a barren wife. This is the only situation in which a wife may retain control over any of her husband's property after his death.

The other exception to the general obligation of a spouse to support an ailing partner occurs when a wife, of her own volition, returns home to seek the aid of her kinsmen in treating her illness. Since a husband's support is in any case tied to co-residence, this move temporarily sets aside his responsibility to provide food and shelter.

A man's duty to support a wife who falls ill includes that of finding the cause of her illness, securing the necessary medicines, and helping her to perform any rites which may be indicated. For divination may reveal that mystical trouble (*mbusu*) involving either a dead parent (*ebuni*) or the personal shrine (*akalibi*) is a contributory cause in illness. Where this is so, it is usually necessary to prepare a ritual meal, and possibly to make a sacrifice in order to restore the patient to a state of grace. Husband and wife are each expected to provide their own sacrificial animals, and where their own resources prove insufficient, to seek

104

the help of kinsfolk. However, while a man does not expect his wife to contribute on his behalf, a woman always hopes that her husband will give her a few shillings towards the cost of a fowl or a goat. While she is living with him, it is usually the husband who will speak to her personal shrine for her. But a kinsman may equally well perform this task and an older woman who wishes to do so may approach her shrine on her own behalf. A man appears to have no necessary role in his wife's communication with her dead parents; indeed, she is in a better position to do this when living with kin who will be more concerned to aid her in finding the things required.

A wife does have an important role to play in her husband's relations with his dead parents. When he wishes to make a ceremonial offering to them, she should be the one to prepare the special meal. A wife who is away on a visit will be summoned back to assist in this rite, and even a woman who has left her husband will try to return to help. While she is not directly subject to their influence, the power of her husband's ancestors to harm her children ensures her concern with their good will. A woman is not concerned with her husband's propitiation of his personal shrine, although she will automatically help to prepare the meat of any animal sacrificed while she is with him.

RIGHTS IN GENETRICEM

In Gonja the kin of each spouse have rights in the offspring of a marriage, and in this sense rights in the reproductive capacity of each spouse are vested in the kin of the other. This diffusion of rights in children is consistent with the absence of kin groups which might act as foci for exclusive rights. The claims which kinsfolk may make on one another's children are necessarily limited by the claims made by and through the other parent. This is the basis for the institution of kinship fostering which occupies such a central place in Gonja social organization. Claims are further restricted to children actually born or begotten by the parent in question. No distinction between *genitor* and *pater* is conceivable to the Gonja; rights and obligations *vis-à-vis* children are recognized only where a 'blood' relationship is known to exist.

A child born before its mother's marriage will either remain with the mother's kin, or if very young at the time of her marriage, may go with her to the compound of the husband. A man must treat such a child, or a child by a previous marriage of his wife's, with every show of affection if he wants his wife to remain with him. As Ajei, a Busunu commoner, explained, "A man will let his wife's child lie on his legs while his own children are sitting on the ground. He will try to find him a good cloth or perhaps the money for a bicycle while his own children go without. For if he does not treat him well, the mother will say he does not want her and go off to her kin."

The position of an adulterine child is essentially similar. The mother's husband at the time of birth is recognized as a pater by the community only so long as he is presumed also to be the genitor. If it is known that the baby is a 'thief's child' (*kayurbi*), the position of mother's husband is that of custodian, and in fact approximates that of a foster parent as I later describe it.

A man does not usually claim custody of his adulterine child from the mother's husband. This reluctance follows from the general rule that a small child remains with its mother. Should the mother leave her husband and marry the child's father, a young child would go with her. But if she remains with her husband the child will be brought up either by him or by the mother's kin. Although a woman will not herself tell a child that he is illegitimate, the husband's kin will see that he learns of it. Directly questioned, a mother cannot deny her child the truth, for sooner or later the spirit of his genitor or one of his ancestors, will be concerned with his welfare, demand sacrifices or make trouble. To attempt to supplicate or propitiate ancestral spirits not related directly through either father or mother would be useless; to fail to give to these spirits what they demand, extremely dangerous. Hence the truth will out.

It is unthinkable to the Gonja that a man would deny a son whom he knew to be his. Because of the mode of succession which characterizes the political system, such a son does not present a threat of direct competition to the senior generation. And as the pattern of inheritance is also characterized by deferred transfer between generations, competition on these grounds is also minimized. On the other hand, the addition of an adult male to the household is an asset: his contribution in labour is considerable, he may also contribute cash from time to time, and, above all, he represents an additional source of support in old age – all this from one whom the father has been spared the trouble of rearing. Seen in this way, the claiming of an adulterine child in infancy is an unnecessary bother. The pattern is not as anomalous as it might otherwise seem if viewed in the context of alternatives of residence open to all youths. For any boy may choose to live and farm with a father's brother or mother's brother rather than with his own father. Due to the remarriage of a mother, others are brought up in the household of a man who is not their father. Above all, residence and allegiance are not determined once and for all at birth, but are settled upon by each individual in accordance with the particular alternatives open to him at a given time and their relative advantages as he assesses them.

True paternity has significance outside the ritual sphere. For both succession to office and inheritance of property are dependent on establishing a direct blood relationship to the property or office-holding kin. Thus, while an adulterine child can succeed through his mother regardless of paternity, he must seek out his genitor to activate claims in the paternal line. Great weight is placed on knowing the people and villages to which one is linked by each parent. Mother's kin and mother's village, father's kin and father's village – mother's side and father's side – together these two principles define the social space within which a man lives and dies. It is undoubtedly in part a wish to find one's place in this system that leads to the emphasis made by Gonja on finding the true father.

In considering the status of an adulterine child, then, it is important to specify both the age of the child and the actors concerned. During infacy and childhood, the mother, and to a limited extent her husband, fill the role of parents and take responsibility for his training and maintenance. The genitor cannot make good a claim, for "the thing a thief steals does not belong to him". In any case he would probably be reluctant to trust such a child to his wives' care. But with the independence of movement attendant on adolescence, a boy will either seek out his genitor or take up residence with his mother's kin. Repeatedly I was told that he would refuse to farm for a mother's husband who was not his own father.

If a man's authority over such a foster child lapses with his maturity, the question arises as to why he is willing to feed and support him in childhood. There are, I think, several reasons. Most important is undoubtedly the mother's influence. As with a pre-marital child, or her children by previous marriages, her current husband must treat them with consideration if he does not want to antagonize his wife and drive her to leave him for another husband or to return to her kin. Secondly, the labour of an older boy or adolescent is a welcome contribution, although not an essential one, to the domestic economy. And finally, there is always the chance that a youth will care more for those with whom he has grown up than for the household of a stranger, even one who accepts him as a son.

SEXUAL JEALOUSY INSIDE MARRIAGE: CO-WIVES (CHAMINA)

The term for co-wife, *chamina*, is used by a woman in referring to other wives of her husband (past or present) as well as to the wives of her husband's full and classificatory brothers. All are her co-wives. In addressing these women she will use their names, or if they have living children call them teknonymously "mother of —". The other wives of her own husband are her companions, her helpers, and above all her rivals. "Co-wives are women who fight over the same man", and "co-wives are women who hate each other", it is said. But the relationship is too complex to be dismissed simply as one of hostility.

The polygyny rate in central Gonja while high by world-wide standards is relatively low for Africa. About 20% of the men in two communities were polygynously married at the time of enquiry (see chapter 4). However, of the women 92 out of 228, or about 40%, were at that time married to polygynists. Thus many women, probably well over half, spend a part of their lives as co-wives.

A man contemplating taking an additional wife must only do so after discussion with his existing wives, and not 'behind their backs'. Should he fail to inform them, and indeed to listen carefully to any complaints they may have, the others have every right to be extremely angry and may themselves leave. For so disrespectful is such a failure that it will be seen as an intentional insult by the husband: his way of indicating that he is tired of them. 'He is looking upon them as worthless' (*e keni bomu jige*), is the implication. A man who has taken another wife without informing the first, will have to go to considerable trouble if he is to persuade the first one to remain with him, finding intermediaries to give gifts and to beg on his behalf.

This situation is the more difficult because, in order to marry, a man must first find a woman whom he thinks is suitable and then court her. And the process of courting a woman involves making her small gifts and usually develops into a sexual relationship. When his wife sees a man paying such attentions to another woman, she is likely to resent it, whatever she may suspect his intentions to be. If it is just an affair, then it is a reflection on her attractiveness, and the time and tokens going to the other woman should rightfully be hers. If she suspects that the affair is in fact a preliminary to marriage, this is a more substantial threat, but at the same time promises her some relief from household tasks. Both these themes appear in the tirade launched against her husband by the commoner wife of one of the BusunuWura's sons when her husband had been sleeping with a lover for several days. The outburst was a noisy one, and when a sufficiently large crowd had gathered, the wife proclaimed her grievances: her husband was neglecting her – he no longer came to her room at night. All right, he could find his comforts elsewhere, but his *jipo* would have to learn to cook. For she would cook no more until her husband either gave up his lover or married her in the proper manner.

The linking of cooking and sexual services is central to the distribution of tasks and privileges among co-wives within a household. All the wives take equal turns, usually of three or four days, to cook for the household and to sleep with their husband, though if there are many it may be for only two consecutive days. During her menstrual period a woman may not cook for any man, nor does she sleep with her husband. Then the wives usually arrange to swop among themselves so that none misses her turn altogether. The wife whose turn it is to cook is also responsible for seeing that her husband's bath water is hot, and for washing his clothes.

This careful working out of the division of tasks between a man's wives serves to minimize the areas of friction between them. The same function is served by the spatial separation of each wife for, however many wives a man may have, each is entitled to a room of her own, as well as her own fireplace. She will also have her own water pot and a separate store of firewood. Each wife is shown a separate part of her husband's farm in which to plant peppers and soup vegetables. If there are two, each will take one side of the central path. A larger number will also divide equally, but each must receive enough space so that she can find room between the yam mounds to plant her condiments.

Ordinarily there is no grouping of wives, although in the very large households of the senior chiefs, women might be paired, or grouped in threes, for the preparation of food since such a large quantity was involved. It is said that those with a great many wives used also to pair them so that none could go outside the compound without her fellow, an arrangement that was intended to make it more difficult for them to have assignations.

The Gonja do not rank co-wives formally; neither the oldest nor the first married directs the running of the household and apportions tasks to the others. In fact where there is an appreciable age difference the older woman does often take the lead, but she must do so with circumspection for it is a privilege and not a right. In any case older wives should be addressed respectfully, greeted first, and generally given the deference due to seniority. But there is no recognized status of senior co-wife, nor the authority (in the sense of legitimate power) which might go with such a position.

Indeed, it is hard to see on what basis a fixed ranking system could be instituted without risking a conflict of the various criteria of status. The obvious possibilities are age, length of marriage, and estate membership. But given a system in which many marriages are relatively brief, and where older wives tend to leave the household (see below, chapter 7), age and seniority will quite often conflict. When the variable of estate membership is added as well, the possibilities for confusion are multiplied accordingly, for there are often wives of two or three estates in the same household. If the oldest, or the longest married, is a commoner (and there is probably a tendency for this to be the case), then a new wife of the Muslim or ruling estate will find herself in a subordinate position if either age or seniority is the criterion of status. But this, though perhaps awkward for some, is less potentially disruptive than a situation in which, say, a new young wife of the ruling estate was placed in authority over older more experienced women of either of the other two groups simply because she was a member of the ruling estate. Again, it could only lead to conflict if an older Muslim woman married into a commoner household and found herself subordinated to a young commoner wife because the latter had been married first. Less tolerable still would be a situation in which there was a clearly recognized position of senior wife that was occupied by whichever wife happened to be oldest at a given time.

The Gonja solution has been to organize households in such a way that each wife is so far as possible autonomous, taking directions from no one, and having authority only over her own children. But each of these mother–child units is related directly to the husband, and not otherwise ordered among themselves.

The two things co-wives quarrel about, it is said, are their husband's favours and their children. Any open favouritism by the father to the children of one wife will be greatly resented, and loudly protested about. Such protests tend to take the form of public complaints that inform anyone within earshot of what has happened in an attempt to enlist their sympathy and support. A strong man will ignore such 'women's noise', but most find it hard not to let it be known that they have redressed the balance, righted the supposed wrong. Quarrels among the wives can start in many ways. If one has older children, these are likely to take the lead in play and to want their own way, which is quite right in terms of the Gonja feelings about deference from younger to older siblings. But to a mother it seems that her children are being bullied, and she may try to intervene. Then her co-wife will side with her own children, and a fight has begun. A husband will separate the combatants in the interest of peace, and if he is skilful he will find a way of satisfying both women. Trouble can also easily start if one wife has many more children than another. In this case the balance is in favour of the smaller family. For since the same amount of food is allocated to each wife, when it is her turn to cook, a wife with one or two children of her own can more easily find extra titbits for them than one who has six or seven hungry offspring. Here there is no legitimate cause for complaint, but feelings nevertheless run high, and relations between the two wives are likely to become strained.

The jealousy of co-wives on behalf of their children is also reflected in the very strong Gonja conviction that a child who is placed permanently in the care of a co-wife of its mother will not flourish. I once commented on the condition of a boy of 8 or 9 who was very dirty and covered with open sores. "Well, what can you expect", was the reply, "his mother has gone off and he has been left in the care of her co-wife. She doesn't trouble to see that he bathes, nor to look after his sores. She probably doesn't even feed him enough. The boy won't last long, you wait and see."

Perhaps because this belief is so strong, one seldom finds young children in this position. If the parents separate children either go with the mother or to a kinswoman of one of the parents. For a man alone cannot be expected to care for young children. Older boys may remain with the father without their own mother, but you can often pick them out by their uncared-for appearance. Anxiety over the possibility of being left with a co-wife was among the themes which appeared very clearly in projective material collected from children in eastern Gonja, so it is a concern felt by at least some of the children themselves.

Sometimes, too, the fear of a woman's hostility towards the children of a co-wife is expressed in gossip and accusations of witchcraft attacks. One youth who was doing much better at school than his father's other sons was sent to live with a 'brother' of his mother's in order to put him out of reach of the supposed attempts of his mother's co-wives to injure him. In an analysis of allegations and accusations of witchcraft (E. Goody, 1970) it was found that the largest single category of believed witches were those affinally related to their victims. These victims were mainly co-wives or the children of co-wives.

This pattern of mystical attack is to be expected in a relationship in which two people are placed in close daily contact where they are clearly in competition for a limited resource, but where there is no formal recognition of their conflict of interests, and no way of resolving the situation (see Marwick, 1965). The same anxiety about the covert hostility of co-wives is apparent in the belief that, during the time when the spirit is unsettled immediately after death, a dead woman may seek to possess and even injure her co-wife. Women who fear this will move out of the house in which the funeral is being performed, and as a further precaution plug their ears with cotton to shut out the taunts of the spirit.

The only recourse open to a wife who feels her husband is paying unfair attention to her co-wife, is to leave the field, either temporarily or (if this brings about no improvement) permanently. But even if she does not wish to end the marriage, a woman often finds that a visit to her mother, or a sibling, will provide some respite from a difficult situation. And perhaps she will indeed be the more appreciated on her return.

One important advantage which both husband and wife gain from the introduction of a second wife is the presence of someone who can carry the burden of the household while one wife is temporarily incapacitated. For a woman is barred from cooking during her normal menstrual periods and also following the birth of a child. Indeed, a wife is supposed to avoid sexual relations with her husband until her infant is able to walk, between the ages of 12 and 18 months. It is partly in order to be free of her husband's demands that a young wife takes a new baby to her mother for the first few months. Women greatly fear conception before the older child is strong enough to walk and eat mainly solid food. It is believed that when a mother becomes pregnant again her milk turns bitter, so a suckling child rejects the breast and may starve or succumb to disease as a result. Yet it is difficult for a woman to refuse her husband's repeated requests for intercourse after the first few months. One solution is to go on a prolonged visit at this point, and this is easier to arrange if there is another wife in the house.[1]

But if co-wives can get on well enough so that they can share in heavy work and take turns in aiding one another, both have much to gain. And most wives seem to have come to the conclusion that whatever their private feelings, it is well worth co-operating in the work of the household. It is not uncommon to see a woman suckling both her own baby and that of a co-wife, while the latter is in the farm or collecting firewood. For, although women do manage to do even very heavy tasks with small babies on their backs, they avoid this if possible. Co-wives also lend a welcome hand in jobs like making soap or shea butter, which a woman does on her own account. These and similar processes are long and tiring, and go the more quickly for someone to talk to, quite apart from the reduction of work involved.[2]

[1] Indeed, the presence of the second wife may mean that the husband is willing to leave the new mother undisturbed, thus avoiding the need for a visit.
[2] No one who has lived always where electricity, running water, automobiles and

SEXUAL JEALOUSY OUTSIDE OF MARRIAGE: RIVALS (DATAPO)

A state of sexual rivalry (*kadata*) exists between two men who have been at one time married to the same woman, or who have both slept with the same woman. The very presence of a sexual rival threatens a man's health and safety. Contact between them, even when accidental, is thought likely to be fatal. For instance, if a drop of blood from one falls on the ground and the other happens to step on it, the injured man will die. Or should their hands touch while eating from the same bowl, one is sure to die. Indeed, virtually any form of contact between them is dangerous: if a man greets his *datapo*, it means he is trying to kill him. This is probably related to the fact that, if a man greets a rival who is ill, it is believed that the invalid cannot recover. One does not know when another is ill, so any greeting between the two is dangerous. There is disagreement as to whether any medicine exists which will neutralize this threat. Certainly it would take a brave man to trust his life to it.

The special abhorrence of adultery with a sibling's wife is in part related to the obligatory greeting and sharing of food between siblings. To continue to share a compound as siblings after becoming *datapo* is virtually impossible, for the enjoined acts are those which kill. The further prohibition on inheritance between rivals simply makes explicit the fear that to take property from a man who was your enemy in life is to risk attack by his spirit. No man would willingly put himself in this position.

While the mystical antipathy between rivals is inherent in the very relationship, they are expected to be overtly hostile to one another as well. They are permanent enemies, and it is assumed that they will come to blows when they meet. Or if too senior to behave in this violent fashion, it is thought that resort will be had to mystical aggression, to the medicines associated with witchcraft and war. No mode of attack is too violent where a rival is concerned. As one member of the ruling estate put it, "When your rival dies, a dog dies."

The vehemence of these attitudes towards sexual rivals, and the severity of the sanctions associated with trespassing on a man's sexual

---

processed flour are the trivia of everyday life can imagine the physical effort, and the tedium, involved in managing a household under pre-industrial conditions. Every drop of water must be carried on one's head, often for two or three miles; every stick of firewood found, and borne home; every item that is needed, soap, pots, cloth, flour, must be made by hand. Co-wives offer some kind of alternative to the division of labour which industrial society has developed so highly.

rights in women, whether wives or lovers, contrasts oddly with the freedom allowed in sexual relations and the absence of any clear transfer of exclusive rights on marriage. On the other hand, perhaps it is the very vagueness with which sexual rights are defined that makes their breach so threatening.

Although a wife is seldom sent away because of adultery, she may well be beaten and is in any case shamed before the kin of her husband who come to know of it. Indeed, the Gonja image of the consequences of adultery is that the woman is apt to run to her kin out of embarrassment, but that unless she wishes on other grounds to end the marriage, she will soon return.

When a wife has committed adultery, a purificatory ritual must be performed. The form this takes varies with estate and in different divisions, and also depends on the shrines held by the husband. A common practice is to demand that the adulterer send the husband a new cloth, pillow and sleeping mat, in addition to a chicken or goat for the purification of his shrines. Some commoner groups force the wife to undergo a public cleansing, which is much resented by the women and tends to prevent reconciliation.

If the adultery occurs before a couple have resumed sexual relations following the birth of their child, it has very serious consequences. Should the husband then sleep with his wife before the purification rituals are completed, it is believed that either the husband or the child will die. This added sanction is significant because of the common pattern of the wife returning to her mother or foster mother for an extended period after the birth of a new baby. This always happens with a first child, and also where there is any special problem, as in the birth of twins, or when two babies come close together. Men are always anxious about their wives' behaviour during such visits home. But as a man ought not to sleep with his wife until their child can walk, it is an added indignity if she goes to another man during this period.

Although there is considerable discussion of adultery, few cases reach either the chief's court or that of the government magistrate. Commoners seldom take adulterers to court, and indeed generally avoid becoming involved in disputes at this level. Muslims and members of the ruling group also prefer to settle such matters 'in the room' where possible. They may, however, take an adulterer to the chief's court 'to show their strength', and if they have clear evidence of guilt can secure a conviction which carries with it a fine of a few pounds. Of this only a small amount for the purification of his shrines will be given to the husband. Where the adultery concerns the wife of a chief or divisional official, the fine will be higher, and a man caught with the wife of the paramount receives the severest fine of all.[3]

AFFINAL RELATIONS

If it were possible to chart the amount of concern invested in the several kinds of relationship, affinity would come very near the bottom. It is not simply that this is a subject which people prefer to avoid discussing. For most people, most of the time, relatives-in-law are of marginal importance. The situation differs, of course, for men and women. For a man the salience of his in-laws is highest before the marriage has been established. At that time a suitor takes pains to show his respect and willingness to serve his wife's parents.

After he has taken his wife to live with him, he should still go for one day a year to help on her father's farm if they are in the same town as her parents (though this will only be expected of a young husband). In general it is felt that after they are married the husband should devote his energy to feeding his wife and children. When a couple lives in the same community as the wife's parents, the husband ought also to send them meat from any animal he kills; when necessary, he should re-thatch his mother-in-law's roof and weave her a grass door-mat. In addition, he must be prepared to assist in any special undertaking should his father-in-law ask it. Finally, he must not grudge the food his wife sends to her parents when she cooks the main evening meal.

Both before and after marriage a mild avoidance is practised between

---

[3] Colonial administrators in the early years of this century complained that the YagbumWura encouraged his wives to entice men to come to their rooms in order to catch and charge these lovers exorbitant amounts in fines. (See letter from D. C. Bole to Commissioner, Southern Province, 22 September 1923, Ghana National Archives ADM 197/234.) Gonja morality would deny this, for a husband ought not to benefit from anything taken from an adulterer. However it is significant that Bowdich made much the same suggestion about the wives of the Asantihene based on his visit to Kumasi in the nineteenth century (Bowdich 1824: 28).

If a chief has many wives, only a few will actually share his sleeping mat. It is the responsibility of the senior *dogte* to supervise the chastity of these women, and as he arranges their turns with their husband and must be told of their menstrual periods, he is the one who pronounces on the paternity of their children. The other wives were allowed to find lovers, who were expected to feed them. Any children were reared in the chief's household, but not considered eligible for chiefly office. They remained to farm for their 'father' and 'brothers' in a status not very different from that of a slave. Only a strong man, i.e. a chief, was able to retain control of his wife's lover's child in this way.

a man and his wife's parents, in that he would never sleep in their compound, but instead should stay with a kinsman or friend if visiting from another village. However, he goes to greet both parents-in-law, and may eat (or more usually drink) with his wife's father. After marriage a man's in-laws do retain the power to insist that their kinswoman leave her husband. It is for this reason that men say they 'fear' (*ngana*) the wife's parents, though it is sometimes added, "we don't fear them as much as we used to do".

When instances of forcing a wife to return are examined, they seem to be of two kinds: either her family has decided that the marriage was a mistake and the husband a poor choice, or there is a major quarrel between the two families of which the snatching back (*soγe*) of the wife is merely one expression. The one instance of the former sort encountered in central Gonja concerned a husband marginal to Gonja society. He was a trader who after a few years moved his trading base from Gonja south to the Ashanti town of Wenchi. His wife's parents felt that their daughter was living too far away, and a brother was sent to bring her home. She was immediately married to a man of her parents' choice, one of a very few instances recorded where a second marriage was arranged. It is significant that the only way in which the parents could effectively finalize a divorce was by seeing that their daughter married someone else. As we shall see in chapter 7, a marriage is only finally ended when a subsequent union is established.

An example of the second sort of recall of a wife occurred in Busunu shortly before my stay there. The youths of another section came to blows with those of the chief's section over the use of the dance drums. For a brief while all the women of the chief's section who had married there were called home. They came, leaving several households without cooked food or water, and remained until a settlement of the quarrel had been negotiated. People spoke of this to me with amusement, and it seems unlikely that marriages would have been permanently disrupted because of a dispute of this essentially trivial nature. But clearly the mechanism is there for dealing with a serious breach.

But friction between families linked by marriage seldom reaches this point for two reasons. In the first place, a man does his best to avoid antagonizing any of his wife's relatives. This may be difficult if, as occasionally happens, her brothers have taken a dislike to him. But with care it is possible. Secondly, as the data on dispersion of marriages show, many men live in a different community from their wife's people. Where this is the case, a man need only scrupulously observe the formal obligations of a son-in-law and he will probably have no trouble.

For couples living in a different village from the wife's parents, most affinal obligations lapse, except that, if his father-in-law sends for him, a man should come and carry out any commissions. The main obligation of a distant son-in-law is to allow his wife to visit her parents at reasonable intervals. The problem which this raises for Gonja husbands will be further discussed in the next chapter, but a man who repeatedly refuses to let his wife go to her parents for a visit is likely to lose her permanently, for they will consider that he is not only unreasonable, but is depriving them of the right to see and know their grandchildren.

All sons-in-law, wherever they may be living, must personally greet the funeral of both the wife's parents, and ought to go themselves to a full- or half-sibling's funeral. These greetings must include gifts. In addition a man must allow his wife to attend these funerals and if necessary to remain afterwards. The failure of a son-in-law properly to observe funeral obligations shows gross disrespect for both his wife and her parents, and is a recognized ground for a wife leaving her husband.

Although the Gonja say that they fear the power of their parents-in-law to take away their wives, what the parents seek is not so much fear as respect. While most people can cite an example of a marriage broken by the intervention of the wife's parents, this does not often happen. Rather, older people like to stress that they could so interfere if they wished, but they will not do so so long as they are properly respected. The elderly BusunuWura was particularly bitter when the YagbumWura failed to stop and greet him when returning from the regional capital at Tamale because he had given the paramount a wife. "What more can a man do, that he should be respected?" he complained.

The obligations due a father- and mother-in-law are completed with the proper observance of their funerals. They do not pass to the successor. As this suggests, the alliance formed at marriage is a particularistic one between individuals occupying specific kinship statuses, and not a compact between kin groups. A man does not farm for his wife's brother, or repair a sister-in-law's roof. Nor can a brother persuade his sister to leave her husband against her will, unless he is also a particularly powerful person in his own right, either through force of character, or perhaps by virtue of an office he holds.

A woman has more direct and constant relations with her in-laws by virtue of the fact that she joins her husband on marriage, and he is usually living with kin of one kind or another. Married sons, however, seldom have their rooms in the same compound with their parents. If this is remarked on, the answer is often that a man does not wish to have

117

trouble arise between his wife and his mother, and the easiest solution is to build at some distance from his parents.[4]

A woman has very different relations with the men and the women of her husband's family. From the first days of her marriage it is to her husband's mothers and sisters that she has looked for advice about local customs and family ways. She probably stayed in the room of such a woman during the early trial phase of her marriage. And it is the senior of the husband's sisters who should have found the things necessary to establish her in a room of her own. Young wives, while slightly awed by their husband's female kin, look to them for support and assistance in a way not possible with co-wives, who are from the first seen as rivals. A mother-in-law does not expect regular help from a daughter-in-law, though she may send for her when some special task is in hand. Each has her own household to run, and is expected to be able to manage on her own for the most part. Yet the mother-in-law retains her close interest in her son, and goes at will into his compound, even into his wife's room. The borrowing and lending of small items between these women is common. For her part, the wife is expected to greet her mother-in-law in the morning and again in the evening, and to send cooked food to her whenever she prepares a large evening meal.

Towards her husband's brothers a woman maintains a certain reserve, at least in the early years of marriage. She is their wife and they her husbands, so far as terms of reference are concerned. Those living in the same compound she feeds together with her husband when it is her turn to cook. Their children are hers, and perhaps more important to her, the children she bears to her husband are theirs as well. Full brothers may share a single compound, but half-brothers often do not. Thus, whether her husband's siblings are also close neighbours varies with the particular residence choice adopted. But so long as he is in the same town, a woman may go to a husband's brother to ask him to speak on her behalf if she has a complaint against her husband. This she will do if she hopes to reason with her husband quietly. If she is really upset, she will take her complaint to his father or another senior male kinsman. This is equivalent to making the quarrel public, and if she is clearly in the right, her father-in-law may call the locally resident kinsfolk together and reprove his son in front of them all. Such a public reprimand is intended to show the wife that her rights will be respected even though she is among strangers. And it makes plain to the husband that his treatment of his wife is not solely his own affair, but of concern to the

---

[4] Such a separation also minimizes contact between a man and his father. This and other aspects of residence patterns are discussed in chapters 10 and 11.

rest of the family who are anxious that 'their' wife shall not be treated unfairly and so be driven to return to her own people. It is perhaps significant that a wife apparently does not ask her husband's sister to intervene in a conjugal dispute on her behalf, although it might appear that their common experiences as women and wives would make her an obvious ally. Nor is a wife usually close enough to her husband's mother to go to her with such a request. This cannot be understood simply as an aspect of the respect and mild avoidance which characterizes relations between in-laws, for the husband's brothers and father are subject to this as well. It does however seem consistent with the concern to avoid friction between kin at all costs. If a sister were to intervene on behalf of her brother's wife, their relationship as siblings could easily become strained in consequence. For a man to speak to his brother is less of a risk, since both sex role and kinship align him with the husband and not the wife.

AFFINAL KIN TERMS

There are only three specifically affinal kin terms in Gbanyito. A spouse's parent of either sex is referred to as *ma sha* ('my in-law') and in turn refers to the spouse of a son or daughter as *ma sha*. While parents may use the name of a child's spouse in addressing him or her, teknonomy is preferred. An in-law of the senior generation is never addressed directly by name. Either a title, a greeting title (where appropriate), or tekno-nomous form may be used. In general it is my impression that a son or daughter-in-law avoids addressing a parent-in-law directly with any name or title.

The other special affinal terms are used for siblings-in-law. A man refers to both his wife's brother and his sister's husband as *m'choro*, and is so referred to by them. The mode of direct address between these men will depend on relative age, and status. Where there are alternatives, the more formal will be chosen unless the two are peers and old friends. A woman refers to her husband's brothers as "my husband" (*ma kul*), and to her husband's sister as "my female husband" (*m'kultche*). Her husband's other wives, the wives of his brothers (and indeed the wives of any relatives of her husband of his generation who live in the same compound) will be referred to as her co-wives (sing. *chamina*). The wife of her brother she refers to as "my wife" (*m'etche*) just as her brother does. As in many African languages (e.g. Talni, Dagari, Twi) the words for woman and for wife are the same; *etche* ('wife/woman') is thus not a strictly affinal term.

119

Male Ego

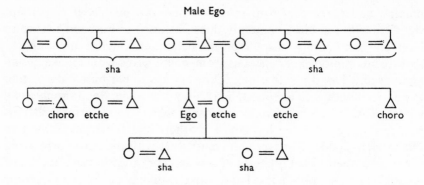

Female ego

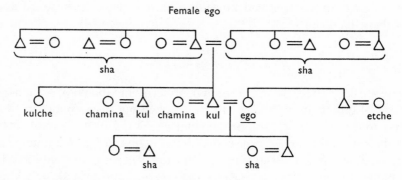

Fig. 4   Affinal terms of reference.

Broadly speaking, the Gonja divide in-laws of one's own generation into 'wives' (ms and fs), 'co-wives' (fs), 'husbands' (ms and fs), and 'those I greet' (ms). The 'wives' and 'co-wives' are always women, 'those I greet' are men, but 'husbands' are both men and women. In-laws of proximal generations are not differentiated at all, but the same term is used regardless of sex and relative status: father-in-law, mother-in-law, son-in-law, daughter-in-law are all my *sha*.

Before turning to an analysis of the dissolution of marriage, there are two further relational idioms, both of which have been referred to in the context of the conjugal relationship, which need fuller development at this point. These are the sharing of cooked food, and the use, or threatened use, of witchcraft powers. While neither of these idioms is limited to relations between spouses or in-laws, both recur repeatedly in the context of these roles.

The conjugal relationship

THE SHARING OF COOKED FOOD

As we have seen, the task of cooking for the household is central to the role of wife. An unmarried girl is not said to 'cook' (*dang*) but to 'help' (*tche*); and when the transition is made from lover, or new bride, to wife, it is indicated by the provision of cooking stones on which meals will now be prepared for sharing not only with husband and children, but also with the compound elders and the youths who help with farm work. The participation of a co-wife in the cooking rota of the household ensures her sexual rights and is inseparable from these.[5]

The wife sends food regularly to the kin of her husband who live in the same compound, since every time she cooks a main meal one large bowl goes to the young men and another to the compound head. She will also send a bowl to any kinswoman of her husband who is staying in the compound,[6] as well as to very close relatives who live elsewhere in the town.

Cooking is an especially wifely function, not only because of its intimate association with other aspects of the conjugal relationship, but because in this way a wife both nourishes her family and at the same time integrates the domestic unit, of which she and her husband are the core, into the wider social nexus. Her husband is thus enabled to participate in the day-to-day affairs of the compound and to meet his obligations to kin. There are also a number of ritual occasions in both the individual and the cosmic cycles when the full participation of the household in the wider community of the village or the supernatural world depends on the sending out or receiving of cooked food.

But the preparation and sharing of food are not restricted to the role of wife. A woman has responsibilities towards her parents, towards a brother whose wife has died or left him, to a sister who is ill, and to a woman who fostered her in childhood. If she is living in the same town with any of these people, she will feel obliged to send them a portion of the food she prepares for the large evening meal, or in the case of a brother who is farming, to prepare separately for him the produce

---

[5] Of course, an only wife cooking for her husband does not sleep with him while her infant is still at the breast: women sometimes cook when they do not in fact exercise their sexual relationship with the husband. But if the opposite occurs, then the other wives feel that their rights have been infringed. Indeed part of the reason that husbands find it difficult to respect the full period of *post partem* abstinence may be because the association in Gonja is so strong between the wife-who-cooks and the wife-you-sleep-with.

[6] A kinswoman of her husband who is a permanent resident and who cooks for herself may or may not receive food.

121

which he brings her. Few of the many ordinary evening meals whose distribution was recorded failed to include a bowl sent to one of these relatives. For certain of the rituals in which the distribution of cooked food plays a central part, it is women acting as sisters or daughters, or in their role as members of a given estate, who are responsible for the cooking. For instance, it is the *ewuritches*, the holders of women's chiefships, who are responsible for preparing the Damba rice which is distributed during the night-long dancing and vigil-keeping which precede the final rites. It is kinswomen, not wives, who are responsible for the making of funeral porridge when a man dies. And some men insist that a sister rather than a wife cooks all food eaten during the dangerous period of seclusion immediately after installation as chief, for "it is your sister whom you can really trust" (*fo suputche e kɔ yerda*).

The preparation and distribution of cooked food is primarily in the hands of women, then, but may be linked to any of a woman's roles, not only that of wife.

OCCASIONS ON WHICH COOKED FOOD IS SHARED

The obligation to share food with parents, siblings, and close kin is a regular one which should be honoured each time a main meal is cooked, and which persists so long as those concerned live in the same community. The distributions of cooked food which mark the transitions in the individual life-cycle are quite different. On these occasions preparations begin days, or even weeks, in advance, and the meal is a special one, being both unusually rich and very large. In some, but not all, communities, the custom is that every household shares either in the provision of the basic ingredients or in their preparation. In the former case, a small calabash containing a few peppers, some salt, some shea butter, and perhaps some grain, will be sent from each house to the one where the food is to be prepared. Such contributions can be a substantial help where a very large amount of food must be made. Alternatively, the household preparing the ceremonial meal may send a calabash of grain to each household in the community for grinding. This is returned the next day as flour, and from this the ceremonial *kude* is prepared.

Despite the fact that yams form the staple food for half the year, a ceremonial meal always consists of porridge (*kude*) and soup. A major ceremony will almost certainly be the occasion for killing a goat or a cow. When this is so, the soup is made with some of the meat, and pieces of cooked meat are placed on the more important bowls. The rest of the meat is distributed among kin or to compound heads, depending on the particular occasion being observed.

The occasions in the individual life-cycle when the sharing of a ceremonial meal is important are those involving the definition of the individual's relation to the community as this is mediated through compound membership. When a new baby is shaved and named, the distinctive sets of triple marks are cut on face, limbs and body; if a boy, he is also circumcised.[7] This is the occasion on which the child is accepted into his own family and introduced into the community.[8] After the shaving and other rites, the women of the household (with the help of female kin – wives, mothers and sisters) prepare a huge quantity of porridge and soup, and bowls of this are sent to all the compounds in the town. Close kin will receive individual bowls as well. The porridge prepared for the naming and head-shaving of a new baby is a 'good porridge' (*kude lele*) and suitable for all to eat.

The only ceremonies associated with the transition from childhood to the responsibilities of adult status are those of marriage. The installation of the established wife in a room of her own is such an occasion. At this time either the bride or her husband's kinswomen prepare a large porridge which is distributed to all the compounds in the village.[9] This act serves to introduce the bride as an established wife, who henceforth will take her turn at cooking in her husband's compound.

From the observer's point of view, the most evident occasions on which bowls of cooked food are sent between compounds are funerals. At such a time, when many people have gathered from miles around, and animals have been killed as a part of the ritual, huge cauldrons of

[7] Some of the commoner groups do not circumcise, but others do. Males of both ruling and Muslim estates are circumcised at seven days. No operation is performed on the female sexual organs. Government opposition has very nearly ended the cutting of tribal marks.

[8] Probably because of the very high rate of infant mortality, the belief is strongly held that some infants are not human but evil spirits who impersonate human children to taunt the parents. A baby who dies before the seventh day following birth is assumed to be such a spirit. The shaving of the hair with which the child was born (*ebuni'min*, 'dead person's hair') symbolizes for the Gonja the child's final decision to remain in the land of the living.

[9] The practice varies slightly in different parts of central Gonja. In the southern area the bride prepares the meal with the help of her kin. In the northern part the groom's kin do all the work. The difference is probably associated with the common practice of either duolocal or uxorilocal residence in the early years of marriage in the south, and the strict virilocality in the north. It is yet another example of the variability of rituals associated with marriage. However, in both parts of central Gonja, bowls of cooked food are sent around to all the other compounds.

porridge and soup are prepared. But these are not intended primarily to feed the guests, many of whom ought in any case to be fasting. Each compound in the town will have sent a pan, and all are spread out by the cooking stones. After the ritual calabash has been prepared and sent into the room of the dead, these other pans are filled and sent back to the compounds from which they came. In this way each compound, and indirectly each household, participates in the sacramental meal which forms a central part of the ceremony. The porridge prepared during funerals is dangerous, literally, 'bad porridge' (*kude libi*), and many fear to eat it.

At each of these points of passage from one status to another, the individual is as it were reintroduced to the community through the idiom of sharing cooked food. Further, the sending of a bowl to a compound head serves to acknowledge his position as representative of the other residents of his compound. Each time such a distribution is made, the structure of the community is stated anew in the act of listing the compound heads who must receive a portion.

There are two festivals of the annual cycle which also employ the same idiom of incorporation through the sharing of food. The most important of these is Damba, with its combination of religious and political themes with those of pageantry and reunion. Twice during Damba cooked food is distributed. The first occasion is when the women of the ruling estate, led by the senior *ewuritche*, prepare a special rice dish (*ameli*) which is distributed just before dawn, a bowl being allotted to each of the compounds in the community. Here again the constituent elements of the local community are made explicit through the allocation of a bowl of food. This is as it were the domestic aspect of Damba. On the following day, when the huge calabashes of ceremonial porridge are brought out and presented to the divisional chief as he sits in state among his councillors and sub-chiefs, the distribution includes the divisions, that is the units, which make up the state as a whole. For the spokesman calls for someone from each division to come and claim first porridge and then a piece of cooked meat. He also calls for a representative of the main Muslim patronymic groups (these vary from one division to another, but always include the Sakparebi, and usually Jebagte), for someone of the spokesmen's people, the war leaders' people, the drummers' people, the blacksmiths' people, the ferrymen, and those who look after the chief's horses. Finally, witches, thieves and rapists are offered a portion as well. In this case the constant elements are not those specific to the town, but rather those which are common to the other divisions of the kingdom. A particular effort is made to see that food is shared with representatives of both the other political divisions, and of the various subgroups based on religion and occupation which constitute the state as a whole. Both Damba porridge and the rice prepared by the *ewuritches* are considered 'good' and suitable for adult consumption.

The feasting at Jentigi has a more private focus, though it also has a dual aspect. In mundane terms, Jentigi is the time when every compound should prepare food in plenty, not only to consume themselves, but also to share with kin and neighbours. Children look forward eagerly to this festival because they are sure to have enough to eat.[10] The Gonja say that one who is not satisfied at Jentigi will never be content. But food is also given to the ancestors. A calabash of porridge topped with a scoop of the richest soup and a piece of choice meat is left out all night for the dead most closely linked to the elders of each compound. On Jentigi, food is sent to close kin, living and dead, so that all should have their fill.

There are at least two other important rituals in which the presentation of cooked food to the ancestors is the central act. Both of these are used by Muslims as well as those who do not pray, and it may be that the general Gonja emphasis on sharing cooked food rather than on sacrifice of animals is related to the Muslim antipathy for sacrifice.

The first of these rituals is a form of alms-giving. The Muslim day extends from sunset to sunset, with Friday (*alejima*) as the holy day. It is at dusk on the previous day, the beginning of Friday, that the supplicant sets out a number of fried millet cakes to be left throughout the night for the spirit with whom he wishes to communicate. At dawn the next morning he will take the cakes outside the compound, or perhaps into the central clearing of the village, and call out "yara yara yara yara . . .". A rush of children from nowhere and the cakes are snatched up so quickly that last-comers must go without. In a moment all is quiet again. Cakes are distributed in this way when a diviner suggests that such an action would please a dead kinsman, or to put right some ritual oversight. But there is usually a specific precipitating event, rather than a desire to improve one's general ritual standing.

The other mode of sharing a sacramental meal with the dead is known as 'making *nyina*' (*wura nyina*). This ritual, which usually involves the killing of a goat, but occasionally a cow, resembles a sacrifice. *Nyina* is

---

[10] As the actual time of Jentigi is determined by the Muslim calendar, it sometimes falls in a period of relative scarcity of food. However, as the economy is based on both root crops (yams and casava) and cereals which ripen several months apart, there is no real hunger period.

not often performed, perhaps once or twice in a lifetime, and then not by everyone. It would be disrespectful to use a chicken unless there was no alternative. Again it is a diviner's diagnosis which determines the offering of *nyina*; those seen as demanding such attention are apparently always immediate ancestors, a father or mother, or very occasionally a parent's close sibling.

Although *nyina* resembles a sacrifice in that a brief prayer may be said as the animal is killed, in Gonja eyes this is not the most important part of the ritual. Rather, the emphasis is on the preparation and offering of a fine meal, and upon the prayers recited by a Mallam the evening before the food is set out for the spirit. The prayers combine general requests that Allah should be merciful and wise, with specific pleas that the dead parent be particularly solicitous for the welfare of the children he or she has left behind, including the one who is offering the prayers and the food. The imagery is direct: parents feed children when they are young; children feed parents when they are old. Each has the interests of the other at heart, and therefore the duty to cherish them. The offering of cooked food is a means of enacting and fulfilling these obligations, and thus of attempting to call the attention of the departed parent to the fact that his children still stand in this dependent role and still need his care.

The filling of bowls with food has a basic or core meaning as the source of daily nourishment for the members of a family. This 'family' in fact consists of several sets of people who eat the food a wife prepares: she and her daughters and small sons form the nucleus, and they eat together from one bowl. Each co-wife receives a bowl to share with her children in the same way. Another set consists of the youths and young men of the compound, and a separate bowl is prepared for them. Finally, a bowl is prepared for the elders of the compound who eat separately from the others, though they may call a younger son or a grandson to bring them water and share their food.

But, as we have seen, the sending of cooked food appears in many different contexts in Gonja social life. The regular obligation to send food to certain close kin of both husband and wife means that the consumption group extends beyond the dwelling group. But in addition, major ceremonies in the individual life-cycle include a distribution of cooked food to other compounds in the community, thereby informing them of the change of status which has occurred and including them in the commensal group. On other occasions, when the community as a whole celebrates events in the annual cycle, cooked food is shared informally among households and formally between representatives of

126

the different elements of the political system. Finally, there are a number of occasions on which cooked food is shared with the dead, by Muslims as well as others.

Radcliffe-Brown remarked (1922) that where a number of different ceremonies share a common ritual element, then we should look for other features they have in common. In Gbanyito there is a frequently heard phrase, *kapulia konle* ('one cooking pot'), which is used to refer to the members of one domestic group and to a single joint household where the wives take turns in cooking the large evening meal. It can also be extended to apply to the members of a single compound whose young men eat together. Those who eat from 'one cooking pot' are usually thought of as related, though by some mixture of cognatic and affinal ties that is irrelevant to the classification. They can also be referred to as *basa konle* ('one people') (see below, chapter 9). But whether or not the speaker knows the exact relationships within such a group, people described as eating from one cooking pot are assumed to be living together, and to be co-operating closely in economic activities. The reference is to an effectively co-operating group, but there are strong overtones of emotional affect derived from the primary meaning of the mother/wife who cooks for children and husband.

It is this core meaning which, I suggest, diffuses to the other occasions on which cooked food is shared. In other words, the sharing of cooked food is a relational idiom whose emphasis is on inclusion, on being a part of a close and interdependent group. There is a special reason for interpreting the sharing of cooked food in this way, which draws on another relational idiom, that of witchcraft. While both men and women may know and practise witchcraft, it is women witches who are feared because they kill maliciously, and they kill those who are not their overt opponents. The main means which women witches use in attacking their victims is placing mystical poison in the food they prepare. The Gonja are therefore extremely careful about what food they eat, particularly if they do not know the woman who has cooked it. To 'eat from one pot' in this context means to trust the women of the house where the food has been prepared.

It is in fact impossible to know all the women who have assisted in the preparation of a ceremonial porridge and the accompanying soup, for the compound is crowded with helpers, each of whom takes a turn at the arduous task of stirring the thick porridge in its huge cooking pot. It would be all too easy for a witch to slip in her poison under the guise of helping. For this reason many people refuse to eat food which is sent during ceremonies, even when it is a 'good porridge'. However, the polite view is that food should be sent to each compound in the community, both as a form of announcement, and to show that on this occasion all are 'of one cooking pot'. To return untouched a proffered bowl of ceremonial porridge would be such a direct denial of trust as to be unthinkable. Instead the food is either thrown out uneaten, or given to children who are believed to be too young to have enemies.[11] Occasionally a man who owns strong protective medicine will eat such food as a proof of his invulnerability.

The sharing of cooked food, then, is a public statement of inclusion in a single moral and social community among whose members there is trust. Yet at the same time individual community members remain cautious about the safety of such intimate bonds. Each compound sends its empty bowl, and carries it home full. Public unity is affirmed. But the people of each compound continue to have their allies and their enemies, and to take precautions against betrayal, even within the community. The extension of the idiom of sharing cooked food as a symbol of the dependability of relations between close kin is only partially successful when applied to the wider community, based as it is on a mixture of many ethnic and religious elements.

WITCHCRAFT AS A RELATIONAL IDIOM[12]

The two relational idioms thus far considered, greeting and begging behaviour and the sharing of cooked food, are both used to bring about a solidary relationship, or to reaffirm one that already exists. Beliefs concerning witchcraft have on the whole the opposite effect. They isolate and exclude.

For the Gonja, the mystical powers attributed to witches (*egbe*) are real. Thus in relating to people it is necessary to keep in mind the likelihood of assistance or injury by witchcraft (*kegbe*) or mystical medicines (especially *korte*). As among the Tiv (Bohannan and Bohannan, 1953) and the Nyakyusa (Wilson, 1951) Gonja witches can act as protectors of the weak and innocent. Indeed, a man who heads a compound ought to know witchcraft in order to be able to guard its occupants against attack by evil witches. If not all compound heads have been initiated into these mysteries, they do not advertise the fact, for this would

---

[11] This is of course inconsistent with the commonly expressed view that witches seek to injure a powerful enemy through his children who have no such protection. The inconsistency is built into Gonja beliefs about witchcraft.

[12] For a full discussion of both male and female witchcraft see my paper 'Legitimate and Illegitimate Aggression in a West African Society' (E. Goody, 1970).

1. A village in central Gonja (Busunu)

2. Chief's council hall and commoner drummer (Busunu)

3. Sub-chiefs dancing Damba at installation of divisional chief (Kawsawgu)

4. Senior women of the ruling estate going to greet the Busunu chief at Jentigi

5. A Muslim greeting a chief

6. Courtship often begins at the dance ground
(Sumpa, Buipe)

7. Cooking: the distribution of food for a ceremony (Jentigi, Busunu)

8. A child carries the evening meal between compounds

invite the very dangers they most fear. Men who hold positions of power on secular or ritual bases, Mallams, hunters, warriors, and chiefs, are widely assumed to be witches as well. One sort of power implies another. And indeed all chiefs are 'known' to have learned witchcraft, for the struggle for office is fought in part on a mystical plane: each contender pits his mystical powers, and his medicines, against those of his rival, and the stronger is the winner. On the whole people are reassured by the knowledge that their leaders are witches. They can then expect them to extend the peace of the political community into the mystical sphere, and to control witches who might wish to injure or kill. For instance, when illness strikes suddenly, the chief will send a messenger into all the lanes and clearings to announce that he, the chief, will not allow another witch to kill in his town. Or again, certain dances are thought to give rise to jealousy which is expressed in witchcraft attacks. They are only performed when the chief is present to protect the dancers. But the clearest indication of the chief's role with respect to evil witches is his obligation to take charge of, and usually to marry, those women who are proven to have killed in this way. Thus they are forced to live in his compound and are under his surveillance and subject to his superior mystical powers, both by day and by night.

Occupants of authority roles in Gonja then tend to be invested with mystical powers as well as those more directly related to their position as the head of a compound, village or division. On the whole these powers are thought to be employed defensively, and thus for good, but at the same time they are a source of fear and awe. For the most prominent attribute of a witch is his power to kill, and to do so secretly. Relations to persons in authority are consequently coloured with a distinct circumspection born of concern. It is much safer to be under the protection of a really strong man, yet his very strength may become dangerous if it should be turned against those close to him.

Women as well as men are thought to be witches, but there is no benign, protective role assigned to female witches as exists for their male counterparts. Women kill, not to protect, but for spite, for meat, or to fulfil a debt to the other witches incurred by sharing their victims. Thus women witches are wholly feared. Nor is there a single role in which women give reign to their evil powers. An analysis of fifty-two believed attacks by witches showed that 40% of the victims were related to the witch affinally, and one-third were kin, while a quarter were unrelated. Thus any woman, mother, sister, wife, co-wife, or stranger may turn her mystical powers against a person. On one level this pattern is predictable in a system which has no strong boundary-maintaining kin groups. For the common proviso that a witch can only attack within her own kin group has little meaning in Gonja, where the main features are the unbounded, overlapping ranges of kin. On another level such a view of witchcraft-potential means that there is no relationship with a woman which is completely safe, whether conjugal, affinal, kin-based, or simply that of friend or lover.

Anxieties are further increased by the belief that the commonest mode of attack by female witches is a special mystical poison, *korte*, which is put on to an object likely to be handled, or is introduced into food. As the preparation of food is the central task of a woman both as wife and mother, this belief places at risk the very closest human relationships. Husbands are 'known' to have been killed by wives in this way, and children by their mothers. Most people, most of the time, take the view that other people's womenfolk may be witches, but their own are not. Nevertheless, the underlying concern is there. Of fifty-one stories told by girls about a picture of a Gonja woman ladling out soup, one-third described her as a witch, or referred to the eating of human flesh. Concern over witchcraft is also expressed, as we have seen, in the reluctance to eat food cooked for ceremonial distribution, when many women will have had access to the porridge and soup during their preparation. Gifts of uncooked food are also suspect, and often accepted only to be passed on or thrown away untouched. People tell of kola nuts given as greetings which were 'really' the poisonous seeds of *akee* apple fruit. And a traveller must be particularly careful to find a woman he can trust to make food for him, as he cannot know the reputations of those in a strange town.

Witchcraft beliefs are here treated as a relational idiom because they are an expression of the element of fear and distrust that exists in relations with women, both from the point of view of men, and that of women themselves. At the same time all power relations among men are tainted with a similar concern. It is as though witchcraft beliefs provide an idiom for expressing distrust which at once gives it a reality outside the individual's own fantasies, and leads to corroborative statements and behaviour from those around him. In some cases, probably a small percentage of all those in which particular witches are discussed, some sort of counteraction follows which may reduce the fear of mystical attack, at least for a time. But the conviction remains that men will use witchcraft in competition with other men, as well as to protect dependants, but that many women are also able to kill in this way, and may do so without apparent motive.

7

The termination of marriage

I have suggested that the very nature of Gonja marriage implies a contractual tie which, in contrast to the bonds of kinship, may be set aside. Since it is the conjugal relationship which provides the usual focus of the household and the domestic group, its disruption must also disturb these units. When patterns of residence and the developmental cycle are considered in detail, it will be clear that separation, divorce and death regularly effect changes in the composition of household and compound. Since relatives tend to be dispersed among several villages, the removal of a woman and her children from a husband's house to the compound of a kinsman or a new spouse may put many miles between parents and children, full siblings, and between children and some of those kin on whom later their rights and obligations will centre.

Because of these implications of divorce and widowhood, it is important to treat the termination of marriage in some detail. In addition to describing the possible ways in which marriage may be ended, there is also the problem of what might be called the pattern of divorce. This has to do with how frequently marriages are voluntarily ended, by whom, what rights are transferred to the new spouse and which retained by the old, and at what stage in the life of a couple they are most apt to separate. For it is not divorce in itself, but a particular pattern of divorce, which may be expected to have important consequences for the structure of the society as a whole.

Attention has been drawn to one sense in which this is true by D. M. Schneider's distinction between jural divorce and conjugal separation (1953).[1] Clearly the society where jural divorce, with full transfer of rights, is rare or impossible, but where conjugal separation followed by a subsequent union is a viable alternative, will look very different from that in which full divorce is freely practised, or from that in which the voluntary dissolution of marriage is impossible.

Another respect in which pattern is crucial has to do with the frequency of divorce or separation. The structural implications of a given form of divorce are quite different depending on whether this represents

---

[1] See also the exchange in *Man* (53: 75, 122, 233, 279, and 54: 96 between Gluckman, Schneider, Evans-Pritchard, Leach and Watson).

a legal possibility or a commonly followed practice. The example which springs to mind is the transfer of rights characterizing secondary marriage, as reported by M. G. Smith (1953) for the Kadara and Kagoro of northern Nigeria. While it is of theoretical interest that this institution exists at all, its impact on the society would seem to depend in part on the regularity with which such unions occur.

However, there is yet another aspect of the pattern of divorce which a consideration of the Gonja material suggests may be important. This has to do with the time at which divorce occurs. As Fortes notes in his discussion of the stability of Tallensi marriage (1949*a*: 84–7), early marriages that are uncomplicated by the birth of children may be lightly treated as experimental, whereas later fruitful unions have a greater tendency to be stable. For an understanding of the Gonja situation it is important to distinguish not only between a high rate of early divorce and a consistantly high divorce rate, but also between frequent divorce during the years of active child-bearing on the one hand and a high rate of divorce in old age on the other.

The unit of reference here is the life span of a woman rather than 'stages' in a marriage, because a consideration of the former seems to throw more light on the significant variables. These variables are the roles available to women, the status accorded to these, and the patterns of residence which result. It is important to distinguish between the effects of the dissolution of marriage during the early phase of a woman's marital career before she bears children, or when she has but one or two very young children, as compared with the effects of divorce during the middle phase of child-rearing, and again with those of the last, post-menopause phase when her children have grown up and when child-bearing and sexuality are no longer primary considerations. For Gonja marriages are ended easily and frequently in each of these phases, but with quite different consequences.

Frequent divorce during the early years of marriage, particularly before the birth of children, may be consistent with high overall jural and conjugal stability of marriage. Divorce in this phase of a woman's life approximates to 'experimental marriage' in that there are no lasting consequences to either partner. Where stable marriage is the general rule a woman may subsequently settle into a lasting union as easily as though it were her first. The importance of distinguishing a pattern of easy early divorce from frequent dissolution of marriage during the middle years of active child-bearing lies in the different sorts of kinship ties which arise as a consequence. For where, as in Gonja, many women have children by each of two or three successive and unrelated husbands, dispersed groups of maternal half-siblings are common. A further important feature is the fact that, once children have been born, the dissolution of a conjugal union can no longer terminate all relationship, for the couple is permanently united through parenthood, through their claims on and obligations toward their children. The regular dissolution of marriages when the wife reaches old age has yet other correlates. At this point divorce is not apt to be followed by remarriage, so that no new maternal siblings will be added to the existing group. But for an elderly woman the alternative to remarriage is residence with a sibling, which influences the composition of residential units and brings the developmental cycle full turn.

It is first necessary to set the discussion in the context of observations on the frequency of divorce and remarriage. Following this, there is an analysis of formal and *de facto* divorce procedures, and of the transfer of rights on remarriage. The next section considers the termination of marriage by death; and the last one considers the regular pattern whereby older women leave a husband to spend their last years with kin.

FREQUENCY OF DIVORCE, WIDOWHOOD AND REMARRIAGE

After only a few months in central Gonja it became apparent that divorce is not only easy to secure but relatively common. However, accurate information on which to base statistical indices of divorce is difficult to obtain for several reasons: the lack of ceremony with which the *jipo* relationship is converted into marriage if the wife has been married before; the brevity of many unions; and the ease with which people move in and out of the community; all contribute to the reluctance to discuss previous marriages and to the vicissitudes of memory. Although there is some numerical material for central Gonja, numbers are low and the information incomplete. These data have been relegated to Appendix III to indicate that too much weight should not be given them. Subsequent visits to eastern and western Gonja made possible the collection of more satisfactory material on marital histories in a reasonably rigorous fashion. The detailed presentation of these figures in a discussion of central Gonja would not be justified as they pertain to different populations, but I have also included summary tables on this later material in Appendix III. The discussion which follows is based on observations in central Gonja and on the trends suggested by the limited numerical data collected there, but the more rigorous material from later studies corroborates these conclusions very closely.

Of the Busunu women who came to us for medicine (the Busunu Health sample), about one-third of those under thirty had been married more than once, but this proportion increased with age until half of those over forty had had at least two husbands. In this group fully established marriages were equally likely to end by death or divorce, thought it must be remembered that many trial unions never reach the stage of the sending of marriage kola. In central Gonja women of both ruling and Muslim estates move more easily in and out of marriage than do commoners, though the difference is not pronounced. Women of the ruling estate also tend to have more husbands than others. It is they who have three and four spouses, while Muslim and commoner women are unlikely to have more than two.

Multiple remarriage is not necessarily due to a series of divorces, however. It may reflect a pattern of early widowhood, due to the difference in age of marriage arising from the greater degree of control exercised by fathers of the ruling estate in arranging marriages for their daughters with older men.

The large number of maternal half-siblings in genealogies indicates that many women bear children to more than one husband. This is also suggested by the finding that three-quarters of the successive marriages of women in the Busunu sample were fertile. Sets of socially, and often spatially, differentiated maternal half-siblings are thus common, since neither widows nor divorcées are allowed to marry a kinsman of any previous husband.

The data from Buipe and Busunu in central Gonja are not adequate for the calculation of divorce ratios. However, for Daboya, in north-central Gonja, the ratio of marriages ended in divorce to all marriages not ended by death (ratio C, Barnes 1967: 61), was 31.6. The same ratio calculated for Bole in western Gonja was 42.3.[2] Similar ratios have been treated as relatively high by Barnes in writing on the Ngoni (ratio C = 36.9, 1951: 53), and Lewis on the Somali (ratio C = 32.0, 1962: 34). They do not, however, approach the extreme levels reported by Turner for the Ndembu (ratio C = 61.4, 1957: 62) and Cohen for the Kanuri (ratio C = 68.0, 1971: 124).

In central Gonja, courtship shades into trial unions, many of which are not converted into marriages. Those marriages which are formally established may last for a few years, or for many years. Couples who survive into old age almost always part then. The picture is one of

---

[2] This figure is slightly higher than that which appeared in an earlier paper (E. Goody, 1969), since a few women have been excluded here whose fathers were either non-Gonja or of uncertain estate affiliation.

fluidity of conjugal unions, but not of chronic breakdown of marriage or anomie.

THE MECHANISMS OF JURAL DIVORCE
AND CONJUGAL SEPARATION

FORMAL REFUSAL

In Gonja there are recognized grounds for formally terminating a marriage and agreed procedures for doing so. A woman is justified in leaving a man who fails to provide her with sufficient food, clothes and medical care, who shows extreme favouritism to other wives, or who constantly quarrels with her. If a man takes a new wife without first telling his other wives and without making each a substantial gift, this is a sign that he hopes they will go. A man may put away a wife who is lazy, disrespectful, repeatedly unfaithful or an acknowledged witch. The spouse taking the initiative may say something like, "I refuse you, you are no longer my husband (wife)" (*N'kine fo, lelingeri n'kul (m'etche) mina la fo*). This act ought to be undettaken through intermediaries, as witnesses are thus ensured. In the case of a woman, the subsequent marriage ought to be from the house of a kinsman rather than directly from that of her husband, and not before an interval has passed long enough for her husband to try to persuade her to return if he wishes to do so. A husband who is irrevocably determined to end his marriage can do so by smashing the water pot kept at the back of his wife's room or by breaking down her fireplace. Reconciliation after this is said to be impossible, but the sanctions are supernatural intervention and injured pride rather than jural process.

Where these usages are followed, it is meaningful to speak of divorce as having occurred in the sense that all parties will agree that a formal act of separation has taken place.

CONJUGAL SEPARATION

Few marriages end in this way, however. One alternative is elopement with a new husband. In this case there is neither a formal refusal nor an intervening period of separation. The third mode of ending a marriage is by far the most common of all, barring death. This is through prolonging a woman's visit to her kin until either the husband ceases to beg for her return, or she remarries elsewhere. Here again no formal renunciation is involved. Ndembu, the young commoner wife of Lansa, who belonged to the Busunu ruling estate, had for several weeks been restive and casual in the performance of her domestic tasks. When her husband finally beat her for refusing to heat his bath water, she took their 18-month old child and went to her father in the near by village of Etchaboinyong. "Her father is an old man and irritable", Lansa said, "and if I go there and beg her to return he will abuse me. Besides, she ran there once before and I had a difficult time getting her to come back. This time I will leave it." Had it been the first occasion no doubt their parents would have tried to bring the two together. As it was, the matter was left to the couple, neither of whom acted to resume the marriage.

The story of Miama of Buipe illustrates another facet of the situation. Now an elderly woman of 65, she described how as a child she had gone with her father to Nyanga, near Bole, when he was appointed Liman to the YagbumWura. From there she married the chief of a neighbouring village and bore him two children. When later she returned to Buipe for her father's funeral, her husband failed to send someone to accompany her home. This failure is a serious breach of a son-in-law's duties and her people prevailed upon her not to think any more of him, but to marry a local man, a commoner. This she did, going to live with him in Morno a few miles from Buipe. After the birth of her daughter there, she came to her maternal home for several months, as is the custom, and never returned to her husband. When the child reached the age of seven, her father took her back to Morno though the girl visits her mother from time to time.

Miama could have returned to her first husband without being sent for if she had been eager to do so. Similarly, her failure to rejoin her second husband in Morno was a matter of her own preference. In each case she used a visit to her kin as an excuse to initiate a separation which the passage of time and later interests finalized. But neither of Miama's marriages, nor that of Ndembu discussed above, could be said to have ended by divorce in the sense of a formal refusal of one spouse by the other.

REMARRIAGE AND THE RE-ALLOCATION OF CONJUGAL RIGHTS

Despite the fact that a woman refers to her husband's brothers as 'husband' while a man uses the term 'wife' for his brother's wives, rights over women are highly individualized. Not only is it equivalent to sibling incest to have an affair with a brother's wife, but marriage to a woman who has ever been in the relationship of spouse to a sibling, parent, or parent's sibling is not allowed. Divorce thus means the disruption of the personal relationship between a man and his wife, but does not deprive the husband's kin of residual rights in a wife.

In considering the rights and duties which form the basis of the conjugal relationship for the Gonja, I have emphasized that complementarity in the roles assigned to the sexes is the keynote in the economic sphere. In the main, productive activities are the province of men and domestic services that of women. To the extent that domestic rituals and *rites de passage* focus on the preparation and sharing of food, the wife's domestic services become ritual services and the complementarity of roles is thus extended into the ritual sphere. The responsibility of the wife and mother for the care of her children further emphasizes the extent to which her role is defined by the performance of domestic services. In view of the stress placed on these services, domestic and sexual, as opposed to exclusive and persisting rights, it is not surprising to find that there is no clear-cut distinction between conjugal separation and jural divorce. For when a couple ceases to live together, services inevitably lapse.

When living apart from a husband, a woman cooks and cares for her children independently of male authority. If she returns to a previous spouse, he resumes his rights in her services whether or not their separation followed a formal refusal, i.e. divorce. On the other hand, if she remarries, her new husband has rights to services equivalent to those enjoyed by any previous spouse, while those of the latter thereby lapse. Since the rights of a previous husband are superseded only on his wife's remarriage, 'divorce' (in the sense of a termination of the rights to sexual and domestic services arising from a marriage) occurs only in the event of a subsequent union. Even this formulation is not perfectly accurate, for there is a sense in which a man's claims on his wife's sexuality persist after her remarriage. This is implied in the continuing relationship of sexual rivalry (*kadata*) which exists between successive spouses of one woman. It is further evidenced by the fact that a woman is not held to be fully widowed by the death of a second husband if her first is still living. Although she must observe many of the funeral rites prescribed for a surviving spouse, she does not bathe in protective medicine. It is said that if the first husband is still living, the one who has died can do nothing since he knows he does not 'own' her. That is, although the second had full rights of sexual access, these were seen as rights of 'use' and not of 'ownership'. There do not appear to be any positive correlates of such 'ownership' rights, in that a first husband has no more control over his wife while their marriage endures than does his successor in his turn. It is more in the nature of a recognition of prior claim. As such it is the representation on the supernatural plane of the situation where a deserted husband has no redress if his wife leaves him to return to an earlier spouse.

If there have been children of the marriage, still other aspects of the relationship persist after separation. Even though an estranged wife has since remarried, she may be called upon to prepare a sacrificial meal for her former husband's ancestors if no other wives are available. The welfare of her children is at stake, since ancestors often vent their anger on the offspring of those who have offended them, and no further sanction is necessary to secure her co-operation. That it is necessary from the point of view of the husband–father indicates the ritual significance given to the domestic role of a wife in preparing food. It also reflects the fact that once there are children of a marriage, the roles of mother and father are added to those of husband and wife. Whatever is the fate of the conjugal union, the ties of parenthood remain. Thus the husband's ancestors are seen as demanding the presence of the 'mothers' of their descendants, regardless of whether or not they are still 'wives'.

The persistence of the parental roles is also indicated by the fact that both parents and their kin continue to have an interest in the children even after a marriage has been ended. There is a widespread custom in Gonja of fostering the children of siblings and of one's own children. This means that from the age of six or seven, usually until marriage, a child may be reared by a parent's sibling or grandparent, living with them rather than with his own parents. Throughout the fostering period, visits are exchanged, the foster child returning for short periods to see his parents, while they and his siblings visit him. The diffuse claims on children of a marriage and the reciprocal claims of the children on their dispersed kin are aspects of the custom of fostering.

Divorce does not nullify these claims. Indeed, it may for reasons of convenience activate those which otherwise would have remained latent. A woman going to a new husband may hesitate to take all of several young children, yet be reluctant to relinquish her right to take with her any who are still too young to fend for themselves. Or the father who has kept with him the older children of a dissolved marriage may wish to avoid leaving the young ones in the care of his other wives lest they be neglected. Under these circumstances, fostering is often resorted to. Yet, whatever the residence of children after the divorce of their parents, the full range of kinship bonds continue to be of significance throughout life.

The custody of children on **divorce** is subject to the same complexities noted with respect to adulterine children and those born before their mother's marriage. Where boys accompany their mother and are reared by a step-father or foster parent, they may later return to the father of their own free will. However, there is a strong feeling that when a father fails to send money for the support of his children, he forfeits his rights in them as adults. But while the mother and her kin can enforce their control during the minority of the child, they cannot do so once he reaches adulthood. Girls constitute no such problem, as they usually remain with the mother or her kin throughout adolescence, and reside virilocally on marriage. The exception here is when a daughter is sent as foster child to a father's sister or other kinswoman.

Custody of children is not a good basis for determining whether or not rights have been transferred in divorce because in any case the genitor's claim is final. Suit for adultery payments is one possible criterion, but leads again to the conclusion that the rights involved in marriage are limited to the period of joint residence. For adultery fines do not appear to be awarded except where the offence was committed while the woman was living with her husband. The Gonja say that a man who succeeds in getting another's wife to come directly to him may have to pay a fine to her former husband. The KagbapeWura spoke of his intention of suing the present husband of his estranged wife, Dongi, and Aboker was violent in his insistence that he would demand payment from Akua's prospective husband in spite of the fact he himself had sent her away. Yet neither threat was carried out. It seems more probable that such claims are a reflection of the very vagueness with which rights *in uxorem* are defined. Because a husband has the right to a fine if his wife commits adultery while she is living with him, and because a separation may be resolved either by divorce or reconciliation, it is difficult for a man to accept the fact that in leaving his house a wife removes herself from his jurisdiction, and that thereafter her lover cannot be made responsible to him.

In this situation it is not surprising that redress may be through supernatural agencies. Retaliation against a man who 'steals' one's wife by elopement is said to take the form of causing his illness or death by the use of medicine (*kuderu*). This is justified by the certainty that no woman would leave her husband suddenly and by stealth unless her head had been turned with medicines. It is partly in order to protect themselves against unscrupulous rivals that men are thought to learn the arts of witchcraft which enable them to know the use of medicines for killing and injury. A wronged husband who obtains revenge by this means is held to be within his rights and is not subject to control or retaliation by the community.

The possibility that an estranged wife who has remarried may some day return to her first husband is a real one, and older men in particular speak hopefully of it. Akuro's wife, Nyomba, had left him for a Moshi man some fifteen years before, the four young children remaining with their father. When she returned to Busunu to greet her grandfather, Akuro did his best to persuade her to rejoin him. Had she agreed, she would have been fully reinstated and nothing further would have been said of the years between. He talked for days about her in- gratitude in refusing, and her lack of maternal affection for her children who, he said, had grown up as orphans (*m'munibi*) in the absence of their mother. And in Buipe, the KagbapeWura continued to speak of Dongi as his wife, although she had remarried and borne children by another man with whom she was still living. When she was brought to a nearby village by her mother's death, he sent a succession of messengers to greet her and finally went himself to beg her to return to him. Her refusal did not finally discourage him and he continued to talk about "my wife Dongi" as though she were absent on a visit.

Some wives actually do return. Pantu was complaining about his wife leaving him for a man in another village, but when asked if he would take his rival to court, he explained that he could not very well do so as it was from this man that she had eloped with him a few months previously. Again, widowhood may precipitate the reunion. When Hawa's husband died in Busunu there was speculation as to whether she would now return to her first husband in Langanteri whose children of 7 and 9 she had with her. But he too died before she completed her mourning period and she eventually went to her mother with the children of both marriages.

Spouses who have separated and remarried continue to refer to one another as husband and wife, and these terms apply also to the wives of a man's 'brothers' and the 'brothers' of a woman's husband. Where children have been born, and sometimes even in barren unions, the termination of marriage does not change even the more inclusive usage. Thus, Seidu, who belonged to the Daboya ruling estate, referred to one of the senior Busunu women as his wife because she had once been married to his father's sister's son and had borne him a child. This boy remained with the father, and his mother subsequently remarried. Yet Seidu continued to think of her as the wife of his 'brother' and as the mother of his 'son'.

This discussion of the usages relating to divorce and remarriage raises the problem of the definition of divorce. Only occasionally is it possible to say that a given couple have 'divorced' in the formal sense of one having refused the other in the presence of witnesses, or, in the more spectacular form, where the husband has broken his wife's water pot or destroyed her fireplace. The far more frequent pattern is one of extended separation in which the husband ceases to sue for the wife's return, or else she persistently refuses to go back. When the situation is resolved by the wife marrying someone else, then the former marriage has ended, at least as far as she is concerned. As Gonja marriage is characterized by rights in a woman's sexual and domestic services (rights *in uxorem*) rather than the jural rights which give the husband and his kin pre-emptive claims to any children she may bear (rights *in genetricem*), it is only the former which can be the subject of transfer on divorce. Therefore, in terms of Schneider's distinction between conjugal and jural dissolution of marriage, it is on the legitimacy of transfer of rights *in uxorem* that we must focus attention. As we have seen, bridewealth does not play a part in the establishment of a Gonja marriage, and thus its return cannot be used as an index of the surrender of marital rights. There would seem to be another possible criterion.

If a man could successfully bring his rival to court, and get the support of the state in securing the return of his wife or the severe punishment of her new husband, then it would be clear that no legitimate transfer of marital rights had occurred. But even today it is very rare for a deserted husband to take his rival to court, although a handful have done so, apparently with a view to inconveniencing their *kadata* as much as possible. Indeed, this use of the court might be seen as a functional equivalent to the traditional use of medicines to injure a rival. The reluctance to employ judicial process in securing the return of a wife, or preventing her marriage to a rival, seems to be due to two factors: in the first place, a judgement would almost certainly be that "if you cannot keep a woman with you by your own efforts, it is no use other people trying to force her to stay". It would be taken for granted that attempts to reconcile the couple had failed before matters would reach the chief's court. Secondly, the strength of the hostility between rivals is such that a woman seldom settles with a new husband in the same town as that of the man she left. Should they both come from the same village, the couple will leave, at least temporarily. Thus, in order to pursue the matter in court, the previous husband would have to follow his wife and her lover, and bring the matter before the chief of the village in which they were living. Unless the first husband himself has

141

kin there, this would be difficult to do successfully.[3] And marital affairs are not considered of sufficient importance to make it likely that he could get his case transferred to a higher, 'neutral' court.

In considering the legitimate transfer of rights between husbands it is important to look at the institutions available for enforcing them. These may be effective either locally, or over such a wide area as to render them virtually inescapable. So far as matters of marriage and divorce are concerned, the judicial system in Gonja does not function above the local level. If it were a divisional chief, or his close relative, the situation might well be different. But in this case the couple would probably take care to move out of the range of the chief's authority. The Gonja are not unique in this respect. In writing of divorce among the Pastoral Fulani of northern Nigeria, D. J. Stenning (1959) describes a very similar situation. What he calls *de facto* divorce seems to occur only when the two husbands do not recognize a common clan or religious authority that is able to reach and enforce a settlement.[4]

Marriages following *de facto* divorce among the Fulani, however, appear to be of the sort (*deetuki*) which Stenning refers to as cicisbean unions, that is, those in which the children of the second husband are not legally his. A woman's remarriage in Gonja cannot be termed a cicisbean union, for a genitor living with the mother of his children has undisputed claim to paternity. This reservation apart, the idea of *de facto* divorce would seem to fit the Gonja situation very well. Both the manner of parting and the lack of a clearly defined end to most marriages reflect a pragmatic rather than a legalistic process.

A similarly pragmatic approach is taken by the kin of those concerned. The authority of a compound head is limited, and kinship authority is split between paternal and maternal kin, with formal final authority over each party likely to be vested in distant relatives. In this situation there may be no consensus as to the best course of action, and even where there is agreement, little chance of enforcing it. If the woman's family are persuaded either that reconciliation is impossible or that it is undesirable, they will be only too pleased that she has found a new partner. The kin of the new husband take much the same view, for another woman in the household means more help and more

---

[3] I have heard complaints in cases to do with theft and witchcraft that a given chief was biased, and that the case should be heard in another division. Even if the chief is in fact prepared to listen to both sides, the stranger always seems to assume that he will be at a disadvantage.

[4] The resort to a Mexican divorce by couples whose national laws do not permit the legal dissolution of marriage is another example of divorce effected by moving out of the jurisdiction of a given legal system into that of another, more amenable.

children. If the first marriage was an arranged match, the wife's kin will make strenuous efforts to see that it does not fail. Paradoxically this effort may not be made if the couple are closely related, as it is considered safer for them to part than to live together on hostile terms. But if repeated efforts at reconciliation fail, there will come a point at which the wife leaves and her kin accept this as inevitable, unless the bride is very young and therefore particularly dependent on the support of her family.

It would seem that from the point of view of the deserted husband there is often a situation in which no legitimate transfer of conjugal rights has occurred, yet the wife and her new spouse behave as though their marriage were fully legitimate, and so do their kin and neighbours. And since full conjugal services are exchanged between the new couple and their children recognized as legitimate, it is difficult to see on what criteria their marriage is not complete. The most satisfactory way of regarding this situation is to consider that, in Gonja, marriage is not a matter of public concern, as it does not enter the political domain where it influences relations between groups.

As a private matter of concern to individuals and their immediate kin, it need only be privately dissolved. For the Gonja, the distinction between jural and conjugal separation is not a helpful one, because the category 'jural divorce' is empty. And this in turn is so because, although there is often personal disagreement and private anguish over a broken marriage, the institutional basis for enforcing conjugal rights, or for controlling their transfer, is absent.

THE ENDING OF MARRIAGE BY DEATH

If there is a sense in which marriages endure even though the partners no longer live together, and indeed have both remarried, what is the situation when their separation is due to death? The institutionalized response to death is best seen in an examination of funeral observances.[5]

When an adult dies, the rites associated with the burial and the following stages of the funeral have three main foci: first, there is the laying aside of the body and the personality, and in this context, the stating of the dead person's various attributes, accomplishments and

---

[5] See J. R. Goody (1962) for a theoretical discussion of the implications of funeral ritual and a detailed study of the mortuary observances of a northern Ghanaian society who, though neighbours of the Gonja, differ radically from them in many ways.

143

roles. Secondly, there is the regulation of the leave-taking between the deceased and the survivors. And finally, relations between the dead person and his or her kin are placed on a new basis, and roles are either terminated or re-allocated. These themes appear at all stages of the mortuary rituals, though at the beginning the emphasis is on the personality of the deceased, while at the end there is more concern with social relationships with kin and, where an office holder has died, with the wider community.

As in so many West African societies, a funeral in Gonja provides a stage on which virtually the whole social system performs in miniature. Even a cursory treatment would require a chapter in itself; a comprehensive analysis, a whole book. In addition, there is an extra aspect of complexity to Gonja funerals because, as with marriage ritual, there is variation in the forms associated with each estate, and some regional differences as well. This chapter will be concerned only with the funerals of central Gonja, and with these only as they affect the widow and widower; that is, with the regulation of leave-taking between the deceased and his spouse, and the subsequent re-definition of roles. A later chapter will touch briefly on some of the ways in which relations among kin are re-oriented during the course of funeral observances.

Although it is not possible to consider the whole sequence of mortuary observances, the following outline may help to relate those which are discussed to one another:[6]

1. The day of death:
   Sounding the death – by drums and wailing
   Seclusion of surviving spouse, eldest son and eldest daughter
   Bathing of the corpse
   Divining the cause of death
   Burial
   Prayers for the dead (*adua*)
   Throughout the day mourners arrive to 'greet the funeral', bringing contributions of kola, drink and money towards the wake-keeping of the next days. Thus begins a week of intensive mourning during which more

[6] The formal nature of this outline should not mislead the reader into thinking that the rituals noted always occur in this order, or that all are always included. No two mortuary sequences are exactly alike, but this general outline probably fits most, at least loosely. It has not been possible to indicate variations in the forms followed by each estate. The situation is extremely complex because different sets of relatives may take responsibility for each of the funerals listed. Thus, if one parent of the dead man was commoner and the other Gbanya, one funeral may be directed according to commoner custom and another follow that of the ruling estate. The possible variations are almost infinite.

parties of mourners arrive from other villages to 'greet the funeral'. The arrival of each new group is heralded by wailing as they come within sight of the village, and this is taken up by those in the funeral house (*kali bu*). No kinsman or friend of the deceased ought to go to the farm or to eat a full cooked meal of soup and porridge until after the three-day funeral.

2. The three-day funeral (*ntchensa*) (four-day funeral for a woman) also called *bu kapulia* (the opening of the pot):

> Following the death of important or very elderly men and women, *awoba* dirges are sung throughout the night before the three-day funeral
> Killing of sheep (or cow) and distribution of meat
> First funeral *kude* prepared and distributed
> Prayers for the dead

A widower is bathed and shaved at dawn after the four-day funeral of his wife, then dressed in new clothes. The eldest son and daughter may be bathed at this time or after the seven-day funeral.

3. The seven-day funeral (*ntchensunu*):

> *Awoba* dirges sung as for three-day funeral
> Killing of sheep (or cow) and distribution of meat
> Preparation and distribution of second funeral *kude*
> Prayers for the dead
> Visit to the 'farm' and testing of the widows
> Reckoning of debts
> Sweeping the room and throwing away of the *akalibi* shrine

The widow 'leaves the room' at dawn of the day following the seven-day funeral, when she is bathed, shaved and dressed in white.

4. The forty-day funeral (*ntchendena*):

> Performed publicly only for very senior men and women. Prefaced by *awoba* dirges, it consists mainly of the killing of a cow, distribution of the meat, and the preparation and distribution of a funeral *kude*. During the sacrifice and preparation of the food, dirges and praises are sung, and certain dances may be performed
> Prayers are said in the evening.

5. The commemoration of the first anniversary of death (*kafe*):

> The observances on this occasion are the same as for the forty-day funeral and, like it, the commemoration of the first year is not often celebrated. It may be this occasion which is chosen for the final allocation of the property of the deceased among his heirs.

The public prayers (*adua*) are offered by Muslim priests, usually all those in the community gathering for the occasion. After the prayers, funeral orations may be made for a person of importance. Although one of the tenets of Islam is that only the faithful should be buried by Mallams, in Gonja these rites are celebrated for members of the ruling estate and also for commoner holders of certain offices. In practice prayers may be said for any adult whose kin wish it. The Sakpare Muslims who are responsible for these performances are the descendants of the Mallam who assisted Jakpa with the conquest of Gonja. Other Muslims sometimes suggest that the Sakpari are not really Muslim any more since they are willing to pray for non-believers. However, the symbiotic relationship between them and the ruling estate is too complete to leave them any alternative. And in most communities such confrontations do not occur because there are no non-Gonja Muslims to complain.

Possession often occurs at some point during the early stages of the funeral rites. The person most frequently chosen by the spirit of the deceased is a matrilateral cross-cousin (sometimes a grandchild); the most likely times are while the body is being bathed, and when the personal shrine (*akalibi*) is being carried out to be thrown away at a crossing of two paths. This event is so much an expected one that, if it does not occur, comments as to the poor character of the joking relatives present are sometimes made. It is generally interpreted as an expression of the reluctance of the deceased finally to leave those he has known and loved. Sometimes he is thought to 'speak' about the distribution of his inherited property (*kapute*) through the possessed person. Possession is an aspect of the first theme of Gonja funerals, the separation of the body and the personality from the land of the living, and the formal statement of their role relationships in life.

The obligations of affinal relatives at a funeral vary in different parts of Gonja. They tend to be expressed in terms of the obligations of a son-in-law when either of his wife's parents dies. During the initial period of mourning, that is, until the end of the seven-day funeral, affines living in the same village come to 'greet' the funeral house, as do kin and friends. At this time they will bring a small contribution to the expenses of mourning and entertainment. But each son-in-law may also be required to bring a party of mourners from his own village to join in the funeral dirges and dancing, and to show by their presence that the dead person was held in great respect by his daughter's husband. If the locally enforced obligation is the provision of a sheep for sacrifice during the funeral, this prestation replaces the bringing of a large funeral party, though to do so would show yet greater respect. The son-in-law's sheep need not be presented during the first week of mourning; particularly if he lives at a distance this is not expected; it can always be kept for the later funerals.

THE REGULATION OF LEAVE-TAKING BETWEEN THE SPOUSES: THE WIDOW

The most consistently recurrent theme in the rituals concerning widows is that of ordeal. Immediately after the death of a man is announced, his wife (or wives) are led away to another room where they remain until after the burial. A wife is thought to be too stricken with grief to be able to assist in the bathing of her husband's body, which might also prove dangerous to her. After the burial she is brought back to the room in which her husband was bathed. There she must remain secluded until the completion of the seven-day funeral, "seeing neither the light of the sun nor the light of the stars." *E lur ebu* ("she enters the room"), it is said.

During the period of seclusion the widow wears an old cloth, preferably one dyed dark blue with the traditional indigo dye. She is allowed to have neither stool nor pillow, but sits on her husband's sleeping mat, legs outstretched and crossed at the ankles. Her ears are stopped with raw cotton "to keep her from hearing the calls of her dead husband, who will try and persuade her to follow him". The only light she is allowed comes from the clay bowl in which shea butter burns with a wick of twisted rag. As the door is kept covered by a mat, the room is dim both day and night. However, a companion is always with her, an older woman who has herself lost her husband. Other women come and greet her briefly, or sit silent beside her on the floor. It is during this lonely, silent and grieving time that a widow is most at risk from her husband's spirit. If they have been very close, he will try to entice her to follow him in death, and if not, he may express his anger by harming her directly.

Although it is said that the widow should not leave the room in which she is secluded, there are a number of ritual performances which require her presence. If her husband was an elderly or important man, *awoba* dirges and dancing will go on all through the night before the three-day funeral. For most of this time she remains shut in the room, but just before dawn she is brought out to sit, silent and with lowered eyes, on the edge of the circle of chanting men and women. The singing of *awoba* is a dangerous time for all, because songs celebrate individuals as well as stating proverbial truths about life and sorrow. It is believed that when those who have previously died hear their names, and those of their kin

147

and friends, they will hurry towards the sound until the darkness round the flickering shea butter lamps is full of spirits. The spirit of the dead man is certain to be present, and again his wife is in danger. As the darkness turns to grey dawn, the singers slip away one by one and the widow too is allowed to return to her room. The night before the seven-day funeral will again be spent in the singing of dirges, and again the widow joins the circle shortly before dawn.

The next ritual of significance for the wife's relationship with the deceased occurs in her absence. Some time towards the end of the week of funeral observances, often immediately before the visit to the 'farm' and the throwing away of the personal shrine, there is the reckoning of the debts of the dead. At this time all the possessions of the dead man are placed on mats outside his room, and kin and friends are asked to claim any that may belong to them. At the same time they are asked to return anything they may have borrowed, and to mention any loans of which they may have knowledge. Any money the dead man owed is claimed and should be paid immediately by the person in charge of the funeral (the *kaliwura*). Any sum owed to the deceased should also be made good. Although the widow is not present, one of her close kinsmen will point out any objects among the dead man's things which belong to the widow, and will return anything of his she may have been using. He will also claim any money that the wife has lent her husband, and this must be paid with the other debts. If the husband has lent his wife money, this should also be stated. Usually the kin will cancel the debt, though they could insist on repayment if they wished. But once the reckoning of the debts is completed there ought to be no further economic obligations outstanding between the dead man and his living spouse.

After the dead man's things have been identified and his debts settled, his room is swept by a joking partner. This must be thoroughly done, beginning at the far corner and finishing at the door. All the dirt is carefully collected and put on top of the personal shrine, so that when the shrine is thrown away at a cross-roads outside the village, the dirt is also disposed of. The dead man's room is now considered to be cleansed of his personality spirit (*kiyaiyu*, 'shadow'). It may be used again without danger.

It is usually at the seven-day funeral that the next event of importance for the widow occurs; this is the 'visit to the farm'. For this occasion a mock farm of a few rows of yam mounds is hastily hoed on the out-skirts of the town. Into several of the mounds are put pieces of yam dug from the dead man's farm. To this 'farm' goes a procession of kin, led by a girl (usually a cross-cousin) carrying the dead man's personal shrine. Directly behind her comes the widow, dressed in her husband's farm clothes, each piece turned inside-out. A strange bedraggled sight she makes, blinking at the unaccustomed light, wan and weak from lack of food and sleep. When they arrive at the 'farm' the little group proceeds three times around it, and the widow is then made to sit on one of the mounds containing a piece of her husband's yam.[7] It is agreed by all that only a woman who had been faithful to her husband would be willing to complete this ritual. For if an unfaithful wife sits on the funeral yam mound, she will suffer some terrible misfortune: perhaps a lingering illness, perhaps death or sterility. Although this ritual of 'going to the farm' is a part of funerals for men of all three estates in central Gonja, it has a special meaning for the Gbanya. For by forcing unfaithful wives to declare themselves, the paternity of children by other men is also brought to light – children who do not have a real right to succeed to chiefship. In the Daboya division, the children of a divisional chief should be fed with funeral porridge for the same reason. For if a child who was not begotten by the dead chief eats this porridge, it will sicken and die. As the party returns from the 'farm' the personal shrine of the dead man is thrown aside into the tangled growth along the path. Wailing again, as on the day of the death, they continue into the village. The widow returns to her seclusion, though for the last time.

Early the next morning, before dawn, she is taken out behind the compound on the edge of the refuse heap which fringes the town. There she is bathed with infinite care, first on the left side of her body and then on the right, then for a second, and then for a final time. After this all her hair is shaved away. With this bath her intimacy with her dead husband is ended. No more of his body dirt (*eyurpe*) can cling to her, and with it goes her extreme vulnerability to injury by his spirit.

Indeed, all these rituals can be seen as separating the widow, in one way or another, from her dead husband and his kin. By the strict seclusion in which she is immediately placed, the widow is prevented from assisting in the funeral itself. Important roles are assigned to the senior man of the deceased's kin, who 'owns' the funeral and is responsible for seeing that all is as it should be; to the old women of the community who know how to bathe the body and who are in charge of the night-long vigil during which dirges are sung; to the Muslims who give prayers for the dead; to the kinsmen of the dead man who arrange

[7] For anyone who has seen a yam tuber, the symbolism of this act is immediately obvious: it is a large, long vegetable.

and perform the sacrifices; to the kinswomen who prepare and see to the distribution of the funeral porridge; and to the joking partners who come and go, singing teasing songs which keep people from becoming too sad, and who perform a number of ritual services during the course of the funeral.

But the widow's role is entirely passive. More than this, each of the rituals with which she is concerned has as its purpose the ending of some aspect of her relation with her husband. At the reckoning of debts any economic interdependence that may have existed between them is ended. The testing of the widow during the visit to the 'farm' establishes once and for all the paternity of her children; since there is no levirate, children she bears subsequently cannot be attributed to the dead man. The seclusion and the dirge-singing are seen as occasions on which her husband will try to re-establish contact with her, either in order to take her away with him or to punish her for any infidelity. During this period the widow is supported, by companions and by the ritual itself, to enable her to resist these attempts of the husband to continue their personal relationship. With the bathing on the morning after the seven-day funeral, the close personal relationship between them is broken, The removal of all body dirt, and the throwing away of the mourning cloth[8] symbolize this severing of all contact between them.

A rite associated with the bathing of a widow, which I saw only once, at Busunu, expresses even more clearly this theme of separation. On this occasion, after the washing and shaving had been completed, the old woman in charge brought out a collection of small objects which she handed to the widow in groups. First, there was a tiny wisp of cotton and a stick. With these the widow pretended to spin. After a few moments, the old woman took them and threw them onto the rubbish heap behind the house near which they were sitting. Next the widow took from her a piece of broken mirror, a vial of eye shadow, a broken comb and some shea butter. With these she pretended to make herself beautiful, as a woman does when preparing to keep an assignation. Then these also were thrown away on to the rubbish heap. Finally she was handed a few pieces of broken calabash, a cup of water, a heap of sand on a leaf and another stick. With these she went through the motions of preparing porridge, mixing the 'flour' and water in the 'pot' with the 'stirring stick'. When the 'food' was ready, she divided it among several tiny pieces of calabash as a wife divides the evening porridge between the pans of the different members of the household.

[8] The cloth is in fact given to the woman who bathes the widow.

Then the older woman took up the pieces of calabash in turn and called out "people of Tuluwe division, come and eat", "people of Kawsawgu division, come and eat", "people of Bole division, come and eat", each time throwing the 'food' on to the rubbish heap. This miming of a public distribution of food followed in abbreviated form that which occurs on the last day of Damba when the ceremonial porridge is offered to representatives of each of the divisions of the kingdom. There it represents the participation of the other divisions in the Damba ceremony; it is a statement of their joint stake in the kingdom. When I later asked the meaning of the mock distribution people could not separate its significance from that attributed to the other mimed acts. All were intended to make the widow free to do these things for another husband. For as a wife, she had spun, taken pains to make herself attractive to her husband, and above all, she had cooked porridge – both for the household and on ritual occasions. My own interpretation of the final 'public' distribution of porridge would be that the widow was being made free to marry anywhere in the kingdom. But as this is in any case true, the point was difficult to confirm in discussing the ritual.

The analysis of the relationship existing between a couple after divorce suggested that the various concerns which continued to link them had to do either with the welfare of their children or with the intimacy of their personal relationship, specifically with sexuality. The leave-taking between spouses that is one of the major tasks of a Gonja funeral is almost entirely concerned with their personal relationship. Other aspects of the funeral re-orient the links between a deceased parent and the children, but these are seen as not involving the surviving spouse directly. Rather, the surviving siblings of the deceased actively assume the parental roles which they already hold in name.

But if the conjugal relationship has so little impact on the kin groups to which each partner belongs, if so few rights are transferred at marriage, why should there be this emphasis on separating the spouses and putting an end to their relationship? In fact it is not prescriptive rights which are cancelled, but the close personal relationship between the spouses which is the subject of these rituals. This emphasis on the personal relationship is epitomized by the stress placed on sexual jealousy, a highly individualized emotion, rather than on either the retention or transfer of rights *in genetricem* which might be vested in a kin group.

Those services which we have seen as defining the marriage bond are particular services between specified individuals. They are not owed to categories of kin. And they cannot be transferred to a relative of a spouse who has died. This is equivalent to incest to the Gonja. They are ended with the death of either spouse. The funeral makes the survivor free to perform them for another, in an entirely new conjugal relationship. This could not be more clearly expressed than in the Busunu ritual I have described.

THE WIDOWER

The regulation of leave-taking between the deceased and a surviving spouse is more prominent in the funerals of men than of women, probably because, as in virtually all societies, marriage plays a more central role in a woman's life than in a man's. Thus, when her husband dies, a woman is more radically affected than when a man loses his wife. Husbands suffer fewer restrictions, mourn for a shorter period, and are thought to be exposed to fewer dangers from the spirit of the deceased than are their wives when widowed. A husband is not usually secluded or, if he is, only for the first period of intensive mourning, until the completion of the four-day funeral. He is bathed the following morning and may be given a white cloth to wear. However, he only wears it until the end of the seven-day funeral, and often not that long. There is no ceremony equivalent to the visit to the 'farm' and the testing of the widow, though his wife's personal shrine will also be thrown away on the final day of the funeral. One reason for the husband's smaller degree of involvement is that wives very often return to their kin when an illness becomes serious, and thus do not die in the husband's house. A part of the funeral must still be performed there – the display of her things, the reckoning of debts, the sweeping of the wife's room, and the throwing away of her *akalibi*. But the husband's compound is not necessarily the main focus of the funeral.

The husband's grief is often very evident, and he must still come to terms with this. However, that he is considered to be in less danger from his wife's spirit than she from his reflects the fact that she was expected to depend on him alone for economic support and sexual fulfilment during their marriage. Fear of his spirit is due to his pre-emptive rights over her in these areas, and hence to fear of retaliation if these rights have been violated by another. But the wife has no such claims on her husband. He has every right to divide his economic and sexual commitments between several wives. When the wife dies, then her spirit is not expected to show jealousy towards her husband, though it is believed that she may threaten a co wife, particularly if there was known to be trouble between them.

THE POSITION OF THE WIDOW AFTER THE FUNERAL

In contrast to accounts of other northern Ghanaian peoples, there is one aspect of a man's funeral which is notably absent in the Gonja rituals. This is the re-allocation of rights in his widows. Among the Konkomba of the eastern part of the region (Tait, 1961), a woman, once married, never leaves her husband's lineage. If he dies, another spouse is found for her within the inner lineage, or if she is very elderly, she is cared for either by one of her children or by her husband's kin. So complete was the transfer of rights in a Konkomba bride that there were no circumstances under which she could legitimately return to her own family, or marry outside the lineage of her first husband.[9] Fortes (1949a) and J. Goody (1962) describe a less extreme situation among the Tallensi and LoDagaa peoples. There a widow is asked if she will marry again in her husband's lineage, and the funeral ritual includes a formal agreement, or if this is declined, a formal release of the widow. If there were children of the marriage, then no bride-wealth need be returned. If the widow is still young and there are no children, one or two cows may be requested, though they will in fact be provided by the next husband. Elderly widows expect to remain in the household of their dead husband, cared for either by their own children, or by those of his brothers.

But a Gonja funeral includes no reference to the remarriage of the widow. Since a second marriage among the kin of her dead husband is prohibited, this is perhaps not surprising, for henceforth neither her sexuality nor her procreative powers are their concern. Instead, the rituals guide the severing of the ties which previously bound man and wife. The marriage relationship is an essentially personal one. With the husband's death it is at an end.

Muslims, divisional chiefs and some ordinary members of the ruling estate expect the widow to remain in her dead husband's house for a period of five months. Among commoners there is no set period of mourning. Nor is there a formal 'handing over of the widow' to her kin at the end of mourning. This too is consistent with the lack of emphasis in Gonja institutions on corporate kin groups. The widow is left to reorganize her life in her own good time. Often she remains for a few

[9] This very extensive transfer of rights begins with infant betrothal when a girl is born. It is against the pre-emption of choice represented by infant betrothal that the Konkomba young men have begun to agitate. However, if they are successful, there are bound to be repercussions on the degree of control over women in later life as well.

more months in her old home. If she is young, she will soon remarry, though sometimes a number of years elapse before a woman takes a second husband. Others do so almost immediately, though this does lead people to comment on the speed with which their grief was conquered. But it is more proper if a woman returns to her own kin for at least a brief period before marrying again. It is probably the gradual decision to try to establish a new life which leads a woman to make the break with her dead husband's home. If she is to receive suitors, this is better done in her parents' or brothers' house than in that of her in-laws. They in turn are not unhappy for her to go. Their own menfolk are not allowed to marry her, nor to have even a fleeting affair. Yet for a young or middle-aged woman without a husband to live for long in a household without establishing a sexual liaison with someone there is considered extremely difficult. It is better for all concerned that she return to her kin before an illicit union is formed.

When a widow is ready to leave her dead husband's house, she is bathed in a special 'medicine' (*jobuni*, 'drive the dead') which has the power to drive off the spirits of the dead. Then she need no longer fear the jealousy of the dead man, but until she has bathed in this medicine, any sexual relations are believed to arouse the spirit's violent anger and to lead to dreadful consequences. The postponement of her release from this threat is one way of guarding against an affair within the dead man's household. Only after this ritual bath may the widow safely receive suitors and enter freely into a courting relationship.

The distribution of children following the dispersal of their family of orientation has already been alluded to, and will be discussed in some detail in the following chapters. The support of orphans falls to those with whom they are living and no separate provision is made for it, apart from the designation, some time after the death, of a successor to the kinship status held by their dead parent. When a father has died, the successor takes over the general responsibility for the children's welfare, regardless of who rears them. They may seek his aid if they are in difficulties, and they must get his permission for important undertakings such as their own marriages. Should it happen that one of the children needed a large sum of money to pay a fine or to secure medicine, it is to this man they will turn.

No economic provision is made for a widow, as it is assumed that if she does not remarry her children or siblings will look after her. This attitude is completely consistent with the Gonja conception of segregation of economic roles during marriage. The one exception is that if a wife of many years has borne no children, she may be given the use of part of her husband's wealth. This is most likely to be a cow or two, which is clearly not sufficient to maintain her for the rest of her life, but it does represent a source of ready cash if she should need it.

A few women are widowed after the age when they are likely to remarry, but before they 'retire from marriage' to live with their kin. There will be fewer pressures on them to leave the house of their dead husband, since they pose no threat to the morals, and thus the welfare, of their affinal kin there. Some widows do remain in old age. But others respond to the same pressures which lead married women to prefer to rejoin their kin as old age approaches.

TERMINAL SEPARATION

Divorce in Gonja is easily brought about by either partner, although most frequently initiated by the wife. It appears to be a relatively common occurrence at all stages of a woman's life. While young women leave their husbands before, and after, children are born, mature women with older children also leave one spouse for another. However, as a wife approaches old age, it becomes increasingly likely that she will leave her husband to settle with kin. In the early and middle stages of a woman's life, marriages tend to be ended by separation which becomes finalized by a subsequent marriage. Up to middle age an active woman will find a new husband. But when an older woman separates from her husband it is highly unlikely that she will remarry and her status continues as that of a 'separated' woman. Since separation in old age is so uniformly final, I call it 'terminal separation' to distinguish it from earlier separations which are in fact a form of transition between one marriage and another. Men, it must be noted, continue to take wives as long as they can persuade women to marry and stay with them. They generally remain married to a more advanced age than women, although elderly men, except for chiefs, are often single.

That elderly women tend to live with kin rather than with a husband is an empirical fact. In Buipe, of nineteen women over 50, fifteen were living with kin as opposed to four who were living with husbands (Table 7-1). All of those with kin had been married. Eight of the fifteen had husbands living, while six were widows at the time of the census.[10] Significantly, the four women in this age group who were still married were all of the commoner estate, providing corroboration for the common belief that marriages to commoner women are more apt to be

[10] Relevant information is lacking for one of the women.

155

Table 7-1. *Residence of adult women in Buipe with kin* or with husband,*
by estate and age

		Living with:	−30	31–50	Age: 51+	All	
Woman's estate:	Ruling	husband	7	3	0	10	N=14
		kin	1	1	2	4	
	Commoner	husband	18	10	4	32	N=42
		kin	3	1	6	10	
	Muslim	husband	11	10	0	21	N=35
		kin	2	5	7	14	
			42	30	19		N=91

* There were no cases in which a widow was living with the kin of a dead husband. Thus 'kin' refers to a woman's own kin.

stable and of longer duration. At the time of the census, no woman over 50 in Buipe who belonged to either the Muslim or ruling estate was still living with a husband.

The withdrawal from married life represented by a woman's separation from her husband in old age does not, however, have the status of an explicit cultural norm. Unlike other customs which influence the patterns of residence and the developmental cycle – the prohibition against a widow remarrying one of her husband's kin, the custom of fostering children and the convention that a son eventually returns to his father – terminal separation was never discussed as though it were generally expected behaviour, or even formulated as something "we Gonja do".[11] Nevertheless, both observation and census figures show that it is indeed something Gonja do.

There are three problems to be considered in connection with the practice of terminal separation. The first has to do with the circumstances which seem immediately to precipitate this sort of separation and the manner in which it is initiated. Secondly, there is the question of what features of the social system facilitate conjugal separation. And finally, we must ask what the implications are for the residence

[11] This cultural 'blind spot' is so marked that it is unlikely to be accidental. It seems likely that for even minimal stability of marriage the actors must assume that, at least in *their* case, it will last.

patterns and the developmental cycle, and for the social system as a whole.

In the instances of terminal separation I encountered, both in Buipe and elsewhere in central Gonja, there seemed to be three sorts of immediate cause. Most dramatic were witchcraft accusations; in the three villages studied there were several older women who had been forced to leave their husbands for this reason. There were other instances of women living with kin on this account, but, being younger, they remarried; in one other case, the husband regularly visited his wife and children in her village during the dry season. Thus, the fact that a woman is accused of witchcraft in her husband's village and is forced to leave, need not terminate the marriage; if it does she may still remarry. But when older women return to their kin in this way, they are unlikely to remarry and the separation becomes terminal.

Another immediate cause is illness. The first response to ill-health is the pragmatic one of procuring the appropriate medicine. This it is a husband's duty to provide. Should it prove ineffective, diviners are consulted and it frequently turns out that more powerful medicine may be had from the woman's kin. In fact, the sequence is a regular one. The husband's aid is first sought and then, if this fails to bring relief, even long journeys are undertaken, regardless of the weakness attendant on serious illness, in order that the help of kin may be secured. Indeed, in some cases the cause of the illness is held to be bound up with residence in the husband's house. Although her intention may not have been to make a permanent break, failure to make a complete recovery is apt to be construed as cause for remaining with kin, rather than as an indication that their medicinal resources are not, in fact, superior to those at the husband's disposal. Conversely, younger women with young families who appear to be happily married tend to return to their husbands in spite of the lack of success of therapy by kin. Increasing illness and infirmity of a husband may also precipitate a separation at this time, if his ability to support a wife is affected. For although a woman's 'brothers' are obliged to supply her with food when she is in need, this is not binding upon them so long as she lives with a husband. While they may help to support a married sister, they may refuse on the grounds that their duty is not to feed her husband and his other dependants, but only toward their sister and her children. For as long as she is in her husband's house, the food she prepares goes to feed everyone there. If she wishes to claim her brothers' support as a right, she must come and live with them.

Polygyny may be cited as one of the factors precipitating terminal separations, but it is clearly so only under special circumstances. For many polygynous unions last for several years, and some women say that they prefer them as domestic tasks are less onerous when shared. But where a second wife joins a domestic unit which has for many years been based on monogamous marriage, it may have a directly disruptive influence.

In each of two cases where this sequence of events occurred, the first wife was mother of well above the average number of living children, in one case seven, and in the other, eight. This circumstance is probably not unrelated to the fact, as Dorjahn (1958: 838) suggests, that in each case she had lived for at least twenty years as the sole wife of the father of her children. Twenty years of a stable monogamous marriage and the rearing of a large family would seem to lower a woman's tolerance for sharing her position with a co-wife. Significantly, the son of one of these women described his mother's fate thus: "My father drove her out. For twenty years she lived with him and cooked for him, then he drove her away by taking another wife." He and his brothers were very bitter about their father's conduct; the details of their elaborate efforts to dislodge their mother's successor lead one to sympathize with the lot of the step-mother.

The second case is a particularly striking one to me because, of all the couples I knew in Gonja, I would have thought them the least likely to separate. Nyiwuleji's wife, Nana, was herself one of seven full siblings and had eight living children, the youngest twins of just under one year, and the eldest just become a father. Superficially this case differs from the previous one in that the break occurred during the courtship of the second wife, before her actual introduction into the household. Significantly, it followed a quarrel about rights over the disposal of yams grown on Nyiwuleji's farm.

All men know that their wives try to put aside a portion of the farm produce allocated for domestic consumption. This they sell in the village for pin-money and, provided the family has sufficient to eat, nothing is said. It was impossible to discover from the allegations and counter-allegations of this quarrel, whether Nyiwuleji chose to take issue with behaviour he would ordinarily have tolerated, or whether Nana really did go too far. Probably there were elements of both. For a wife of a long-standing monogamous union comes to assume a community of property and interests with her husband which is not in fact justified. No such identity of interests could long survive the constant challenge of a co-wife's competing claims. In the same way, I suspect, she comes to assume an exclusive right to his affections which grows out of their close relationship but which is not supported by the jural

with Shetro. 1st wife = head wife + has her
own responsibility for allocation of resources.
Her status is enhanced by a junior wife + her
sphere of control enlarged.

norms of the society. For these norms positively sanction plural marriage for men, and their extra-marital affairs are accepted as long as they do not involve adultery with the wife of another.

Thus when a man in Nyiwuleji's position anticipates converting a monogamous domestic family into one based on plural marriage, he may feel that he must see his first wife does not exceed the limits of a wife's prerogatives. For if a second wife took similar liberties, he would be bullied if not impoverished. And to deny one wife what is allowed another is out of the question. Similarly, Nana seems to have said, in effect, "If I stay, it must be on the same terms as before, otherwise I go." And if these 'same terms' include sole claim to a husband's resources and affections, they are manifestly impossible. But as this is not an accepted basis for complaint in a polygynous society, the actual break occurs on some other pretext.

Ordinarily a husband's affairs do not lead to the departure of a first wife. Nor does the introduction of a second wife, otherwise there would be no polygyny, but rather serial monogamy. But where the first wife is an older woman, and particularly where she has been an only wife for a long time, the tensions arising from the transition to plural marriage tend to precipitate a separation.

It appears that witchcraft accusations, the increasing illness and infirmity of old age, and the taking of additional wives are the most apparent immediate causes of the termination of marriages when the wife reaches old age. This return of a woman to live with her kinsfolk as old age approaches, and her consequent withdrawal from married life, is well-nigh universal among women of the Muslim and ruling estates and frequent with commoner women, as indicated in Table 7-1. In citing the precipitating causes, I have interpreted this pattern from the actor's point of view. One woman could not remain with her husband because there she was considered to be a witch. Another found that in order to obtain proper treatment for illness, she had to seek the medicines of her kin. And still another resented her husband's taking a second wife. Yet witches, illness and polygyny occur in many societies where a woman expects to live out her life in her husband's house. In order to deal meaningfully with the question of why terminal separation is a significant feature of Gonja social organization, we must consider how other aspects of the social system function in such a way that as a woman approaches old age, these crises are resolved by the termination of marriage.

Here the absence of the levirate or any form of widow inheritance is undoubtedly a key factor. This operates in two ways. On the one hand, a woman knows that, should her husband die first, she will in any case return to her kin in old age. Although her husband's kin have an obligation to support her if she wishes to remain with them as a dependant, this solution is not a preferred alternative. As one elderly Muslim woman put it, "If I had stayed there, they would have expected me to fetch water, carry firewood and cook for them. But here in my brother's house I can sit in the shade of my room and spin thread for my shroud in peace." If she has any kin who are able to provide for her, a widow will claim support from them. And such a claim may not be denied without risking the ire of the ancestors. In this situation, for a woman to withdraw from a marriage which she no longer finds rewarding is but to anticipate the inevitable.

But this course would be impracticable if the role of the divorced sister were not a recognized one in Gonja society. That it does receive recognition is made inevitable by the return of widows to their kin, and also by the fact that since women past child-bearing age are not wooed, they become the responsibility of their kin.

Here it must be noted that men do not as a rule encourage an ageing wife to leave. Even when she can no longer bear children and has ceased to be interested in sexual relations, a wife is valued both as a companion and for the domestic services she renders. Furthermore, it is hard on a man's self-esteem to lose a wife, whatever her age, and the older he gets the less complacent he is about it, for he knows it will be hard to find another. Today it is the old men who complain most bitterly about the difficulty of persuading modern girls to accept arranged marriages, "For how else are we to find wives?" they say. "If we court a girl, it doesn't matter how many gifts we give her, she will take them and then marry a young man." The regularity with which men express regret when their older wives desert them, leaves no doubt as to their feelings. Let me cite but a few of the many confirmatory instances. Earlier I described how the KagbapeWura still hoped that his estranged wife, Dongi, would consent to return to him. Yet this woman was at least 45 years old and if she did return, she could not be expected to remain for more than a few years. Then there is the instance of the concession made by an elderly chief to his twelve wives when he begged them to remain with him until his death, saying that he didn't care if they took lovers so long as they stayed in his house to cook for him.[12] Or, again, neither the BusunuWura's 'sister', Supini Wuritche,

---

[12] These women varied between 70 and 30 years of age. If cooking had really been his major concern, one or two of the younger wives would have sufficed to fill his needs and he could have released the other ones. But the number of his wives was a matter of great pride to him and he could not bear to reduce this by even one.

nor her two ex-husbands were married at the time I knew them. Although she was at least 55 and a grandmother, both men complained that since she had left them, they had been wifeless (*kagbau*), and each strongly resented the other as a possible obstacle to securing her return.

But whether or not men are glad to see the last of elderly wives, the fact that in Gonja these women may and do return to their kin in old age, is in direct contrast to the pattern reported for the LoWiili (J. Goody 1956) and the Tallensi (Fortes 1949*a*), their patrilineal neighbours to the north. The matrilineal Ashanti to the south, however, follow much the same practice as the Gonja (Fortes 1949*b*). There too terminal separation is associated with a relatively high divorce rate, but it is one facet of a traditional system in which many marriages were duolocal, the husband and the wife each residing in their lineage compound, with the wife visiting her husband at night and sending him food when it was her turn to cook. Further, while the ideal is for sons to grow to manhood in the father's house, on his death they tend to join their mother's brothers and assume their roles as adult lineage males. As soon as her sons are able, they are expected to build their mother a house of her own which then becomes the nucleus of the minimal matrilineage. It is, Fortes contends, a desire to consolidate her position as founder of a segment of her matrilineage that leads the ageing Ashanti wife to separate from her husband and live with her brothers or sons.

No such explanation is possible for terminal separation among the Gonja, for no lineages of either sort are present. What other factors make this shift of residence desirable from the woman's point of view? We must look at two things: firstly the attributes of the roles of sister and wife as these are affected by increasing age; and secondly the residence of a woman's children and grandchildren.

It is significant that none of the five women I knew who held chiefly titles, the *ewuritches*, lived with husbands, although all still had ex-husbands in the same village. Dambayiri Wuritche was a partial exception to this. She had not yet passed the age of child-bearing and considered herself married. However, although she was nominally a wife, she cooked for and slept with her husband irregularly, and lived not in his compound but in that of her brother. This is the only instance of mature non-resident marriage which I found in central Gonja, and in fact more closely resembles the Hausa 'marriage of taking up the staff', as described by M. G. Smith (1955: 53). These cases suggest that women who hold formal positions of prestige prefer to maximize this role by withdrawing, at least in part, from that of wife. This situation finds an echo in the Gonja saying that "two chiefs cannot stay in the

161

same house" (*Bawura banyo, ba minan tchina langkonleto*). For a husband is the 'chief' in his own house, so far as his wife is concerned. When a wife becomes a chief indeed, she is no longer content to remain under the jurisdiction of a husband.

The cases of the *ewuritches* emphasize the point that authority and prestige are important in determining the choice of residence for older women. This factor affects the women of each estate somewhat differently. While both men and women intermarry freely between estates (Table 4-3), women of the ruling estate more frequently marry either commoners or Muslims than they do men of their own group. And indeed Gbanya men say that women from their own estate make difficult wives and it appears that either the men marry accordingly, or the women themselves prefer to marry out. In this case, when a woman of the ruling estate returns to her kin in old age, she is not only maximizing her status by activating her role as sister, but she is associating herself with brothers who are likely to hold major chiefships and thus sharing in their glory. The present paramount chief has moved, as custom demands, from his own division of Daboya to the capital. His establishment there includes not only his wives and children but also several 'sisters' who have chosen to leave their husbands and their natal division in order to participate in the life at court. There are tangible rewards for so doing. At the enrobing of the new chief of Kawsawgu division, I met two of the YagbumWura's 'sisters' who had been sent to represent him at the ceremony and who were treated throughout with the greatest respect. At the capital each has her own compound and attends daily her 'brother's' audience.

Another trend observed in Table 4-3 was the somewhat higher degree of intra-estate marriage which characterized Muslim women. This tendency almost certainly has to do with their religion. For while Muslim men who marry pagans insist that their wives learn to pray and prepare food in the prescribed ways, Muslim women have no such control. It is recognized that those who marry non-Muslims have great difficulty in keeping to the ways of the Book. In many villages there is no mosque and no Mallam to lead prayers. And while it is possible for a woman to pray privately and to avoid pork and all meat which is not ritually killed, her life can be a real hardship in a household where these prohibitions are not otherwise observed. These same considerations would seem to apply to the very high rate of return of Muslim women to their kin in old age. To the factors which affect all women alike, is added the wish to die in the faith and among believers.

Terminal separation for women of the ruling estate, who tend to marry out, serves to maximize status by associating them with kin in positions of power. For Muslim women the same consideration may be present, but in addition there is the return to the religion of their fathers. That neither of these forces operates where commoner women are concerned is reflected in the fact that, although they also return to kin in old age, they do so less consistently than women of other estates. Commoner women who exchange the role of wife for that of sister better their status in the domestic domain but not in the community as a whole.

The status accorded an elderly woman approaches that of a male elder. She possesses the wisdom and ritual knowledge associated with age, and is accorded commensurate respect. The Gonja are very conscious of seniority as the basis of respect and deference. Siblings and cousins are designated by two terms, *nda* and *nsupo*, meaning respectively older and younger relative of the same generation, regardless of sex. An older sibling may reprove or physically chastise a younger, but never the reverse. This principle operates jointly with the deference of the junior generation to that directly above it. By the time a woman reaches late middle age there are apt to be few members left of her parents' generation. Her surviving kin tend to be mostly younger siblings, her own children and those of her siblings and cousins. When living among kin, she is thus in a genealogically superior position. In her husband's house, however, she is not only subordinate to him, as is every wife, but she is surrounded by his kin; with these, unless she has married a kinsman, considerations of birth order are secondary to the constraints of affinity. The role of wife is defined as subordinate, while that of sister is not.

An obvious limiting factor in an older woman's choice of residence is the location of her children. In a society where the domestic family is based on the localized patrilineage, a wife who remains with her husband in old age is assured of continual contact with her sons and their children, although her daughters will disperse on marriage. Should she return to her own patrikin, an older woman would be separated from sons, daughters and grandchildren, except where patrilateral cross-cousin marriage is commonly practised. In the case of the matrilineal Ashanti, the tendency of adult sons to reside with their maternal kin means that the wife who separates from her husband to live with her lineage kin is likely to be living with her sons (as well as with any daughters who are living with maternal kin while married duolocally). And although sons' sons will eventually leave to join their matrikin, this loss will be compensated for by the arrival of daughters' sons.

Table 7-2. *Residence of elderly unmarried women in Buipe by source of support*

		Supported by:				
		Son living neolocally	Son with his maternal kin	Natal kin only	Husband of ex-foster child	
Resident with:	Maternal kin	—	3	2	—	5
	Paternal kin	—	3	5	—	8
	Chief	1	—	—	1	2

N=15

The Gonja situation falls between these two ideal types, as might be expected in the absence of lineages of either sort. The headship of a compound traditionally passes in the agnatic line, usually from father to son or to dead brother's son, should he be the elder. Yet it is unusual to find a woman living as the dependent of a son who is resident in her dead husband's house. As Table 7-2 shows, of the fifteen elderly women in Buipe living with kin,[13] none was supported by a son living in his dead father's house, and one only by a son living neolocally, that is, who was not resident with either his paternal or his maternal kin. Of the remaining fourteen, one half were supported only by their natal kin, brothers or mother's brothers, and slightly less than half by a son living with his maternal kin. Of the women living with sons, half were living with their maternal kin and half with paternal kin. The women without sons tended to live with paternal kin rather than with their mother's people.

Now it might seem that the gains from such an arrangement were not sufficient to balance the losses accruing from leaving a husband's house if sons are likely to remain behind. But the picture is more complex for several reasons. Firstly, if a woman has married more than once and has borne children in each marriage, then the home of her natal kin provides a neutral ground where the children of each union may visit her and where she may equally well rear any foster children

[13] This figure includes two women who are dependants of chiefs. Neither has natal kin in the village or elsewhere that I was able to discover. Both are almost certainly of slave descent, although no mention was ever made of this. Such people are referred to as belonging to the kin of those who originally owned them – "they are our family (*kanang*)" is the expression. They are here treated as dependants only because no direct kinship connection can be traced. In another generation or two, they will have become indistinguishable from distant kin.

entrusted to her. For, as noted earlier, the termination of a marriage by death or divorce almost always results in the dispersal of the children. Although young sons may accompany the mother when she remarries, they are unlikely to remain there under the control of a step-father. Reluctance to do so is expressed in the formal refusal to farm for a step-father. This practice does not have the status of a prohibition, but the refusal of a step-child to farm is accepted as justified. Hence the adolescent and adult sons of previous marriages are most unlikely to be living with the mother and her present husband when in late middle age she begins to consider a terminal separation.

Secondly, one or two sons may have been sent to their maternal kin as foster children. In this case they may have married there and settled down to farm with a mother's brother. Although it is nearly always the case, as the Gonja insist, that a man who has grown up with his maternal kin will eventually return to the house of his father, this move is frequently delayed until after the death of the foster parent. Where this pattern is followed, a woman who leaves her husband to join her brothers goes to the village or compound where her son and his young family are living.

Youths of the Muslim and ruling estates frequently spend the years of early adulthood 'roaming about'. This wandering may take the form of selling trade goods in the more remote villages, of going south to seek work, or of becoming a day labourer with one of the departments or firms in northern Ghana which hire casual labour. Or it may involve extended visits to kin in other villages or divisions. Protracted dry season hunting takes small groups of men off to temporary bush camps. Mobility at this age is a response to three sorts of pressures. On the one hand, there is the reluctance of adult sons, particularly eldest sons, to live under the daily constraints of paternal authority. And secondly, the pattern of succession to office, which goes by seniority of birth order among those eligible, means that a young man who has older brothers must look forward to a waiting period of several years or even decades before he can expect to enter even the lower ranks of chiefship. For he will not be given a title until his older brothers, paternal half-brothers, and patrilateral parallel cousins have themselves succeeded to one. In central Gonja it is possible for a man to succeed to a junior title while his father is still alive, but in practice this usually happens only to the sons of very old men, who are themselves approaching middle age.

Finally, there is the fear that witchcraft may be used against them by fellow villagers. The Gonja are confident that no one is subject to witchcraft when he is among strangers, although travel has its own dangers. But witchcraft, in the sense of premeditated injury through mystical agencies, is only a threat where people know one. Members of the ruling estate are in particular danger, not only from their own rivals for office, but especially from attempts to injure their senior titled kinsmen by an indirect attack. For one of the axioms of witchcraft in Gonja is that when a witch finds the victim's defences impenetrable, she will injure the original victim by harming someone close to him who is less able to protect himself. Fear of witchcraft in their father's village was several times given by young men of the ruling estate as the reason why they had temporarily left home.

For these reasons, the mothers of young men of the Muslim and ruling estates cannot count on their sons' continuous residence with their father. That these sons will almost certainly return after his death has little bearing on their mother's decision to leave him, because she would already have left after the funeral unless a son was present and in a position to support her. In my records of the three divisional capitals there is no instance of a widow living with kin of a deceased husband other than her own son. Of the three instances in which a widow lived as a dependant of an adult son in his father's house, two of the sons occupied senior chiefships and were in a better position to support her than her own kin. Also, these two women were old and no longer had even classificatory siblings still alive. Their choice then fell between living with their own children or with siblings' children and, understandably, both preferred the former. The third instance was a case of kinship marriage where the widow was living at the same time with kin and with affines.

If sons tend to be an undependable source of support for their mother, adult daughters are no more predictable in their movements. To begin with, they are living in virilocal marriage, perhaps in their natal village but more likely elsewhere (Table 4-5). Furthermore, the possibility of divorce both before and after the birth of children means that, whatever their residence at a given time, it is apt to change. In these three villages there was only one case where an elderly woman was living as a dependant of her married daughter and her husband. This woman was considered insane, and her daughter was the only person who could handle her. Married daughters eagerly look forward to visiting their mothers, and do so daily if they are in the same village, several times a year if in nearby villages, and every two or three years, often for several weeks at a time, if they live at a distance. The period immediately following the birth of a first child is always an occasion for such a visit, which is expected to last until the baby can walk, and this may be repeated at the birth of subsequent children. And it is to her mother that a young woman goes for preference when she separates from her husband for, I was told, "Your father will be trying to make you go back to your husband, but your mother will let you sit quietly until you marry again."

If a woman has married in her natal village, there is virtually no change in her relations with her children when she leaves the house of her husband for that of her brothers. So long as they remain in the same village, all her children will come to greet her and to gossip, and will continue to defer to her wishes.

To summarize, a woman does not greatly prejudice her close relationship to her own children and grandchildren by leaving her husband in old age to reside with kin. Her daughters will be living in virilocal marriage and will continue to visit her wherever she is. In fact, they will do so more freely and for longer periods if she is living with her kin than would be the case if she were with a step-father. In early adulthood men of the Muslim and ruling estate are apt to be away from their father's village for long stretches of time. And in all three estates, one or more may be living with maternal kin. If their mother has remarried, they are likely to feel constrained in the house of a step-father, whereas they are welcomed by their mother's kin.

In discussing the residence of a woman's children, we must also consider the children of siblings in order to do justice to Gonja custom. For in a very real sense, these are felt to be one's own. This attitude was stated and reaffirmed again and again; it is reinforced by the institution of fostering and by the lines of inheritance of property which tends to pass between 'siblings' in order of birth. Hence the body of kin for whom wealth is held in trust is composed of siblings and their children. The obligations which are associated with such a range of kin include economic support, succour in illness or trouble, and contributions to the costs of litigation or funerals. A woman who leaves a husband to reside with a sibling is reasserting her position in this kin group, especially the rights of herself and her children with respect to its property and its personnel. Rights in the personnel include the right to a brother's daughter or granddaughter as a foster child, upon whose help a woman is particularly dependent as her own strength fails.

There is one final aspect of the social organization which is relevant to women's residence in old age. This has to do with the personal shrine (*akalibi*). A woman's shrine is established on her first marriage and thereafter follows her, wherever she may live. She always bears the major burden of finding money for sacrificial animals and although a husband usually performs the sacrifices for a young wife, her brother may do so equally well. And so may the woman herself, especially in maturity and old age. Not only is she independent of a husband for spiritual ease, but the latter has no role to play in her rapport with her ancestors. These she may approach (*nyina*) wherever she is living, but if she is with siblings she may do so more frequently and at less personal expense by contributing to joint offerings. Thus a woman's spiritual well-being is enhanced by her residence with kin.

In discussing the roles available to old women, the residence of their children and grandchildren, and the relative independence of women in their relations with the supernatural, we have again worked largely within the actor's frame of reference. For such factors enter into a woman's assessment of what is the best course of action. However, they are relevant on another level of analysis, for at the same time they are the 'givens', the constant features, of the social system within which these women live. That is, this system is one in which marriage to the kinsman of a deceased husband is not permitted, and in which there is a positive obligation on men to support their full and classificatory sisters when the latter choose to live with them: it is one in which full siblings, half-siblings and cousins share the same set of obligations and are apt to be scattered through several villages, and even two or three political divisions.

Finally, there is the problem of the sort of effects which the institution of terminal separation may be expected to have on the social structure. In other words, what happens when women regularly return to live with kin in old age rather than remain in their husbands' compounds? The results are far reaching and must not be considered solely in terms of the chronic disruption of marriage. For, as both Forde (1941) and Gluckman (1950) have pointed out, the fixed framework within which kinship and domestic relationships operate need not necessarily be based on the conjugal family. Turner (1957: 69) makes a similar point in discussing Ndembu divorce, when he says that the return of women to their kin on divorce or widowhood may in fact constitute a functional prerequisite for a given type of social system. What does constitute the fixed framework of kinship and domestic relations in Gonja? And if the return of women to their kin has become an integral part of the society, to what other institutions is it closely linked?

The functions of terminal separation are in some ways similar to those of a high incidence of divorce or widowhood at other periods of a woman's life. However, the particular significance of terminal separation lies in its inevitability: many women remain with a single husband all their married lives, but, however happy their marriage, if they live to old age they will spend their last years with kin. There is a final and permanent identification of a woman with her own kin rather than with her husband's family. By the very act of terminal separation the children are forcibly reminded that the parents do not form a permanent unit. With the disbanding of the family of orientation, father and mother are each identified more closely with their own natal kin and villages. The children must now relate to these directly and no longer through the domestic family based on their parents' marriage.

Divorce, a widow's return to kin, and terminal separation, all serve to limit the generation span of the intact domestic family. A man and his wife (or wives) do not live in old age surrounded by their sons (or their daughters) and their families. There may indeed be children and grandchildren living with a man. But his wife (their mother) is almost certainly elsewhere, perhaps being supported by another son who is living with his maternal kin. And some of the sibling group of young adults in the compound (and indeed of the generation below them) are in other compounds, villages and divisions. There is no single, clearly defined group which stays together over time. The termination of marriage, by whatever cause, is not only consistent with this dispersal, but makes it inevitable in the Gonja system. For since the rights of both parents in their children persist after conjugal ties are severed, the children tend to be distributed among kin on both sides when a marriage breaks up. And as we have seen, in central Gonja this means that they are scattered in different villages and at considerable distances from one another.

This situation has certain clear similarities to Ndembu, Bemba, Lozi and other central African groups. But except in the Lozi case, these moves occur within a framework of small, relatively temporary villages, and it is the ideology of matriliny which provides the integrating framework. Among the Lozi the economic importance of the mounds in the flood-plain means that the villages associated with these are, like those in Gonja, relatively permanent. For both Lozi and Gonja villages are firmly anchored in a political and administrative context. It is my impression, however, that the Gonja divisions, serving as they do as the primary focus of citizenship, provide more of a fixed point of reference than the Lozi mounds. In any case, in Gonja the movements of kin are seen as occurring between communities with distinctive socio-political identities, and great efforts are made to retain links between them: thus a woman who leaves on marriage will return in old age; meanwhile she and her kin exchange visits, whatever the distance

169

which separates them. If a woman takes young children with her on divorce, the boys will almost certainly return to their paternal home. Even if girls marry from their mother's village, they must seek the consent of their father to the match, and they may later return to their village to live with a kinsman, either temporarily between marriages or permanently in old age. Where boys have remained with their agnatic kin, they will visit their mother in her own village.[14] These visits may be connected with future expectations of inheritance, which is determined by seniority of age within a group of classificatory siblings, and not by the closeness of a particular relationship. But contact by one member of a sibling group serves to reassert the rights of the group as a whole. In the same way, children who disperse at the end of their parents' marriage continue to keep in touch. It is between full and maternal half-siblings, wherever these may be living, that the closest ties in adulthood lie.

The fact that people who are united by these strong primary bonds of siblingship and parenthood are often living in widely separated villages, and that such ties tend to be maintained regardless of intervening distances, is one of the main features of Gonja social structure. It is to a closer consideration of these bonds between parents and children, and within the sibling group, that the following section is devoted.

In stressing the need to describe not only the frequency but also the pattern of divorce which characterizes a given society, I do not imply that the variables suggested are necessarily the only ones that should be considered.[15] The frequency with which women of various ages change marital partners must always be important because the bearing of children to successive unrelated husbands leads inevitably to dispersed groups of maternal siblings; also, ties of parenthood are less likely to be completely severed at divorce than are ties pertaining solely to the conjugal relationship. The importance of distinguishing divorce in old age from that which occurs earlier lies in the fact that where divorce, or terminal separation, is a regular feature of women's old age, this must have direct repercussions on the definition of roles available to adult women, the composition of residential groups, and the territorial distribution and definition of role obligations of members of kin groups.

[14] This again may be the village of either of her parents.
[15] Any sufficiently detailed ethnography will probably include information on relevant points. See especially Gluckman (1950), Djamour (1959), Stenning (1959) and R. T. Smith (1956). For a specifically numerical approach see Forde (1941), Turner (1957) and Fortes (1949*b*), who distinguishes explicitly the marital status of women at different ages. Mitchell and Barnes (1950) present data broken down by age, but do not consider the implications in any detail.

8

Parents and children

From the discussion of marriage in the preceding section there should have emerged a sense of the conjugal relationship; not only of the formal complex of rights which define it, but, equally important, of the quality of the conjugal bond. It is against this background that parent–child relationships must be viewed. For to discuss mother–child or father–child interaction without bearing in mind the relationship between the parents themselves would be artificial. This will be clearer once we turn to the subject of fostering, for when a child is sent to a kinsman of one parent his attachment to that parent is thereby emphasized with the inevitable result that ties with the other parent and his kin are lessened. Just as in the conjugal relationship itself there is always present an opposition between the two partners, which is crystallized around the balance between their separate kin, so in the relations between parents and children this same opposition is present.

The potential conflict is resolved on one level by the primary identification of children with the parent of the same sex. But cutting across this dichotomy is the unique warmth of the mother–child bond for children of both sexes, and the complex attachment between father and daughter. The latter is complex because it is at once warmer than that between father and son – affection is openly demonstrated by a man toward his daughter in a way which is impossible between males – and at the same time the father is the supreme authority figure for his daughter in a more absolute sense than for his son because the parent–child dominance is superimposed upon that of males over females.

This is to say no more than that there exist strong affective attachments between each parent and their children of both sexes. The bases for these attachments noted above are not peculiar to Gonja parent–child relationships, although the difference between male and female authority is undoubtedly more pronounced in traditional West African societies than in contemporary Euro-American ones.

Two sorts of injunction concerning the obligations of filial piety are made explicit. The first of these has to do with the tendering of obedience and respect. For a child should under no conditions answer back when reproved or corrected by a parent, nor ever lift his hand against them

171

in anger. It is difficult to convey fully the absolute nature of these commandments. To flout them is simply unthinkable, and the same sort of incredulity met queries as to what would happen if this occurred as I encountered when referring to parent–child incest. A positive correlate of 'Respect thy Father and thy Mother' is the obligation on a child to greet them night and morning so long as they are in the same village. The Gonja attach great significance to greeting as a general mode of conveying respect; of all one's kin, to greet one's parents is held to be the most important.

Respect to one's parents is also expressed by punctiliously observing the obligation to send a leg of any animal killed to a parent who is living in the same village. The regular sending of bowls of cooked food also has this dual function of expressing respect and providing sustenance.

Providing elderly parents with food is only one aspect of the second moral imperative of the parent–child relationship: care in old age. As one man put it, "When you were weak (young), your mother fed you and cleaned up your messes, and your father picked you up and comforted you when you fell. When they are weak, will you not care for them?"

When an aged father is living with an adult son, he continues to be treated as the head of the compound. Everything is done in his name, and he makes, or appears to make, all the decisions. As the farm is also 'for him', it is said that he feeds the people of the household, rather than that they feed him. In fact his sons may be doing all the farming, though an elderly man often continues to walk the considerable distance to his farm to oversee its cultivation. A man without sons of his own may occupy a very similar position in a compound where his brother's sons live. He is their 'father', and they farm for him and defer to him in the same way. A man who has neither sons nor brother's sons must continue to farm on his own as long as he is able. By attaching himself to classificatory siblings in neighbouring compounds, he can usually manage to get help with the heavy jobs of clearing the farm and making yam mounds. But the planting and weeding he must do himself, and this limits the area under cultivation. A man who cannot farm and who has no close kin, will be fed by neighbours out of charity. In practice only those crippled by blindness or disease accept this role. Other old men who live alone continue to farm even if only a small field on the exhausted land near the village. The few old men I met in this situation in the villages studied did not have *nyeribi* ('foster sons') with them. The lack of kin with whom to live and farm, apparently meant a lack of kin from whom foster children could be claimed.

172

The residence and support of elderly mothers is more complicated. As we have seen, if both parents survive to old age, the couple is likely to separate. If they remain in the same town, one son can go with his mother when she moves to her 'brother's' compound, while others remain with the father. This was the solution adopted by the mother of the KagbapeWura's four adult children. The one son who lived with her continued to farm with his brothers on their own and their father's farms. But the produce he grew went to feed his wife, his children and his mother, while that from the other brothers' farms went to their families, their father and his wife.

Often, however, a widowed or divorced mother returns to her own people in another village. When this occurs, one or more of her adult children may already be living with their maternal kin. Such a son, or a daughter's husband, will provide a woman with grain and yams from his farm. At the same time the daughter or daughter-in-law sends a bowl of porridge or mashed yam and soup for the evening meal. In other cases her 'brothers' will find food for her. The source of support for fifteen elderly women in Buipe is indicated in Table 7-2, p. 164.

SANCTIONS ON FILIAL PIETY

The distinction between the institutionalized and affective sanctions that reinforce parental authority will later contribute to an understanding of how the role of foster parent differs from that of real parent. Institutionalized sanctions are themselves of two sorts. On the one hand a parent can enforce his wishes while his children are young, by threatening to withhold food, shelter, financial help in paying debts or contracting marriages, as well as by the use of physical force. With respect to the last, we have seen that a child may never raise his hand against a parent, who is thus able physically to chastise even a grown son. However, of equal if not greater importance is the position a parent occupies with respect to the ancestors. For it is thought that either parent can bring illness and misfortune to a wilfully disobedient child, both while living and after death. This retribution need not even be intentional, for if a man's ancestors hear him complaining, even to himself, that his children are not fulfilling their filial obligations, his anger may lead them to retaliate without his consciously willing this to happen. Thus a father's apparent good nature is no insurance against trouble sent by the dead.

Affective sanctions are those deriving from the affection which marks most parent–child relationships. Where strong ties of sentiment exist

173

between father and son, and where the latter does not fulfil expectations of what is the proper behaviour, guilt feelings inevitably result. This seems obvious enough. It is, however, precisely this element which is often lacking in the relationship between a child and his foster parent.

The hostility between parents and children, which is an inevitable component of their relationship, is given relatively little recognition in the form of institutionalized avoidances in Gonja society. There is for instance no prohibition on the eldest son's access to supplies of stored grain as is found among the Tallensi (Fortes 1945: chs. V and VIII). However, the eldest son and daughter are distinguished from other children in a number of ways which emphasize the inevitable succession of one generation by the next.

Perhaps the clearest single expression of this avoidance is found in the prohibition on a father attending the ceremony at which his first-born child, of whichever sex, is shaved and given a name and tribal marks. With these acts the child is declared a human being, and the next generation is formally given recognition.

The eldest son is set apart from all a man's other children by the customs regarding eating. He alone may never eat from the same bowl as his father. Interestingly enough, this prohibition is of little relevance except during a boy's childhood and early adolescence. For while a man may share his portion with young sons, he seldom eats with those old enough to farm. Adolescents and young men usually eat together, often in large groups whose membership corresponds to those which co-operate in farm-clearing work. Men old enough to have grown sons hold aloof from such groups, eating alone or perhaps with a child – a younger son, or grandson – for company.

The insistence that a man and his eldest son never eat together emphasizes that the two represent different generations, and perhaps counteracts a tendency to make a particularly close companion of the first-born son. In fact, in establishing their own domestic groups, sons tend to separate themselves spatially from their father. This separation may be explained (if attention is called to it, it is not normally a subject for discussion) by the comment that a man and his eldest son are uncomfortable if they live too close to one another. For, as one man put it, "A man sees his son growing strong and bearing children to fill his house and this makes him (the father) feel weakness". The implication here is that there is a single pool of vigour upon which father and son must both draw. As the son's share increases, the father's must diminish. No man, it is felt, wishes to be reminded of this fact.

A comparable notion exists with respect to a woman and her children, and is formulated in terms of fertility. Thus, when Akua gave birth to her first child, a woman of her mother's compound remarked that henceforth her mother would bear no more children. "When the daughters begin to bring forth", she said, "the mother's child-bearing is at an end." A related prohibition is based on the belief that if an adult child, of either sex, calls from behind the house to the mother while she is inside, and if the mother answers, then fertility will be transferred to the child. This prohibition may be equally well interpreted in terms of the authority relationship between a mother and her children. There is nothing offensive in a small child calling to its mother; as elsewhere, this merely expresses dependence on the mother for succour and guidance. But for an adult to summon or question a parent by calling from a distance is considered disrespectful. To do so implies a reversal of roles, for it places the parent in a subordinate position. Thus it is not strange that such an act is seen as threatening the mother's status as a woman in full possession of her youthful strength and capacities. For it heralds the approach of the time when, as an elderly woman, her position of authority and respect in the community is challenged by the next generation.

The prohibition on a grown child calling to his mother inside the room can be purposely broken if a son or daughter fails to have children after some years of marriage. In this case it is seen as a way in which the mother can help by giving up her own fertility, and this is quite appropriate once her own children are themselves married. There is a rather similar prohibition, however, which lacks any such benign aspect. This is the taboo on a first child of either sex sitting on an up-turned cooking pot and calling its mother by the familiar form 'maa', always used by children for their own mother. If a first child does this at any age, it is firmly believed that the mother will die in the very near future. Here again there is the role-reversal implied in a child summoning the parent, when it ought to be the adult who summons the child. But, unlike the beliefs about fertility, where only grown children are a threat, even a toddler cannot call 'maa' while sitting on a cooking pot without causing her death. Here, as in a number of other contexts, the bringing together of images about food, maternal care, women and authority relations appears to create an extremely threatening pattern of symbols. In this case, the threat is perceived as coming from the child and as being directed towards the mother. Other instances see the threat as coming from the woman, either as mother or co-wife endangering the child, as in witchcraft attacks; or the wife threatening her husband, as

175

when a woman attempts to fight back when her husband strikes her, or far worse, hits him with the stick used for stirring porridge (E. Goody 1970: 241).

These prohibitions concerning eldest children, and the constraints surrounding adult children and their ageing parents, apply only to their own children and not to those of 'siblings'. This is so even when a man or woman fosters the child of a kinsman.

The ultimate act of filial piety is participation in the funeral of each parent. All the sons and daughters ought to return during the last illness, or at least for the funeral itself. It is the duty of the children to provide a cloth in which to bury the body, and often several are contributed by children, both own and classificatory. The children fashion bracelets, anklets and wreaths of dried grass to wear during the long series of observances. Such garlands distinguish the very close kin, including siblings of the deceased.

At the funeral of either parent the children are represented by two special roles: the *ewurikung* (eldest son) and the *ewurikuntche* (eldest daughter). If the actual eldest son and daughter are not present, 'siblings' will be chosen to take their place, but there must be an 'eldest son' and 'eldest daughter' at the funeral of an adult. Both are secluded for either four or seven days. At the funeral of an important chief the seclusion may last until the end of the forty-day funeral, and it is the *ewurikung* who sits on the skin (throne) of the divisional chief until the successor has been installed.

Like the widow, the children are thought to be in danger from the attempts of the dead parent to persuade them to follow him or her into the land of the dead. While in seclusion they should never be left alone, and their fasting and vigil-keeping are intended to guard them from the temptations of the spirit. Like the widow, the eldest son and daughter are cleansed of the dirt of the funeral by being shaved and bathed on the final day, but they cannot bathe in *jobuni* medicine as they must remain accessible to the spirit of a dead parent who may later communicate with living descendants. Relations with the spirits of dead kinsmen, as distinct from affines, are never severed.

Throughout the funeral rituals, both the eldest son and eldest daughter keep by them a small iron model of handcuffs of the sort formerly used for slaves. When they join in the dancing and singing of dirges during the nights before the three-day and seven-day funerals, the handcuffs are carried with them and may be flourished as they dance. These small trinkets are part of the funeral paraphernalia of the eldest son and daughter throughout Gonja. The directness of the symbolism is striking:

176

it is said that as a child is the slave of the father and mother during their lifetime, anything they ask must be done, however difficult. When the parent dies, this servitude is ended, at least in its overt form. But the shackles are a reminder of the debt a child owes its parent for care and guidance, indeed for life itself.

The equivalent in Gonja of the 'wicked stepmother' is of course the mother's co-wife. Whatever the mother's own relations with a co-wife, the Gonja are so explicit about the risks to which children are subject if left in such a woman's care that they cannot help being apprehensive. Such is the strength of these feelings, and the institutional arrangements made to avoid entrusting children to a co-wife, that it is unusual to find a child who has become close to one of his father's wives as a substitute mother. However, so long as the mother is also present, the children's relations with her co-wives may be cordial, at least if hers are. They call their mother's *chamina* by the familiar form for mother (*maa*), and to do otherwise is insulting. If they are not on good terms with a mother's co-wife her name will be added: for instance *maa Hawa*. The mother's sisters are also called 'mother', but the formal term *niu* is used instead of the familiar *maa*. In reference, and sometimes in address, a suffix indicating the sisters relative ages is added: those older than the child's mother are *niu gbung* ('older/big mother'), while those younger are *niu ker* ('younger/small mother'). In address, the term *niu* is usually used with the name of the mother's sister. Among these women may be a future foster parent. Whether or not they go to live with her, the children feel that a mother's sister, particularly a younger sister, is an ally and a friend. The father's sisters are more respected and probably less affectionately regarded. They are referred to as *tana*, and no distinction is made according to their age relative to the father. A father's sister who lives in the same house and whom the children know well may be called by this term with her name as a suffix: *tana Miama*. Otherwise *tana* alone is used.

Terms of address for the parents' male siblings follow a similar (bifurcate collateral) pattern, with the father's brothers given the same term as the father while the mother's brother has a special one (*wopa*). This usage stresses the identity of each parent with his or her siblings of the same sex, based on the similarity of their adult roles. The term in each case is independent of the cross-sex term, unlike the usage in societies where descent group membership is a critical factor in identity; there a mother's brother is often called 'male mother' and the father's sister 'female father' to emphasize their common descent with mother and father respectively. Among the Gonja, on the other hand, the

G   177

terminology stresses the disjunction based on sex difference rather than identity through common descent.

There is another general aspect of these terms which merits comment. Parents' siblings of the same sex (father's brothers, mother's sisters) are differentiated according to age as 'older' or 'younger' mother or father. Those of cross-sex are not. These differences are always relative to the parent, who is of course called by the same term, and the usage represents a method of distinguishing true parents within a broader category of 'fathers' and 'mothers'. It also separates very clearly those mothers and fathers to whom the parent must defer, ('older fathers' and 'older mothers') from those who are themselves subordinate to the parents ('younger fathers' and 'younger mothers'). This point is often commented on by the children, who tend to attribute a more authoritarian manner to 'older' mothers and fathers, while they see 'younger' fathers and mothers as being relatively indulgent.

The attitude of a son towards his mother's subsequent husband has already been referred to (see chapter 5). As we have seen the two are likened to sexual rivals and not expected to get along. They will seldom be found in the same compound, for nothing but misfortune is expected to follow. A boy avoids referring to or addressing his step-father; a girl uses the form 'father Seidu' (*ntuto Seidu*) for both reference and address.

The terms of reference and address used for the parents' brothers are the mirror opposite to those described for their sisters. The brothers of the father are distinguished as 'fathers' who are older or younger than he: 'elder father' (*tuto gbung*), 'younger father' (*tuto ker*). The mother's brother, on the other hand, is referred to as *wopa*, for example, *wopa Seidu*, regardless of whether he is older or younger than the mother. The complex relationship between a child and the mother's brother has been discussed in part in the context of cross-cousin marriage. In central Gonja this relationship is neither that of joking between a man and his sister's son that one finds in some patrilineal African societies, nor is it the extreme respect and authoritarian pattern characteristic of matrilineal systems. For despite the fact that the mother's brother is said to have the power of life and death over his niece and nephew, it is the father and his kin who in fact hold the day-to-day authority in most cases, as well as being the source of primary citizenship and thus of major rights to office. The result of this balance is that, while Gonja children respect their mother's brothers rather than joke with them, they tend to be on fairly easy-going terms. Much depends on both the character of the man concerned, and on whether he is a familiar or a distant figure.

Grandparents and grandchildren share in a reciprocal joking relationship; they are *kitcherpo* to one another. This is most strikingly demonstrated at funerals when the grandchildren (*nanabi*) of the deceased gather together and roam the town singing merry songs. If the bereaved of other generations want them to stop, they must pay them off with small coins.

The dominant note in relations between grandparents and grandchildren is one of anticipation of mutual indulgence. A grandparent is usually a soft touch, good for a bowl of porridge or a few pennies if teased insistently. Grandparents appear to delight in pleasing with such small favours, but in turn look to their grandchildren as a potential source of support in old age. For when they grow elderly, their children will delegate a young boy or girl to care for them, the former to farm for a grandfather and the latter to cook, wash and fetch water for a grandmother. A man or woman who lives to ripe old age may have a succession of such foster children. Unlike children who are raised by a parent's 'sibling', no possibility of inheritance or direct conflict of authority complicates the fostering relationship between alternate generations. And it is widely held that grandparents are less demanding in this role than are parents' siblings.

Although indulgence characterizes the exercise of domestic authority by grandparents, in jural or ritual matters their word is law. While a parent may be able to prevail upon a sibling to alter his position with regard to the arrangement of a marriage or to allow a foster child to return to his natal home, he will be reluctant even to approach his own parent with such a request. However, such constraints do not directly affect grandchildren as jural minors, but are worked out between the successive generations represented by their parents and grandparents.

It is necessary to lay emphasis on both the strength and complexity of affective ties between parents and children as well as on the formal aspects of their roles because of the very fact that children, both as adolescents and adults, must often relate to their parents separately. For a high proportion of adolescents are children of dissolved marriages.

However, this situation is less disruptive than might be expected because it is anticipated by the norms of the society; not anticipated explicitly, it is true, but taken into account in the provisions made for residence of single women with kin and of the distribution of children among kinsfolk. Nevertheless, children are frequently placed in a position where they must hear one parent denounce the other and yet maintain good relationships with both. A number of instances of this sort occurred in the course of field work. For continuity's sake I shall discuss the effects on the children in the two cases described in chapter 7 in which parents separated after many years of marriage and the birth of an unusually large number of children.

When Nyiwuleji and his wife Nana quarrelled over his mistress and Nana's sale of farm produce, Nyiwuleji's older children sided with their mother. They told their father that the yams whose sale he resented had been grown only with their help and so far as they were concerned belonged to their mother if she had need of them. Further, they announced that if he did not apologize and placate her, they would accompany her to her brothers' compound, also in the village of Busunu, settle there, and farm for their maternal kin. I do not know how the situation was resolved, but even if the sons carry out their threat and take up residence with their maternal kin, most of them will return to their father's house. They may do so as the result of falling out with a member of their new compound, or they may await the time when a 'brother' there succeeds to the role of compound head. Should this happen, residence with the father may well be viewed as more attractive.

The situation at the separation of the KoroWura and his wife was more complex because of the distances involved. The sons felt that their mother was 'driven out' by their father's second marriage and greatly resented his treatment of her. Yet they all divided their time between the village of Katangi where they fished for their father who, as a chief, did not fish himself, and Buipe, some forty miles away, where their mother lived with her 'brother'. Seidu, as the oldest son, considered himself responsible for his mother and elder sister "because they are women", visited them frequently and sent them money. But, although outspoken in claiming that his mother had been ill-treated, he considered Katangi as his home and held his father in great reverence.

It may seem strange to begin a discussion of parent–child relations with the consideration of how they are affected by the parents' separation. But the virtual inevitability of separation, as well as the constant distinction between mother's kin and father's kin, cannot but colour the domestic scene. And the two cases discussed above are atypical in one respect, for in them separation occurred only after many years of marriage and the birth of several children. As the figures in Table 8-3 indicate, sibling groups of seven and eight are rare; only seven out of 103 sibling groups in the Buipe census had five or more members. With the figures on the proportion of adolescents whose parents are no longer living together, this suggests that separation frequently occurs after only a few years of marriage.

The opposition between parents can be used to influence the children themselves. This is what happened when Boipo declined to farm for his father, Maman, because he felt that his refusal to help him marry was unjustified. Maman held Boipo's mother, Wuritche, responsible, saying that she encouraged him to be lazy and flout his father's authority. Her tears finally succeeded where Maman's threats had failed, for Boipo said he could not stand to see his mother so abused on his account. Although no reference was made to the possibility that the quarrel might lead to his parents' separation, this happens so frequently that it cannot have been far from Boipo's thoughts.

KINSHIP FOSTERING

In discussing the rights *in genetricem* transferred at marriage, and the residence of children on the divorce or death of their parents, reference has been made to the role of proxy and foster parents. For during late childhood and adolescence many children live with adults other than their own parents. Indeed, one of the first entries in my first Gonja notebook reads "*kabita* – a girl given to someone; *kaiyeribi* – a boy given to someone". These terms of reference, not address, are frequently heard in conversation; like the institution they refer to, that is the sending of children to be brought up by kin, these social roles are explicitly and universally recognized.

This is not, as might at first appear, a form of adoption, for adoption as it is usually defined involves a legal change in status of the adoptee, which is specifically not the case in Gonja. Unlike adoption, fostering by kin involves no permanent forfeiting of rights or duties in order to assume a new set, no change in the kinship terms used between the people involved, and no permanent change of status in any sense. This is so because the transfer of residence and of immediate jurisdiction occurs within the group in which these rights are already held.

In societies where adoption is regularly practised, as in classical Indian and Chinese cultures, ancient Rome, and today in rural Japan, the explicit intention is that by conferring membership on a selected individual, the continuity of the group, whether represented by ancestral shrines, name and titles, or economic assets, may be secured.[1] But the institution of kinship fostering cannot act in this way. Firstly, there are no descent lines or corporate units to be perpetuated. Secondly, fostering takes place *within* the range of kin who already share rights to office and property. And in a system of lateral inheritance, such as that

[1] See J. R. Goody 1969, for a comparative discussion of the functions of adoption.

found throughout West Africa, there is rarely a scarcity of heirs. For these reasons I use the term fostering, from the Anglo-Saxon *fostre*, to nourish or feed. For it is the duty of Gonja foster parents to feed, clothe and train their foster children, to raise them (*belo bomu*) to be good people (*esa pa*). As the Gonja send their children to relatives and not to strangers, the institution is best described as 'kinship fostering'. When 'fostering' is used in the following pages, it is to be understood in this modified form. I shall speak of a child brought up in this way as a foster child, and those who rear him as foster parents, but this fostering relationship is always superimposed upon one based on direct kinship ties. In order to learn about a person's background one must ask both, "Who bore you?" (*Wane kurwe fo?*) and "Who reared you?" (*Wane bela fo?*).

In central Gonja fostering is spoken of as though it always occurred between kinsmen standing in certain relationships to one another. In this paradigm a male foster child goes to his mother's brother, and the female to the father's sister. In fact this is a highly idealized picture of what occurs, but because the Gonja attach such importance to these two models, and because they serve as a charter by virtue of which other kin may put forward claims, it is worthwhile describing in detail the procedure followed in these two ideal types of fostering.

THE FATHER'S SISTER AS FOSTER PARENT

When a marriage is contracted, the one most immediately concerned, aside from the partners and their parents, is the sister of the groom. If she lives in the same compound as the new husband, it will be in her room that the bride spends the first months of her marriage. And when the trial period is over and the bride is given a room of her own, it is the husband's sister who must find the cooking stones and the large water pot which together symbolize the wife's position. It is by virtue of these services that the first girl born of the union should be given to the father's sister. On the birth of his daughter, a man sends a messenger to his sister to tell her that the girl who will become her foster child has been born on such and such a day, and that, when she is old enough to leave the mother, the aunt may come and claim her. The future foster parent sends kola for the naming ceremony which is held on the seventh day after birth, and thereafter supplies the waist beads worn by a girl as well as an occasional trinket or piece of cloth. Not until the child 'has sense', that is, until the age of about 5 or 6, will the foster parent come to take her new charge home, traditionally with a gift of cloth for the mother and for the child. From that time, the child lives with the foster parent, learning from her the women's tasks that her mother would otherwise have taught her, and taking a growing part in the domestic life of the compound.

There is a special term for a female foster parent, essentially a term of reference, though sometimes used as a term of address to convey particular respect. This term, *tchepe*, literally means 'the place of the woman' (*etche*, woman; *pe*, place), but the meaning given is 'the one who looks after you, has charge of you'. Foster parent is then a fairly exact translation. In everyday conversation, however, both foster parent and foster child continue to use the kinship terms which they would employ if the child were living with her own parents. There is no question of the foster parent completely taking over the role of the child's mother, although she does perforce assume those functions of a mother which are dependent on co-residence. Such a child will accompany her foster parent when she goes to visit her brother, the child's father, and later she will visit her parents' home by herself. These visits may last for as long as two or three months, and if the mother should need her help, for instance at the birth of a younger sibling, the foster parent may allow the girl to return for even longer periods. In this way, a daughter keeps in contact with her natal home, though it is always assumed that she will return again to her foster home. In fact, while everyone agrees that a foster parent is a far stricter task-mistress than one's own mother, a girl seldom runs away, although some complain bitterly. If she is too badly treated, the parents will refuse to let her return, either directly (as in one instance where the girl was overworked and beaten into the bargain), or indirectly by pleading that her help is needed at home. Generally, however, a small amount of discipline is considered to improve the character and must be endured.

When a girl begins to have suitors, it is to her foster parent that she shows their gifts, and to her that the suitors address their pleas. For, although the suitor's final gift of twelve kola nuts and twelve shillings which seals the contract is sent to the parents and distributed by them to their siblings as well as to the foster parent, the latter's consent to the match should first be won.

The bonds between a girl and her foster parent vary with the particular people involved. Little love will be lost between a woman and the child whom she treats like a household drudge. But many are very close; especially if the child's mother subsequently dies, so that the foster parent becomes in fact a proxy mother, the relationship develops into a close one. Where the two have grown fond of each other, their relationship will be kept up after the girl's marriage by constant visiting, and it may be to the house of her foster parent that the young wife will return after the birth of her first child. The point to stress here is that, while the relationship between a mother and daughter is by definition one of deep and lasting affection, that between a girl and her foster parent may be but is not so necessarily.

THE MOTHER'S BROTHER AS A FOSTER PARENT

In normal circumstances the first son of a marriage is not sent away to be brought up by kin.[2] Although a mild form of avoidance is practised between a man and his oldest son, this boy belongs pre-eminently to his father and may never be claimed by his mother's kin. A second son may be so claimed by the mother's brother, and to refuse such a request is thought to endanger the life of the child. In this case, the boy is not likely to be designated at birth as belonging to a foster parent, though if the mother's brother wishes to press his rights, he may insist on being allowed to pay the expenses involved in the naming ceremony. More often he will come and beg (*e kule mu*) for the child when he has grown enough to leave his parents, again at about the age of 5 or 6, though if anything a bit later than in the case of a girl. If the father's people agree, and the pressures on them to do so are strong, the boy takes up residence in his uncle's compound.

As in the case of a girl and her foster parent, there is a term used reciprocally with *kaiyeribi*, to refer to the male foster parent. This term is *nyenipe* and means literally 'the place of the man' (*enyen*, man, and *pe*, place). Its meaning in use is the same as the equivalent term for a woman, 'the one who looks after you, has charge of you'; and again it is used primarily for reference, the ordinary terms for mother's brother and sister's child being retained in address.

The foster parent is responsible for teaching the boy to farm, to hunt, to build houses and to acquire the other crafts practised by all Gonja men with a varying degree of skill. It is also his duty to impart such moral education as is considered necessary, though this it is felt any

---

[2] At least, not in the central Gonja divisions in which I worked. In western Gonja members of the ruling group used to send the eldest son to a sibling of either father or mother. Compare this western Gonja practice with that reported by E. Skinner for the Mossi of Haute Volta where eldest sons were traditionally sent to the mother's father or brother to be reared (Skinner 1964: 45). Fostering of sons in eastern Gonja appears always to have been relatively uncommon. See Appendix IV.

normal boy will pick up for himself through watching the behaviour of others and from the reactions of the community to it. A foster parent will be held responsible for any misdemeanour or felony committed by a boy in his care. In practice, he would expect the father to contribute to any fine which might be levied, although he would be reluctant to request such aid, and unless the trouble were serious he would try to handle it quietly himself.

A boy is expected to remain with his foster parent at least until marriage, when it is the foster parent's duty to help the youth get a wife, sometimes, but not necessarily, by arranging a marriage himself.

When the mother's brother arranges the marriage on behalf of the sister's son who is living with him, the bride may be related to her prospective husband. In any case the usual courtship and marriage gifts are given. Once a boy has reached the age where he is ready to take a wife, his obligation to remain with his foster parent is ended, and he may reside where he wishes. Most men eventually return to their father's village, although in some cases not until their foster parent dies, by which time they may be well into middle age. The whole career of a male foster child is more problematical than that of a girl in the similar role. A youth has more freedom of movement and is more independent than a young girl, and consequently a boy who feels that he is being maltreated will often return home. The first or second time he may be sent back again, but to send him back a third time would be foolhardy indeed, for triple flight indicates that his mother's ancestors do not wish him well and will try to harm him if he returns.

On the other hand, while there is no possibility of a girl remaining with her foster parent beyond adolescence, for virilocal marriage is the universal lot of young women, a man who treats his sister's son well may hope that he will remain to farm with him until he dies. Both these factors, the greater independence of the boy, and the possibility of his remaining in his foster home as an adult, tend to give him preferment at his uncle's hands, often to the detriment of the mother's brother's own sons. In one instance of this kind, a man had so alienated his two older sons by his preference for a sister's son resident with him that the two boys refused to farm for their father at all. Such a situation is possible because fathers and sons alike accept the fact that a man's place is ultimately in the compound of his father. Whatever their differences, this tie is in the end the binding one. On the other hand, if a foster child quarrels with his *nyenipe*, he will soon return to his own father, even during the period of his jural minority. If he is to stay once his obligations have been met, it will be because of the affective bonds with those

185

in his foster home.[3] This possibility of conflict between a man's own children and his foster children raises the question of why it should be so important to retain a sister's son that a man will endanger his relations with his own children. Firstly, although always latent, such conflicts seldom seem to reach the proportions in the situation quoted above. This accepted, the answer must be sought on two levels. On the one hand, such behaviour is expected. A man whose foster child refuses to stay with him will be censured by the community at large for what must have been bad treatment, and he will be blamed by his kin for letting down a trust. For it is partly through foster children that ties are maintained with the children of the women who marry out of the community.

However, any answer in the form, 'the norms of the community specify such behaviour', begs the question – why should the normative system be so structured? Before turning to a consideration of this point, let us take a closer look at the institution itself.

The first male and female child of a marriage are traditionally for the father and his kin; the Gonja say they are for the father's people (*tutopebi*) or the father's place (*tutope*). With the birth of a second son, the claims of the mother's people begin to be pressed. But the sending of a boy to be brought up by his mother's brother does not satisfy these claims for all time. If the union is a fertile one, it is the prerogative of the mother's people to ask for additional foster children; two out of a total of four or five, three if there are five or six, and so forth. By whom these children will be reared depends above all on their sex. For the rights exercised over foster children are essentially rights to their labour, and the duties of a foster parent pertain to instruction in these tasks. If a boy were to be given to the father's sister, he would not in fact come under her tutelage but under that of her husband. Should a girl be given to the mother's brother, she would be placed under the immediate jurisdiction of his wife. Just as it is recognized that a parent's sibling is less permissive than the parent himself, so it is accepted that a foster parent related by affinity rather than kinship would be an even harsher master. And this is almost never allowed to happen. Instead, if the child

---

[3] There would appear to be a contradiction between the image of the foster parent as a stern taskmaster and as indulging his foster child at the expense of his own children. Fostering relationships which corresponded to each image were observed, and both views thus appear to be based on fact. It is also the case that the relationship is characterized differently depending on the experience of the actors and the particular role with which they identify. Thus a man who thinks of himself as a foster parent emphasizes the capriciousness of foster children and the necessity of treating them well. Another, remembering his own or a son's treatment while living with a foster parent, may stress the disciplinary aspects of the relationship.

to be fostered by the mother's people is a girl, she will go not to the mother's brother's wife but to a sister, preferably a younger sister, of the mother. Or she may be sent to care for the mother's mother or her sister in their old age.

The situation with respect to the father's kin is somewhat different. A girl is sent first of all to the father's sister though she may also go to his mother. But a boy is not usually given to a brother of the father in the way that he is to a mother's brother. In pressing this point in Buipe, I was met by incredulity. As one man said, "Why should I do that? My sons are for my brother in any case. When I die, he is the one who owns them all. If they roam about in the bush, it is to his house that they will return." And to clinch the point, he remarked, "My brother would never beg for my son."

In the only instance I encountered where a girl was sent to her mother's brother, she remained only a few months and then managed to return to stay in her natal home.

In fact, a few scattered instances were recorded in which a man was reared by an elder brother of his father during the latter's lifetime. In two cases, the father was living away from his natal village and apparently took this means of seeing that his son was familiar with his paternal kin. The YagbumWura himself spoke at some length on the desirability of a man's sending his sons to be reared by a brother. "The brother will in turn send his own sons to you and thus the children of each will be well brought up", he concluded.

But the fact that fostering by a father's brother is relatively rare and seldom discussed reflects again the difference in time perspective which applies to the fostering of male and female foster children. In the case of the latter, it is only the period before marriage that is affected by fostering. With male foster children, there is always the possibility that they will remain after marriage to farm and reside with the foster parent. But since the father's kin anticipate the eventual return of the boys who have been sent away as foster children, there would appear to be less need for them to insist on their rights during the period of adolescence and young adulthood than there is for a boy's maternal kin. For the latter can have little hope of establishing any claim once this period has passed.

A boy is sometimes sent to the father of either parent to help him farm in his old age. But here the issue of adult residence is not expected to arise. If the foster parent is the father's father, he is probably living in the village in which the youth's agnatic rights are vested. This is the village to which he expects to return in any case, unless his father is so well established in another (usually his mother's) that he chooses to consider this his paternal home. If the foster parent is the mother's father, adult residence is still not likely to be a problem, because of the differences in ages involved in alternate generations. Thus it is thought unlikely that a man will reach the age where the responsibilities of parenthood and jural majority lead him to seek out his father's home while his grandfather is still living.

We have so far been concerned with the claims of particular kin of each parent to certain children. And this is how fostering is discussed by the Gonja themselves, for the initiative is usually left in the hands of the potential foster parent. This pattern means that the possibility only becomes real when a kinsman of either parent actually asks for the custody of a particular child. If, however, we consider the institution from the position of the child in the network of kinship relations, we see that this picture of individual claims is by no means a complete one.

In enumerating his kinsfolk, an individual differentiates them into 'people of his father' (*ntuto pebi*) and 'people of his mother' (*niu pebi*). Both are equally kin, and when his child makes a similar enumeration he will rarely distinguish between his father's father's and his father's mother's people or between his mother's mother's and his mother's father's people. They tend to be grouped respectively into his father's kin and his mother's kin. Or to take the opposite point of view, a person considers the children of his sons and the children of his daughters as being equally related to him, although he may sometimes distinguish between them, referring to the former as men's children (*enyen pibi*) and the latter as women's children (*etche pibi*). A very simple diagram of this situation (Figure 5) demonstrates that from the point of view of the senior generation the children of any marriage fall into two groups of kin. To the father's people, they are men's children, and to the mother's, women's children, but both number them and their children among their kin. In this sense the kin of each parent claim all the children of the union and these claims necessarily overlap. One way of resolving this built-in contradiction is the particularization of rights which I have described. Furthermore, every child who is resident in the role of foster child acts as a reaffirmation of the claims on his sibling group as a whole.

I have considered in detail the procedure followed in the two cases that provide the models for male and female foster children respectively, because foster parenthood is discussed in central Gonja as though it normally occurred between these relatives. At the same time I have suggested that, from the observer's point of view, the institution of kinship fostering is best considered, not as the result of claims of indi-

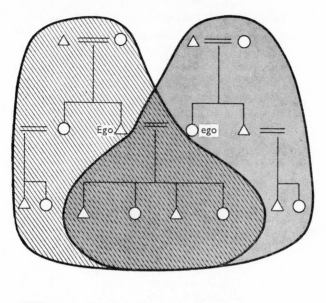

	'father's kin' for the children of Ego and ego
	'mother's kin' for the children of Ego and ego
	'women's children' for ego's kin and 'men's children' for Ego's kin

Fig. 5   Overlapping claims on the children of a marriage.

viduals to particular children, but rather as expressing the claims made by the kin of each parent on the offspring of a given union. It is thus not surprising to find that successful claims for foster children are made by a wider range of kin than the model would lead us to expect.

There were thirty-four foster children in Buipe at the time of the census. Table 8-1 shows how they were related to their foster parents.

From this table it appears that the ideal pattern of fostering, with girls going to the father's sister and boys to the mother's brother, is far from being the most frequently practised. Exactly one-third of the female foster children are with a father's sister, the remainder going mostly to the mother's kin. And of the male foster children, not even one-fifth are with their own mother's brother, the largest proportion, nearly half, going not to the mother's kin but to that of the father's mother; two to their father's mother's brother and five to a maternal half-sibling or maternal cousin of the father, that is, to a classificatory father's brother.

189

Table 8-1. *Distribution of male and female
foster children among various
categories of kin*

Foster parent is:	Sex of foster child: Female	Male
Real or classificatory mother's brother		3
Real or classificatory father's sister	6	
Father's mother's brother		2
Father's maternal sibling or maternal cousin		5
Mother's sister	4	
Real or classificatory parent of father	1	2
Real or classificatory parent of mother	5	3
Own paternal half-sister	1	
Father's paternal sibling*		1
Mother's brother's wife	1	
	18	16

N=34
* Own father still living

However, if the pattern of relationships is considered in terms of the generation of foster child in relation to foster parent (Table 8-1a), the picture is not too far from the model. About two-thirds of the

Table 8-1a. *Generation of foster parent in
relation to foster child*

Foster parent is:	Female foster child	Male foster child
Parents' generation	11	9
Grandparents' generation	6	7
Child's generation	1	—
	18	16

N=34

fostered girls are with a parent's real or classificatory sibling. The majority of male foster children are also with a member of the parental generation, but nearly as many are with a grandparent.

The next point that requires comment is the wide range of relationships linking foster child and foster parent. The thirty-four foster children are distributed over ten categories of kin, and even these groupings lump together full and classificatory siblings, and full and classificatory grandparents. Thus, while the 'model' on which the institution of fostering is based prescribes the parents' opposite-sex siblings as the proper foster parents, successful claims are made by a wide variety of kin.

Table 8-2. *Residence of foster children*
with agnatic or uterine kin

| | Sex of foster child: | | |
Resident with:	Female	Male	
Mother's kin	10	6	16
			47%
Father's kin			
(a) uterine	—	7	18
(b) agnatic	8	3	53%
	18	16	100%

N=34

As is indicated in Table 8-2, if male and female foster children are considered together, they are distributed almost equally between maternal and paternal kin. The balance results, however, from matching the higher proportion of female foster children who are with maternal kin, against the greater number of male foster children with paternal relatives. The material from other parts of Gonja also suggests a rough balance in the allocation of foster children to relatives of both parents (see Appendix IV).

The thirty-four Buipe foster children represent a relatively small proportion of the 187 children and adolescents in Buipe at the time of the census, about 18%. Apparently the number of children living with foster parents at any given time is not large. This situation reflects, however, two related characteristics of the institution of kinship fostering itself.

191

On the one hand any particular foster child–foster parent relationship represents claims with respect to sibling groups and not to individuals. These rights are not exclusive or exhaustive; the institution would take on quite a different character if all children were fostered. If this were to be the case the sibling group itself would disappear. But this does not occur in Gonja. Rather, for each generation the extended sibling group, including half and classificatory siblings, constitutes the single most important set of ties. Thus in a given population one would expect to find that foster children were in rough proportion to the number of sibling groups whose members have not yet reached adulthood rather than to the total number of children. The 187 children in Buipe in September 1956 belonged to 103 full sibling groups. There was thus about one foster child for every three sibling groups.

There is yet another factor which might be expected to limit further the incidence of fostering. Although it is said that a son ought to go to the mother's brothers, it is also held that the maternal kin only have rights to a second or third child, and that their claims will be hardest to resist where there are several children in the sibling group. Similarly, a father's sister's claim to a daughter is unlikely to be pressed so long as the girl remains an only child. In other words, sibling groups of one or two children are in a sense 'ineligible' for fostering. Of the 103 full sibling groups in Buipe, thirty (31%) consisted of a single child, and another twenty-seven children are recorded as only children but information on their siblings may not be complete. At a conservative estimate, half of this latter group are probably only children. Something like 40% of the sibling groups, then, are unlikely to have claims made on them for foster children. Only twenty-five full sibling groups (24%) were recorded as having three or more members, and would thus fall into the category most 'at risk'. A ratio of thirty-four foster children to twenty-five large full sibling groups comes much closer to what one would predict from the explicit norms of Gonja fostering.

However, although the Gonja tend to speak as if foster children were always sought out by a would-be foster parent, and belong to large sibling groups, in fact many children are fostered as a direct result of the dissolution of their family of orientation. A parent dies, or there is a divorce, and then decisions must be made about who shall rear the children. These instances in which fostering was precipitated by the break up of the conjugal unit are best referred to as *crisis* fosterage. Where the child has been begged by a relative in the traditional way, this is described as *voluntary* fosterage.

The Buipe sample, the only one from central Gonja based on a

Table 8-3. *Size of full sibling groups of infants, children and adolescents in Buipe*

One child only	30	
One child? if more*	27	78=76%
Two children	21	
Three children	16	
Four children	2	25=24%
Five or more children	7	
	103	

Number of full sibling groups=103
Total children and adolescents in sample=187
Total extant marriages of parents=54

---

* These children are all sole representatives of their sibling group in Buipe. They are nearly all children of divorced or widowed parents, and foster children from other villages for whom information on full sibling groups is lacking. Many in the former category appear to be only children of transitory marriages. Those in the latter category are more likely to have full siblings elsewhere. Unfortunately, at the time the census was taken the importance of fostering was not fully realized, and no systematic enquiries were made as to children currently brought up in other villages.

complete village census, gives some basis for generalization. The parents of nearly two-thirds of the fostered children from this sample were no longer married, and most of these marriages had probably ended before the children were fostered. The relatively small number of people in the Buipe census raises the question of the general validity of such a high level of crisis fosterage. Samples from western Gonja have somewhat lower levels of crisis fosterage (43% for males and 52% for females); however, data from north-central Gonja show similarly high proportions (75% for males and 67% for females, see Appendix IV).

The frequency of crisis fosterage suggested by this material must, however, be seen in the context of overall likelihood that a child's family of orientation will be intact until he reaches adulthood. For, as we have seen in the analysis of Gonja marriage, there are many possible causes of its dissolution. In Table 8-4 adolescents and children are compared as to the proportion whose parents were still living together, and the proportion whose parents had separated through death or divorce.

The first thing to be noted from this table is the relatively high proportion of cases in both age groups whose parents are no longer living together. If only children under 12 are considered, in 30% of the

Table 8-4. *Relationship between age of children* and status of parents'*
       marriage

	Adolescents	Children	
Parents together	40 (42%)	44 (70%)	84 (53%)
Parents separated by death or divorce	55 (58%)	19 (30%)	74 (47%)
	95 (100%)	63 (100%)	158 (100%)

* Because of the age categories employed in collecting census data, this is not an easy comparison to make. Non-adults were recorded in one of three age categories: infants, 0–1½ years; children, 2–11 years; and adolescents, 12–20 years. It has since become clear that a more useful division would have been between young children of up to 6 and 'children who are old enough to have sense' or roughly those of 7 and over. It is the latter group from which foster children are drawn.

cases the parents are no longer married. And for the older age group (12–20), this figure has nearly doubled – 58% come from unions which are no longer extant.

The difference between the two age groups is in itself of interest, for it suggests an ongoing process; the implication is that the older a child, the less likely his parents are to be living together. The threats to a marriage from death and divorce are continuing and cumulative; the longer it persists, the more it is exposed to them.

This raises the question of what happens to the children when the marriage of their parents is ended. Table 8-5 records the residence of the seventy-four Buipe children whose parents are no longer living together. The definition of the categories under which this material has been analysed requires a brief digression. Residence with the surviving parent is an obvious alternative on the death of the other, although it is worth noting that the practice of virilocal marriage in itself does not prescribe the residence of the children on the death of either father or mother. On the death of the mother, some may go to her kin; and on the father's death, the mother may take some with her when she returns to her natal home. In this table residence with a foster parent refers to present residence. Not all these children were sent to foster parents because of their own parents' separation; some are known to have joined them while their parents were still together.

The term 'proxy father' has been adopted from Fortes (1949a: 140) to denote the man who 'automatically' cares for the children of a deceased kinsman; that is, the one to whom the responsibility passes unless some special arrangement is made. There were five youths in the

Table 8-5. *Residence of children whose parents are separated by death or divorce*

Child with:	No.	%
Surviving parent	41	55%
Proxy father	5	7%
Foster parent	28	38%
	74	100%

sample living with male proxy parents and they have not been included among the foster children. For the foster parent does not jurally replace the real parent as the proxy parent does. Neither proxy nor foster parent is thought able to replace the true parent in the child's affections. As long as the true parents remain alive, they retain their place as the closest kin both in terms of affect and in terms of the strength of the claims which may be made upon them or through them. One's mother and father are always addressed as parents, as foster parents are not. And at their death, they are more deeply grieved, and mourned in distinctive ways. A foster child often visits his parents and is frequently visited by them. They are always there as an alternative refuge should the treatment of the foster parent become too severe. The proxy parent, usually a father's 'brother', continues to present this alternative after the father's death.[4] He is still conceived of as a 'father' in contrast to the foster parent, be he mother's brother, father's mother's brother, or more distant kin.

A consideration of the distribution of female foster children raises the question of whether there is a role of proxy mother complementary to that of the father's 'brother' as proxy father. For, as indicated in Table 8-1, of the eighteen girls living as foster children, four are with a mother's sister and four with real or classificatory mother's mother.

[4] Though a proxy father is usually a man whom the father called 'younger brother' (*supo*), he may be a maternal or paternal half or classificatory sibling. 'Brother' in this context does not necessarily mean either full brother or agnate.

195

On some criteria the answer is yes, and on others, no. To begin with, a girl whose mother dies 'belongs' to the father or proxy father in the same sense that her brothers do, and must be 'begged' for by a mother's sister or mother. If the father has no other wife, and thus no one to look after the girl, and if the child is very young, he will probably be glad of an arrangement which ensures she will be well cared for and relieves him of the responsibility. But if she is nearly adult and there are younger children, he will expect her to remain and care for them. Jural and moral authority remain with the father unless specifically relinquished. Furthermore, there are alternatives to sending a motherless girl to her mother's female relatives. The father may give her to his sister to rear as a foster child, or he may entrust her to the care of another of his wives. This last possibility has the greatest claim to being termed proxy motherhood, for the father's wife is called 'mother' and fills the same role *vis-à-vis* the father and paternal half-siblings that the child's own mother did. Yet this is very seldom found, for it is recognized that a polygamous wife cannot help but prefer her own children to those of her husband's other wives and there are no ties of kinship to soften her treatment of such a ward.

As is consistent with the bilateral nature of Gonja kinship terminology, the mother's sisters are called 'mother' and distinguished in reference by whether they are older or younger than the mother (but not consistently so distinguished in address). Thus a girl living with her mother's sister does not alter the kinship terms she uses; neither does a girl living with the father's sister, but in the former instance the term is one of those used for her own mother, while in the latter it is specific to the father's sister. In this sense the mother's sister is a parent from birth in a way that the father's sister is not; she might for this reason be thought of as a proxy parent rather than as a foster parent. Furthermore, it is generally, though not universally, agreed that in their treatment of a foster child the mother's sisters are apt to be milder and more permissive than are those of the father.

In speaking of the male foster parent, it was said that the father's 'brothers' always presented an alternative haven to a boy living with a foster parent. The mother's sisters do so, but to a lesser extent. This difference is due to their being women and thus economically dependent on their husbands, as well as less effective jurally (although by no means jural minors). In short, the role of the father's 'brothers' as proxy parents is jurally defined in a way that only men's roles are, while the role of a female proxy parent must, at least in this society, be primarily defined in terms of sentiment.

An individual speaks of all the children of his siblings of either sex as his children, and thus both foster parents and proxy parents speak of their wards as their 'children'. But the descriptive term for female foster child, *kabita*, is applied to a sister's child or daughter's child where its counterpart, male foster child (*kaiyeribi*), is not used for a brother's son by a proxy parent.

Taking into account the ways in which the mother's female relatives resemble proxy parents and those in which they are more like foster parents, they must be considered as potentially both, in a way that does not hold for any other category of kin. If a mother's sister or mother's mother begs a child to rear while the mother is still living, they will do so as foster parents. For the real mother is there, visited and visiting, and the foster parent–foster child relationship is, as it were, mediated through her. But should the mother die, the sister who was a foster parent becomes a proxy parent in a sense in which the father's sister cannot. This is so because of her close identification with the mother herself, and because structurally, in the network of kinship ties traced through the mother, she occupies an identical (or, in the case of half-sisters and classificatory siblings, a very similar) position.

The basic difference between the role of proxy father and proxy mother, however, is that the former is the designated heir of the dead man who inherits responsibilities along with his property; there is no such explicitly recognized successor to a woman's responsibilities toward her children. For the purpose of the present analysis, then, no distinction will be made between a female foster parent and a proxy mother.

To return to Table 8-5, it is clear that when a marriage is ended by divorce or death, there are a number of possible alternatives for the children. They may go to either parent at divorce, to the surviving parent of either sex when the marriage is dissolved by death, or they may go to a representative of the father (a proxy father) or to a foster parent. Let me emphasize that each member of such a sibling group may be living with a different person, that is, the residence of each may have been determined on a separate basis. The possible complexities are reduced by the fact that comparatively few full sibling groups have more than three members.

While many foster children are claimed on the dissolution of their parents' marriage (as Table 8-6 shows) this is not in any sense a forced choice. In only two of the thirty-four cases were both parents dead, that is, in only two cases was residence with a parent not an alternative to fostering. And even in these two cases, residence with a proxy father remained a possibility.

Table 8-6. *Status of parents' marriage of thirty-four foster children in Buipe*

| Foster children: | Status of parents' marriage at initiation of fostering: | | | | | |
	Parents separated	Mother dead	Father dead	Both dead	Parents together*	Total
Male	4	2	6	1	3	16
Female	3	6	2	1	6	18
	7	8	8	2	9	34

* Three of the twenty-eight children of dissolved marriages (Table 8-5) to my knowledge joined foster parents while their parents were still living together. Others may have as well; the data are not complete.

When foster children are claimed on the dissolution of their parents' marriage, where do they go? When the mother dies, her kin might try to make good their loss by claiming a foster child from among the offspring of the union, and on the death of the father his kin might make the same demand. The figures in Tables 8-7 and 8-7a are too small to be conclusive, but certain trends are suggested. These differ, however, for male and female foster children.

So far as female foster children are concerned, the mother's kin appear to have more success in making good their claims, regardless of which parent has died. Thus of the eight girls in Buipe who have lost one parent and are living with foster parents, only one is with her father's kin. The picture is less clear for male foster children. While no boy has gone to his maternal kin on the death of his mother, male foster children seem more likely to go to maternal than paternal kin on the death of the father. This suggests the possibility that the mother's brother becomes

Table 8-7. *Relationship of residence of female foster children with kin of father or mother to status of parents' marriage*

| Child with: | Female foster children: | | | | | |
	Mother dead	Father dead	Both dead	Parents separated	Parents together	Total
Mother's kin	5	2	0	2	1	10
Father's kin	1	0	1	1	5	8
	6	2	1	3	6	18

the person with the greatest responsibility for a youth on the death of his father.

However, a consideration of male foster children gives an incomplete picture. As we saw in Table 8-5, residence with a proxy father was an alternative for five fatherless boys in the Buipe sample. These cases

Table 8-7a. *Relationship of residence of male foster children with kin of father or mother to status of parents' marriage*

| | Male foster children: | | | | | |
Child with:	Mother dead	Father dead*	Both dead	Parents separated	Parents together	Total
Mother's kin	0	4	0	1	1	6
Father's kin	2	2 (+5)	1	3	2	10 (+5)
	2	6 (+5)	1	4	3	16 (+5)

* Figure for boys resident with proxy parent given in brackets.

represent a successful claim by the father's kin and for this reason the figure has been entered in parenthesis in Table 8-7a. If those resident with a proxy father are included, it will be seen that the mother's kin may receive custody of the sons on the death of the father, but that they are not so likely to do so as are the kin of the father.

The one marked correspondence in the residence of sons and daughters of broken marriages is summarized in Table 8-8. This is the relationship between the sex of the foster child and the sex of the parent through which the fostering relationship is traced.

Table 8-8. *Children whose parents are no longer married: sex of child and whether with maternal or paternal kin*

| Child resident with kin of: | Sex of child: | | |
	Girls	Boys	
Mother	9	5	14
Father	3	8 (5)	11 (16)
	12	13 (18)	N=25 (30)

Girls are more likely to be fostered by maternal kin than by their father's relatives, while boys are more apt to be with paternal kin – either with a foster parent or a proxy parent – than with a relative of their mother's.

To recapitulate, the Gonja think of foster children as exemplifying the rights held by siblings in the children of a marriage; for example, the first daughter ought to go to the father's sister, and if there are three or more children, the second son is for the mother's brother. Moreover, they discuss the fostering of children as though this always occurred while the parents were living together. However, foster children are more likely than other children to be the issue of dissolved marriages, so that the institution of fostering also serves as a charter for claiming children by kin when a marriage ends.

CHANGES IN THE INCIDENCE OF FOSTERING

The question of the extent to which modern conditions have affected the traditional form of an institution is always a difficult one, because people often tend to feel that things were 'better in the old days'. But there is little doubt that ease of travel, with the introduction of roads, bicycles and lorries, and the freedom from bandits and slave raiders, has made it more difficult for the senior generation to impose its will on the young people. This mobility is frequently mentioned in connection with the lack of success of arranged marriages, and with the difficulty of keeping children with foster parents. The threat of running away to the South, the land of wonder and opportunity, is all too often carried out. The consequent reluctance to force children against their will would partly account for an apparent decline in fostering as compared to one or two generations ago. Of a group of sixteen adults for whom I have life histories, eleven had been brought up by foster parents. Of these eleven who were fostered, six were sent while their parents were still living together. Although the sample is very small, the proportions are surprisingly close to those found in several samples of adults from other parts of Gonja. The ages of the adults in these later samples ranged from twenty to eighty, and between 45% and 55% of each group had been fostered. Again, about half had been sent voluntarily, while the other half had been fostered following some family crisis (see Appendix IV). These more inclusive figures, showing about 50% of adults as having been fostered, give a reasonable approximation of the prevalence of the institution in the period immediately following the advent of colonial over-rule.

200

THE ENFORCEMENT OF FOSTERING OBLIGATIONS:
SANCTIONS

It would seem more difficult to be sure that a reluctant child remains with a foster parent today than it used to be. When foster children visit their own homes, or when their kin come to see them, complaints may be made and pleas lodged for a permanent return to their own parents. In the villages studied there were several children and young men and women who had lived for a time with foster parents, but who succeeded in persuading their kin that they ought not to be forced to remain. Some returned to their natal homes while others went to live with another relative. Significantly, most of those who succeed in leaving a fostering relationship have parents who are still married. This is far less important once a child reaches adolescence. Judging by the instances recorded in case histories, there must be several children and adolescents in the Buipe sample who have lived as foster children, but who had returned to their parents at the time of the census.

For the child who wants to return, there are two sources of support: his parents and the ancestors. Indeed, fostering is similar in a sense to cross-cousin marriage, in that both offer an opportunity to link siblings through the bringing together of their children. But both also create the risk that these very children will become a source of friction between the siblings, and of danger from ancestors if there is quarrelling between them. Two examples illustrate this. When Miama went to her father's sister as a foster child, no one was surprised to find that she found the situation difficult. A father's sister is expected to be more strict than a maternal kinswoman, and many girls have been through this experience, which is considered good for the character. However, when her father heard that the girl, who was about 14 at the time, had been beaten on the path when she could not carry her load of firewood any further, he was furious. He went himself to the village where his sister lived, ordered his daughter to follow him home, and told his sister that she could never expect another *kabita* from him. The open expression of anger between siblings is most unusual and gives some indication of the strength of feelings in this case.

The second example concerns a boy who had been sent to a maternal relative of his father's. He was also attending school in the village at the time, and found it difficult to study when his foster parent continually sent him on errands. When he fell sick, this illness was interpreted by his parents as being due to the annoyance of the dead that their descendants were quarrelling. It was decided that if the boy returned home, the

201

ancestral spirits would stop troubling him, because there would no longer be the daily friction between him and his father's 'brother' to anger them. In more general terms, the possibility that ancestral spirits may cause trouble is also recognized in the convention that, if a child runs three times to his parents, the ancestors do not wish him to remain with the foster parent. The advantage of introducing the ancestors into such a situation is clear: neither party need be judged at fault.

There is another aspect to the operation of sanctions which concerns the wider problem of why parents should agree to part with a child. I was once sitting talking with an older woman about fostering when her 'sister's' son, a youth of 18 or so, intervened saying, "I will never send a child of mine as *kabita* or *kaiyeribi*." My friend just smiled and replied that he should wait and see. When the time came, he would not be able to refuse. How does this work out? When the initiative comes from a would-be foster parent, the request is first put to the parent to whom he or she is related, and then that parent is expected to press the request with the other spouse. The major sanction behind the claims of the father and his kinsfolk (while the marriage endures) is based on the superior authority of men over women, and thus of husbands over their wives. Table 8-7 shows that five out of six of the girls sent to foster parents during the time their parents were married went to paternal kin. Once the parents have separated the situation is reversed, with nine out of twelve going to the kin of the mother.

The same pattern appears for male foster children (Table 8-7a), but here we can also see the intervention of another factor. Even excluding those boys living with proxy parents, there are more with paternal than with maternal kin. This is the more puzzling because the Gonja explicitly identify a male foster child and a sister's son in concept and in conversation. But even stronger is the identification between a boy and his father. It is through his father that he will succeed to his place in the political structure of the society, that is to primary citizenship and to office. He is a member of the same social estate as is his father, and whoever rears him, and wherever he grows up, it is to his father that he is expected to return. And it will be one of his father's kinsmen who on his death inherits not only his property but responsibility for his children. Since final authority over the children as a group remains vested in their paternal kinsmen, it is not surprising that foster children more frequently go to paternal kin.

Although female foster children also remain under the final authority of paternal kin, primary citizenship and adult roles in the political domain are much less important for them than for their brothers. There are a few exceptions among the daughters of chiefs, but for the most part women function in the domestic domain. It is perhaps for this reason that paternal kin do not press claims to girls with the same success as they do their claims to boys, who will ultimately succeed to their positions in the community.

How then does it happen that maternal kin ever succeed in claiming male foster children? The primary sanction for such claims lies in the fear of the maternal ancestors. For it is held that only the ancestors of the mother (*niupe bubini*) can cause death. Mystical trouble (*mbusu*) may come through the ancestors of either parent but, while that mediated by the ancestors of the father may be inconvenient, it is said never to be fatal. This theme recurs constantly in a variety of contexts. It is cited to explain the widely felt reluctance to marry cross-cousins. It serves as the charter for norms of conduct between kinsmen; a father's brother may abuse his brother's child with impunity, but a mother's brother and sister's son dare not quarrel lest they be killed by the anger of their ancestors. It is to fear of the boy's maternal ancestors that the Gonja attribute the fact that a man could not sell his own son into slavery to pay a debt but might so use his sister's son. For the debt is no concern of his wife's kin whose refusal to agree to the loss of one of their children on this account will be supported by their ancestors. The mother and her brother, on the other hand, share the same ancestors who have a common interest in the welfare of their descendants. And since it is primarily maternal ancestors who are to be feared, the Gonja feel that to refuse a man's legitimate claim to a sister's son as foster child would be to endanger the boy's life.

Indeed, this sanction can be invoked whenever there is a dispute over jurisdiction of children. When MoroWura's daughter died of malaria, he insisted that it was through the spite of her maternal ancestors because he had refused to let the girl go to the dead mother's sister as a foster child. The maternal kin, however, had quite a different view of things; so far as they were concerned, one might expect this to happen when a man insisted on keeping a child under the care of a co-wife of her dead mother.

One of the clearest indications that foster children represent claims on the sibling group as a whole lies in the belief that failure to fulfil fostering obligations to maternal kin will jeopardize the safety of the entire sibling group. Nyiwuleji, one of the few Busunu men of the Muslim estate, accounted for the institution of kinship fostering in the following way: "First you take a wife and make her pregnant. If she is sick, you pray to God and perform the rites necessary to send away the

203

trouble. And if she brings forth and the child is good, you get medicines to help it grow strong. The father's people take two (children) and the mother's people take two. Now Europeans insist that a man owns all the children, but we used to divide. If not, all the children will die because of trouble sent by the mother's ancestors."

It appears, then, that the father and his kin retain control over the children through the combined influence of (1) possession, following from the fact that marriage is virilocal; (2) the authority exercised by a man over his wife; and (3) the recognition by all parties that the ultimate identification of a boy with his father is among the strongest of all influences upon him. The maternal kin do, however, succeed in pressing claims to boys, and more frequently to girls. The most effective sanction they have is the threat from their maternal ancestors to all the children of the union should the father refuse a legitimate claim. That maternal kin more often foster girls than boys seems to be related to the strong identification between a woman and her daughters and a correspondingly slighter emphasis on the tie between a woman and her paternal home. This last is clearly the corollary of the minor role which women play in the political system. While the paternal home is the touchstone to office for their brothers, only very occasionally do they have such interests there.

THE POSITIVE SIDE: IMMEDIATE AND LONG-TERM ADVANTAGES IN FOSTERING

While these sanctions may help to explain why parents can be brought to part with their child, it is only one side of the problem of persistence. For to adult Gonja, the institution of fostering is seen as having many advantages, some of which benefit the parents, some of which work to the advantage of the foster parents, and others for the child itself.

In the case of female foster children, these gains are fairly straightforward. If the girl goes to a kinswoman of her mother's this can only be at the mother's wish, either because she has been convinced that the child's help is needed, or perhaps because she wishes to take only her infant child with her on entering into a new marriage. A father's reasons for wishing to send a daughter to his sister are more complex. Akurɔ put it this way: "You give a child to your sister, the one who follows you and listens well to you. You trust her well. The mother's people won't keep the child as it pleases you but in their own ways . . . That is why they divide. The mother's people will teach them their secrets and the father's people will teach them theirs." This is an unusually clear expression of the consequences of a marriage between members of different estates; however close their personal relationship, the partners still view one another as belonging to a group whose ways are alien. Thus a man knows that his wife will bring up their children in the ways of her people ('teach them her people's secrets'), and this will affect girls more strongly than their brothers, for children above the age of 6 or 7 spend most of their time with members of their own sex. It is inevitably women, and particularly the mother or foster mother, who will teach girls not only how to carry out their domestic tasks, but how to be adults. By sending a daughter to his sister, a man ensures that she learns these things after the manner of his own people.

Table 8-9. *Ages of male and female foster parents*

Age of foster parent:	Women fostering girls	Men fostering boys
25–39	6	—
40–54	4	7
55 and over	8	9
	18	16

N=34

Female foster children go both to women who are in the process of rearing their own families, and to older women whose children have grown and married. The women in Buipe currently fostering children were fairly evenly distributed between young, middle-aged, and older women; foster mothers may clearly belong to any of these three categories (Table 8-9).

When a woman is infirm or is tied down by several young children, the services of a foster daughter are very welcome. The tasks of carrying firewood and water, most often delegated to the older girls, are tiring and may involve carrying heavy loads for several miles. For the older woman particularly, a foster child may mean the difference between an assured supply of these necessities and an uneasy dependence on the other women of the compound. Where a woman has returned in old age to live with her kin she will be in a much stronger position if she has her own *kabita* with her. As with a woman who has never borne children of her own, but is still young and strong, she values a foster child both for the companionship and for the help.

205

Here it must be remembered that a valid claim to foster children exists only when they have more than one sibling. Thus, they do not represent too great a loss to the labour force of their natal domestic group. However, it does happen that a daughter goes away as a foster child just at the point when she might have begun to help, leaving her mother with several younger children, none of whom is old enough to contribute much assistance. The mother may at best be able to delay her daughter's departure by a few months. If she is lucky, she may be able to claim a foster child to replace her. There was one instance in which the foster child arrived on the very day when the woman's own daughter herself joined a foster parent. In another, an older woman about to give birth was able to borrow her daughter, being fostered at a village about fifteen miles away, to help her with preparations, but only for a few days. She had to return before the birth occurred, though an older paternal half-sibling came later from another village to help with the cooking for the household.

As we have seen, it is often the case that fostered girls come from domestic groups which have dispersed following the death or divorce of a parent. Sometimes the mother would prefer her daughter to stay with her, but it is felt that earlier promises, particularly those made by a dead father, should be honoured at this time. Often the mother is relieved not to have to bring older children with her into a new marriage. For, while a daughter does offer a certain amount of assistance with domestic chores, she may also be a potential source of friction in the new family.

The situation with regard to male foster children is in many respects quite different. While a woman also wishes to see a son brought up in the ways of her own people, she lacks the authority to enforce her preference. The effectiveness of her ancestors' wrath may well be deferred until some illness or accident to one of the children reminds their father of its power. It is again significant that the claims of maternal kin are held to apply only to a second or third son. That is, they do not come into force until there are several children, any one of whom may become the target of such supernatural retribution.

On the other hand the father has less to lose, and the male foster parent less to gain, so far as the transfer of the labour of a son is concerned. Until their early teens boys do little on the farm except run errands and take turns at scaring away birds and monkeys during the time when the grain is ripening. From then on their contribution increases until the man with two or three sons in their twenties need do no farming unless he wishes. However, the Gonja never force a boy to go to the farm. Or rather, they may carry him, protesting, along the path when he first refuses to accompany a hoeing or weeding party, and even repeat this once again. But it is held to be useless to force a youth three times against his will. Subtler pressures are of course applied, and he who consistently remains at home while others farm is known publicly as a lazy man (*tɔlpo*). Yet several times I remarked on the presence of youths lounging about the village during a busy farming season only to be told that, if they did not wish to go to the farm, it was impossible to force them. The import of this for fostering lies in the fact that the period when a boy begins to be of some use about the farm is also the point at which his independence of movement must be reckoned with. If he chooses to farm for a foster parent, then his help will be considerable; if he declines to go to the farm, or works sporadically, criticism or discipline may cause him to return to his paternal home. Thus, while it is true that boys may remain until a much later age with a foster parent than is the case with the female foster child who inevitably leaves at marriage, his return is always a contingent possibility. Even where the youth's own father is dead, a proxy father always provides an alternative residence.

So far as the labour of a male foster child is concerned, it is doubtful whether he earns his keep for several years. Thereafter his contribution may be sizeable, but how long he will continue to help is problematic. In agreeing to part with him the father is as aware of this as the foster parent, who tempers his discipline with caution.

As with a fostered daughter, the foster father has prior claim, even where the father needs his son's help. The elderly ZabogoWura was himself no longer able to farm, but he had three sons of 18, 15 and 12, as well as a wife and young daughter. Three such youths could have farmed enough for the family's needs had they all worked together. However, the eldest and youngest boys were both with foster parents in different towns, leaving Lansa, the fifteen-year old, to manage as best he could. The oldest son paid a visit to his parents in October, as the grain was beginning to ripen. There was little he could do to help them, except to join his brother in scaring birds and monkeys from the fields. His father hoped that his mother's mother's brother, by whom he was being reared, would allow him to stay and help with the harvest. But he sent for the boy, saying his help was needed 'at home'. The harvest was gathered successfully, but only by calling neighbours to help in return for a large harvest meal. This meal in turn meant substantially less grain to store for the six months until the first yams ripen. An economically 'rational' allocation of the ZabogoWura's sons would have kept at least the two oldest at home to farm for their father in his old age. In the event, the claims of their maternal 'grandfather' were stronger than those of the father himself.

The possibility that a youth may remain with his foster parent in adulthood raises the question of the implications of fostering on the juro-political level. For while female fostering relationships terminate at marriage, and pertain in any case to the domestic level, the fostering of boys concerns a relationship between and about males and might be expected to have implications within the wider, external, sphere.

There are two ways in which this might occur. First, foster children might be monopolized by the higher status groups in such a way as to increase the followers of important chiefs and religious leaders. This concentration could easily come about in the ruling estate if commoners who had Gbanya wives systematically sent their sons to their chiefly mother's brothers in the hope of securing preferment. Something of this kind appears to be institutionalized among the Mossi of Upper Volta (Skinner 1964). The distribution of cases in Table 8-10 suggests that in Gonja this does not occur, however, and that foster parents and their wards are to be found in all three estates. This is what one would predict for a system in which marriage between estates is the rule, and fostering relationships determined by kinship roles.

That there is only one case of a foster parent of the ruling estate, despite the presence in Buipe of several Gbanya chiefs, is clear evidence that there is no great concentration in chiefly households. It is true that the senior Buipe chief, the BuipeWura, is omitted from this list since he was living in New Buipe. He had one adolescent foster child as well as the adult *kaiyeribi* referred to below. Observation of senior chiefs in other divisions confirms that while they do have foster children (the MankpaWura had two, as did the BusunuWura), they do not have a disproportionately high number.

However, it is also possible that the important factors determining who receives foster children are such attributes of achieved status as wealth and political office, rather than the ascriptive status represented by estate membership. There is a certain amount of evidence to support this suggestion. In Busunu, two commoners who each had more than two foster children were the two wealthiest men in the village, although neither held political office. In Buipe two men had between them seven wards. One of them, the KagbapeWura, was the senior commoner chief of the Gonja state. The four foster children with him and the three with Jina, the Buipe spokesman, were all there by virtue of kinship ties. But in selecting among possible foster parents, the choice went to kinsmen whose position in the community made it likely that the boys would eat well and be in a position to observe the affairs of important men. Nine men acted as foster parents to the remaining nine male foster children; all of these men, and the two mentioned above, had sons of their own.

Table 8-10. *Relationship between estates of foster parent and foster child*

Male foster children

Estate of foster parent:	Ruling	Muslim	Commoner	Not known	Total
Ruling	1	—	—	—	1
Muslim	1	4	4	—	9
Commoner	2	1	2	1	6
	4	5	6	1	

N=16

Female foster children

Estate of foster parent:	Ruling	Muslim	Commoner	Not known	Total
Ruling	2	—	1	1	4
Muslim	1	3	1	1	6
Commoner	—	1	7	—	8
	3	4	9	2	

N=18

For the child, the basic function of fostering is educational; the teaching of skills, the ways of parents' kin, the ways of the world. Perhaps this fact is made inevitable by the absence (at least in the beginning) of the affective content which characterizes relations with the child's own parents. There remains the instrumental, training, aspect for the foster parents' role.[5] It is certainly the training received which is

[5] I have considered the various components of the parent–child role relationship in some detail in E. Goody, 1971.

stressed as the main advantage to the foster child. Usually such training is part of the daily routine of domestic work and farming. Fortes' description of the direct link between the child's world and that of the adult in his discussion of education in Taleland (Fortes 1938) is entirely appropriate here. Occasionally training assumes a specialized form, as when Muslim boys are expected to attend daily lessons in the Koran. The senior Muslims in Buipe were both too old to have pupils, but among those who did a number had foster children who were also pupils.

Specialized teaching is the second way in which fostering might impinge on the politico-jural domain. Unlike the Dagomba, their neighbours to the northeast (Oppong 1965), the Gonja do not regularly send their sons as foster children to learn the craft skills of their maternal kin. Nor are drumming or divining passed on in this way. Occasionally, however, a chief may arrange that his son go to another chief in a different territorial division, to 'learn chiefship'. Such a one was Denkeri who lived in the BuipeWura's old compound in Buipe. A man of about 30, he farmed for his wife and child and apparently acted as the BuipeWura's 'eyes and ears' during his absence in New Buipe. He had been sent as a boy by his 'father', the old chief of Kawsawgu, in order to get a wider experience of the ways of chiefs than if he had remained at home. Neither the MangpaWura nor the BusunuWura was currently participating in fostering relationships of this sort when I knew them. However, the current chief of Daboya division had lived with the present MangpaWura's father when he was MangpaWura many years ago.

The practice of sending a chief's son to live at another divisional court coincides with the custom that young men of the ruling estate should spend some part of their political minority visiting their kin in other parts of the kingdom. This is held to fulfil the dual purpose of avoiding the attacks of witches at home, and of familiarizing them with the system within which they may eventually hold office. This 'roaming about' is not usually begun until after adolescence and provides a man with an alternative to living and working as an adult under the authority of his father.

However, the significance of fostering in reinforcing the tie between two divisional chiefs must not be overemphasized. There are few ways that such an alliance can benefit directly those who establish it. Except for Sister's Son chiefships, there is no possibility of succession between divisions, save to the paramountcy itself. Furthermore, since succession is often deferred until middle age, it is unlikely that foster child and foster parent will both occupy their respective divisional chiefships simultaneously, even supposing that the foster child should actually reach this office. Indeed, in order to ensure their sons friends in high places, each dynastic segment of a division's ruling estate would have to send foster children to all the dynastic segments of the other divisions. The figures in Table 8-10 make it very plain that this does not occur. There were several minor chiefs representing both segments of the ruling estate resident in Buipe. None of these men had a foster child from the ruling estate of another division.

The use of the term for male foster child (*kaiyeribi*) in the context of non-kin fostering arrangements between the chiefs of different divisions is an illustration of the wider usage this word occasionally receives. In certain contexts a political subordinate may be referred to as a chief's *kaiyeribi*, and here the sense is of someone who attends on the chief, and may render him small services. In the larger villages of central Gonja one of the younger men is usually given the unofficial title of KaiyeribiWura, and the role of leading the youths and 'young men' (*mberantia*) in such task as the clearing of paths or preparing the chief's farm.[6]

Although we have seen that it has both economic and political aspects, it would be a mistake to try to reduce kinship fosterage to either a primarily economic or a primarily political institution. It is more than either of these. The emphasis on the difference between the ways of maternal and paternal kin represents another level on which fostering has effects throughout the system, through the maintenance of kinship ties. There are several ways in which this happens. Fostering acts to reinforce the bonds between physically dispersed kinsmen who may live in villages anywhere from two to two hundred miles apart; it serves to bridge the gap between generations by giving a more concrete meaning to the ties of classificatory siblingship between first and second cousins; and it helps to diminish the social distance between estates by familiarizing members of each with the ways (the 'secrets') of the others. People assume that each patronymic group has its own ways, and there are a number of minor differences in ritual and diet which tend to reinforce this view. Yet in fact the degree of cultural uniformity in central Gonja, and indeed in the state as a whole, is quite striking considering the varied origins of the population. It is probable that the

---

[6] This collectivity of younger men has certain affinities with the *mmerantia* (Young-men) of Ashanti, but lacks their political role in approving the choice of a new chief. *Kaberantia* in Gbanyito is also used as a general term for a young or middle-aged adult male who holds no office.

combined effects of open connubium and fostering largely account for the high degree of cultural uniformity observed.

Each of these dimensions, physical space, genealogical distance between generations, and the social distance between members of different estates, constitutes a potential limitation to the extent and integration of the bilateral kinship system. Should kinship ties cease to be of importance between villages and different territorial divisions; should they cease to be traced between collaterals of successive generations except where those concerned also lived in the same community, then the local community would become even more important, and much more isolated, than it is now.

Given the great and lasting importance of the sibling bond it follows that the experience of one member of a sibling group is in a sense available to the others. But the diffusion of the experiences derived from the fostering situation is not only accomplished vicariously, for the visiting which is such a prominent part of the Gonja scene ensures that children, adolescents, and adults spend time in the households where their siblings are staying. A child who is living with a parent's sibling or parent's parent will visit his natal kin as frequently as he can, joining a party of adults who are going in that direction, or sending a message asking that someone come and meet him on the path, if the distance is not great. And his stay-at-home brothers and sisters will look for a chance to come and join his household for a while, whenever they can prevail upon their parents to spare them from domestic or farming chores. Such visits take on added glamour as courting becomes the dominant pastime in adolescence. Both boys and girls express a preference for finding partners outside the village where they have grown up, and trips to neighbouring villages provide an excellent opportunity to do so.

Finally, it is the hope of parent and foster parent alike that the child may marry in his foster home. Although the senior generation complain that they can no longer enforce such marriages, the chances are still good that this will happen. A male foster child is more likely to do so because of the help given by the foster parent in arranging a youth's first marriage. But even if the parental generation takes no part, the role played by courtship is such that a spouse is most likely to be selected from the village in which a child grows to marriageable age.[7]

Where such marriages do occur the cycle begins again. Fostering may

[7] The figures given in chapter 4 might seem to contradict this. However, they refer to the villages of the fathers of marriage partners, and not to the villages in which the pair were living at the time their marriage was contracted.

be said to have permanently, rather than temporarily, reinforced kinship ties within the sibling group. This is so whether or not the marriage is to a kinsman, for contiguity is of prime importance in determining the content of kinship ties. Where a foster child marries and brings up his own family in the village of his foster parent, those aspects of kinship roles which are dependent on contiguity will have meaning there and there only. Furthermore, the kin of his foster parent will be known to and meaningful for a man's children, which is generally not the case where two generations have intervened since more than casual contact occurred.

Any analysis of an institution must take into account the actual pattern as well as the ideal type. As we have seen, many fostering relationships involve children whose parents have separated. Kinship fostering in Gonja clearly provides the model on the basis of which claims are made by the kin of each parent to the offspring of a marriage; and this is the model employed whether the marriage is intact or whether it has dissolved. Hence, to discuss fostering is to discuss claims to jurisdiction over children during their minority which is pre-eminently a matter of the rights and duties defining kinship roles. It is for this reason that the institution cannot be fully understood except in the context of kinship.

It is to the analysis of kinship roles that the following chapter is devoted. Various aspects of the key kinship roles have been referred to in the course of the discussions of village and domestic organization, marriage and fostering, mainly aspects having to do with rights and duties attendant on co-residence. While the next chapter will deal with these briefly, it will be primarily concerned with those obligations of kinship which are independent of contiguity.

213

9

Kinship and sibship

The Gonja kinship system is organized, like all others, on a bilateral base. That is to say, besides the ties of conjugality and affinity that flow from marriage, there are ties of filiation to mother and father and to sons and daughters. In addition, there are ties to one's own siblings as well as to the siblings of one's parents and to the parents of parents, and to the children of siblings and of parents' siblings. Relatives reckoned in this way, with respect to a central actor, constitute an 'ego-oriented kindred'. In a few social contexts the descendants of one person through both males and females may be relevant for specific purposes; in this case we have what is formally a 'descending kindred'. However, while it is possible to describe such units in Gonja, they are of peripheral importance as groups. What we find in practice is a range of kin extending from ego and merging into non-kin. Indeed, the distinction between kin and non-kin is not at all clear. After about two generations from living persons specific genealogical ties cease to be important. This is because intermediate links become vague. After this point people are classified by the kin terms in daily use. But as there is often doubt as to which term to use, and as this doubt tends to be resolved by selecting the term most appropriate to the age and generation status of those concerned, this sort of reckoning cannot be considered as genealogical.

BASA ('RELATIVES')

It seems best to begin with an analysis of the categories used by the Gonja themselves for classifying kin. The word ordinarily used for 'people' in Gbanyito is *basa* (sing. *esa*). This has a number of forms. It is used for 'human beings' in general (*enyen basa*), as well as to refer collectively to any group one seeks to identify with, as "all Gonja are one people" (*Gbanyabi kike le basa konle na*). It also simply means people, as "all the people had gone home" (*basa kike ba dan yope na*). A very frequently heard usage, however, is the same as the English 'relatives'. "My mother's relatives" (*n'niu ba basa*) or "he is my relative" (*m'esa na*) are examples.

Used in the sense of 'relative', *basa* (like the English term) can mean either one or a few relatives, or it can be used to designate a collectivity. In both Gbanyito and English one can say "My relatives are arriving tomorrow", and mean not that every relation is coming, but that an unspecified sub-set is going to appear. We can equally well use the collective meaning, as when one says, "My mother's relatives are very generous (or from Yorkshire)." Relatives, in one or another sense, are constantly referred to in conversation. The term is as ubiquitous as it is imprecise.

When the term for relatives is used collectively for all a person's kin, it corresponds to an ego-oriented kindred, since the reference is from ego outward in all directions. However, more commonly a person will designate a sub-set of relatives to which he is linked through a particular parent or grandparent. "They are my father's mother's people" or "My mother's relatives come from that village." Here the speaker sees himself as belonging to the personal kindred of a parent or grandparent, and this is expressed by citing the filial link with the person from whom the kindred is reckoned.

This usage, which treats each parent's own ego-centred kindred as a separate set of relatives linked directly to ego, is illustrated by an argument about whether a person has four or six *basa*, which my questions precipitated. One man contended that he belonged to four kin sets (*n' kɔ basa ana*): to the people of his father's father, and those of his father's mother, and the kin of his mother's father and those of his mother's mother. "No", said a bystander, "you must have six because there are the relatives (i.e. affines and descendants) of your father himself and also your mother's." Both these men were using *basa* to describe a range of kin reckoned with respect to individuals of senior generations. The first man considered that he was a member of four such sets of which his father belonged to two and his mother to the other two. His friend's contention that six sets of kin were involved gave implicit recognition to the fact that for his own children, the perspective would be different. The argument was finally resolved by agreeing that the father's descendants were to be identified with his father's *basa* and the mother's with her mother's kin.

That the number of distinct sets of kin should be a matter for argument is itself significant, for it underlines the fact that the relatives being collectively designated as 'one people' (*basa konle*) have no existence as a group apart from their various relationships to ego's parents.

This conceptualization of kin into those related through particular

215

parents and grandparents is reflected in the frequently made distinction between mother's kin (*niu pebi*) and father's kin (*ntuto pebi*).[1] Both these terms have a strong element of identification with locality – the village and division from which the parent in question came. But because such a kin set tends to be dispersed throughout several villages the spatial referent is only metaphorically inclusive of all the kin concerned. In fact a person's identification with the village in which he was born gives rise to a form of quasi-kinship. Thus, if a man's mother came from Buipe, the town is 'his mother's town' (*mu niu pe*), and the town's people presumed to be his kin, although he may not know how they are all related to her. It is in this sense that a man will maintain that the people of Buipe are his *basa* and mean by this something very different than when he uses the same term to identify his parents' full siblings and their children.

The material on marriage patterns (chapter 4) makes it clear that most people will have relatives in more than one estate, since two marriages in three were between a husband and wife of different estates. It is also true that many people will have kin in different villages and even different divisions. The proportion of marriages within the town of Buipe itself varied by estate from 24% for commoners to 41% for Muslims, with the ruling group intermediate at 31%. Villages outside the capitals are smaller, and marriages more frequently between villages. Children of such marriages will have kin sets identified with two or even three estates, and with a number of villages. If their kinsfolk are considered individually, even more estates and villages will be represented.

Relatives can thus be thought of collectively as sets or ranges of kin identified with each of four grandparents, or in many contexts as only the two opposed sets of 'mother's kin' and 'father's kin'. In this case there is a spatial referent. Although a person will know that all the kin of a given set do not actually live in a given village, in speaking collectively a local focus is assumed. This usage is a reflection of the fact that citizenship rights (for some primary, for others secondary) are defined in terms of this locality.

Relatives are also individuals. "My father's brother's son, Maman, with whom I grew up" or "My mother's sister, Hawa, who used to visit at Damba time but died last year." In this particularistic usage, the

---

[1] In *Gbanyito* the word *pebi* is a compound of *pe* meaning 'place' and *mbia* meaning 'children'. Thus *Buipebi* (a contracted form) means 'children of Buipe'. It is in this sense that *niupebi* means both 'people of mother's place (town)' and 'mother's kin'. *Pebi* is often used to mean people, in the sense of 'people of . . .'.

primary identity of a given relative is less important than individual attributes: Maman with whom I grew up; My 'small mother' Hawa who died last year.

The importance of the local focus of the kin sets identified with parents (and sometimes with parents' parents) can perhaps best be suggested by referring to these as locally anchored ranges of kin, though the wider reference clearly includes non-kin as well.

KANANG ('FAMILY')

The central connotation of relatives (in the collective sense) is of an open, unbounded set of kin. When a different emphasis is intended the collective term used is *kanang*, which I have translated as 'family'. Like family in English, *kanang* in fact is used of a group whose limits are unclear, but where the sense of unity is important. Thus, one often hears the phrase, "we are one family" (*anye le kanang konle*), in explanation of some other shared feature, perhaps a physical resemblance or a common dietary prohibition. The expression for marriage to a kinswoman, for instance, is *kanang ta etche*, "to take a wife in the family". As the discussion of preferred kinship marriages will have shown, such a wife is thought of as a cross-cousin, a close relative, but specifically not unilineal kin.

Sometimes, however, 'family' is used for a dynastic segment of the ruling estate, or for a localized element of one of the Muslim patronymic groups (both usually referred to as *mbuna*, 'gates'). When this happens an agnatic slant is given to the term. For instance, it is felt that all members of the ruling estate are descendants in the agnatic line of the founder of the kingdom, NdeWura Jakpa. In some contexts all dynastic segments of the ruling estate are referred to as one family (*kanang konle*), as when it is said that the family (*kanang*) of Jakpa do not lie, for fear of his spirit.

The commoner groups in central Gonja identify themselves by their original languages (a number of which are no longer spoken) by traditions of local origin, and by special relationships with the Earth or other shrines. A few have specialist occupations; where, as with ferrymen and blacksmiths, these are small in number and identified by a special greeting, the patronymic group may in certain contexts be termed a *kanang*. Most commoner groups are not internally differentiated in this way, however. In these cases, an office tends to go from father to son (or sometimes from a man to his sister's son) without being associated with a wider kin group; kinship ties are associated simply with anchored kin ranges identified with each parent or grandparent.

MBUNA ('GATES')

The word used for a doorway into a council hall or a private room is *kabuna*, which we have rendered as 'gate'. In eastern Gonja the main entrance into a compound is through the large reception room of the head; in some cases this is the only entry. Here the gate to the hall is also the gate to the compound. In western Gonja the same pattern in fact exists, although the architectural forms are very different. But in central Gonja there is no such restricted access to a compound (see diagrams in chapters 3 and 10), though the metaphor of the 'gate' is still prominent. In a political context this same word, *mbuna*, is used to designate the dynastic segments from which divisional chiefs are taken in turn. And on the national level, the divisions which supply the paramount are also referred to as gates. The vividness of the metaphor was expressed in the traditional layout of the cemetery in which the paramount chiefs of Gonja are buried. There used to be a wall surrounding the cemetery, which lies on the outskirts of Mankuma, a village near the capital which has important ritual associations with the paramountcy. In this surrounding wall a separate gate was cut for each division from which a paramount had come. When a YagbumWura died, it was through the gate of his own division that he was carried to his grave, just as it had been through the gate of his dynastic segment that he had succeeded to the chiefship of his natal division, and through the gate of this divisional chiefship that he succeeded to the paramountcy itself.

Within the division, there are usually two or three dynastic segments (or gates) of the ruling estates. Each is known by name. Sometimes this is a name associated with the putative founder, but in other cases it is the chiefship name of a relatively recent divisional chief from that segment. Each gate usually maintains a compound in the divisional capital, and in a political context the compound as well as the segment may be referred to by the same name.

The patronymic groups of Muslims are not usually differentiated internally in this way. The Sakpari Muslims in Buipe are a partial exception to this rule, for there are two *de facto* gates to the office of divisional Limam. However, while *kabuna* can be used to describe two segments of the Buipe Sakpari, this term is rarely heard. The same holds true of a few of the commoner priesthoods. The idiom of gates is used in describing succession where this alternates between two groups, or

218

circulates among several. The right to hold chiefship is the main identifying characteristic of the ruling estate, and the gates to office are important in organizing relations between segments and with the other estates. For the Muslims and commoners, office plays a less central role, and gates are correspondingly less important.

SIBLINGS AND THE 'SIBLING GROUP'

SIBLING TERMINOLOGY

The prototype of solidary relations in the Gonja idiom is *niu pibi* (literally, 'mother's children'). Latent hostility is recognized to exist between paternal half-siblings; in fact the quarrelling between co wives is often laid to this cause. Their children fight and, in taking each the part of their own offspring, the mothers fall to abusing one another. But between maternal siblings, whether full or half-siblings, such hostility is disclaimed and in any case cannot be openly expressed. The fact that behaviour between siblings is strictly prescribed has the effect of minimizing such tensions. Thus an older brother or sister may correct, chide, or even abuse a younger sibling of either sex and the latter ought to accept this in good grace. This submission is the more significant as the Gonja are such a proud people that failure to chastise – either physically or else by taking to court – a person who abuses you is considered a crime against your kinsfolk and an indication of lack of character (*da*). Yet, if an older sibling abuses a younger it is done, the Gonja say, only that the latter may learn the correct way to behave. Under no circumstances may the younger lift his hand against his senior, or return his abuse. Should he feel anger about to overcome his self-restraint, it is better to run away.

It is to minimize the possibility of quarrelling between siblings that the Gonja never allow two sisters to marry the same man, or to marry two brothers; nor may a man marry a girl and her first cousin, at any time. In other words, the prohibition endures even after the death of the first wife. The same repugnance is expressed at the notion of a man sleeping with his brother's wife as is characteristic of the thought of sexual relations between brother and sister. Indeed, it is said that in either case both man and woman would die. An indication of the degree of identification between full siblings is to be found in Supini Wuritche's statement, illogical as it appears to the outsider, that, "If a man were to sleep with the wife of a full brother, it would be the same thing as sleeping with his own sister, because if your brother were a woman and both were to sleep with the same person, it is as though they had slept with each other." She went on to say that this would also be true for either maternal or paternal half-siblings.

So strongly is the term 'mother's children' identified with affectionate, positive and dependable relations that it is applied in conversation to all close kin, to all those related in any way through the mother, to the people of the mother's village, and often of her estate, and to close friends who are not related at all. It is derogatory to apply its complement, 'father's children', to one's father's kin except in explaining a particular relationship. To use 'father's children' in a general sense would be to define relationships as relatively distant, less warm and dependable than if the term for 'mother's children' had been employed. As one man explained, "We Gonja, we don't say father's children, all are mother's children – anybody, from either your father's side or your mother's side."

There is one further distinction possible within the category 'sibling'. This is based on the opposition between the children of same sex siblings (parallel cousins) and the children of siblings of opposite sex (cross-cousins). The Gonja speak of the joking between cross-cousins as occurring between women's children (*etche pibi*) and men's children (*enyen pibi*), when they say that women's children and men's children play together. The same relationship can be expressed descriptively as 'father's sister's children and mother's brother's children play' (*tana pibi ni wopa pibi, ba pol na*). Cross-cousins are the prototypical joking relatives (*mitcherpo*) in Gonja.

Both parallel and cross-cousins are ordinarily referred to and addressed as elder or young siblings (*da* or *supo*). Parallel cousins may be described as "child of my (younger or older) father" or "child of my (younger or older) mother". In exactly the same way, cross-cousins may be described as "child of my father's sister" or "child of my mother's brother". Such clumsy forms are not used in address, only in explaining a particular relationship as when the ethnographer asks, "Why are you joking with that man?" Here the answer, "He is a child of my mother's brother", is felt to be self-explanatory. For with one's mother's brother's children and one's father's sister's children, playful abuse, sexual allusion and the appropriation of small personal items are allowed and enjoyed. Marriage is permitted with this category of classificatory siblings, in spite of the fact that the Gonja simultaneously maintain that to marry or have sexual relations with siblings is forbidden.[2]

[2] See chapter 4 for discussion of cross-cousin marriage.

220

However, in day-to-day life there is little difference in behaviour between parallel and cross-cousins. True, there is an element of joviality in the behaviour of the former which is absent in that of the latter, but 'siblings' of both sorts are sought out for companionship in the evening, to aid in some task (such as the clearing of new farm land or the preparation of a batch of shea butter) and for advice and support when difficult decisions are to be made.

This situation is reflected in the complete absence of any kinship terms which indicate degree or extension of a relationship. All siblings, half-siblings and cousins, indeed all those of a man's own generation whom he considers kin are his 'siblings'; all those of his parents' generation are 'parents' siblings' of various kinds and all those of the next ascending generation, 'grandparents'. The same principle applies to kin of descending generations – a man's own and his 'siblings' children are alike 'children', and their children, his 'grandchildren'.

The terminological grouping of kin by generation in the typical Hawaiian pattern reflects the fact that intra-generational alignments, that is, sibling groups, are structurally of great importance in Gonja kinship relations.

Terminologically, the sibling group is internally differentiated by its members on the basis of two principles which are to some extent contradictory: sex and age. There is a single term, *da*, used both in reference and address for all older siblings, and another, *supo*, for those who are younger. In addition, the standard suffixes for male and female, *enyen* and *etche*, may be added to indicate sex. Genealogical position is extremely important, for within the sibling group the younger must defer to the older, the latter succeeding to office and inheriting property first, and being followed in turn by their younger siblings. However, it is held also that "women are always younger", as one informant expressed it. That is, they neither hold nor transmit full rights in office, and hold modified rights in inheritance, although full rights to certain sorts of property pass through them. Most important, both political and domestic authority are primarily the concern of men.

Thus, while men always refer to an elder brother as *nda* (my elder brother) and a younger brother as *nsupo* (my younger brother), they may refer to all their sisters, younger and older, as *nsuputche* (my younger female sibling). If, however, a sister is several years older, or if her brother wishes to show his respect for her, he will call her *nda* or occasionally (in reference) *ndatcheso* (elder female sibling). Although the compound term *ndanyeniso* ought to be possible, I have never heard it.

221

To recapitulate, within a man's own generation all his kin are designated both in reference and address as either elder sibling (*da*) or younger sibling (*supo*). The closest sibling ties are felt to exist between mother's children, and this positively valued term of reference has an extended use, being applied to the following categories of kin: full siblings, maternal half-siblings, maternal cross and parallel cousins, anyone related through ego's mother and, by courtesy, to any kinsman and to close personal friends.

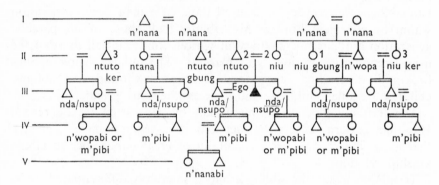

Fig. 6 Kin terms of reference: male ego. Generation II: numbers indicate birth order. Generation III: either *nda* or *nsupo* for all siblings regardless of sex depending on age with respect to ego. *Nda* if ego is younger, *nsupo* if ego is older. All forms are inflected in the first person singular.

The mutual obligations obtaining between siblings are those which one would expect to find between close kinsmen of the same generation. While within the sibling group respect is due from junior to senior, the general character of sibling relations is egalitarian companionship, solidarity in time of trouble, and economic, jural and ritual support in time of need. In a very real sense, the universe of a man's kin is structured in terms of sibling groups. As a child, it is the sibling groups centering around his father and mother, and to some extent those of his grandparents, which are important; their rights in one another's children are probably the single most significant factor in maintaining the solidarity of the sibling group. As a man's generation matures, the central role of his parents' siblings yields to that played by his own, and this in turn is reinforced by the rights he claims in their children, and they in his. Thus, sibling relations and the rights emphasized vary with the ages of those involved and the resulting position they hold in the community.

222

THE DEVELOPMENT OF SIBLING BONDS

It is recognized that, as small children, all siblings fight and quarrel among themselves, maternal siblings most often over objects in their mother's room which they covet, and paternal half-siblings over food and chores. At this age the cleavage between full siblings and paternal half-siblings is already apparent, both in the source of friction and in the fact that, when the children of a compound fight, maternal siblings side together. Responsibility of older for younger siblings also begins early. It is formally prescribed for girls, for one of their main tasks from the age of six or seven is to tend and carry younger siblings. For boys, it is just as real if not so readily observable, and they are often to be seen playing with a younger brother or sister in the courtyard outside their mother's room. I remember one disgusted youth of eight bodily removing his three-year old sister from a group of youngsters waiting for titbits at a sacrifice, because, he explained, she kept teasing the other young children who would go and get their elder brothers and then he would have a fight on his hands.

In childhood and adolescence, friends and companions are drawn from those of one's age and sex who live close by. They will include both 'siblings' and non-kin, contiguity and shared interests taking precedence at this time over kin relations. Kinship for the adolescent, and hence his sibling ties as well, is seen rather as obligations to one's elders than as the basis for association with one's peers. This is inevitably so as the adolescent's participation in the formalized activities of the wider social system is mediated by his elders. As a jural (and economic and ritual) minor he acts not on his own behalf but in response to the claims and obligations of his kin of the parental generation – his parents and their respective siblings.

In this role both boys and girls may be sent to live with a parent's sibling, or, in the event of their mother's remarriage, may accompany her to a new home where they will come under the immediate though limited jurisdiction of a step-father. In the event of a father's death final responsibility for them will pass to their father's heir who will usually, again, be 'a father's brother', full or classificatory. Here immediate destinies are determined by the claims of parental sibling groups. However, even as a jural minor, a man's concern with his own sibling group is expressed through the visits which its members exchange when they are spatially separated. Already in childhood and adolescence, the maintenance of sibling ties calls for frequent journeying between villages.

For both men and women, marriage marks the assumption of adult status, although for both independence of action and importance in the community gradually increase throughout adulthood. When a girl marries, neither her brothers nor sisters have formal roles. This is almost certainly related to the fact that, except in the extreme south, a wife moves into her husband's household on marriage. Her own kin have little to do with her husband, and need not make an effort to bring him into their world. When a man takes a wife, however, his eldest brother sponsors the dance at which she is introduced to the men of the section and his eldest sister provides the pots and fireplace which symbolize her status as a wife.

In adulthood, relations between siblings take on an increased importance, commensurate with their widening sphere of activity. Gradually, rights and duties vested in the parental generation devolve upon the senior representatives of the sibling group. While men become increasingly independent, women continue to seek the support of a man, either a husband or a kinsman, throughout their lives. Thus, sibling relations are inevitably characterized by an imbalance between male and female sibling roles, the former bearing the responsibility for their sisters' welfare, and holding, in return, certain rights in her children and property.[3] In most instances a claim is first made by a woman on her husband – for economic support, food and shelter, medical and ritual assistance – and he holds immediate rights in their children. However, even while his sister is married, a man exercises certain rights and responsibilities towards her and her children, and if she leaves her husband, or when she is widowed, her brothers become the primary source of support.

While a woman actively fills the role of wife, many of the rights and duties which characterize the relationship between brother and sister are held in abeyance. However, their importance, and indeed their very existence, is reinforced by various observances.

When a woman and her brother are both married and living in the same village, cooked food is frequently, although not regularly, exchanged between the two households. The fact that this exchange occurs in time of plenty but not when food is scarce indicates that it is in no sense viewed as a primary source of support, but rather as a gesture of

[3] Property (*kapute*) is said to be inherited by siblings in order of birth, regardless of sex. However, where a man's *kapute* falls to a woman her next youngest brother appears to hold it on her behalf, although she must be consulted about major expenditures and important decisions concerning the dependents (see below pp. 229ff). Similarly, a man will not hold a woman's *kapute*, though he may take responsibility for her children.

good will. So long as the sister is married, responsibility for providing her with food falls upon her husband, and she in turn is obliged first to feed him and her children before contributing to the meals of her brother's household. However, if her brother is without a wife (*kagbau*), either temporarily or for a long period of time, a woman may assume the job of feeding him. This she will do from grain, yams and meat which he himself supplies. ZabogoWura's elder children say they were brought up by their father's maternal half-sister (*ebe belo anyi*, 'she reared us') because after their mother died, she sent them food each evening which she had prepared on the hearth in her husband's compound at the other end of the village. Conversely, when a woman becomes a widow, or when she leaves her husband, her brothers are obliged to support her, to find a room for her in their compound and to bring her food from their farms. Even while his sisters are married, and live nearby, a man often sends them grain and yams, or a portion of an animal he has killed, to augment their food supply.

When women owe money, it is most often to their brothers that their creditors apply for payment, as illustrated by the case of Dari's sister (chapter 6). A husband has no obligation to make good his wife's debts, although he may voluntarily do so. On the other hand, a man is unlikely to seek small loans from a sister, although if a large sum is urgently needed he will certainly enlist her help in finding the money. In pre-colonial times, the most usual way of raising a large amount quickly was through pawning (*terma*) a child as surety for the sum borrowed. The child's labour then paid his keep and acted as 'interest' on the loan, at the same time that his presence ensured that an effort would be made to repay the principal. In Gonja law a man has no right to pawn his own children in this way, nor to sell them into slavery. His sister's children, on the other hand, are at his disposal should the need arise.

These occasional services, the payment of debts and the provision of extra food, are earnests of the claim a woman has on her brother's support in her old age or in a crisis. This last is of more than academic interest, for if a woman is driven from her husband's home as a witch, it is her brother who is responsible for sheltering her. Reference was made in chapter 7 to six reputed witches, five of whom were living with 'brothers' and one who maintained her own compound. The trial of another woman for witchcraft occurred, before the chief and his assembled elders, during my stay in Busunu. Mumuna had previously fled her natal village of Daboya to escape her reputation as a witch and had married in Langanteri, some five miles from the capital. Recently her brother, Gunguni, had followed, establishing his compound on the path between Langanteri and Daboya, about three miles from the former.

When her child died, it was rumoured that Mumuna was responsible, and when, shortly afterwards, her husband died suddenly, his kin in Langanteri were certain that he had been a victim of his wife's witchcraft. Mumuna was brought before the divisional court at Busunu by a 'brother' of her dead husband and several of his male kinsmen. Her own brother, Gunguni, also appeared at the hearing, but was seated across the room from his sister and her accusers, together with another man from his compound. The proceedings fell into two parts. First the Busunu chief raised the question of Mumuna's guilt. This was resolved very simply by questioning her. "Yes", she replied, "they all say I am a witch, so, although I didn't intend to harm anyone, I suppose I must be one." Then the problem was what to do with her.[4] The Langanteri people insisted that she should come and live in the compound of the Busunu chief where she would be at a safe distance and where he could employ his own mystical powers to control her homicidal tendencies. For whatever reason, the BusunuWura raised a series of objections to this solution and finally turned to her brother and enquired whether he was willing to take her to live with him. "Yes", he replied, "she can come and stay with me. Her children are mine and mine are hers. If she kills my children, it does not matter."

It would seem that Gunguni was willing to have his sister live with him, not because she was powerless to harm him, but despite this fact, and despite the fact that any attack was thought most likely to be aimed at his children who would be more vulnerable than Gunguni himself. It must not be supposed that to accept the presence of a known witch in one's compound is an easy thing. The atmosphere at the trial was heavily charged. Macabre jokes about the treatment of witches in the old days were greeted with raucous laughter of a sort I heard at no other trial, nor for that matter at any other gathering. Everyone was on edge, the Langanteri people grimly determined that the witch who had killed two of their kinsmen should not remain anywhere near the village, and the Busunu folk anxious at the suggestion that she be

---

[4] There is no doubt as to what would have happened in pre-European times. The commoner elder who holds the title of KabiaseWura was the executioner for the Busunu chief, and the present KabiaseWura had been sent to examine Mumuna's room for evidence of her crime. During the hearing, he constantly made reference to the fact that in the old days he would have been given her possessions in payment for executing her. This case is discussed further in my paper on Gonja witchcraft (E. Goody, 1970).

brought to live in their midst. I was struck by the impression that the most natural solution was felt to be the execution of the witch, each alternative appearing fraught with danger to one of the parties. In this atmosphere, Gunguni's calm assertion that he would take Mumuna to live with him seemed almost unbelievable. Yet the very matter-of-fact way in which he answered belied any element of personal heroism. He really appeared to take it as natural that, as Mumuna's brother, he was the one with whom she must live.

Besides being an unequivocal statement of the solidarity of siblings under stress, the theme of the holding by siblings of rights in one another's children is clearly enunciated in this case. As we have seen, rights in the same group of full siblings are held by two sets of siblings of the parental generation, the father's and the mother's. The sending of a child to live with the kin of either parent represents and partially discharges their claims against the sibling group as a whole. The limiting case is where, once a man has pawned a sister's child, he cannot again ask her for a foster child. Indeed, I once heard a man loudly proclaim that he owned his brother's children and could pawn them if he wished. As this is directly contrary to the usual pattern, I asked how this could be. "We have given one boy to his mother's brother – now the rest belong to us", he insisted.

But shifts of residence and pawning are the extreme form of emphasizing rights in siblings' children. Even when the sibling group remains intact and continues to reside with their parents, the parents' siblings retain a keen interest in their welfare, and often verbally assert their 'ownership'. In this sense, 'ownership' of a brother's or sister's children means two sorts of things. One may request services of these children and have a say in arranging their marriages. "If your mother's brother calls you to do something for him, you must go", the Gonja say, whether this be help in clearing a farm, carrying bush meat to the nearest market or taking a message to a distant village.

Ownership also has to do with transfer of authority on the death of a parent; his rights and obligations with respect to the children devolve upon the members of his sibling group. And there is an additional meaning of the 'ownership' of siblings' children which is one aspect of the authority exercised over his juniors by the eldest member of the sibling group. Thus, although an older sibling may not inherit from a younger, the eldest member of the sibling group 'owns' the children of his brothers and sisters, in that he is responsible for them as for the welfare of their parents. But his younger brother will just as readily assert that he 'owns' the children of the eldest brother (*mu da*). In this

227

case, what is meant by ownership is that the younger brother will be consulted before important decisions are made during the latter's lifetime and will assume the role of proxy parent at the real parents' death. Thus, of three adult male siblings, A 'owns' the children of B and C, but B 'owns' the children of A and those of C, while C also 'owns' the children of A and B.

This reciprocal sharing of rights in the children of siblings is part of what I have called final authority over members of the junior generation. During a man's lifetime, the interests of his siblings in his children are mediated through him. Except under such special circumstances as when a child is fostered or pawned, they remain interests rather than primary rights. But on his death, the senior male among his 'siblings' assumes authority over his children, 'on his behalf'. This man, be he full, or maternal or paternal half-sibling or cousin, has always been called 'father' (*tuto*) and now assumes the role of proxy father.

However, a dead sibling's child may be living in another village or compound. Where this is the case, immediate authority is vested in the kin with whom he resides, while the proxy father still retains his rights of final authority as expressed in rights to labour and obedience.

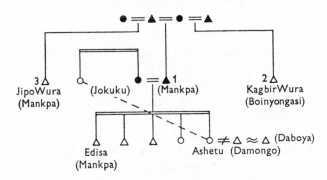

Fig. 7   Genealogy showing siblings of Ashetu's parents. Numbers indicate birth order.

An example of how such a distribution of authority works in practice is provided by the negotiations which prefaced Ashetu's second marriage. On the death of her father several years before, the final authority over Ashetu and her full siblings passed to their father's maternal half-brother, the shrine priest of the village of Boinyongasi in the division of Kawsawgu. Ashetu herself was living as a foster child with her mother's sister in Jokuku, a village south of Kawsawgu. The shrine priest concurred with her foster parent's insistence that she marry a suitor from Damongo whose gifts and attentions she had accepted for several months. Although she was reluctant, she agreed to the marriage, but after the birth of a son she left her husband and joined her full brothers in Mankpa, where they were living with the JipoWura, a paternal half-brother of their father. It was in Mankpa that she was wooed by Abudu. Her 'father', the JipoWura, agreed to the match but insisted that Ashetu and Abudu go to Boinyongasi to inform the shrine priest and secure his consent before the ritual kola was accepted. Abudu was working for me and as I was reluctant to lose his services during the time such a visit would take, I suggested that possibly a messenger could be sent with 'kola nuts' (i.e. a monetary gift) to inform the shrine priest and ask his approval. However, it was thought that this would not convey the necessary degree of respect; only a personal appearance would suffice. And so Abudu reluctantly agreed to go.[5] It is interesting that the sanction which the shrine priest had invoked when persuading Ashetu to agree to her first marriage was the threat of the withdrawal of his protection. He warned her that if she did not accede to his wishes, she could never again come to him in Boinyongasi, for shelter, for medicine or to seek his help in interceding with her ancestors.

The exercise and transfer of authority between siblings is one aspect of the pattern of inheritance. The Gonja formula for the transfer of property on death is a deceptively simple one. "The younger sibling takes", they say, and when these are finished it goes to the children in order of seniority of birth. However, enough has already been said about the extension of siblingship to show that this formulation only begs the question. In fact, it is subject to several limitations. As noted, an older sibling may not inherit from a younger. Further, full siblings should not inherit from one another because 'they are too close'. The question then becomes, which of the half-siblings and classificatory siblings may inherit? "Oh, the mother's children (*niupibi*), they are the ones who take", one is told. But here again, this is not a finite category of persons. The extension of the term has been discussed above. Among the instances recorded there is in fact a strong bias towards the passing of property between children of sisters, and from a man to his sister's child. This is formalized in the common statement that chiefship, that is political office, is inherited among father's children while property goes to mother's children. And if we waive the question of just what

---

[5] He was reluctant on several grounds: confrontations of in-laws are always felt to be difficult, and the visit would inevitably involve small gifts to Ashetu's kin in Boinyongasi.

degree of relationship this involves, and this is so variable as to require separate analysis, such a formulation is a reasonably close approximation of the pattern of inheritance in central Gonja.

That portion of a man's property which is passed on intact and not parcelled out among secondary heirs, is known as *kapute*. This portion should include all valuables and wealth which he himself inherited. The main store of wealth is in cows. Valuables consist of iron manufactured objects (needles, guns, hoes) and gowns of locally woven cotton, indigo dyed. Also included in the *kapute* are certain of a man's kinship obligations. Thus his heir takes over nominal responsibility for the support and control of the dead man's siblings and children, what I have called final authority, and must use the wealth which he has inherited on their behalf should the need arise. They in turn owe respect to him and must contribute their support and labour if he requires it. Because inheritance should not occur between full siblings, this form of authority may come into conflict with that exercised by closer, co-resident, kin. In fact, unless the children have gone to reside with their father's heir, they remain under the immediate authority of the dead father's siblings, while the heir retains residual rights to their labour and support.

Thus, when Mallam Aleidu, a senior Buipe Muslim, died, his *kapute* was inherited by the son of his mother's mother's sister's daughter, the GbampeWura, an office-holding member of the Mankpa ruling estate. The GbampeWura took the money and personal belongings which composed the *kapute*, but refused to make his home in Buipe because it was the town of neither of his parents; both his mother and Mallam Aleidu's had come from the town and division of Daboya in north-central Gonja. Since their father had been very old when he died, and they themselves were adults with families established in Buipe, the children refused to join the GbampeWura, and the eldest of them, Mallam Moru, assumed headship of his father's compound and *de facto* authority over the children and grandchildren who lived there. But the members of this group are still obligated to visit the GbampeWura regularly, and if they are in need, they may appeal to him for help.

Figure 8 shows the relationship between Mallam Aleidu and the GbampeWura. On it are also indicated the agnatic kin in line of succession to the Kante Mallamship which Mallam Aleidu had occupied. There was doubt for a time as to which of three men had the strongest claim to the office. Siibu was of the same generation as the previous incumbent but younger than the other two candidates, his 'brothers'' sons. The eldest of the possible candidates, Adamu, was a member of the police force and had lived far away in Bamboi for several years. When he failed to return for any of the funeral observances it was decided that he had forfeited any right to succeed.[6] As the eldest of the remaining contestants, Moru was favoured by many but the position finally went to Siibu.

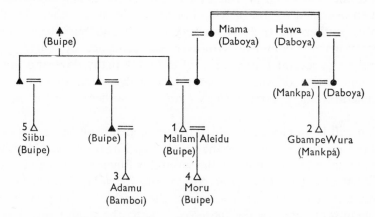

Fig. 8   Genealogy showing kinsmen of Mallam Aleidu: those through whom inheritance passes and those concerned in the succession to his Mallamship. Numbers indicate birth order.

Both the succession to the Kante Mallamship and the inheritance of Mallam Aleidu's *kapute* were described as going to the children of siblings: the Mallamship to father's children and the *kapute* to mother's children. In this particular instance both passed to classificatory siblings of the dead man. If Mallam Siibu's successor to the Kante Mallamship is Moru, it will go not to a 'sibling' but to a 'sibling's child'. However, Moru too will be classed as a 'father's child', since it is through their respective fathers that he and Siibu are related. This case shows particularly clearly that the 'siblings' concerned with succession to office are not those who have an interest in property. Any example of succession to a divisional chiefship in the ruling estate would show a similar split, with the new chief coming from another dynastic segment altogether, while the *kapute* passes to 'siblings' whose parents were either full or maternal half-siblings. Only with very old men like Mallam Aleidu is the reckoning of inheritance likely to be pushed back as far as the deceased's grandparents.

[6] Since the object of succession was an office whose incumbent must live in Buipe, this was no more than a recognition of the fact that Adamu would be unlikely to accept if appointed.

When a person dies, the balance between the *tutopibi* and the *niupibi* is maintained in another way. Each kin set takes responsibility for one or more of the major funerals of the sequence of mortuary rituals. The observances on the day of death, including burial, preliminary divination of cause of death, and the first prayers, are the responsibility of the head of the compound in which the death occurred. The Gonja do not have an extended period of lying-in-state as do many other Ghanaian peoples. Rather the body is washed, dressed and buried as soon as preparations are complete. However, the sequence of rituals which comprise the several funerals are spread over many days and involve the congregation of kin from considerable distances. In many cases, the funeral itself is 'carried' (*ba sɔl kali*) to another town for the next stage.

Who will be in charge of which funeral depends on the status of the dead person and where he or she was living. For instance, a divisional chief is responsible for holding the seven-day funeral of his predecessor, and must also bear the major cost of the forty-day funeral and the celebration of the first anniversary of the death. This responsibility is doubly appropriate, for the successor inherits the wealth vested in the divisional chiefship, and may use a part of it to defray the expenses of the funerals. But in addition, it is appropriate in Gonja eyes because, as a member of another of the dynastic segments of the ruling estate, the successor is a 'brother' and *tutopibi* of the dead chief. Thus the ownership of the later funerals can be expressed in both the political and the kinship idiom. So firmly is the performance of the seven-day funeral associated with succession to the divisional chiefship, that one of the ways a competitor can seek to pre-empt the choice is by installing himself in the capital and beginning the seven-day funeral. Since the *tutopibi* of a divisional chief perform the seven-day funeral, the *niupibi* have the right to make the three-day funeral.

More frequently, a man dies in his *tutope* and the three-day funeral is performed by his 'siblings' there who will represent his *tutopibi*. It is then said that his *tutopibi* 'own' the three-day funeral. In this case, it is the *niupibi* who will 'own' the seven-day funeral. If the senior sibling among the *niupibi* lives in another village, the funeral will be carried there, usually by bringing some dirt from the grave. The widow, eldest son and eldest daughter do not accompany the funeral to the *niupe*, but are bathed and released in the compound of the dead man. If a man was living with his maternal kin, then the allocation of funerals is reversed, with the *niupibi* performing the three-day funeral and the *tutopibi* the seven-day rituals.

232

The allocation of responsibility for the funerals of a woman is more complicated, because she may be living as a wife in a village where neither her maternal nor paternal kin are represented. In this case, her husband's people may see to the performance of the three-day funeral in addition to burying her. The seven-day funeral will then be sent either to the *niupibi* or the *tutopibi*, depending on which held final authority over her. If she has any full siblings still living, they will expect to assist in the performance of the seven-day funeral, and this fact may determine where it is performed.

When one of the later funerals is 'carried' to a town so that the 'siblings' there may perform the rituals, the wailing and the singing of dirges begins as though the death had just occurred. The dirt from the grave is buried in the usual cemetery, unless the death was a bad one[7] when it may be thrown away or buried at a cross-roads. Afterwards the various rituals are carried out as though the death had occurred in that town.

In contrast to the widow and the children of the deceased, the siblings do not play individual roles at the funeral. Rather, in their collective status of 'father's children' and 'mother's children', they 'own' the funerals. The person responsible, the *kaliwura* ('funeral owner'), is the senior among the 'siblings', or parents' 'siblings', on either the father's side or the mother's side of the personal kindred of the deceased.

At a funeral the *niupibi* and *tutopibi* of the dead person act towards one another as though they were joking partners. Like cross-cousins they are 'siblings' related through links of the opposite sex. They might be called 'courtesy joking partners' and the Gonja do use the term for joking partner in this way. *Niupibi* and *tutopibi* also have the kind of common, yet divergent interests which Radcliffe-Brown long ago identified as a source of the permitted aggression which characterizes institutionalized joking.

While death precipitates realignment of the authority and property relations within the 'sibling' group, the serious illness which often precedes it is the occasion above all others at which the solidarity of

---

[7] The deaths of certain categories of people, or deaths diagnosed as due to certain causes, are referred to as 'bad' (*libi, k'man wala*). The main examples are deaths of witches, habitual thieves, women who die in childbirth, suicides, and some infant deaths. If a person is found to have died because of breaking an oath to a shrine, this is also a bad death. These are all people whose behaviour or condition places them outside the moral community, and hence deprives them of the rights of full burial. There is often an element of punishment of the deceased in the rites that are performed, or the emphasis may be on cleansing the community of his influence.

siblings is expressed. If a woman falls ill in her husband's house, she first informs him and he endeavours to find medicine with which to effect a cure. If his efforts do not prove successful, the husband should send one of his siblings to inform her brother so that he may *ler mbusu* on the woman's behalf. If this fails, she may take up residence with her brother until she recovers. This recourse to kin and the shift in residence are explained on two levels by the Gonja. On the one hand, it is said that in serious illness the help of the ancestors is required to discover the underlying cause and to work a successful cure. While a woman may try to make the necessary sacrifices herself with her husband's help, it is considered that a male kinsman is likely to have more success. And on another level, it is held that a woman has little chance of recovery while in her husband's house, as she is dependent for food on her co-wives who will be annoyed that her illness has increased their share of the domestic tasks. They are unlikely to see that she gets the food and rest she needs, while her brother will ensure that she is well cared for in his house.

A woman's move to her brother's compound is the more striking when brother and husband live in the same village. For where this is the case, it would seem that she could benefit from a brother's knowledge of medicines and his ritual intercession with the ancestors while she continued to live in her husband's compound. When questioned, the Gonja explain that often rites must be performed early in the morning, and it is more convenient to have the sick person close at hand. A sufficient supply of food is clearly not the reason here, as cooked food could easily be sent between compounds. It seems, rather, that in illness a woman wishes to be surrounded by kin.

When an illness becomes serious, all the members of the sick person's sibling group, full and half-siblings, must be notified wherever they are living. All those who can, come and stay until the crisis is past or death intervenes. When Dari first fell ill in Buipe, she took to her bed in her husband's compound, and her full brother DanyampaWura, who also lived in Buipe, notified her only surviving full sister Bumunana, and her maternal half-brother Ajei, who were both living in Kabalipe, as well as her mother's sister's daughter, Kipo in Mankpa. Bumunana came at once and remained for the next six weeks except for short trips home. When Dari grew weaker, Ajei and Kipo also journeyed to Buipe and were there when their 'sister' died. Ten days before her death, Dari was moved from her own room to that of her brother. From then until she died, all the 'siblings', DanyampaWura, Denkeri and Ajei, her 'brothers', and Bumunana and Kipo, her 'sisters', slept there with her – in spite of the fact that the ostensible purpose of the move had been to give her greater privacy than her own room afforded.

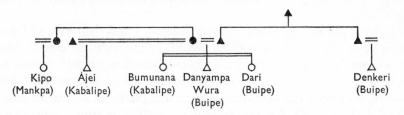

Fig. 9   The 'siblings' who gathered during Dari's last illness.

At the illness of a man his siblings are similarly notified and again they gather at his side. In this case too the obligation to be present at the death-bed falls most heavily on full and half-siblings, although classificatory siblings will be summoned if they are near at hand. I was unable to discover whether or not the GbampeWura was summoned when Mallam Aleidu was dying, but, although he was ill for several days, his 'brother' did not come to Buipe until some weeks after his death.

It appears that, as with authority, involvement with crises has both formal and informal aspects, and that these affect a different range of siblings. Full and half-siblings are more concerned with the person, his feelings and his welfare, while more distant, classificatory, siblings have formalized rights and obligations with respect to his property and dependants.

When I saw Dari's sister, Bumunana, some five months after the funeral week was completed, the inheritance of Dari's *kapute* had still not been arranged. The *kapute* of a second woman whose funeral I attended in December 1956 had not been allocated a year later.[8] The *kapute* of most women consists of little beyond an iron cooking pot or two and the much prized collection of enamelled pans that line the back wall of a woman's room. Older women who spin local cotton will have a few cloths as well as the shroud they have so carefully set aside. A reserve supply of peppers and shea butter, and perhaps a string of carnelian waist beads will probably complete the list. Some older women have one or more cows, and a few pounds, but the rest of the things

[8] The funerals were held in Mankpa by the MankpaWura, who was the dead woman's father's 'brother'. A year later I had moved to Busunu, but the 'sister' who expected to inherit was married there, so I was able to keep track of the process of allocation. By then my own pattern of residence had begun to reflect the fluidity of the Gonja pattern!

are used by and for women, and will be inherited by a sister, or if there is none, a daughter. Any items of wealth, as opposed to personal property, should go to the next youngest of the *niupibi*, whether a man or a woman.

Neither of the two women whose funerals I was then able to follow from beginning to end had either wealth or the status of eldest sibling to pass on. The inheritance of their *kapute* was thus a matter for women as it concerned only women's things. Nevertheless, it was not to be done hastily. Although the long delay was at first puzzling, I came to understand it later. For the assumption of a dead person's *kapute* is a dangerous act, in that if the person who inherits does so against the will of the deceased, then trouble is sure to follow. So serious is this threat that a person who has cause to believe that the dead person was displeased with him will waive his turn to take the *kapute* and insist that it go to the next younger 'sibling'. This renunciation can cause problems too; since a full sibling must not be the one to inherit, it may mean skipping over the second in line as well. In a few cases, the result has been to leave the *kapute* unclaimed until the rightful but reluctant heir himself (or herself) has died. Then the next in line can safely take. Disagreements about who should inherit are likely to be resolved in the same way. Unless the dead person's wishes can be ascertained through some sign, it may be judged wiser to leave the *kapute* 'in its box' than for the wrong person to risk possession against the will of the dead.

A further reason for the frequent delay is undoubtedly the fact that a person who holds important *kapute*, is very likely to be elderly and the last survivor of his full sibling group. When he dies there is no one in a position of authority who has the responsibility and right to initiate action until the successor is appointed. The local kinsfolk can hold councils and consult diviners, and it is the obligation of the senior among them to do so to discover the cause of death. But it is quite likely that the heir to the *kapute* will not be one of these people, and that there will be other interested parties who are not represented. Such meetings can reach consensus as to the best heir, but they have no way of enforcing their decision. In time, a choice will be accepted and the heir will agree. If not, the property is left until there is another death, or until some further crisis forces the issue.

The anxiety which surrounds the transmission of *kapute* is based on the fear that *mbusu*, mystical danger, may exist if the relations between the living and dead kin are not good. *Mbusu* is a major sanction on behaviour among close kin, particularly those linked through women. However, it has a wide and complex range of referents which extend beyond kinship. Indeed, *mbusu* forms one of the key idioms in terms of which social relations are interpreted.

MBUSU WUTƆ: *THE STATE OF MYSTICAL DANGER AS A RELATIONAL IDIOM*

The phrase *mbusu wutɔ* is often offered as a warning or as an explanation of why something must or must not be done. Its meaning is not easy to pin down, except gradually through examples and their contexts. Basically, *mbusu* is a state of mystical danger. The verb used with it, *wutɔ*, is a form of the verb to be, and connotes existence. *Mbusu* is, or rather, inheres in certain situations. At first these situations appear to be so many and so various that it is difficult to see any pattern. A scorpion's sting, certain dreams, an accident on the farm, illness, death – all are likely to be included. Such happenings are not themselves *mbusu*, however; rather they are signs that a state of mystical danger exists. They are expressions and warnings that something is wrong in the relations between men and the supernatural agencies which surround them.

It is for this reason that such misfortunes, large or small, send the victim to a diviner. The present trouble is only a warning. What must be discovered is the underlying cause of the state of danger. The cause again is likely to be complex. In the first instance, it must have been an act, or a failure to act, or worst of all a refusal to act. Wrong behaviour generally can be interpreted by the Gonja in many ways. A theft is wrong, and is punished by the elders who demand restitution and apology. There is no mystical danger involved here. Prohibited acts (*akishi*, 'hated things') are of many sorts. Those learned from the previous generation, and observed because 'our grandfathers did so', are sometimes called 'things of old' (*ashieng dera*). To break these prohibitions would be wrong but not mystically dangerous.

An example may make this clearer. It is thought that a woman should not try to grow from seed the red hot peppers which form the basic flavouring for soups and stews. If she wishes to introduce peppers into a new field, then seedlings should be transplanted from an old farm. Thereafter the birds will scatter the seeds and the pepper plants will quickly become established. This prohibition is adhered to because it is thought that people will get sick if they eat soup made with sown peppers. But there is no mystical danger (*mbusu min 'to*); it is a matter of 'things of old'.

Other prohibitions have more serious consequences for, if they are not observed, a state of mystical danger is thought to be the almost inevitable result. The prohibition on quarrels among close kin, especially uterine kin, is sanctioned in this way, as are the claims of kin to their sisters' and daughters' children, and of elderly women to shelter and support. A few of the prohibitions on sexual relations, both within marriage and outside it, are also of this kind. Less serious mystical danger is feared when personal shrines 'ask' for gifts or sacrifices, and when the owner of a hunting or war shrine fails to observe the rules associated with it. This distinction between serious and minor mystical danger was repeatedly made in attempts to explain *mbusu* to me.

People think of *mbusu* as being 'sent' by a particular supernatural agency, in the sense that proper relations with this power have in some way been disturbed. The dangerous situation which results may be due to direct malevolent action against the human concerned. It may involve only the removal of protection, leaving the individual vulnerable to many sorts of attack; or it may be seen as a loss of control over mystical powers which thus become capricious and wilful. *Mbusu* is sometimes said to be of two kinds – that from shrines, and that sent by the ancestors – but the implicit premiss that there is an ongoing relationship between a person and a given supernatural force underlies all such situations.

MBUSU FROM SHRINES

Shrines (*agbir*) are of very many kinds: some held by individuals, some vested in kin lines, some endowed with an apparent will of their own which 'climb' (possess) the shrine owner; some associated with spirits of the wild, or of trees or rivers, some with the earth, and some with the dead founders of a village, a division or, in the case of the grave of NdeWura Jakpa, the Gonja kingdom itself.

Those shrines held by individuals which are believed likely to bring mystical trouble are of two sorts. The first includes all the important shrines for protective or aggressive medicines; it is thought that, if the prescriptions and proscriptions linked with the shrine are disregarded, it will either fail to give proper aid and protection, or may even turn against its owner. Even the withdrawal of protection can be very dangerous, as when a man depends on his hunting shrine for the ability to disappear in the face of a charging buffalo. The mystical trouble brought by an unfaithful wife is primarily due to her power to 'spoil' (*jegge*) her husband's shrines in this way.

The other personal shrines likely to bring mystical trouble are those which express an individual's particular identity. For example, there are twin shrines (*mborebi ba agbir*) which are first fashioned at the birth of twins and thereafter inherited by their descendants. Shrines for those conceived too soon (*mankɔr*) or born in breach deliveries (*bɔlemba*) are similarly transmitted. All link living individuals with a special supernatural force. This force is believed to be very active and to intervene constantly in the lives of those tied to it. It is the task of the holder of a twin shrine to learn what his shrine requires of him. He must bear the burden of seeing that the relationship between him and the force represented by the shrine is in balance. When a diviner reports that mystical trouble comes from the twin shrine, he means that the shrine is trying to communicate with its holder, to let him know that something must be done to restore the relationship. The closeness of the link between a twin shrine and its holder is likened to that between twins themselves. Like many other people, the Gonja feel there is an intangible bond between twins which leads each to know what the other is thinking and feeling, however far apart they may be. This oneness in two bodies continues even when death intervenes. Mystical trouble from a twin shrine is a sign that the closeness of this relationship is threatened.

The most common source of minor mystical danger, however, is the *akalibi* shrine.[9] The shadow soul (*kiyaiyu*) is believed to speak out before birth and ask God for a particular destiny. At this time it may also require certain observances during its period of human existence. The *akalibi* shrine is the means by which a person communicates with the shadow soul. Relatively minor misfortunes, particularly the stings of scorpion, are often seen as an indication that the *akalibi* shrine is asking for something. As this demand was in a sense pre-ordained as part of the destiny of its human life, the shadow soul is thought to have a right to receive what it wants. There is a sense of inevitability, of unfulfilled obligation, about requests made by a person's *akalibi* shrine. The mystical trouble is said to be relatively mild (in this, it is always contrasted with the kind sent by the ancestors), and is seen as a temporary condition easily dispelled by the required sacrifice.

The widest definition of *mbusu* sees it as a state of mystical danger brought about by some sin of omission or commission which throws the relationship between man and the supernatural out of balance. Failure

---

[9] The *akalibi* shrine is similar in many ways to the Good Destiny shrine among the Tallensi (Fortes 1959: 41ff). However, the Gonja do not see the personal destiny as linked to protection by the ancestors. It has perhaps more in common with the *kra* of the Ashanti. The present account is a very incomplete treatment of *akalibi*, only as it relates to *mbusu*.

to follow the rules associated with protective/aggressive shrines clearly produces such a state of imbalance. But the balance involved in relations between a man or woman and their personal shrine is of a more complex kind. These shrines are seen as concrete manifestations of forces which act on the person concerned. Only through the shrines can the individual communicate with and control these forces. Neither inherently good nor inherently evil, they are as it were personalized fragments of supernatural power motivated from somewhere outside the individual. In fact protective/aggressive shrines are in this respect very similar. Through them, the individual seeks to control mystical forces which exist 'out there'. By owning the shrine he puts himself into relationship with these forces. The rules with which such shrines are surrounded are best seen as ways of attempting to keep the relationship in balance, to retain control over the mystical power which, as it continues an autonomous existence outside of the shrine, can all too easily get out of hand.[10]

Mystical danger from shrines, then, inheres in the very nature of the relations between men and supernatural power. As one Buipe elder put it, "All shrines have their *mbusu*." If the rules are not followed, or if the shrine makes a demand which is misunderstood or allowed to go unheeded, then the mystical forces are likely to turn on its owner. A state of mystical danger exists: *mbusu wutɔ*.

Community shrines, including Earth shrines (usually *adamang* in central Gonja), also may bring *mbusu*. While special 'medicine' shrines like those at Jembito, Bute and Chama have their own particular prohibitions, there are few general avoidances associated with Earth shrines. For whatever reason, mystical danger from community shrines is seldom associated with specific breaches of these prohibitions. Instead, such shrines are 'repaired' (*ba long kagbir*) at a certain time every year, as well as when some particular trouble threatens, for instance when an especially severe drought brought a plague of bees on Mankpa during the dry season of 1956–7. At the 'taking out of danger' (*ba ler mbusu*) at the Kabalipe Earth shrine in February 1957, both the ancestors and the Earth were asked to remove the mystical condition giving rise to the drought. This association between the Earth and the ancestors who lie buried there is seldom made explicit by the Gonja. Nevertheless, it underlies beliefs about fertility of the land as among a great many West African people, including the Ashanti, the Tallensi, the LoDagaa and the Ibo.

---

[10] See also the section on protective and aggressive medicines in 'Legitimate and Illegitimate Aggression in a West African State' (E. Goody 1970).

The concept of *mbusu* associated with community shrines combines aspects of beliefs about mystical danger from other kinds of shrines with beliefs about trouble sent by the ancestors. The chief and elders act on the premiss that the mystical forces emanating from the Earth and the dead must be kept in balance by annual sacrifice. If there is a natural crisis such as a drought, or if there are many deaths in the town, then a diviner may find that some particular act has disturbed the balance and brought about the state of mystical danger of which the drought or deaths are one expression. When this occurs a sacrifice must be made to 'take out the *mbusu*'.

MBUSU FROM THE ANCESTORS

Unlike many West African peoples, the Gonja do not establish shrines to particular ancestors, nor are there collective ancestor shrines, apart from a few symbolic graves of culture heroes and early chiefs. The term used for the spirit of a dead person is the same, *ebuni*, as that for a dead body.[11] There is no special connotation of either spirituality or lineal ancestry. And indeed references to the dead are usually collective unless the outcome of a specific divination is being discussed. Such undifferentiated grouping together of those who have died is consistent with the bilateral kinship system. Ancestors are either an undifferentiated collectivity of the long dead, or one's own immediate forebears: parents, occasionally grandparents, and close siblings of parents and in one's own generation. There are no established shrines to any of these dead kin, which has the effect of making them equally accessible to all descendants, wherever they may be living.

There is general agreement that the most dangerous states of *mbusu* occur when the ancestors are angered. Mystical danger not otherwise specified is usually taken as being from dead kin, and indeed people sometimes simply equate the two: "*Mbusu* is when the ancestors are angry." Unlike the trouble sent by personal shrines, which is usually seen as initiated by the shrine itself, the ancestors appear to send danger only when their living kin have broken a moral norm. The list of situations in which mystical danger is felt to inhere shows these to be norms governing close relationships between kin. *Mbusu* is feared if a man and his sister's son quarrel, a younger sibling strikes an elder sibling, a son stays with his father following his parents' divorce, if there is quarrelling

[11] This is very reminiscent of Tutuola's use of 'deads' and 'dead town' in his books written in West African English; see especially *The Palm-Wine Drinkard* (1952).

between a husband and wife who are also relatives, or if a man fails to welcome and support an elderly female relative.

While some of the rules reflected here are quite specific (a younger sibling must never use force against an elder; a man must support his female kin), they are themselves aspects of a more general ethic. Kin must not quarrel, but must accede to requests for aid and support. To 'refuse' (*kine*) a relative carries the same kind of moral stigma as did Peter's triple denial of Christ. This in turn serves to sanction the honouring of specific obligations between kin, and the mechanism is of some interest.

There are two main ways of describing 'talking' or 'speech' in Gbanyito. Conversation, general discussion or gossip is *gbiri gbari*, but more serious talk is *maliga* ('to speak'), and this form is used for court cases (*kamaliga*, 'a speaking') or for a serious consultation or announcement. The implication of *maliga* is that it is serious, and that people ought to pay attention. If a person has been wronged by a relative, he may speak about it to himself, or even simply have angry thoughts 'in his chest' (*kagbunto*). But the speaking does not go unheard, for those relatives who have died are thought to be very concerned with the good relations of their descendants, and are believed to pay special attention to such words of righteous anger. This notion was behind the words of a commoner chief in Buipe when he remarked to me, "You must give plenty of food to a sister living with you or else she will be talking and you will die."

As this comment of the KagbapeWura implies, it is generally the breach of obligations between the living which is thought likely to anger the ancestors and lead to a state of mystical danger. This is usually because the dead relative concerned in sending *mbusu* has a direct relationship with both the offender and the injured party among the living. Thus a brother who struck an elder sibling would greatly upset their dead mother and father, who demand amity among their children and support the authority of the elder over the younger, just as they did as living parents. Similarly, a stingy brother fears the muttered complaints of an aggrieved sister because he believes that their mother (or common ancestor) will hear and be offended that she is not being properly cared for.

The importance of the ancestor's link with both parties is most explicit in the lack of concern over mystical danger following quarrels between husband and wife. Where the couple is unrelated, quarrels are considered unfortunate but free of mystical danger. If they become continual or too severe, the couple will separate, and that will end the matter.

Quarrels between related spouses are an entirely different matter. They are greatly feared, as the ancestors' annoyance is likely to lead to the death of the children. This conviction is shared by members of all three social estates, and held equally by men and women. It is often cited as a deterrent to arranging marriages between kin, and is undoubtedly one reason why the dissolution of kinship marriages is not prevented by the families concerned. The conjunction of kinship and marriage in 'family marriage' is the focus of such strong anxieties precisely because kinship bonds are seen as indissoluble, and this is sanctioned by the ancestors' continuing enforcement of norms of kinship amity. Marriage, on the other hand, is subject to disruption at any point, and the assumed outcome of friction between spouses is their separation. Friction in marriage is seen as probably inevitable, and at the same time tolerable as long as it is not confused with kin ties. When such a confusion does occur, serious *mbusu* is the result.

Mystical danger which is diagnosed as sent by the ancestors due to the breaking of kinship norms is the most difficult to remove. A sacrifice is required, though among Muslims this takes the form of preparing a ceremonial meal which is set out for the dead, following the recital of prayers. Close kin will be invited to the observances, for they are felt to share in both the danger and the responsibility for setting things right. The removal of mystical danger sent by the ancestors is particularly difficult, however, because their demands are less precise than those of a medicine or a personal shrine. Basically, they are causing trouble because kinship norms have been broken. While a diviner can recommend sacrifice or prayers, the living cannot be sure that they will suffice to convince the dead of their good intentions. If further misfortunes follow, this is an indication that sufficient amends have not been made.

Indeed, the uncertainty over the satisfaction of the dead with the behaviour of their living kinsfolk is made inevitable by the very general way in which kinship norms are defined. How well must one look after a dependent relative? Who has not felt angry with a sibling? The difficulty of being sure that kinship obligations are fully met means that one can never know that a state of mystical danger does not exist. For this reason, when a potentially dangerous undertaking is imminent (for instance, the birth of a child or the assumption of office), a diviner is often consulted to see if it is necessary to 'take out *mbusu*'.

The intractable nature of ancestral *mbusu* is also indicated by the belief that it is the form of mystical danger most likely to lead to death. The divination which follows nearly every death is aimed at discovering the cause. Once witchcraft is ruled out, ancestral *mbusu* is the probable diagnosis; so the attribution of the death of close kin to sins against other kin is a regular experience for the Gonja. Such a pattern of belief imposes severe burdens on its followers. The tendency for kin to ascribe deaths to witchcraft, at least in discussions during the funeral period before the final divination is made, is probably one result. "If a witch is responsible, then we are not", is the implication.

Another consequence is the extreme secrecy which attends the final divination for the cause of death. It is generally done in another town from that in which the deceased lived and died, and only the very close kin know when it occurs and what the conclusion is. For if the verdict is that ancestral *mbusu* was responsible, then the initial cause lies among these living kin.

Not all mystical danger sent by the ancestors is fatal. In general the spirit of a dead man is less dangerous than that of an ancestress. A father, for instance, is said never to kill a child: "If you refuse (*kine*) your father's younger or elder brother, and your father is dead, he will trouble you. He will spoil your farming, and the things you want, you won't get. But he won't kill you" (Muslim, Busunu). And, "Your father, if you do something very bad, he will not kill you. But your mother, even if you do a very small thing which is wrong, she will kill you" (ruling estate, Busunu).

Indeed, a man's dead father or father's brother may try to warn him through dreams that a state of mystical trouble exists. A dead man is thought unlikely to try and warn his sister's son through dreams unless they were particularly close. This protective role of the dead father is a direct extension of the part he plays in life. For "a man whose father is alive doesn't know trouble", say the Gonja. If there is a state of mystical danger, then the father is responsible for making the necessary sacrifices. He stands between his children and the anger of the dead. When he dies, they must themselves be responsible for correct relations with their dead forbears. The father may still try to help them by sending warning dreams; he may chastise, but he cannot kill.

However, the mother and maternal kin generally are more feared. The ancestors believed most dangerous are the mother, the mother's brothers, and the elder and younger sisters of the mother. Women who are maternal kin are more trusted in life but more feared in death; the reverse is true of paternal kinswomen, at least so far as the father's sister represents this group. She is regularly described as stricter and less sympathetic than a mother's sister. But mystical danger is not greatly feared from her after her death. This fact shows very neatly that the concern is not that a wronged kinswoman will take revenge after death, for father's sisters are often in the category of dependent women who are very vulnerable to neglect. It is rather the spontaneous reaction of those already dead to maltreatment or quarrelling among their living kin that is dangerous.

There is no way of obtaining a representative sample of misfortunes attributed to *mbusu,* nor of the broken norms diagnosed as ultimately responsible. From the occasional examples recorded, and from texts and discussion, the relatives most likely to be instrumental in sending mystical danger appear to be as indicated in the following figures.

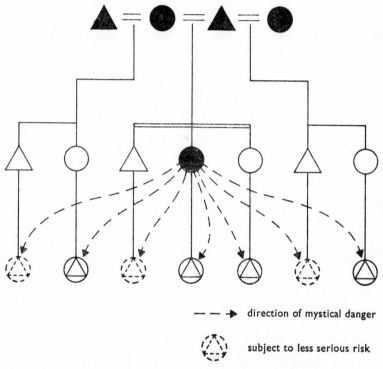

— — ➤ direction of mystical danger

subject to less serious risk

Fig. 10 Vulnerability to serious mystical danger from a dead 'parent'.

As this schematic figure shows, women are thought likely to kill the children of their full siblings and of half-siblings related through either parent. Texts and statements do not agree as to whether a dead brother may kill his sister's children, though he is known to be able to cause serious trouble. As a maternal relative he is dangerous, but as a man unlikely to cause death. The scope of effective intervention against siblings' children is relatively narrow for a kinship system in which

245

third, fourth and fifth cousins are recognized as 'siblings'. The dead are believed to take a strong interest only in their own children and those of their immediate siblings.

When the pattern of mystical sanctions against siblings themselves is considered, the picture alters in two respects. In the first place, dead men as well as women are able to kill a sibling who neglects kinship obligations. The example frequently given is the danger liable to occur when a sibling fails to care properly for the children of a dead brother or

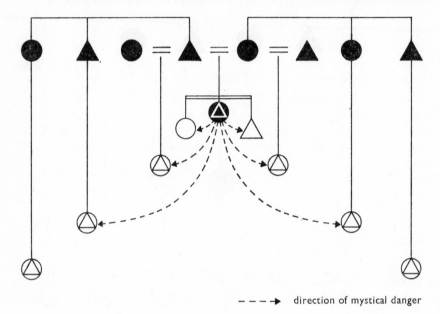

Fig. 11   Vulnerability to serious mystical danger from a dead 'sibling'.

sister. Secondly, it is obligations of classificatory as well as full and half-siblings which are liable to this sanction. However, mystical danger is only feared between the children of brothers (*tuto ker pibi*) and the children of sisters (*niu ker pibi*), that is, between parallel cousins. This difference is quite explicitly because the children of cross-cousins are joking relations and thus, as one man put it, "they know how to be angry without causing harm" (*ben ting nyi agbo na, n'ka minan wura shĩa*).

Like mystical danger from shrines, that sent by dead kin reflects a disruption in the balance of relations between the living and supernatural forces. But while mystical danger from medicine shrines indicates a failure to keep the stipulated rules, and that from personal shrines is a sign that something must be given to the shrine to retain control of the force it represents, neither of these forms of *mbusu* implies moral failure or arouses guilt. Mystical danger from the ancestors is more serious and does always imply a failure to fulfil kinship norms. Where such a failure is held to be the indirect cause of a relative's death, some degree of guilt would seem inevitable.

The absence of important descent groups which might structure relations between kin is reflected in an absence of shrines to specific ancestors, or indeed of any ancestor shrines. Nor are dead kin identified with personal shrines, despite the common occurrence of a modified form of reincarnation.[12] The only dead to take a direct interest in the living are recently deceased and very close kin, as indicated in Figures 10 and 11. It is possible that the strongly moral nature of their interest in the living is related to the recentness and directness of the links between them. It may also be related to the relative weakness with which kinship authority is institutionalized in central Gonja. In the absence of either descent groups or established ancestor shrines, the sanctions available to the occupants of senior kinship status are weak and difficult to invoke. In the last analysis they rest on two things only: the direct recollection of help and affection received as a de-

---

[12] A child is named at the ceremony of 'shaving off the ghost hair' seven days after birth. This name is chosen differently by members of the three estates. However, if the baby is sickly or cries a great deal, a diviner is likely to find that it has been 'climbed' (*dii*) by a dead relative. This is usually a parent or parent's sibling of the child's own parent. A person who had an important position or dominant character in life may climb several children in the years immediately following his death. This is explained as due to the strength of his spirit. At a simple private ceremony, the baby is re-named for this dead kinsman or woman, and thereafter the two are identified in certain ways. For instance, the children of the name ancestor never call the child who has been 'climbed' by their parent's name. It is extremely rude, and indeed unheard of, to call one's parent by name, and to call someone 'climbed' by a parent by this name is said to be the same thing. Thus one hears an adult calling to a small child, "Mother, come and take this . . .". Should the child resemble its name ancestor, either physically or in character, this is explained by their special relationship, but a resemblance is not expected in every case of 'climbing'.

Despite this close relationship, the name ancestor is not believed to interfere directly in the affairs of the person he has 'climbed', once he has been acknowledged by the re-naming of the child. The name ancestor is not mentioned at sacrifices to the personal shrine, or in *nyina* rituals. Repeated attempts to discover any active relationship between the two always met with puzzled denials. The feeling seems to be that the name ancestor *is* his descendant, and to expect a further influence from outside is redundant. The initial re-naming ceremony establishes this identity once and for all.

pendant; and the fear of the anger of those with whom one acknowledges close kinship.

Mbusu and inheritance both concern maternal kin. Is this fear of death from the uterine ancestors due to guilt over wishing that a kinsman would hurry and die so that his property might be inherited? Probably in part. Certainly this factor seems possible in cases like that of a man who complained that his father's 'brother' (actually, a maternal relative of his father's) had taken property which included several cows and, since he had lived to such a ripe old age, he was eating them all. "It is when a man lives too long that he spoils the *kapute*", he concluded. But this instance is not typical, since few men have any cows to pass on when they die. Inheritance between maternal relatives is a matter not only of wealth, but of certain ritual items, and of responsibility for kin. The cases in which mystical danger was spontaneously mentioned as a serious threat, or in which it was revealed by divination, concerned the care of dead or absent siblings and siblings' children. To the extent that fear of *mbusu* is an expression of guilt, then, it is guilt about obligations to and relationships with maternal kin. Property relations are only a part of these relationships.

CENTRIPETAL AND CENTRIFUGAL FORCES

The dispersion of kin in space and the pattern of open connubium mean that relatives are unlikely to be concentrated either in a single community or a single social estate. Several of the institutions already discussed can be seen to express the obligations and rights which nevertheless continue to hold between kin. The sharing between maternal and paternal kin of rights to perform funerals, the vesting of rights over children in the kin of both parents, and the circulation of office between dynastic segments, depend on the recognition of rights of office relatives who may be neither neighbours nor (except where office is concerned) members of the same estate. Beliefs about mystical danger provide one kind of sanction for these claims, and dependence on reciprocal support constitutes another, no less forceful. These may be seen as centripetal forces tending to counteract the diffusing effects of open connubium.

There is another theme which appears in the same institutions and demonstrates a contrary, centrifugal tendency. For there are a number of distinct situations in which close kin must be passed over in favour of more distant relatives. The clearest examples are the avoidance of marriage to first degree cross-cousins, despite the general preference for cross-cousin marriage; the prohibition on a widow remarrying in her dead husband's kindred; the prohibition on a son succeeding his father in office; and the feeling that a full sibling ought not to inherit until the property has been held by a more distant relative. A study of fostering relationships shows that parents' full siblings seldom serve as foster parents, despite the use of mother's brother and father's sister as models for the foster parent role. This is said to be due to a reluctance to jeopardize the amity between them. Indeed, the rationale offered in explanation of all these prohibitions is likely to be that the people involved 'are too close'. The implications of kinship proximity have been discussed in the context of *mbusu*. Quarrelling between close kin is thought to anger the ancestors, and carries a risk of serious mystical danger. It is safer to separate those relationships likely to involve friction (marriage, fostering, inheritance) from those in which quarrelling is subject to mystical sanction.

In effect, this is a system which operates in the idiom of primary kinship relations, stressing the importance of bonds between parents and children and between close siblings. But at the same time that these primary relationships are used as a charter for ties with more distant kin, any self-sufficiency of the nuclear relatives themselves is prevented by a series of prohibitions. At the level of kinship institutions the system functions largely independently of statuses in the wider economic and political systems. Nevertheless, relations based on residence and status in a wider social system do effect the balancing out of the centripetal and centrifugal forces noted here. In the final section we will look more closely at this interdependence.

10

Residence: the synchronic view

In Gonja, patterns of marriage and child-rearing lead to a circulation of persons of all ages, male and female, between the fixed points in the social system: division, village, compound and household are constellations of people anchored in physical and social space. This chapter looks at the composition of the smallest of these units, the household and the compound, at a given point in time. These are units which hold, as we have seen, a key position in articulating the individual and the institutions, political, jural, economic and ritual, of the wider social system. A second purpose in looking at the composition of households and compounds is to give concreteness to the processes which bring about movement between them. This theme is further explored in the following chapter, where the processes themselves are reconsidered in a developmental sense, and as they vary between estates.

Any discussion of residence in Gonja raises acute problems of classification. Designation of village and division is clear enough, since these are spatially discrete. Villages differ greatly in their composition, however, which raises the issue of selection among them. Further, although it is often possible within the village to distinguish section and compound by name, as well as physically, the difference between them is frequently blurred. Nor is it always clear whether two adjacent clusters of rooms form a single compound, or separate ones. The household is an analytically important unit; yet this has no necessary physical correlate, and indeed some compounds consist of a single household, while a few households are split between two compounds. Such difficulties are far from academic when it comes to presenting and analysing data on residence patterns, because the form of classification used largely determines the results obtained.[1]

There are then two kinds of problems which arise in analysing the residence patterns. The first has to do with the representativeness of the sample used. The second concerns the problem of defining the units with respect to which residence is studied.

In a society which is internally differentiated, no single community is

[1] See exchange between Fischer and Goodenough on their conflicting census results for the same Truk village (Goodenough 1956; Fischer 1958).

likely to be a good basis for generalizing to the others. The villages within a division exemplify to some degree the sort of functional integration to which Durkheim referred as organic solidarity. In Buipe, while political institutions are focused on the capital, the Morno ferrymen transport people and goods across the Volta and look after the river shrines; Frufruso is a centre for spokesmen (the *dogtes*), while Katangi provides an income from the excellent fishing of the White Volta marshes. On the national level each division has a special role which is a composite outcome of its history, its economic and ritual resources, and the people who happen to be centred there.

Such an overview of the special roles of divisions and their constituent villages is, however, the end result of a period of research, and unfortunately not available to the fieldworker in making his initial plans. So one is left with material on a few communities and an appreciation of their non-representative nature.

Buipe is used as the basis for the following analysis of residence patterns for two reasons. It is the only one of the three divisional capitals in central Gonja for which a total census is available. As will become increasingly evident in the latter part of this chapter, the relations between compounds are often crucial in understanding the pattern of residence *within* a compound. So a complete census is vital. Secondly, of the three capitals, only in Buipe was there a permanent Muslim population. As one of the most interesting aspects of residence is the difference between estates, the Muslim element cannot be omitted. However, the very fact that many communities in central Gonja lack a Muslim population raises in acute form the issue of bias. Buipe is clearly not typical of villages which have no Muslims. Any conclusions from this analysis, then, cannot be generalized without extreme care.

A second source of bias lies in the very fact that Buipe is a divisional capital. As such, it contains a number of compounds belonging to the dynastic segments of the ruling estate. Again, this is a point of importance if differences between estates are to be examined. However, other villages in these divisions contain much smaller elements of this estate, and some only a few individuals. Patterns of residence typical of the ruling estate in the capital cannot be generalized to the outlying villages. Indeed, such patterns have a special significance just because they identify the dynastic segments with the divisional centre; they are not typical of all enclaves of the ruling estate, wherever found.

The ways in which commoner residence in the capital is likely to differ from other villages will be indicated in the course of the discussion. There are fewer obvious systematic sources of bias. In the absence of office as an important factor, residence is more often determined by considerations that lie solely within the domestic domain than is the case in the other estates who share the same domestic institutions but take into account status and pedigree. However, commoner residence is also effected by the wish to exploit links with those in positions of relative importance, even where direct access to the power positions themselves is not at issue.

The choice of a community for analysis is determined by a mixture of theoretical and pragmatic considerations, but it is a choice irrevocably made in the field. When it comes to analysis, one can only take any bias into account and work within these limitations. The selection of units within a sample is partially controlled by the way the data were initially collected. But in grouping and analysing the material, there are often a number of possible approaches. In the present context, the problem is how to reckon residence, that is, what should be taken as the basic unit, and with respect to whom? Individuals could be classified in relation to household heads, or to compound heads. Households themselves could be taken as the unit of analysis with respect to compound composition. Or compounds could be related to one another and an attempt made to look at the history of compound headship. Whichever approach is chosen, the problem of identification of the units must still be faced. Before people can be assigned to households and compounds, these must be clearly designated.

Yet in both social and spatial terms, one is dealing here with a merging series. Rooms are the fundamental elements of the system, and a household consists of a number of rooms; but some households contain only one. Households are the constituent elements of compounds, which may contain from one to six or more such units. The word for compound means also courtyard (*langto*). Many compounds consist of rooms built around a single courtyard, but others include two or three courtyards. And in practice the social criteria are variably applied to these physical units. The paradox is clear: one must assign people to some kind of unit in order to count them and analyse the relationships between them. Yet the fluidity of the units in which the Gonja live and work is an essential feature of the system. There is a danger of reification here; of giving too great a concreteness to the units in order to have a means of classifying the data. Again, having identified the problem, one can but go on and work within its constraints. I have tried to do this in two ways; firstly, by discussing the essential criteria for household and compound, and considering the degree to which co-operation and authority are necessarily related to these as physical units. Secondly,

I have tried to see the household and compound as related to other households and other compounds. Tried, in other words, to keep the analysis as fluid as the patterns of residence themselves.

A TYPOLOGY OF RESIDENCE?

The Gonja provide a particularly clear example of the limited usefulness of a typology based simply on residence at marriage. For, although at the beginning and end of a marriage a woman often remains with or returns to her kin, this absence of conjugal co-residence has to do with how marriages are established and terminated. Otherwise marriage is unequivocally virilocal. However, as we saw in chapter 7, not all women are married. The residence of their husbands is still more problematic, not only because of the problems of bias and classification, but because even within an estate there is no single norm.

The first step would seem to be an examination of the smallest functionally independent unit of domestic organization – the household.

THE HOUSEHOLD

Households have been defined as the units within which daily farming activities are jointly carried out, and within which women take turns cooking the evening meal using the produce from these fields. The basis of this unit is the conjugal family, a man and his wife (or wives) and their children. Where full brothers live in the same town, they appear always to live in the same compound. As young men they usually form a single household, their wives sharing the task of cooking the evening meal, as do the wives of one man. However, perhaps because of the small size of full sibling groups, full brothers are seldom found living together as mature adults, and here it is difficult to know what the pattern is. Of the four instances I have on record, two groups of full male siblings of the commoner estate in Busunu and one in Buipe farmed separately and their wives cooked separately, but a high degree of co-operation existed between the households. Another pair of full brothers of the ruling estate in Busunu farm jointly, but only one of the brothers is married and his wife cooks for them both. As we have seen, households centering on a conjugal pair often include young children of the wife from an earlier marriage and foster children of either spouse.

There are two sorts of *partial* household, corresponding to the two criteria of farming and cooking groups. Where a divorced or widowed woman and her children are living with kin, they form a partial house-

254

hold because, while the mother cooks for herself and her children, she does not feed the kinsman from whose farm the produce comes. Similarly, an adult man who has no wife to cook for him, but who continues to farm, is treated as a partial household. He may cook light meals himself, but he will give grain and yams to a kinswoman or brother's wife as a contribution towards the large evening meal. There is no additional woman from this household, however, to share in the rota of cooking. The single man is a dependant in this respect, as is the single woman, on a kinsman's farm.

Partial households centering around a woman depend for farm produce on her kinsman. A father, brother, or son, usually living in the same compound, will be responsible for supplying her with food. Support of this kind is a woman's right so long as she is not living with a husband. The beliefs about mystical danger discussed in the last chapter are undoubtedly the major sanctions enforcing this right between kin who are not closely related. Sentiments of affection for the woman and children appear to forestall the resentment of her own father, brother or son.

Partial households headed by men depend for cooking services either on the wives of other men in the compound, or on kinswomen who cook as a part of another household. In either case, the man will bring produce from his farm to the woman. If it is a brother's wife, she will add this food to her other supplies and cook a single meal. This may also be done by a kinswoman. However, if she is married and cooking for her husband's household, she may be concerned to show that she is not taking her husband's food for her brother. In this case she will cook two separate meals.

While the household typically centres on a conjugal pair or a polygynous family, this is not one of the criteria of a complete household. The limiting case shows why. For occasionally a man without a wife and a kinswoman who has no husband will co-operate as a *de facto* household, although there is no conjugal or sexual relationship between them. I refer to this as an agamous household since no marital tie is involved. In the cases where this arrangement was found, both man and woman were living in the same compound. Thus, while co-residence is not logically a necessary condition of household composition, in practice complete households are co-residential in central Gonja. Partial households, in contrast, are often spatially separate from the unit on which they depend.

In all three estates the majority of households are complete and based on a conjugal pair. Both types of partial household are also present in

255

each estate. For Muslims and the ruling group, that based on a woman and her dependants is more common than the partial household represented by a man with no wife. Among commoners, men and women are about as likely to head partial households. This reflects the fact that commoner men are more likely in old age to be without a wife than the men in other estates. It is not easy for an elderly man without

Table 10-1. *Type of household by estate of household head: Buipe*

Household type:	Ruling		Estate of household head: Muslim		Commoner	
Complete*		62%		57%		60%
Polygynous	2		4		4	
Monogamous	6		20		21	
Partial		38%		43%		40%
Male head	1 (7%)		4 (10%)		7 (16%)	
Female head	4 (31%)		14 (33%)		10 (24%)	
	13	100%	42	100%	42	100%

N=97

* Two commoner men and one Muslim have established an agamous inter-dependence with single women (of the same estate in each case). Both men and women have been treated as partial households for the purpose of this table.

either office or wealth to replace a wife who has died or left him. On the other hand, commoner women are somewhat less likely to be living with kin rather than a husband. This last pattern is reflected in the slightly lower incidence of commoner women in partial households in Table 10-1. Although I do not have figures on divorce for the Buipe sample, there was no apparent difference between estates in this respect. The difference in proportion of partial female headed households is due almost entirely to the greater tendency of women of the Muslim and ruling estate to return to kin in old age.

While the exchange of farming and cooking services, and thus the interdependence of food production and preparation, are the basic criteria of household viability, these activities are not restricted to the household. The sharing of cooked food has been discussed in some detail. The consumption group includes not only compound members outside the household, but kinsfolk outside the compound. Similarly, while daily farming activities are the responsibility of the personnel of the household, there are times in the agricultural cycle when the co-operation of men outside this unit is required. To what extent can the household be considered as independently viable?

HOUSEHOLD VIABILITY AND BASIC PRODUCTIVE RESOURCES

No one would mistake central Gonja for the biblical land of milk and honey. Much of the soil is too poor to farm at all, and the rest has to be allowed to return to bush after a maximum of four years. However, there is plenty of land; new farms are made wherever unused land looks fertile and is conveniently near a path and not more than an hour or two from the village. No one need be asked, and even the Earth priest is not concerned with either existing land rights or the clearing of new farms. The basic productive resource, apart from land, is a lien on labour for this heavy task, which is in fact undertaken about every two years, since farms are phased so that a man has fields at all stages of use. A man who belongs to a large compound can count on the help of all the men for clearing, although he must be prepared to feed them well. A man in a small compound may still have close kin on whom he can call for this work. Even if he does not, he can rally his peers and their dependants for a co-operative farm-clearing (*ndɔ kule*, 'farm (work) begging'), but again in exchange for plentiful food. So far as routine tasks are concerned, a man who is in good health can grow enough on his own farm for his immediate family, and indeed there are instances of young men who are supporting two wives and their children. On the other hand, an elderly man farming alone is a sad thing. The area he can mound is small, and he is hard pressed to keep even this weeded. However, even such a modest farm at least allows him to function as a partial household, contributing produce towards his cooked food.

Household viability was discussed in the context of the distribution of male foster children. The point to be stressed here is that, if there is a scarce resource, it is adult labour rather than land or cattle. Even so, it is not usually household viability that is at stake, but rather the margin of extra food which more hands makes possible. This produce may be set aside against the delay or failure of the next harvest; it may be sold to provide a little cash or, in tsetse-free areas, invested in a cow; or it may go to feed guests and support dependants. Such dependants enable a man to act as host and provider in his old age rather than himself declining into a semi-dependent status.

Access to a regular supply of labour depends on retaining the services of sons and foster sons in early and middle adulthood. This in turn depends on a range of factors all the way from temperament to formal political status. However, so long as there is a secure source of the occasional heavy labour needed for clearing new fields, a household can make do with the regular work of one man.[2] Further, joint residence is not a necessary prerequisite for assistance even in daily farming tasks. Particularly when a father and son are concerned, joint farming can continue although the two live in separate compounds. The household represented by a man and his wife and children is a potentially detachable unit which can subsist on its own within any community in which it can secure co-operative assistance in heavy farm work.

SPHERES OF ACTIVITY AND SPHERES OF AUTHORITY

The ease with which partial households can become viable by linking on to other households, either partial or complete, and the virtual autonomy of the complete household, raise again the question of the necessary conditions for interdependence in the domestic sphere. In considering the conjugal relationship, co-residence was shown to be a requirement of continuing marriage, since conjugal rights (though not those of parenthood) lapse once a couple ceases to live together. This dependence on co-residence clearly does not hold for the rights and obligations which exist between kin. As we have noted, the members of the various dynastic segments of the ruling estate tend to be dispersed throughout several villages as a result of the system of succession to office. And in practice sets of siblings, and the children of siblings, of the other estates are also dispersed. Further, women are not incorporated in their husbands' families but continue to be important in the affairs of their natal kin whatever their marital status. And we have also seen that there are many important events – naming ceremonies, marriages, illness, the removal of mystical danger, the proper observance of funeral rituals, and finally succession and inheritance – with which not just co-resident kin, but all close kin are concerned. Thus, the development of the physical units and their personnel, households and compounds,

[2] Two instances were noted in which men newly returned to settle had to find a lot of help in a short time so as to establish farms to feed their families through the coming year. Both came back at the beginning of the dry season, that is, when new farms are cleared. Each made use of rather distant ties to join a large compound and so secured the necessary labour in exchange for their own help on the farms of the other men. In one case the newcomer had close ties with smaller compounds, and seemed likely to build his new rooms there, rather than among the men with whom he was farming. In other words, a largely pragmatic view of sharing labour is taken by at least some. It is not necessary to be closely related, so long as a man can pull his own weight.

does not reflect directly the basic lines of obligation and authority which order the central events of people's lives.

There are in practice three spheres of activity, each with its characteristic patterns of rights, obligations and its own sphere of authority. A few of these activities are shared only by those who live in the same compound. Several are limited to those residing in the same village, and in this case they may or may not occupy a single compound. Others may relate to people living in several villages, although here again those concerned may all dwell in a single village, or conceivably even in the same compound. The group which participates in the first set of activities (and their implied obligations) may be termed co-resident, the second, localized, and the third, dispersed.

Spatial definition of groups sharing key activities and associated authority spheres

	The group participating:	
Is always co-resident	*Must be localized, may be co-resident*	*Is usually dispersed*
Cooking	Distribution of cooked food	Succession to office
Daily farming	Distribution of farm produce	Final jurisdiction over kin
Conjugal relations	Farm clearing	Final responsibility for kin – jural and ritual
Domestic authority	Immediate jurisdiction over kin	
	Immediate responsibility for kin – jural and ritual	

It will be seen that the obligations and activities depending on co-residence include those which were found to be essential to the conjugal relationship. The obligations defined in the second column derive either from kinship ties or those of immediate affinity. In the latter case they are usually limited to the parents of a spouse, occasionally including a spouse's foster parent, or spouse's parent's full or half-sibling. The obligations these relationships involve are few. Where distance intervenes they are virtually limited to support in emergencies, and funeral attendance and contributions. With these exceptions, the only obligations involving a dispersed group are those between kin. These the Gonja define as obligations between siblings, mother's children (*niu*

259

pibi), although, as has been shown, this in fact also refers to classificatory siblings, related either through men or women, and to the children of siblings.

It follows that, while the village in which a man or woman resides automatically limits the kinsfolk from whom regular co-operation and support may be sought, within a village the choice of the particular compound does not restrict most of the rights and duties derived from kinship, nor determine the locus of immediate authority. However, with occasional exceptions, and these occur at the very beginning or the very end of a woman's marital career, co-residence does determine domestic authority and it *is* a prerequisite of the conjugal relationship.

An appreciation of the degree to which residence does not restrict claims over kin is important for an understanding of the structure of compounds. For fission can occur within the residential group without disrupting certain of the relationships upon which economic co-operation is based. And although domestic authority is largely dependent on co-residence, jural and ritual jurisdiction based on kinship are not, and they continue to be vested in the head of the original residential group so long as he is the eldest living kinsman. However, when fission takes the form of removal to another village, immediate authority, that is, first recourse in adjudication of wrongs (room cases), help in meeting debts and in finding medicines, either devolves upon the individual who has seceded or upon his closest senior kinsman in the new village. What I have termed final authority, the right to be informed and to consent to marriages, rights in inherited property, and claims to support in times of crisis, is dependent neither on co-residence nor on localized kinship ties. These rights persist in spite of the dispersal of kin so long as contact is maintained between them.

THE ASSOCIATION OF HOUSEHOLDS IN LARGE UNITS: THE COMPOUND

Compounds are verbally identified by the name or title of a compound head, that is a person, nearly always a man, who is described as *lang-wura*, the owner or 'chief' of a compound (*langto*). However, rooms are often distributed around a number of courtyards (also *langto*), with no boundaries to indicate where the jurisdiction of one compound head begins and that of another ends. Other compounds are much more discrete.

For the analysis of residence I have used the two criteria of name linked with a compound head, and spatial distinctness. Where both criteria apply there is no problem. Where two or more courtyards are called by a single name, or commonly designated as under a single compound head, these have been treated as one compound even where spatially they appear separate. A man who holds a political or ritual office occasionally commands the sort of assistance from other compounds that is usually reserved for a compound head. In these cases, however, he is not described as *langwura*, but his authority is attributed either to a remote kinship link or to his office. For the Gonja the role of compound head has connotations of both joint residence and authority.

Of the eighteen compounds in Old Buipe in 1956, over half contained between twenty and thirty residents. However, while almost all the compounds with heads of the ruling and commoner estates fell into this modal category, the Muslim compounds were more evenly distributed. The mean number of people in compounds with heads of each estate was very similar.

Table 10-2. *Number of residents in eighteen Buipe compounds*

		Range	Mean	Modal category
Estate of	Ruling	9–26	20.4	20–9
compound head:	Muslim	6–46	22.4	10–19; 20–9
	Commoner	13–29	19.7	20–9

Of more interest than numbers of residents, however, is the way in which households are grouped into compounds. If we again consider compounds in terms of the estate of the compound head, we find that half of the commoner compounds have only two households, the largest contains only five, and the mean number of households per compound is the smallest for any of the three estates, at 2.3. The compounds headed by members of the ruling group contain between two and six households, but are very evenly distributed within this range, with a mean of 3.4 households per compound. The distribution for Muslim compounds is bimodal, with nearly half containing only a single household, and the same number six or more. The mean number of households per compound of 3.7 for the Muslim compounds is the highest for any estate.

As shown in Table 10-1, men and women of all three estates are found as heads of partial households. Do they choose with equal frequency to live in compounds headed by men of each estate? In Table 10-4 the number of partial households headed by men, and by women, is expressed as a proportion of all households in compounds identified with each estate. Partial households headed by men account for twice as many of the households in commoner compounds as in those of either

Table 10-3. *Complete households in compounds by estate of compound head: Buipe*

		Range	Mean	Modal category
Estate of	Ruling	2–6	3.4	2
compound head:	Muslim	1–7	3.7	1 and 6/7
	Commoner	2–5	2.3	2

of the other two estates. Indeed, in commoner compounds there are about as many incomplete male households as those headed by women. This is not at all the case for compounds of the Muslim and ruling estates in which partial women's households account for almost one-third of all households (Table 10-4).

Table 10-4. *Compounds of each estate: partial households headed by men and by women: Buipe*

		Proportion of all households represented by partial households headed by:	
		Men	Women
Estate of	Ruling	.10	.31
compound head:	Muslim	.09	.30
	Commoner	.20	.24

Now that we have looked at the types of household and their distribution among the compounds of the three estates, as well as the size of the compounds themselves, we are in a position to consider by what kinds of links households relate to the compound head. The question assumes that the relationship to the compound head is meaningful. That this is so for central Gonja will become clearer from an examination of the structure of particular compounds in the last section of this chapter.

There is no pronounced difference between the three estates in the relationships between household heads and the compound head with respect to generation: about one-fifth of those in the ruling and commoner compounds are 'brothers' of the head and the remainder 'sons' (including sister's sons and a few grandsons). Muslim compounds in Buipe contain slightly more men in the category 'brother' but these are mostly accounted for by the several men in Abokerpe who are distant classificatory brothers but resident in the Muslim section because of maternal links with the main Sakpare compound (see below, pp. 270 ff). It is likely that ruling and Muslim compounds differ less than the figures in Table 10-5 suggest, since the generation classification of distant kin is to a certain extent arbitrary.

Only in the ruling estate is there an instance of a household head in a generation senior to the compound head. Normally this would be very awkward for all concerned, as a 'father' should always have seniority over a 'son'. In this case, however, the father is a commoner who is related through his mother to the compound head who is also a chief. Here the chiefship over-rides generation status sufficiently to make living under the authority of a 'son' tolerable.

Table 10-5. *Generation relationship between male household heads and compound heads of each estate: Buipe*

		Generation of household head in relation to compound head:								
		Senior		Same		Junior*		None or unknown		All	
Estate of	Ruling	1	5%	3	18%	11	65%	2	12%	17	100%
compound head:	Muslim	0	—	8	35%	15	65%	0	—	23	100%
	Commoner	0	—	3	22%	10	71%	1	7%	14	100%
	All compounds	1	2%	14	26%	36	67%	3	6%	54	100%

* Includes grandsons

If, however, we look not at generation but at the kinship tie which links heads of households to their compound of residence, a curious pattern appears. For compounds of the Muslim and ruling estates these links are mainly cognatic (that is, traced through males and females), while two-thirds of the households in commoner compounds are related only through agnatic links to the compound head. These are households of full or paternal half-brothers and sons of the compound head.

Table 10-6. *Relation of male household heads to compound heads of each estate: Buipe*

		Relationship between compound head and household head is:			
		Agnatic	Cognatic	Not known or unrelated	Total
Estate of	Ruling	4 24%	11 65%	2 12%	17 101%
compound head:	Muslim	10 43%	13 57%	0 —	23 100%
	Commoner	9 64%	4 29%	1 7%	14 100%
	All compounds	23 42%	28 52%	3 6%	N=54 100%

In part this difference reflects the fact that there are fewer households in commoner compounds, and thus fewer distant relatives. But Muslim and ruling compounds might well contain even more paternal half-brothers, sons, and brothers' sons, and maintain the same ratio of agnatic to cognatic ties as the commoner compounds. The major cause of the predominance of cognatic ties in Muslim and ruling compounds lies in the fact that there are relatively few brothers and sons, but relatively many 'women's children'.

How is the predominance of cognatic ties in compounds of the Muslim and ruling estates to be reconciled with the fact that offices for which members of these estates are eligible pass in the agnatic line? Surely we would expect to find a concentration of agnates in the divisional capital, looking after their rights and advancing their claims? Instead it is the commoner compound heads who manage to keep their sons and brothers living with them, while in the compounds of the other two estates these heirs apparent are poorly represented. Although there are a number of villages in the division besides the capital, Buipe is unusual in having no village chiefships of the first rank. The four major chiefs all live in the capital. Thus, unlike the other divisions, dynastic segments do not establish local foci in outlying villages because the men hold chiefships there. But where are the men of the ruling estate?

So long as we retain a synchronic view of residence patterns it is difficult to explain this seeming paradox. Without anticipating too greatly the diachronic arguments of the following chapter, we may, by looking at the pattern of succession to compound headship, consider how extensive is the bias towards cognatic links in the ruling and Muslim estates. The data in Table 10-7 show the pattern of succession to the eighteen compounds in Old Buipe plus a further fifteen from

Busunu and Mankpa. Compound heads of the ruling estate are all living agnatically, nine in their father's compound, and one in a new compound in his father's village. It is true that residence in a capital is for a member of the ruling estate of that division, residence in his father's village. However, it is significant that in three divisional capitals there

Table 10-7. *Relation of compound head to previous compound head for thirty-three central Gonja compounds*

Estate of present com- pound head:	Dead father's compound	New site in father's village	Village or compound of maternal relative	Neo- local	Not known	Father still living	Total
			Site of compound:				
Ruling	9	1	—	—	—	—	10
Muslim	3	3	—	2	—	—	8
Commoner	3	1	4	1	2	4	15
Total	15	5	4	3	2	4	

N=33

is no man of the ruling estate living as a compound head in his maternal home. And further, while the establishing of new compounds is a regular pattern for men of the other two estates, those in the ruling estate seem rarely to do this.

Muslims show a similar bias towards living in maturity in their agnatic home; none of the Muslim compound heads in Buipe or Busunu was in either the village or the compound of maternal kin. Two senior Muslims had, however, established compounds in a village where they had no kin. Both of these men were traders living for the time in Busunu, and both were prosperous enough to have their own compound rather than having to rent rooms in someone else's.

The commoner compound heads provide the greatest contrast with those of the ruling estate, for less than half are living in the village or compound of a father. The two cases which are recorded 'not known' are almost certainly neolocal, but it was not clear whether their fathers had for a time lived in Buipe where the sons now have their compounds. The heads of the remaining four of the thirty-three compounds were

265

relatively young men whose fathers were still alive. All four had established compounds in the village and section where their fathers were living.

The picture here is quite different to that suggested by the kinship ties linking households to the compound in which they are located (Table 10-6). It appears that, although there may be only a few agnates living in compounds of the ruling estate, they form a permanent core group within which the compound headship passes. Even the establishment of a new compound in his paternal village is unusual for a man of the ruling estate. Muslim compounds in the paternal village are newly established as often as they are taken over from a dead agnate. And as often again, a Muslim compound may be a temporary base in a strange town. Finally, the commoner compounds are about evenly divided among those where a paternal kinsman previously was the head, those previously under a maternal kinsman, and those established by the present head himself. And here the reversal of the picture is completed. For, while two-thirds of the households in commoner compounds belong to agnatic kin, only one-fifth of the present heads succeeded an agnate. This suggests a pattern in which young married men remain to farm with a father or mother's brother until they have a household mature enough to establish in a compound of their own. It fits also with the lower mean number of households in commoner compounds. These themes will be picked up in the following chapter, when movements between compounds, and villages, are looked at over time. First, however, I want to examine the composition of compounds of each estate.

COMPOSITION OF SELECTED COMPOUNDS

Of course no one compound is really typical, even of those with compound heads of the same estate. However, numerical summaries are not entirely satisfactory as a way of describing or expressing differences between estates. For this reason the synchronic view of residence concludes with brief sketches of three compounds, one identified with each of the social estates. In order to understand the pattern of residence within a compound it will sometimes be necessary to discuss other compounds as well, which in itself provides an important insight into the meaning of residence.

Burumbupe, a commoner compound (Busunu)
Many of the older people in Busunu still refer to Burumbu's compound as Boduape, for his father, Bodua, was a famous hunter. In a way,

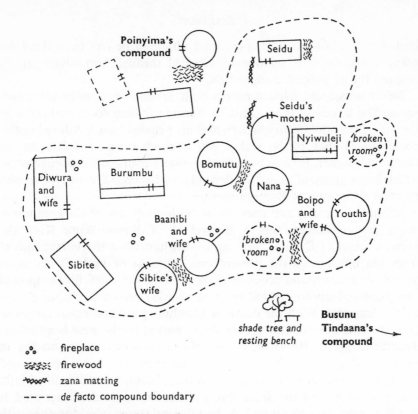

Poinyima's compound

Seidu

Seidu's mother

Nyiwuleji

broken room

Diwura and wife

Burumbu

Bomutu

Nana

Boipo and wife

Youths

Baanibi and wife

broken room

Sibite

Sibite's wife

shade tree and resting bench

Busunu Tindaana's compound

- ° fireplace
- firewood
- zana matting
- - - - *de facto* compound boundary

Fig. 12 The compound of Burumbu.

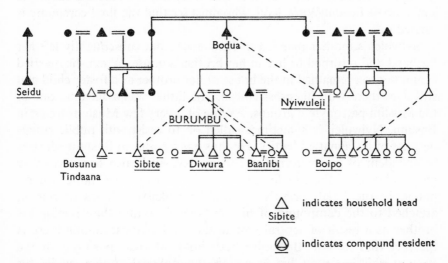

Seidu

Bodua

Nyiwuleji

BURUMBU

Busunu
Tindaana

Sibite

Diwura

Baanibi

Boipo

△ indicates household head
Sibite

⬤ indicates compound resident

Fig. 12a Genealogy of adult males of Burumbu's compound. Villages lived in by
adult compound residents: Busunu, Kawsawgu, Frufruso.

Bodua still dominates the compound although he has been dead for many years, for it is relationships traced through him which largely account for its present composition.

This compound includes rooms built around three adjacent courtyards. The largest of these contains Burumbu's own room and those of his wife, their adolescent children and his married 'sons'. Adjoining this courtyard is that of Nyiwuleji whose mother was a full sister of Burumbu's father, Bodua. Next to Nyiwuleji's courtyard lies the third, in which live a group of unrelated dependants descended from a slave who married a kinsman of Bodua's mother.

Burumbu's father, and thus Burumbu himself, are of the commoner Anga group. Bodua was a dependant of BusunuWura Kofi, the previous chief of Busunu, and came with him when the village moved from the old site to the present one. Because of Bodua's status as household retainer and provider of meat to the old chief, his compound was allocated another retainer, a slave who served as BusunuWura Kofi's drummer. With the death of the chief, jural and ritual responsibility for the descendants of his slaves passed to the new head of his dynastic segment. However, the people themselves continue to live in the same place. Burumbu speaks of them as his kin, but when pressed for the exact relationship explains that there is only a remote affinal link. When Seidu, one of the descendants of the first slave drummer died, it was Burumbu who performed the first funeral ceremonies, together with the kin of the dead man's mother and wife. But it is another man, the son's son of BusunuWura Kofi, who must see that the final ceremony is carried out.

Nyiwuleji's mother married in Kawsawgu, but subsequently left her husband and returned to live in her brother's house. When she married again, her son remained in the house of her brother as a foster child and still lives there with his cross-cousin. His father was a Jebagte, one of the Muslim patronymic groups. As one of a very few Muslims living in Busunu, Nyiwuleji is sometimes called on to assist with public rituals because of his agnatic identity. He thus has a status in Busunu which is independent of his maternal ties there. Nyiwuleji also has a younger maternal half-brother, Gelli, who lives in his own dead father's compound in the Earth priest's section. Nyiwuleji continues to remain attached to the compound of his cross-cousin rather than joining his brother as a result of several circumstances. Foremost among these is the fact that he and Burumbu both hold informal positions in the Busunu chief's court; his is within the political system, while his cousin's is a particular relationship of a personal kind. Their independent yet equivalent status is also expressed by the fact that Nyiwuleji's rooms centre around a separate courtyard from those of his cross-cousin, and that the two men farm separately.

Of the six rooms which centre on Burumbu's own courtyard, two are occupied by his household and the rest by other households. One room belongs to Burumbu's eldest son and his wife, another is occupied by a son of Burumbu's dead brother, with his wife and young children, while two rooms are used by Sibite, his wife, children and foster child.

Sibite's father, now dead, was a paternal half-brother of the father of the Busunu Earth priest, whose compound lies across a path from that of Burumbu. Sibite and the priest are thus parallel cousins and Sibite is next in line of succession to the title. However, Sibite's mother was a full sister of Burumbu's father, who 'begged' him as a foster child when he was a boy. So he continues to live in the compound where he was reared, as a 'son' (in fact a 'sister's' son) of the present compound head. When he succeeds to the position of Earth priest, Sibite will almost certainly move into the compound where his agnates live.

Boduape is typical of other commoner compounds in having household heads who live there as cognatic kin as well as agnates of the compound head. It is also typical in containing individual members of all three estates, as well as of more than one commoner group. With five complete households, it is larger than most commoner compounds, but this is probably a temporary situation. For there are indications that it was at the high point of a developmental cycle and likely to contract considerably in the near future. The courtyard containing the rooms of Seidu's household was already nearly deserted, although the seven-day funeral had not yet been performed. Nyiwuleji's eldest son had just married,[3] and his younger brothers would do so within a few years. Once Nyiwuleji found himself in a position of kinship authority over several households, it would be unlikely that he would choose to remain under Burumbu's headship for long. And Sibite's departure was only a matter of time, until he succeeded his 'brother' as Earth priest.

While it is clear that the residents of this compound have links of several kinds with kin living elsewhere, these ties are particularistic, leading in many different directions. The compound temporarily provides a physical focus for similar particularistic ties, which are thus given a greater concreteness by co-residence. Several of the households might equally well take up residence in different compounds, however, and these would in turn assume the added importance that goes with co-residence.

[3] His wife is living with her mother following the birth of their first child. She has not yet begun to cook 'as a wife'.

Limampe, a Muslim compound (Buipe)

The current head of this compound, Limam Krantomah, is himself the son of Limam Famolle, and both served as the Limam to the Gonja paramount, the YagbumWura. Now, however, Limam Krantomah is old and blind, and the Limam of the Muslim town of Larabanga serves the YagbumWura's court. His deputy in Buipe is his paternal half-brother, Mallam Kamoshi, whose room faces that of the Limam across the single courtyard. These men are the only ones of their generation in the compound. The other rooms (all square 'men's rooms') which surround the Limam's belong to their 'sons', one for the unmarried young men, the rest for couples and their children. Like the young men at the other extreme of life, the Limam has no wife.

As in compounds of other estates, we find that some of the 'sons' are in fact related through women; one a classificatory sister's son, and another a daughter's son of the compound head. Both these men are practising Muslims, though only one belongs to the Muslim estate, by patrifiliation. Three of the households are headed by the Limam's own sons, each of a different mother, and the last by the eldest son of Mallam Kamoshi. While the apparent compactness of this compound is not due, as it at first appears, to an entirely agnatic pattern of relations between the household heads, this feature is markedly stronger than in most compounds. The cognatic kin also seem more firmly settled than in Burumbu's compound. It is true that Landeni speaks of his 'fathers' among the Bole Muslims, and may one day return there. But Abudu (like his two younger full brothers who sleep in the Limam's room as his *nyeribi*) is unlikely to return to the compound of his dead father's people since they are commoners, and hunters who do not follow the Muslim rules of diet and prayer.

One feature of the architecture which contrasts markedly with that of both ruling and commoner compounds is the absence of round 'women's' rooms, or indeed of any separate rooms for women and children. The choice of square or oblong flat-roofed rooms is undoubtedly a matter of Islamic tradition in the Sudan (Prussin 1969), and women's rooms can be of this shape as well. Therefore the absence of separate rooms for wives is due not to Islamic architectural tradition, but to the fact that Muslim men do not hold the type of shrines, found with commoners and chiefs, which are endangered by the presence of a menstruating woman.

Limampe has seven complete households and thus falls in the larger of the two modal categories for Muslim compounds. Yet in other respects it is atypical: there is one partial household centering on a man,

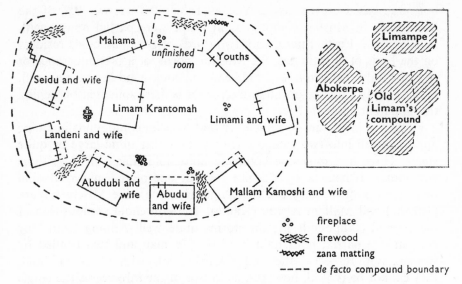

Fig. 13 The compound of the Buipe Limam (Limampe). The inset shows position relative to other Sakpare compounds.

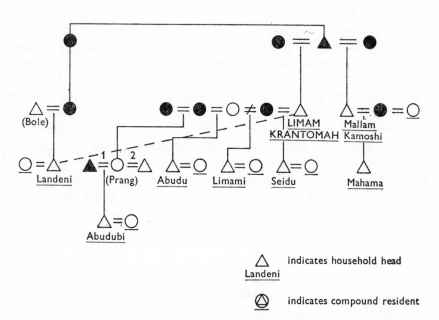

Fig. 13a Genealogy showing relation of household heads to Limam Krantomah. Villages lived in by adult compound residents: Prang, Morno, Bole, Boruasi, Larabanga, Nyanga, Mpaha, Mankpa, Bonduku, Abonyipe.

but none based on a woman. Yet, as Table 10-4 shows, 30% of the households in Muslim compounds in Buipe were partial houses with female heads. Furthermore, with two-thirds of the households resident on the basis of agnatic ties, the Muslim 'norm' of a preponderance of cognatic links between household head and compound head is reversed. Is this simply a matter of random error, or is there some reason behind this apparent anomaly?

First, it is important to remember that Muslim compounds in Buipe appear to fall into two categories: they are either quite large or quite small. Three had only one complete household. Each of these three compounds is headed by a senior man of one of the minor Muslim patronymic groups: they are the Dogte (Nafuna), the MiserassiWura (Jebagte) and Mallam Aleidu (Kante). The household composition of these small compounds fits the norms quite well. Among them they contain one partial household headed by a man and two headed by women. With respect to the kind of kinship links within the household, they cannot be typical, however, as in two of the three cases the single household is that of the compound head himself; that is to say, there is no link between households of any kind, agnatic or cognatic. In the third case, the household head is the son of the compound head who is without a wife.

But what of the large compounds which, apart from Limampe, contain a high proportion of complete households related through women, and of partial households headed by women? Here the critical factor is that three of the four remaining Muslim compounds are associated with the Sakpare patronymic group. These are descendants of the Mallam Fati Morukpe who helped NdeWura Jakpa to conquer Gonja. They hold most of the divisional Limamships as well as serving the paramount. Their very substantial numbers in Buipe testify to their long association with this historic town and to the importance of their position in the state. All Sakpare in Buipe are considered to be one family (*kanang konle*), though there is not a single genealogy linking those now living. While following the same rule as the Gbanya, that a son may not directly succeed his father in office, the Sakpare do not have distinct, named, dynastic segments as does the ruling estate. On the other hand office often passes in a similar manner. In Buipe there were two branches of the family, one currently holding the Limamship, and the other which had supplied the previous incumbent.

If the three compounds associated with the Sakpare Muslims are looked at as a whole (inset in Figure 13), it is possible to see how the agnatic bias of the Limam's compound and the predominance of cognatic ties and partial households headed by women both figure in a larger pattern. The largest of the three compounds, Old Limampe, includes rooms built around two main courtyards. Those around the first courtyard are all occupied by sons, or brother's sons of the previous Limam. This agnatic core is very similar to that found in the present Limam's compound. The second, larger, courtyard contains the rooms of nine women who are related (half agnatically, half through women) to the old Limam. Although there are a few rooms of men as well, this courtyard is largely dominated by the partial households of divorced or widowed women.

The third compound, Abokerpe, although an integral part of the Muslim section of Buipe, is headed by a commoner convert to the religion of his mother's people. Here live several other households of Muslims who are 'women's children', some of them the sons of the women in the old Limam's compound. Most of these are in the same generation as the compound head (so far as generation can be reckoned, for ties are often distant or unclear). This is in effect a compound of classificatory brothers.

Some of the men in this compound are almost certainly of slave descent. Others just as clearly are not. Persistent enquiries on this subject are much resented, and given the general lack of interest in genealogical matters, it is virtually impossible to establish whether a commoner was originally of slave stock. The pattern of marriage between villages and between estates makes it improbable that most, or even very many, commoners living in the capital were the children of slaves.

In the same way that Abokerpe can be seen as a compound of 'brothers', the Old Limam's compound could be seen as consisting of one courtyard of 'sisters' and 'daughters' and another of 'sons' of the previous compound head.

If we consider the several Sakpare courtyards as a whole, we have a pattern of two agnatic cores, with two attached groups, one of sisters and the other of sister's children. That these two attached groups are very substantial is clear from the figures already given. But the way they are attached differs radically from what we found in the case of the commoner compound, Boduape. There ties were direct and particularistic; here there are nine 'sisters' and a whole compound full of 'sister's children'. Of course, there are the same individual kinship links between these people and other compounds in Buipe and elsewhere that we found for Boduape. But in this Muslim population the links between compounds are not confined to the particularistic sort. Indeed,

Limampe seems anomalous until we take into account the pattern of relations in all the Sakpare compounds.

SilimaWurape, a compound of the ruling estate (Buipe)
There were three compounds in Old Buipe headed by chiefs of the ruling estate. Another belonging to the present BuipeWura was partly empty following his move to New Buipe. The SilimaWura's compound consisting of two complete households is neither the largest nor the smallest of the four. That it used to be a little larger is shown by the two broken rooms, and the broken council hall (*lembu*), used by two previous chiefs of Buipe, Chenchanko, and his son, Konkonte. The present compound head is a paternal half-brother of the late BuipeWura, Konkonte, though not the oldest of the surviving sons of BuipeWura

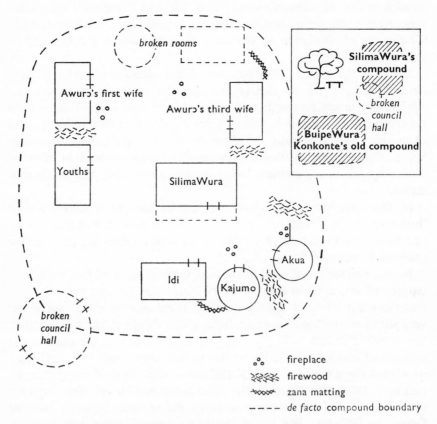

Fig. 14   SilimaWura's compound. The inset shows position in relation to Buipe-
Wura Konkonte's old compound.

274

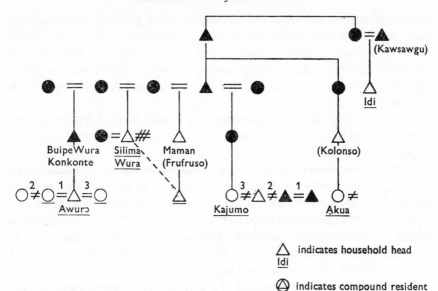

Fig. 14a Genealogy showing relation of household heads to SilimaWura. Main villages lived in by adult compound residents: Benyalipe, Kolonso, Yapie, Jembito, Kabalipe, Frufruso, Damongo, Abonyipe, Larabanga, Kawsawgu.

Chenchanko; this position is filled by his elder half-brother Maman, who lives with his maternal kin in Frufruso. Maman declined to accept the Silima chiefship when it fell vacant, preferring to let his younger brother return and take charge of the family compound. However, Maman has sent his son to grow up with SilimaWura and visits him there from time to time.

There is only one complete household based on a conjugal family in SilimaWurape, for of the three adult men there, only the youngest, Awurɔ, is married. Idi's wife died some time ago and he has remained a widower. The SilimaWura appears to be between wives, a not un-common state for him judging by the fact that each of the four sons who live with him has a different mother. SilimaWura and Idi farm, but have no wives to cook for them. They give produce from their farms to two adult women who are without husbands and living with their children in the compound of their maternal kin. These women cook for their children and send bowls to their 'grandfather' Idi, and to the Silima-Wura who is mother's brother to one (Kajumo) and father's 'brother' to the other (Akua). In one sense the two older men have exchanged the services of wives for those of sisters. The situation is completely charac-

275

teristic of such domestic arrangements in being partially a permanent, and partially a temporary expedient. SilimaWura and his 'daughter' Akua will both remarry, later if not sooner. Idi and Kajumo are probably through with marriage and the siting of their rooms suggests that they may have settled on a *modus vivendi* which suits them both very well.

The genealogical chart showing the relationship between room-owners in the SilimaWura's compound falls neatly into two halves (see Figure 14a). The SilimaWura and his dead brother's son, Awurɔ, form an agnatic core which has a solid foundation in the next generation in the young and adolescent sons of the SilimaWura and his brother. The other three households, all partial, are linked through women to this core.[4] These people have a right to live here, and fulfil useful functions in balancing the domestic economy. They are nevertheless referred to as 'women's children', meaning that they are not of the ruling estate and cannot provide future office-holders.

There remain two aspects of the SilimaWura's compound which, though not apparent from the diagram and the genealogy linking its occupants, are just as important as those already mentioned. First, the residents who are living here represent only a few of those who have a right to be here. Maman, the elder brother in Frufruso, is one such absentee. There are three more sons of the SilimaWura's father living in other towns in Gonja, and any of these four men could return and make his home in their father's compound if he wished. The same right applies to the sons and sons' sons of BuipeWura Chenchanko's brothers, and it holds also for the daughters in old age, and for their children. That this right is a genuine one is shown by the fact that the SilimaWura himself was reared elsewhere and only returned to take up the chiefship. Of those resident through maternal links, Idi came back with his mother from Kawsawgu when she left his father, and he has lived in Buipe ever since; Kajumo has been here for a few years, but Akua only for a few weeks.

The other factor which is not evident from Figure 14 is that, although SilimaWurape qualifies as a compound by the criteria of having a name, a designated compound head, and physical discreteness, it is in fact closely linked with another adjacent compound now known as Bakeripe, after the eldest son of the senior woman living there. Many people, however, still refer to it as Konkontepe, for it was the compound of the

---

[4] Two of these partial households have a longstanding pattern of co-operation but are treated in the numerical analysis as partial households. See above pp. 255–6.

late BuipeWura Konkonte, the SilimaWura's elder paternal half-brother. So far as the daily domestic and farming routine is concerned, those living in the two compounds are quite independent. But there are certain occasions (Damba and Jentigi in the ritual cycle, and the clearing of new farms and harvesting of grain in the agricultural cycle) on which the authority of the SilimaWura extends over both compounds. This is so by virtue of his being the senior man of Konkonte's generation resident in Buipe. This status carries with it no title; it is simply said by those in Bakeripe that "SilimaWura owns us" (*SilimaWura e be wɔ anye*).[5]

There is no agnatic kinsman of the late chief living in his old compound now; the several households are all headed by men related through maternal links. This is so despite the fact that a son of Konkonte's lives in the SilimaWura's compound, who at thirty-five, and with two wives, could assume the role of compound head if he wished. Instead, he lives under the authority of the SilimaWura, apart from the several households of distantly related cognates. The SilimaWura's compound appears to serve as a focus for the dynastic segment of the ruling group represented by the late chiefs Chenchanko and Konkonte, and currently by the SilimaWura. While close cognates also live there, those more distantly related have joined together in a separate compound. Two other much smaller compounds also fall under the Silima-Wura's authority; they belong to men who were dependants of the old chiefs, and who still acknowledge this relationship on certain occasions.

As in the case of the women's children living in Sakpare compounds, some of those in these loosely associated compounds were probably originally of slave descent. However, one can see the same kinds of links at an earlier stage in SilimaWurape; in these cases, paternity is known, and there is no question of slave origin. Again, resident in the Buipe-Wura's compound while he was in New Buipe were two households of commoners whose father was a maternal relative of the chief from western Gonja. Now the relationship is known, but in another generation people will say vaguely, "they must be women's children". This inevitable ambiguity of the relationship of some residents to the compound head is reflected in Table 10-6 where a small proportion of households in both ruling and commoner compounds are listed as unrelated or unknown. This table also shows that two-thirds of the

---

[5] The position of the old council hall between the two compounds (see inset, Figure 14), suggests that BuipeWura Konkonte's compound may have at one time extended this far to incorporate the hall. I neglected to establish this point at the time.

households in compounds associated with the ruling estate are linked through women to the compound head. The genealogy for Silima-Wurape gives some indication of the kind of links involved. Here we are again confronted with the contradiction between the preponderance of cognatic kin living in compounds of the ruling estate and the importance for this estate of being in the house of one's father. It is only by examining patterns of residence in time and space that this paradox can be resolved.

11

The developmental cycle

The patterns of residence which have been outlined in the last chapter must be considered from a diachronic as well as a synchronic point of view. I do not have enough time-based data to deal in detail with all the ways that social changes are affecting the domestic groups in Gonja society. The synchronic aspects referred to are those resulting from the working out of the developmental cycle. The object of this chapter is to outline the forces operating on individuals through the life cycle to produce the kind of residential patterns that we have seen in the last chapter.

Fortes' discussion of the developmental cycle (1958) sets out the successive stages of the maturation of a new member of society, from totally dependent infant to an adult who himself heads a domestic group and begets new recruits. This development is expressed in terms of widening spheres of competence, and steadily increasing involvement of the maturing individual in the affairs of his society: not only domestic affairs, but the ritual, political and economic activities which are the very stuff of social life. There are thus two parallel themes. On the one hand, the individual matures and gradually extends his own sphere of activity and competence from the narrow confines of his mother's room through compound, neighbourhood, village, and beyond. And on the other hand the re-creation of new domestic groups with marriage, and their expansion and eventual dissolution occurs, must occur, within the economic and political constraints of the society. The developmental cycle is a way of conceptualizing the articulation of individual maturation with the career of the domestic group. It also highlights the dual role of the domestic groups themselves as socializing agencies and as units of the wider system.

I have discussed a number of institutions which are related to the shift of personnel between domestic units: voluntary fostering sends children from one household to another; crisis fostering, following the death or divorce of the parents does the same; the ousting of a widow from her conjugal home means that the next household of which she is a part cannot be within the compound of her late husband; the brief duration of many marriages also limits the existence of many domestic groups;

279

and terminal separation ensures that many compounds contain partial households centred on an elderly man or woman, often with a child or grandchild. It is this movement of individuals between households, and households between compounds, which is the main feature of the developmental cycle shared by the three estates. These institutions, and the circulation of personnel to which they lead, create the conditions for both individual maturation and the developmental pattern of domestic groups. It is with the latter process that the present chapter is primarily concerned.

THE BASIC FORM OF THE DEVELOPMENTAL CYCLE

In the discussion of residence patterns 'on the ground', it was necessary to distinguish between three spheres of authority. Domestic authority is vested in the household head and refers to control over household members in the pursuit of daily economic and housekeeping tasks. The authority of a husband over his wife, and of parents over their children, has been discussed in the earlier sections.

Immediate authority means responsibility for assistance in meeting debts, finding medicine and providing food if the household is in need. In return the elder who exercises this authority expects regular expressions of deference and respect through greeting and a willingness to perform services. He will, for instance, expect male household heads to assist him with the clearing of new farms, and adult women to help with the preparation of the large meals given to those who co-operate in heavy farming and required for certain rituals. Immediate authority is held by a closely related senior kinsman who is living in the same village. This person is usually a man, and the head of the compound in which the household is established. There are, however, a number of situations in which immediate authority is not vested in the compound head. Where an elderly couple has separated but continue to live in the same village, a son often accompanies his mother, lives in her natal compound and farms with her kin. If his mother's own brother is there as well, he will assume immediate authority over the sister's son. However, if she has joined more distant kin, the youth's father will continue to hold immediate authority over him. A related case is that of a mature man who establishes his own compound while his father is still alive. Although he himself is a compound head, he will still defer to his father, assist him with labour and support, and consult him in important matters. Here it is the independence of domestic authority which a son has secured by establishing his own separate compound. This situation does not occur frequently and usually follows the return of a married son with his own family after a period of living elsewhere. Immediate authority can only exist with respect to those in the same village, between those who regularly co-operate and consult.

Final authority, on the other hand, is a matter of kinship and not proximity. There are two separate spheres in which final authority operates, the political sphere and the sphere of inheritance of property and kinship responsibility. Final authority in the political sphere seems to function only for those patronymic groups in which office is vested. It is exercised by the senior office-holder of the group or segment, and when he dies, it passes to his successor along with the office. In the political sphere final authority controls the relations of agnates in matters with which they are jointly concerned.

Throughout Gonja it is the mother's brother who is held to 'own' the children of the next generation. In central Gonja inheritance tends to pass between maternal kin, and final authority over these people is vested in the senior maternal kinsman. The earlier accounts (chapter 9) of the negotiations preceding Ashetu's second marriage, and of the transmission of authority over Mallam Aleidu's adult children on his death, provide examples of how this works in practice. The kinsman who holds final authority over an adult is his last recourse in trouble and has the deciding voice in major decisions. The sanction behind his position is the threat of mystical danger should dead maternal kin see that their representative is not being respected and obeyed.

The importance of this divisibility of authority is seen most clearly in the pattern followed by the father-son relationship as the son reaches adulthood and establishes his own household. The element of respectful avoidance which characterizes relations between men of adjacent generations is not often made explicit, nor is it formalized to any great extent. It is nevertheless one factor in the determination of residence of men whose fathers are still alive. In the eighteen Buipe compounds, there were thirty-six heads of household in the generation below that of the compound head (see Table 10-5). Of these, only nine (25%) were sons of the compound head. In twelve of these eighteen compounds, there were no married sons of the compound head; in four cases there was a single married son, and in two compounds there was more than one. The way in which this pattern differs among the three estates is discussed below.

Avoidance is strongest between a man and his eldest son (*ewurikung*). The opposition between successive generations which is focused on this relationship is frequently expressed in separate residence once the son becomes head of his own household. This separation make take several forms. So long as father and son reside in the same village they continue to participate in the same farm-clearing group, and the father continues to hold ultimate and often immediate authority over the son and his household.

In several cases, where the parents had separated and the mother lived with kin in the same village, the eldest son and his wife and children lived in the same compound as the mother and farmed for her. Instances of this pattern were recorded where the parents belonged to all three estates. A similar form of separate residence occurs in all estates at the time when a man's father dies and the headship of the compound passes to a proxy father. After a suitable period of mourning, his mother will return to her own kin. When they live in the same village, one of her sons, usually the eldest, may remove his household to the compound of his maternal kin, without severing the jural, ritual and economic ties with the members of his dead father's compound.

In other instances, the establishment of their own households during their father's life-time means that eldest sons take up residence with a father's 'brother' in the same or a near-by village. This type of move involves transfer of immediate authority and economic co-operation to the new compound head, although ultimate authority remains unaffected. If, as is likely, the brothers co-operate in farm clearing and turn to one another for jural and ritual support, such a shift in residence results in little change unless removal to a different village is involved.

Although the pressure to remove himself from the father's immediate domestic authority falls most heavily on an eldest son, it is not confined to him, nor is it universally acted upon. But because an eldest son is usually the first to head a domestic group of sufficient size to be independently viable, he is frequently the first to move away. Furthermore, it is 'safer' from the father's point of view to detail an eldest son to reside among his maternal relatives and farm for his mother, because at the father's death this son will be more likely than a younger brother to return to his paternal compound.

Occasionally a man will establish his own compound during his father's life-time. In all the recorded instances the new compound is in the same section as that of the father, and in some cases it is a moot point whether it constitutes a separate compound or a detached court-yard of the father's compound. This ambiguity in fact reflects a transitional position in the developmental cycle. However, so long as a man's father or proxy father is alive, he is subordinate to him in certain ritual and jural contexts, even though head of a separate compound. The situation is transitional, because at his father's death this dependence lapses. Either two discrete compounds clearly emerge, or a single compound is again formed and one of the sites abandoned.

Establishment of a separate compound in the same village during the father's life-time is rare. It appears to happen in one of two circumstances: if a mature son returns to his paternal home he can, by building his own compound, continue to enjoy a measure of the independence from paternal authority to which he has become accustomed, while at the same time reaffirming his ties with his parental family and agnatic kinsfolk. Secondly, if an elderly man has several adult sons living with him at the same time, full siblings (or those relatively close in age) may form a separate compound.

However, the most common pattern is for sons gradually to break away from the immediate authority of the parental generation by utilizing the flexibility of Gonja architecture. When youths approach puberty they no longer sleep in their mother's room. This prohibition is not heavily stressed; it is rather the case that young men eagerly anticipate the independence signified by joining other adolescent boys in whatever room they have managed to claim for their own. These youths may appropriate an old room no longer considered habitable by their elders, or, if no such room is available, they may join the youths of a nearby compound or sleep in the council hall of the compound head. Some time before he marries, a young man either appropriates, or builds, a room of his own. If he is preoccupied with farming and hunting, it may be some years before his first wife has a separate room, since youths are unlikely to have shrines which must be kept from contact with a menstruating woman. But unless he is exceptionally lazy, or has no kinsmen to help him build, by the time a youth has one or two children he will be the head of a household consisting of two rooms. These two rooms can usually be positioned in such a way as to form a subsidiary courtyard next to that in which his father lives. Sometimes this rearrangement is accomplished by sealing up the old door and cutting a new one on the opposite side of the first room. Alternatively, the building of the second room may serve as an occasion to abandon the husband's own room, in which case not one but two new rooms will be constructed, enclosing a space which becomes the new courtyard.

The clarity with which the new courtyard is distinguished architecturally from the old varies greatly. If the compound already has two or three courtyards, the rooms of the son may be added to a subsidiary courtyard. Where this happens, the son simply joins his generation peers. If the compound is small and compact, the new rooms must be built outside its previous limits; to one familiar with the old layout of the compound, they indicate immediately that a new household has been formed. On the other hand, many compounds are open, surrounding a single central courtyard. Here the separation may be achieved by placing the new room in the centre facing toward one side, and hence towards one group of rooms and simultaneously away from others. The result is a two courtyard compound created out of one.

Sometimes other factors take precedence over generation in determining the placing of rooms. An example is shown in the diagram of Burumbu's compound (Figure 12). This consists of three courtyards, one occupied by an unrelated dependant of slave descent, together with his wife and children, another by Burumbu's cross-cousin, Nyiwuleji, and his family, while in the third live the compound head and the members of three households headed by his 'sons'. Here the 'distances' between the compound head, an unrelated dependant, and a cross-cousin are greater than between adjacent generations. The position of the rooms and doorways of Awurɔ's household and of the unmarried youths' room in Figure 14 suggests that a new courtyard may soon be formed within SilimaWura's compound to separate the 'sons' from the 'fathers'.

The basic pattern of the developmental cycle at the domestic level, then, is the establishment of subsidiary courtyards by members of the generation below the compound head, with the eventual assumption of headship of the original compound by the eldest son. The return to a father's compound represents not only the assumption of an established compound headship. It is also desirable because the dead father is felt to be still present as a spirit, keeping watch over his children just as he did in life. Paternal half-brothers, more distant 'brothers' and other dependants who made up the subsidiary compound are not likely to return to the dead father's compound. The eldest 'brother' remaining assumes headship of what becomes a distinct compound, although the men in both are likely to continue cooperating in major economic tasks and family ritual.

This is the pattern likely to be followed where a son grows to adulthood in the household of his father or in that of a proxy father. The relation of present to previous compound head (see Table 10-7) may be used as an index of the return of a son to his dead father's compound. Here we see that the headship of half of the compounds has passed to a son. However, in several of these cases, the son was not in fact raised in his father's village, but returned from elsewhere to head the paternal compound. In well over half the cases the pattern is clearly a different one.

ALTERNATIVE FORMS OF THE DEVELOPMENTAL CYCLE

There is no need to refer again to the processes which lead to the dispersal of sons among paternal and maternal kin. We saw, in chapter 8, that thirteen out of sixteen male foster children were with either their own, or their father's maternal kin. Those who are reared away from their paternal compound usually remain until they marry, though a few persuade parent and foster parent that they should return earlier. Others defer the responsibilities which go with marriage, and spend up to two or even several years 'roaming about' before establishing a domestic unit of their own. The decision to marry may be precipitated by the foster parent presenting the youth with a bride from among his 'daughters' or 'grand-daughters'. Or, as we have seen, a young man may court a girl for himself. Either way, marriage does not necessarily mean a decision about where a man will finally settle, since he may return to his paternal home at any time. If he chooses to stay with his foster parent, contact with his natal family is still maintained through visits, and later perhaps through the return of a son or daughter as a foster child, or by means of an arranged marriage.

If we take the developmental cycle as that process which leads to the establishment of domestic groups in the next generation, then for those who leave the paternal home in childhood or as adolescents, the critical question is, under what conditions will they return, and under what conditions will they remain to settle elsewhere, with non-agnates? For those who do come back, the basic developmental cycle has been, as it were, stretched out of shape. The time dimension is distorted but the pattern is still that of a man first establishing domestic independence elsewhere, and finally assuming headship of his own compound and immediate authority over his dependants in his paternal village. For the man who settles permanently with maternal kin, there is, in addition to the gradual assumption of independence, a basic shift of identity, which also affects the identity of his children. The household they grow up in may be the same, whether it is part of a compound of maternal or paternal kin. We have seen that the household is a highly independent, potentially mobile unit. But the external domain of economic and political relations to which the child ultimately has access through his membership in household and compound often differs radically, depending on whether it is the world of his agnates or of other kin.

FACTORS INFLUENCING DECISION TO RETURN TO AGNATES

The same two dimensions are reflected in the factors influencing a man's decision as to whether or not to rejoin his agnatic kin. On the one hand there are relations with and role obligations towards close kin: the internal, domestic domain. Other factors are more properly seen as aspects of the external domain; economic, political and ritual constraints and considerations are all relevant. I outline here what seem to be the major considerations, first in relation to kinship roles.

KINSHIP CONSIDERATIONS

The interplay between a youth and his foster parents' own sons was discussed earlier. Particularly if there has been a certain amount of latent hostility between them, the shift of immediate authority within the compound on the death of the foster parent may be critical. While this man is still alive, loyalty to him (and indeed often his active support against his own sons) controls the overt expression of hostility. Once he dies, the sons may find ways of letting their 'brother' know that he is no longer welcome. He, for his part, may be unwilling to accept the authority of older kinsmen of his own generation, whereas he was willing to acknowledge it from a member of the senior generation.

A related factor is the residence of a man's mother. By the time her son has married and begun to establish his own family, she will probably have left his father, either as a widow or in terminal separation. If she has come to join his foster parent, the son will have a strong obligation to remain and farm for her. Furthermore, he could not now leave his foster home without leaving his mother behind. A very strong reason would be needed to justify his return to his paternal kin. If a man remained out of respect to his mother, her death would soon be followed by his departure. It is most unlikely that he would fear the anger of her spirit, since it is thought that every man will eventually wish to join his father's people.

But it is not unusual for a man to marry and rear his own children in the compound of a foster parent, and to remain there after both this man and his mother have died. By this time, he is likely to be well-established in the community in his own right, and indeed may even have his own compound. There is still another set of factors which may bring the head of even a mature, apparently settled household, back to his paternal village. These are pulls associated with paternal identity, rather than pressures to leave the foster home. One such pull is the death of his own father. If there has been a pattern of avoidance between them, this is now at an end. For as we have seen, the spirit of a dead father is believed to guide and warn his sons, and even if he chastises, to do so in a relatively gentle way.

Avoidance is strongest between a man and his eldest son, but any son who lives in the same compound with his father will find it hard to establish autonomy even within his own household. The father is likely to continue to treat him like a youth long after he has married. Once the father has died, a son can return to live in his paternal compound without coming under the domestic authority of any member of the senior generation. Finally, for the eldest of the siblings, the death of the last of his 'fathers' (that is, of his father's brothers) marks an even greater transition. He is automatically placed in a position of seniority over his younger siblings. He will hold this status wherever he is living, and it is his right to be informed and consulted on important matters where they are concerned. If, however, the elder brother is living in the paternal compound, he will have in addition to the final authority conveyed by his seniority, immediate authority over those of his 'brothers' and 'sisters' who live there, and over their children. Even where the compound is small and kinsfolk few, the opportunity to succeed to a compound headship is among the most important things that can happen to a man. For as a compound head he has a form of title, he is Langwura, and represents his people in the affairs of the village. Indeed, for a man who has no access to political or ritual office, compound headship probably offers the nearest thing to a position of prominence to which he can aspire.

POLITICAL CONSIDERATIONS

The authority conveyed by the convergence of kinship status and compound headship comes very close to political authority, for even if they hold no formal office, compound heads are recognized as elders and men of importance. But for members of all three estates, succession to office is often a critical factor in the decision as to where to live. The commoners who succeed in securing one of the few chiefships reserved for sons of women of the ruling estate tend to have been reared by their mother's 'brothers' in the divisional capital. The irregular succession of the previous chief of Busunu is an extreme example of the advantage which may be gained by a sister's son who becomes a favourite of a chief. There are enough cases of commoners who have been given chiefships by their maternal kin to lead the ambitious to hope. Even if they are unsuccessful in their suit for office, living with maternal kin means the relative excitement of life in a chief's compound at the capital instead of the routine of a rural village.

But what kinds of pressures are exerted on men of the ruling estate by their eligibility to office? Such men do not lose their chance of office by living elsewhere, though they must be prepared to live in the capital or the village to which they are appointed, once they take office. There are many examples of men who returned to their father's division after prolonged absence and almost immediately succeeded to a chiefship of importance. Of the three men in Buipe who held chiefships of the first rank under the BuipeWura, only one had been reared in Buipe. The heir apparent to the Busunu skin had only recently returned from his mother's town, Bole, in western Gonja, and taken a title; during my stay in Busunu, the middle-aged son of the BusunuWura returned after many years of 'roaming about' to take a chiefship during the Damba celebrations. Even the refusal of a less important chiefship does not render a man ineligible to take the divisional skin later on. The elder brother of the SilimaWura had declined to take that office when it was offered to him, saying that he was happy where he was in the village of Frufruso. However, when the divisional chief died (after we had left the town) he returned to join his brother, and so rigidly observed is the rule of precedence for the elder sibling that he, a man without even a title, was given the Buipe skin instead of the SilimaWura.

The fact that a member of the ruling estate does not lose his right to chiefship by prolonged absence from the division still does not explain why so many do not return until middle age. One aspect is undoubtedly the greater personal freedom of life away from the fathers and older brothers who hold chiefships in the capital. For if it is difficult for any son to establish his independence of his father's domestic authority on marriage, it is much more difficult if the father has an office which endows him with political authority as well. However, more important, at least for the Gonja, are the dangers of living in the capital for a man who is not confident of his ability to withstand the mystical aggression of his rivals. "Your father's house is good if you are strong, because some day you will be an important man there. But if you are weak you will suffer greatly." In his mother's home, a man is relatively safe from witchcraft attacks, since her people are not competing with him for office. It should be stressed that it is not so much his own close agnates that a man fears as those of the other dynastic segments. Within his own segment, seniority by age is strictly observed and precedence thus clear. But between segments, this is not so and competition for a vacant chiefship may be intense. Even if a man does not wish to participate in political life, he may fear the attacks of those who do not trust his professed withdrawal. If his father holds a chiefship, his enemies may attack him through his children. Sons of chiefs are thus especially vulnerable.

In central Gonja, Muslim offices tend to circulate within a much smaller group of agnates than the chiefships of the ruling estate. In Buipe only the Sakpare have segments which alternately supply the Limam. Office should go in order of seniority within a generation before dropping to the eldest of the next generation. And as with chief-ship, residence in the divisional capital is not a necessary criterion for eligibility, though one must come and live there on taking office.

RELIGIOUS CONSIDERATIONS

Since there are very few Muslim offices succession can only occasionally be a factor in residential choice. Religion does have a direct influence, however, in that most central Gonja villages have no resident Muslim population, and thus neither mosque, priest, nor congregation. Although a man normally prays by himself, except on Fridays and on special occasions in the annual ritual cycle, there are two fundamental rules of Islam which cause the faithful great anxiety if they are isolated from other Muslims. One is the prohibition against eating meat that has not been properly killed. By Gonja non-believers this is seen as a rule against eating the meat of dead animals, that is, those shot or trapped in the bush rather than killed in the market by a Muslim butcher. There are no markets in central Gonja and a proper diet is difficult for a Muslim living on his own. The second source of concern is that a man will be overtaken by death far from a priest, and be buried in un-consecrated ground without the prayers which ensure his salvation. Considerations of this kind probably underlie the relative infrequency with which Muslim boys are sent to be fostered by commoner relatives in the outlying villages. They are also important in understanding the tendency for those who are fostered by non-Muslims to return home at an early stage.

The converse of the situation in which a man of the Muslim estate seeks to avoid isolation from his religious community, is that where the sons of Muslim women by 'pagan' fathers tend to take up residence with their maternal kin. There were two sets of brothers in Buipe who had left the compounds of commoner fathers to live with their mother's people who were Sakpare. For these converts, continued residence with their paternal kin meant daily embarrassment over the sharing of food among the young men of the compound. They remained on cordial terms with their paternal kin, but found it easier to co-operate with other Muslims. When a commoner youth has been fostered by a Muslim kinsman, he will have learned the Koran as a normal part of his childhood. Although he still visits his paternal village and may well marry there, it is very difficult for such a man to return to live in a rural village away from those who share his values and the rules which govern his daily life.

ECONOMIC CONSIDERATIONS

We have seen that the main constraint affecting household viability is the requirement of a man to farm and a woman to cook; the household is usually also a conjugal unit. If this unit breaks down, then either of the partial households may become viable again if attached to another household able to supply the missing service. Household viability also depends on both farmer and cook doing their jobs effectively. Thus only a healthy man can support his wife and children on his own. An elderly man, or one who is unwell, will need help from sons or foster children. All men seek assistance with the clearing of new farms. This help can be secured by exchanging one's own labour on other men's farms for their help in turn. Or a man unable to farm himself can summon a working party by providing a feast at the end of the day. Neighbours, kin of all kinds, even strangers, may provide the basis for such a work force. While it is every man's hope that he will have his adult sons living and farming with him, many do not achieve this. And it is possible to maintain an independent household alone so long as strength lasts.

(i) *Sons and 'sons'*
As a man grows older, the viability of his household becomes a potential problem. If his own son is living with him, or even living in the same village, he will work his father's fields. A brother's son ought to do so as well, but in practice this is limited to cases where he is living in his 'father's' compound. Otherwise, he will give his 'father' produce, but not work fields in his name. The same holds for a sister's son. If he is

290

living with his mother's brother he will continue to farm for him even when he has his own fields and family. Thus for an older man the residence of married 'sons' in his compound can augment or replace the help of his own sons. A compound head is in a stronger position still, since all those of a junior generation to him in the compound are his 'sons'. In practice, distantly related 'sons' will not farm for a compound head regularly, but they may be depended on for a few days concentrated work at intervals.

From the point of view of the junior generation, the decision as to whether to return to the paternal home seems to be little affected by considerations of land or labour. Only if he were to settle in a town where he had no kin would a man have trouble in establishing his farms. If he takes the long view, however, and is concerned about what sons he may draw to settle with him, his father's village has an important advantage. While his own sons will probably be equally likely (or unlikely) to remain with him wherever he lives, and his sister's son will do so only on the basis of special bonds forged through fostering, his brothers' sons are tied to the paternal compound through sentiment, supernatural protection, and their agnatic identity. We shall return to this point when we come to look at the variations in the developmental cycle which characterize each estate.

(ii) *Inheritance*

The basic productive resources, then, are land and adult labour. Neither of these is transmitted to a man's descendants. Wealth and kinship authority are inherited together, as a single trust, known as *kapute*. In fact, if a man has several items of wealth, some may be distributed among his favourites and closest kin. But *kapute* is thought of as impartible, and ought never to go to the primary kin, own siblings and own children. Thus the relationship between inheritance and residence can only be indirect. Further, as the example of the inheritance of Mallam Aleidu's *kapute* illustrates (and there are a number of similar cases on record), there is no need for the heir to live in the same town as the previous holder. Indeed, the prevailing pattern of inheritance between maternal kin means that residence in different towns is probably the norm, especially where it is the children of sisters who are holder and heir. Inheritance of property is central to the maintenance of the pattern of obligations among close maternal kin, but only occasionally does heirship coincide with residence in the same compound.

The problem of transmission of property from a man to the sister's son he has raised is more complex. This relationship is not considered too close for inheritance safely to occur. Some indeed maintain that, when a sister's son remains to farm in adulthood with the maternal uncle who reared him, it is only right that he should take the *kapute*. Others dispute this, saying that he may have an elder sibling, also a descendant in the maternal line, but entitled by age to inherit before his younger brother. If such selective transmission does occur it is among the Dompo and possibly the Mpre of south-central Gonja and not among the Hanga of the more northerly areas; and certainly not in the ruling and Muslim estates. Where it does occur, selective inheritance by a fostered sister's child would constitute a very strong incentive for remaining with the foster parent in adulthood. The four commoner compound heads who are living in the village or compound of a maternal relative (Table 10-7) may have inherited property in this way, but data on this point are not available.

'ROAMING ABOUT'

'Roaming about', which has long been customary for young men of the Muslim and ruling estates, reflects a mixture of economic and status motivations. For Muslims, learning to read the Koran is only the first step in a scholarly and religious education. Many go no further, but those who aspire to more than a life of farming will continue, and often seek teachers in other centres. This period of later training may be supported by farming for the teacher, or the young man may take up trading. The links between Islam and long-distance trade are old and well recognized in the Sudan, and even from a remote area like central Gonja Muslims move easily into the trading communities of the larger towns in Ghana and neighbouring countries. Opportunities for trade in thinly populated central Gonja are now few.

Young men of the ruling estate may also take up petty trading for a time. Before the widespread use of guns led to the virtual extermination of large game, many became skilled hunters. This occupation had associations with the traditional role of the Gbanya as warriors, and the correspondence between skills and medicines used in hunting and in war is close in a number of ways. Either as a trader or a hunter, the youth of the ruling estate could escape the drudgery of farming. There is a rule, never I think strictly enforced, that chiefs do not farm. As all men of the ruling estate are potential chiefs, some use this to justify a refusal to farm. A number of the divisional chiefs, and at least one of the recent paramounts, are spoken of as never having been to the farm. As youths they would not have been forced to go against their will, and as young men a period of roaming about postponed the time when they had to find a way to support a household. For those who try so hard to avoid farming, the eventual decision to settle down is probably precipitated either by the wish to establish a household of their own, or by the opportunity to succeed to chiefship, with the associated headship of a compound and thus the promise of assistance from the young men. In the days when the chiefly families owned slaves, the economic motivation behind roaming about was almost certainly less central than the desire for independence and fear of witchcraft, though the taking of slaves certainly fitted into this pattern, since they occupied themselves with raiding rather than trading.

These are the main considerations influencing a man's decision to remain with non-agnatic kin, to travel or trade in other parts of Gonja or in southern Ghana, or to return to his paternal home. Each man must calculate the gains and costs of the possible courses of action from his own point of view. The most systematic intervening variable is probably his estate identity, and that of his maternal kin.

The choice of compound in which to establish his household determines in large measure those with whom a man will farm and share his food. For his children, the compound provides companions in early years and is still the major determinant of the peer group even in adolescence. His wife will be among strangers wherever her husband chooses to settle, unless the couple are themselves kin, or unless they live in her village or one in which she has relatives. But for most women most of the time married life is lived with in-laws and co-wives. No man would admit to settling in a given village in order to please his wife. And indeed, the marriage tie is fragile enough that if a woman feels strongly about being with her kin, she simply goes.

But in addition to providing the setting for daily economic and social activities, the compound is strongly identified with one of the three estates, usually, though not always, the estate of the compound head. Thus residence in a given compound may either reinforce or mask the estate identity of the constituent households. In order fully to understand the developmental cycle, it must be seen as underlying the pattern of growth and fission of compounds, as well as in terms of the individual's decision about where his own best advantage lies.

VARIATIONS IN THE DEVELOPMENTAL CYCLE AMONG THE THREE ESTATES

The kinship institutions, such as fostering, terminal separation and the ousting of widows, which have the effect of moving people between households, compounds and villages, are important in each of the three estates, as would be expected in a system where open connubium leaves few barriers between them at the domestic level. While the constant circulation of personnel may be a factor in the basic developmental cycle, the variations between estates arise instead from the different roles played by men and women of each estate in the political and economic domains.

The models of the developmental cycle for each estate presented here are, of course, only applicable to the compounds in the divisional capitals of central Gonja. While this must obviously be the case for the Muslim and ruling groups, since they are often poorly represented in the outlying villages, it is also true of the commoner compounds. In the capitals, these latter are often headed by men with a special role in the divisional court: drummers, councillors, war leaders and Earth priests. On the other hand, in a village having only a single chief or shrine priest, the position of a commoner compound head is enhanced by his relatively greater voice in village affairs.

We have seen (Table 10-2) that the compounds associated with all three estates are very similar in the number of residents: the mean varies between nineteen and twenty-one. Despite this similarity, the discussion of residence has suggested that there are three key areas in which the developmental cycles of compounds differ characteristically for each estate. These are (1) the core relatives in the senior generation; (2) the kind of 'son' who remains in adulthood; and (3) the ways in which a compound is related to the others around it. In other words,

Table 11-1. *Relationship of household heads of junior generation to compound head*

		Own son	Agnatic 'brother's' son	Cognatic 'brother's' son or 'sister's' son	
Estate of compound:	Ruling	0	3	7	10
	Muslim	5	0	8	13
	Commoner	6	1	3	10

N=33

the three estates appear to differ systematically in the pattern of kin ties within, and between generations, and in the extension of kin-based relations to other compounds.

THE DEVELOPMENTAL CYCLE OF COMMONER COMPOUNDS

The typical core of a commoner compound is a pair of male 'siblings'.[1] They may be full brothers, paternal or maternal half-brothers, or sometimes parallel or cross-cousins. They frequently have living with them a 'sister' who is either between husbands or has retired from marriage. In the generation below that of the compound head, the junior generation, the head's own sons, his brother's sons and his sister's sons are all apt to appear, though commoner compounds have a higher proportion of the head's own sons than do those of any other estate. A commoner compound head often succeeds in keeping his sons with him even after they have married and established their own households. The classificatory sons are typically closely related to the compound head, being children of a full or half-sibling.

Commoner compounds have a relatively tight structure, centering on close kin. Nevertheless, the junior generation tends to place the rooms of its households so as to form a separate courtyard. Fission into two separate compounds may occur following the death of one or both of the 'fathers'. Where the 'brothers' of the senior generation are themselves cross-cousins, as in Burumbu's compound (described in chapter 10), fission tends to follow quickly on the marriage of the junior generation, or even to be precipitated by a quarrel before this time. There is apparently a natural limit to the size of commoner compounds, not in terms of numbers, but of kinship distance. While full or half-brothers may remain together all their lives, and their children continue for a while in the same compound, mature cousins rarely occupy the same commoner compound. It seems that there are no constraints keeping mature cousins together in the same compound which might balance the advantages of autonomy. And since their own sons are likely to remain with them as adults, they can afford to break away from their 'brothers' and their sons.

Relations between commoner compounds are expressed in terms of particularistic kin ties: "Our fathers were 'brothers' so we still co-operate in farm clearing" or "My mother's brother and I clear farms together." Similar links may also exist between individual household heads in

---

[1] This is not apparent in Table 10-5 because only complete households are analysed in this table. Many commoner men are wifeless, and live with a married 'brother'.

different compounds. Only occasionally, when the commoner compound head holds an important office by virtue of his seniority in his localized patronymic group, will relations between commoner compounds be expressed in terms of common agnatic identity. Even here the relationship is extremely general, and does not necessarily involve reciprocal farm clearing. Thus, the compounds in the Earth priest's section of Busunu are all described as being the 'people' of the Earth priest, but farm clearing groups are based on particularistic kin ties.

THE DEVELOPMENTAL CYCLE OF MUSLIM COMPOUNDS

The picture for Muslim compounds is more complex and, though both large and small compounds are based on an agnatic core, it takes very different forms. The small Muslim compounds in Buipe all belonged to patronymic groups with specialized ritual functions. Three of the seven Muslim compounds were of this type, none containing more than a single complete household. In one case the agnatic core was represented by an elderly Mallam and his adult son, only the latter being married. In another the elderly Muslim and his own wife comprised the single household, but the married son was absent. In the third case the household was polygnous, and headed by the divisional spokesman. His adolescent sons would provide a second generation of agnates in due course, assuming they remained in Buipe. In these three compounds there is no question of explaining a variety of kinship links in the junior generation. There is but a single married son of any kind among them, although two were headed by elderly men. Yet there is evidence that absent sons do return to fill the offices vacated on a father's death. Mallam Aleidu had himself returned to take up the Kante Mallamship in just this way after living many years in Daboya. The office in such cases acts as a focus for absent sons' paternal identity, while allowing them to seek more favourable trading and scholarly opportunities elsewhere in youth and middle age.

In these small compounds there is no room for fission; in fact the provision of a successor in the next generation is a potential problem. At the same time, the office and the patronymic identity with which it is linked provide an incentive for the lone elder to retain his residential autonomy by maintaining a separate compound instead of moving in with cognates, as each of these men easily could have done. For they all had widely ramified cognatic links with individuals in compounds associated with all three estates, but no outside agnatic ties.

The second type of Muslim compound in Buipe is that found in the

Sakpare complex. Although there are several compounds which function almost entirely as independent units, in developmental terms they are best seen as consisting of two agnatic male cores, a courtyard of 'sisters' and a compound of 'sisters' ' and 'daughters' ' sons. The agnatic cores contain paternal half-brothers and parallel cousins, and in the next generation, sons of the compound head. Despite the fact that there are several 'brothers' of the two compound heads, none of their married sons are living there; only immediate ties of filiation to the compound head seem to be of sufficient strength to keep younger Sakpare men in a remote area like central Gonja. The obligations on brothers' sons to stay and farm for a compound head are weaker than those on sons of the head himself. And perhaps they see fewer of any benefits there may be from their 'father's' Limamship. For whatever reason, this group has gone elsewhere. 'Sisters' and cognatically related 'brother's' sons, however, are well represented over the three compounds of the Sakpare cluster. Two-thirds of the households of the junior generation are of this type.

The two agnatic cores alternate in providing the Limam to the Paramount, though now he stays in Buipe. The compound of the segment holding the Limamship retains his sons, though not those of his brothers. The other segment is represented by the surviving younger brothers of the previous Limam, who are now of the 'fathers' generation. Their married sons are also elsewhere. It ought to be one of these 'fathers' who next succeeds to the Limamship. At that point, on the death of the present Limam, his segment will be represented by his sons, but most of their own sons will probably have moved out to the centres of trade. If this is in fact the process underlying the Sakpare residence pattern, what we have is a constant sloughing off of brothers' sons who leave to trade and study elsewhere. The sons of the Limam himself feel obliged to remain and farm for him, and thus do not establish themselves in the Muslim communities of more prosperous centres; when their father dies, they remain in the same way as the sons of the previous Sakpare Limam.

All of the large number of returned 'sisters' and 'daughters' claim some relationship to the previous Limam because the compound in which they have their rooms is still designated as belonging to him. Many of them, however, are sisters of the men who have left to trade or settle elsewhere. The apparently disproportionate number of women thus represents the female members of sibling groups whose males have moved out. These women have returned because they cannot follow the laws of Islam in the outlying villages where there are no other

Muslims, and they are afraid of dying without the benefit of ritual services. Some are supported by 'brothers' and others by sons who have accompanied their mothers. These younger married men have a separate compound where they and their wives can live apart from the surveillance of mothers (and mothers-in-law). It is unlikely that many of these men will return to the more remote villages, though some no doubt will do so when their mother dies. Others will move out and set up their own compounds as *tuba* (commoner converts to Islam) elsewhere in the town. There were two compounds in Buipe which had probably originated in this way. One is considered to be Muslim, but, although they use the Sakpare patronymic, they do not fit into any Sakpare genealogy, except through women. Those in the other compound have lapsed in the present generation and are no longer practising Muslims; three of the more determined converts have returned to live with the Sakpare.

Very broadly, most of the brothers leave, some permanently; a few remain to provide the Limam and maintain the agnatic core of the two Sakpare segments from which the Limam is chosen. Many sisters and daughters, probably a high proportion of those who live to old age, return. Many bring with them sons who settle and to some extent replace the Sakpare men who move out. These sons of sisters and daughters live as Muslims, but most of them in a compound separate from those of the agnatic cores. Some will return to their paternal compounds or villages when their mothers die. Others will move out to establish their own compounds, some to become accepted as Muslims, others to revert to commoner ways.[2]

THE DEVELOPMENTAL CYCLE OF COMPOUNDS OF THE RULING ESTATE

Chiefs must live either in the divisional capital or in the village which they rule. Thus, the core of the compounds of the ruling estate in the capitals consist of chiefs and their agnates. Unlike compounds of the other estates, those headed by chiefs seldom contain their full or paternal half-brothers, or father's brothers' sons. If there is another man of the chief's own generation, he is almost always a 'woman's child'.

The residence of sons in the ruling estate is the mirror image of that

---

[2] For acephalous societies the conversion of Muslim traders into pagan farmers has been documented for the Mafobe Dagarti of Jirapa (J. Goody 1954: 32) and the Hen'vera clan of Isala (Rattray 1932: ii, 472). Here too intermarriage appears to have been an important factor.

found among the Sakpare Muslims. None of the five compounds of
the ruling estate in Buipe contained a married son of the compound
head, although there were a number of sons of 'brothers' and 'sisters',
who had established households. In part this difference may be due to
the delayed age at which men of the ruling group begin to raise their
families, for there were several adolescent sons of these chiefs living with
them. But there were also married sons who had chosen to live elsewhere. Sons of chiefs appear to prefer the safety of other villages,
often of other divisions, to the risks of mystical attack in their fathers'
capital. Brothers' sons often make the same choice, but a few have
decided to be on the spot to press their own claims to office; they might
feel that a father's brother will be less assiduous on their account than
where his own sons are concerned.

Sisters and daughters return to compounds of the ruling estate, as
to the others, and for much the same reasons. Where Muslim women
come back to seek the comforts of religion, women of the ruling estate
may hope for office, for themselves or for their sons. As with the
Muslims, the sons of 'sisters' and 'daughters' account for two-thirds
of the complete households of the junior generation in the compounds
of the ruling estate. These are men for whom a distant connection with
an office-holder is preferable to unembellished commoner status. Their
relatively remote relationships with the chiefs who act as compound
heads is expressed by residence either in a separate courtyard or in a
separate compound.

Here, as in the Muslim compounds, fission among agnates has been
anticipated by the residence of many brothers, sons, and brothers'
sons outside the capital. Those who do return stress their paternal
identity by living in the compound of their 'father', the chief.

To recapitulate, in commoner compounds the core in the senior
generation is either one man or a pair of 'brothers', but these 'brothers'
may be related either agnatically or through a woman. The compound
head's own son is likely to live with him as an adult, but so is a
brother's or sister's son. Either may succeed to the headship of the
compound, which is linked only through particularistic ties to other
compounds.

Muslim compounds always centre around an agnatic core. This may
depend for continuity on the return of an absent son to succeed his
father when he dies. Among the Sakpare, the only large Muslim
patronymic group in any of the three villages studied, the agnatic core
consisted of paternal half-brothers and patrilateral parallel cousins.
In the next generation, only the sons of the acting Limam remained

in adulthood to farm. They were assisted by the sons of returned Muslim women who lived mainly in a separate compound.

The compounds of the ruling estate also centre on an agnatic core, but in the senior generation this rarely contains more than one man, almost always a chief. 'Sons' in the agnatic core tend to be brothers' sons rather than those of the chief himself; the latter come home when it is their turn to succeed to office. This movement produces an oscil-

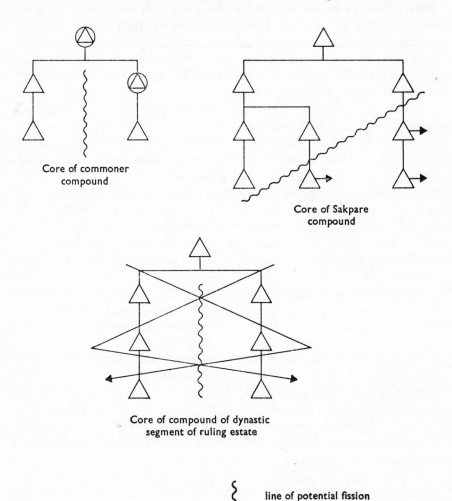

Core of commoner
compound

Core of Sakpare
compound

Core of compound of dynastic
segment of ruling estate

line of potential fission

movement in and out of compound

Fig. 15 Models of kin cores of the compounds of each estate, showing links between generations and lines of fission.

lating pattern of residence, which corresponds to the circulating pattern of succession to office in the ruling estate (J. Goody 1968). Sisters and daughters return between marriages and in old age, and their sons provide a following which usually occupies a separate compound.

Yet, however slender the agnatic core, the headship of compounds of Muslim and ruling estates passes from a man to his own or his brother's son. Commoner compounds, on the other hand, are as likely to be headed by a man living among maternal kin as by a son succeeding in the agnatic line. For, with few exceptions, paternity for commoners is not reinforced by the conveying of important status in the domain of political and ritual affairs.

12

Conclusions

The concept of the developmental cycle allows for consideration of cyclical change in the domestic group, with the birth and maturation of a new generation, its own entry into the reproductive phase, and eventual independence – and the repetition of the pattern. In central Gonja this cycle is worked out not within single or adjacent compounds, but by utilizing ties with a number of villages. Cyclical change incorporates spatial mobility.

In the context of the shaping of domestic groups, this mobility is directly related to marriages between communities, for it is the kinship ties of the next generation with villages of both parents that form the paths along which move foster children, and later sisters and daughters who return after divorce. These kinship ties also supply much, though by no means all, of the motivating energy of the system. A system based on calculated alliances between different communities, ratified by marriage between the families of officials or the well-to-do, would require firm control over marriages of both sisters and wives. It is quite clear, beginning with the institutionalization of courtship, through the middle years of marriage when divorce is endemic, to the final return of older women to their kin, that this control is absent in Gonja.

Open connubium refers to marriages contracted freely between social groups as well as between communities. Although these estates are seen as being different from each other in certain important ways, for example, in having their own 'secrets', constant marriage between them has removed the sense of foreignness. Even in the remote villages of central Gonja, most people have kin in two or even three groups. Again, this is not the outcome of a deliberate policy of alliances but rather the unintended consequence of courtship and of an absence of barriers between groups.

In a society as ethnically and linguistically heterogeneous as Gonja, open connubium itself has certain consequences. The bringing together in a domestic unit of husband and wife from different backgrounds means that the conventions and rituals of family life have somehow to accommodate the ways of both. The balancing of the kin and customs of both spouses appears in many of the domestic institutions considered in this study. One example discussed in some detail was the reduction of the key legitimating rite in marriage to a common minimal factor, namely the marriage kola, which has no economic value but serves as a universally accepted acknowledgement that the marriage has agreement from the kin of both partners. It would seem that marriage transactions must tend towards a common norm if groups of different origin are constantly being brought together by unions between them. It would be impossible for one group to maintain one set of bridewealth transaction (high) and another a different set (low) in the face of continued intermarriage.

The dual orientation to maternal and paternal kin continues to be of immediate relevance throughout a person's life. It is expressed in the institution of terminal separation and widow return, and is a major factor, I believe, in the high level of divorce. Residence with their own kin remains a real possibility to women throughout their early and middle age, even while they are married. Residence with kin in old age is expressly seen as desirable by many women, and experienced by most. Thus, even children who remain with their own parents into adulthood are constantly relating to two separate, but dispersed, sets of kin, and to the communities in which these people live.

For those who are reared by foster parents the picture is the same, but with figure and ground reversed. They grow up with one kin set, but through visits in both directions retain their involvement with paternal kin and the siblings living there. As we have seen, fostering occurs across estate lines as readily as marriage, and its significance for the accommodation of potentially 'foreign' ways is perhaps even greater. For the child, who grows to maturity in a household of a different estate from his own, will come to accept the ways of his foster family as quite ordinary. In his parents' view, however, he is learning the 'secrets' of this group, and can later be expected to explain each to the other.

The balancing of funeral roles and obligations between mother's people and father's people is a particularly clear instance of accommodation to a situation of open connubium. For each set of relatives is responsible for a separate funeral sequence, and can thus perform their rites in their own way. The categories are shared: Burial, Three-day funeral, Seven-day funeral, Forty-day funeral. But there is room for variation in the form of the rites within each category. This balance even appears with respect to the character assigned to ancestors: dead 'fathers' guide and warn their children, and, although they may punish, do so relatively gently. Maternal ancestors, on the other hand, are greatly feared and thought quite likely to cause serious illness or death.

Perhaps the most critical balance of all is that between the transmission in the paternal line of primary citizenship, identity with respect to division and estate membership, and the transmission to maternal 'siblings' of final kinship authority and personal property. In this way the power and wealth which office-holding segments tend to acquire are systematically diffused among maternal kin who belong to any, and often all, of the three estates.

What are the effects in the political sphere of open connubium and the associated institutions which maintain a balance between the kin of mother and father? At the village level, the main units of internal structure are the compounds, that is, clusters of domestic groups represented by a compound head. Through their head, the people of a compound relate directly to the village chief and council. Although the compound is identified with a segment of one of the social estates, the compounds themselves are of heterogeneous composition, and there is no effective polarization of estates in affairs within the village.

Despite remoteness and poor communications, villages outside the capital are not isolated, nor is traffic with them restricted to the formal role they occupy within the divisional constitution. Coming and going is constant between the outlying villages, and with the capital. Perhaps because many people have lived for some time in both types of community, one does not hear disparaging comments about 'country cousins'. Relations between village and capital are experienced as relations with specific people who are kin, or mediated through kin, 'my mother's people' rather than being abstractly categorical, with 'those Bute people'.

Very much the same pattern holds for the mode of relating to people in other divisions. They are not generally grouped into categories in terms of language or region, nor do people ordinarily distinguish between estates within another division in the abstract sense: 'the Mankpa ruling group' or 'the Buipe Muslims'. Rather a Buipe man will say, "My mother was a Mankpa person, she was of the ruling group" or "My father's mother's division is Mankpa, her people could become chiefs there." Again, ties are particularistic, to individuals, or through individuals. In practical terms this means that travel between villages and divisions is facilitated by making use of kin ties to find a host and perhaps a sponsor for one's errand. Even in the mid-1950s when trade caravans and markets were only a dim memory, it was not at all unusual, in any of the three capitals I studied, for a party to arrive from Daboya in the north, Debre to the east, or Bole to the west within the space of a week or two. This mobility is not a universal pattern in northern Ghana, as can be seen from Fortes' observation that in the 1930s many Tallensi had never travelled more than five or ten miles from where they were born. At the individual level each person has an internal map of the society which is based on his own kin ties to people in a few villages. Just as no two people have the same kindred, so in Gonja this map of effective social space is also personal. More than this, the kind of contact on which it is based ensure that it has an immediacy and centrality which also parallel the personal kindred.

At the level of the political system, there is a pattern of opposing fields of force. On the one hand, the division is virtually autonomous *vis-à-vis* the paramountcy, and has no formal links with other divisions except through their joint involvement in the national polity. Yet this interdependence of the divisions at the national level is fundamental. It is perhaps clearest for those divisions which are eligible to supply the paramount himself. But the other divisions also have special roles to play. Mankpa's status as councillor to the paramount, Busunu's reputation for leadership in war, and the special position of Buipe as sanctuary, peacemaker and enrober of the YagbumWura: none of these would have a meaning if there were no state of Gonja. The separatist tendencies latent in any divisional system have been held in check by rewards for each division of filling its allotted role.[1] While the individual has primary citizenship only in his father's division, he has rights as a woman's child in the division of his mother. If his mother was a member of the ruling estate, these rights of secondary citizenship include eligibility to certain minor chiefships. If his mother was a Muslim or a commoner, these rights provide him with a compound to live in and people who will readily support him, an essential prerequisite for farming. He has a right to live there and an identity as a 'woman's child'. Some men use rights of secondary citizenship as a basis for extended periods of residence in their maternal home. Others settle permanently.

It seems probable that this 'dual citizenship' in divisions of both the mother and the father has an effect on the individual level that is analogous to that arising out of the inter-relationships between divisions at the national level. Where a man has rights in two divisions, he is unlikely to wish to see them become enemies. Particularly where a

---

[1] Attempts at secession and rebellion have occurred, and in one case led to the absorption of a division by the others and the banishment of its ruling estate. But the state survives, though at times there has been a gap between eastern and western regions.

man is living with maternal kin but cherishing the hope that one day he may be in line for an office in his paternal home, he will have a vested interest in mediating any disputes that might arise.

In writing of African kingdoms, many authors have tended to stress the role that unilineal descent groups play in their organization, though the function of descent groups is seen as different in these states from that played in the acephalous or segmentary systems found so widely in this continent: African societies, of whatever degree of political development, have often been described as built around a system of descent groups. For example, in the standard collection of studies *African Political Systems* (ed. Fortes and Evans-Pritchard 1940), the accounts of the Zulu, Tswana and Ankole all emphasize the unilineal character of their kinship groups. The fourth account, of a part of the Nupe kingdom, is by Nadel, and it is significant that he, like other writers on northern Nigeria is in doubt about whether he is dealing with a unilineal or a bilateral system (Nadel 1940, 1942; see also M. G. Smith 1955). However in other studies of West African kingdoms such as Ashanti and Yoruba the role of clans and lineages has again been much emphasized (Rattray 1923, 1929; Busia 1951; Fortes 1950; Lloyd 1962).

When we first approached the Gonja, we were struck by the importance of an agnatic genealogy, stemming from the conquering hero, NdeWura Jakpa, as the main calculus of eligibility to high political office. But on looking at the structure of domestic relations, it was the bilateral character which came to the fore. The institutions which proved to be fundamental to domestic and kinship relations are all, in some way dependent on ties through both parents. These institutions are associated in Gonja with a different kinship system from that of their southern neighbours, the matrilineal Ashanti, as well as from the more northern acephalous groups like the Tallensi, the Konkomba and the LoDagaa. However, the Gonja are very similar in many ways to the Lozi of Zambia whom Gluckman has specifically contrasted to the strongly patrilineal Zulu of South Africa. In making this contrast, Gluckman has drawn attention to several features of the same kinship system which I have analysed for the Gonja. These he has recently summarized as follows (Gluckman 1971: 236):

Zulu	*Lozi*
Very rare divorce	Frequent divorce
Marriage endures beyond death of spouse, in true levirate, or sororate (deceased still married to relict, but pro-husband or pro-wife)	No endurance of marriage beyond death

Zulu	*Lozi*
Marriage contractable by dead man or by woman to woman, or by group to woman	No such marriage contractable
Sororal polygyny encouraged	Marriage to near kin of spouse forbidden
Adulterine children to wife's husband	Adulterine children to their genitor
If goods available, high marriage payment	Even if goods available, high marriage payment is unusual

In a paper comparing several societies in northern Ghana (E. and J. Goody 1967) we found that three of these variables (high bridewealth, low divorce and widow inheritance) characterized the acephalous systems while the absence of these features and the presence of widespread fostering and lack of exogamous groups were found among the centralized states and the commoner groups incorporated in them. In other words the complex of bilateral institutions first identified in an African kingdom by Gluckman, and documented in the present study for the Gonja, has a wider distribution in centralized states of northern Ghana, where it contrasts with the kinship institutions of the acephalous unilineal peoples.

In Africa, bilateral systems occur among certain hunting groups such as the Bushmen. But we also find a whole category of important states that seem to be characterized not only by the virtual absence of unilineal descent groups (although they often have dynasties recruited agnatically), but also by a series of other features of the kind noted for the Lozi and the Gonja. We do not expect that these features will always be linked together. But there is growing evidence that this 'bilateral' element is a significant feature of the organization of a number of important states in Africa, in which little reliance is placed upon unilineal groups. This category of 'bilateral states' appears to include not only the Gonja and the Lozi, but probably the other states of the Mossi group – Mamprussi, Dagomba, Nanumba, Wa, Gurma, and Mossi itself.[2] It may also include the Hausa and Nupe of northern Nigeria and some of the small state systems of the interior of Sierra Leone (Mende, Limba, Kuranko).[3] The list is speculative but whatever the particular constellation of traits and the specific names on the list, it is clear that such a category does exist, and that, as Gluckman has insisted for southern Africa, it stands in contrast to kingdoms of the Zulu or Ashanti type.

Can we go further and point to any factors associated with the

[2] See E. and J. Goody 1967.
[3] See Little 1951; Finnigan 1965; Jackson 1971.

difference between 'bilateral' states and those in which unilineal descent groups continue to play a central role in both the political and domestic domains? Any answer must be tentative. But enough has been said in the detailed analysis of kinship in central Gonja to show that it is marked by a continual circulation of men, women and children between compounds whose heads are members of different estates and which are often located in different villages. Such a circulation has political consequences of the kind I have stressed. It also has cultural consequences of the kind I have noted in discussing the formalities of marriage and funerals. This circulation of persons appears to lead to a merging of norms in such a way as to stress the highest common denominator for the groups involved. In kinship terms this is the bilateral component, as can be seen by comparing the matrilineal Dompo and Vagala living outside the Gonja sphere of influence with people of the same groups who have been incorporated into the state. Only those outside Gonja retain unilineal descent group organization at the domestic level.

But the forging of a centralized state does not, as we have seen, always lead to the emergence of a bilateral kinship system. If groups of basically similar culture are brought together in one state, as appears to have happened in Ashanti and in Zululand, then unilineal descent groups are often of continuing importance in the social structure, including at the domestic level. But if a series of ethnic groups of widely different customs are brought together in a state system marked by frequent intermarriage, then the resulting tendency towards a merging of norms appears to facilitate a shift of the kinship system towards the 'bilateral' pole.

In West Africa, Islam has undoubtedly encouraged some of the features among the cluster of kinship variables we have noted. This is especially true of low bridewealth (since Islam advocates a dowry system) and non-exogamous groups (since marriage to a father's brother's daughter is approved). But the Lozi case, as well as the peripheral position of Islam in many of these states, suggests that we must look further. Throughout this account I have tried to stress the inter-relationship of political and kinship variables, the interpenetration of of these two domains by a similar set of factors. Even if the processes by which this association has come about are in doubt, it is important to recognize the existence of a set of African kingdoms whose kinship systems have a pronounced 'bilateral' emphasis. It is equally important to see the implications of bilateral kinship institutions for the political system as a whole, especially as concerns the links on the domestic level which bind together politically differentiated groups.

Appendix I
Distribution of Ethno-Linguistic Groups in Gonja

Language	Geographical position Western Gonja	Central Gonja	Eastern Gonja
Gur languages			
Mossi (Mole-Dagbane) sub-group	Nome Batige Dagari Safalba Mara	Hanga	Dagomba
Grusi sub-group	Vagala Degha (Mo) Kira	Tampolense	
Gurma sub-group			Konkomba Kparli
Senufo sub-group	Nafana		
Kwa languages			
Guang sub-group	Choruba Gbanyito	Dompo Ntereto Mpre? Gbanyito	Nawuri Nchumuru Nterato Mpur? Gbanyito

* Based on: Westermann and Bryan 1952; Manoukian 1952; J. Goody 1954 and 1963.

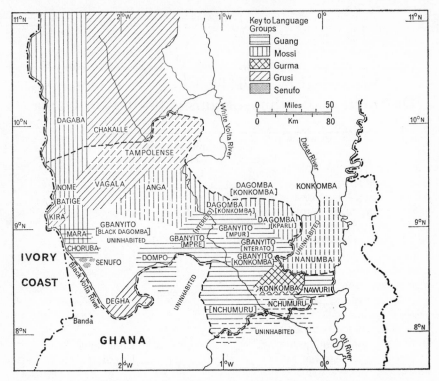

Map IV. The distribution of languages in Gonja. The shading indicates the language of the commoners throughout the State of Gonja; the ruling estate speaks Gbanyito (Gonja). The languages in square brackets are extinct or almost extinct.

Appendix II
Numerical Data on Marriages from other Regions of Gonja

The two surveys on which the following tables are based were made in 1965 and 1966 respectively. The first, the Women's Marriage Survey, was carried out while I was in Bole in western Gonja. It consists of two sub-samples, one from Bole and the other from Daboya in northern-central Gonja (see Maps II and III). For the Bole sub-sample, the town was mapped and a stratified random sample of compounds drawn so as to include the same proportion identified with each estate. All the adult women in these compounds were then interviewed to obtain marital histories and several kinds of related information. For the Daboya sub-sample this was not possible in the time available, so compounds identified with the Muslim and ruling estates were selected, and again all the women interviewed at length. Commoner compounds (apart from one belonging to a Sister's Son chief) were not included in Daboya, since I had no opportunity to study the characteristics of two of the three Daboya commoner groups at first hand. Both Bole and Daboya contain very substantial Muslim populations.

The Men's Marriage Survey is very different. During the early stages of analysis of the Women's Survey, I became concerned about the implications of working with material gathered only from women. By this time I had left Ghana and there was no prospect of an early return. However, my husband was to spend some time in Gonja during the summer of 1966, and he offered to get in touch with a number of our old assistants and arrange for them to carry out a very simple survey. By deciding to confine this survey to three divisional capitals, in each of which I had previously worked for several months, it was possible to pre-select compounds to represent each of the three estates. The interviewers were given the list of compounds to be surveyed, and they filled out a simple questionnaire with each of the adult men ordinarily resident there. Although it was possible for me to clear up a few ambiguities later by letter, for the most part these data could not be checked as in the Women's Survey. While it probably gives a fair indication of differences between regions and estates, the detail and relative precision are not as good.

311

(*a*) MODE OF INITIATING MARRIAGES

Table 1. *Men's Survey: proportion of first marriages initiated by arrangement and by courtship, for three regions of Gonja*

		Region of Gonja:			
		Western (Bole)	Central (Busunu)	Eastern (Kpembe)	
First marriage initiated by:	Arrangement	27 36%	0 0	6 10%	33
	Courtship	48 64%	33 100%	57 90%	138
		75 100%	33 100%	63 100%	N=171 NA=4

Table 2. *Women's Survey (western and northern Gonja): proportion of first marriages initiated by arrangement and by courtship for women of each estate*

		Wife's estate:			
		Ruling	Muslim	Commoner	
First marriage initiated by:	Arrangement	14 42%	22 73%	18 31%	54
	Courtship	19 58%	8 27%	41 69%	68
		33 100%	30 100%	59 100%	N=122 NA= 9

Numerical data on marriages from other regions

(b) FIRST MARRIAGES: WHETHER TO KIN OR UNRELATED SPOUSE

Table 3. *Men's Survey: proportion of first marriages to kinswomen by estate of husband for combined sample*

	Ruling	Muslim	Commoner	
Not kin	56 73%	21 52%	19 59%	96
Cross-cousin*	7 9%	2 5%	4 13%	13
Parallel cousin*	1 1%	1 3%	0 —	2
Other kin	13 17%	16 40%	9 28%	38
	77 100%	40 100%	32 100%	N=149 NA= 26

* Including both first degree and classificatory cousins.

Table 4. *Women's Survey (western and northern Gonja): proportion of first marriages to kinsman for women of each estate*

		First marriage to kinsman:			
		Yes	No		
Estate of wife:	Ruling	16 53%	15 47%	31	100%
	Muslim	16 67%	8 33%	24	100%
	Commoner	17 33%	34 67%	51	100%
		49 46%	57 54%	N=106 NA= 25	100%

(c) ESTATE ENDOGAMY

Table 5. *Men's Survey: proportion of estate endogamous marriages for three regions of Gonja*

		Region of Gonja:			
		Western (Bole)	Central (Busunu)	Eastern (Kpembe)	
Husband and wife are:	Same estate	34 45%	16 53%	29 45%	79
	Different estates	42 55%	14 47%	36 55%	92
		76 100%	30 100%	65 100%	N=171 NA= 4

Table 6. *Women's Survey (western and northern Gonja): estate of husband and estate of wife on wife's first marriage, showing percentage of husbands of each estate with wives of same estate*

		Estate of husband:			
		Ruling	Muslim	Commoner	
Estate of wife:	Ruling	14 33%	10	9	33
	Muslim	4	18 43%	8	30
	Commoner	24	14	19 53%	57
		42 100%	42 100%	36 100%	N=120 NA= 11

Numerical data on marriages from other regions

(*d*) DISTANCE BETWEEN SPOUSES' NATAL VILLAGES

Table 7. *Men's Survey: distances between parents' towns,*
by region of father

		Western Gonja (Bole)		Central Gonja (Busunu)		Eastern Gonja (Kpembe)		
	Same town	35	46%	12	37%	39	61%	86
Distance between towns:	→ 29 miles	23	31%	11	33%	19	30%	53
	30 miles +	17	23%	10	30%	6	9%	33
		75	100%	33	100%	64	100%	N=172 NA= 3

Table 8. *Men's Survey: distances between spouses' towns*
by region of husband

		Western Gonja (Bole)		Central Gonja (Busunu)		Eastern Gonja (Kpembe)		
	Same town	37	50%	14	42%	29	48%	80
Distance between towns:	→ 29 miles	20	27%	6	18%	21	35%	47
	30 miles +	18	23%	13	40%	10	17%	41
		75	100%	33	100%	60	100%	N=168 NA= 7

Table 9. *Women's Survey (western and northern Gonja):
distances between spouses' towns (wife's first
marriage) for women of each estate*

		Wife's estate is:			
		Ruling	Muslim	Commoner	
Village of first husband:	Same	20 56%	14 47%	22 37%	56
	→ 29 miles	7 19%	5 17%	14 24%	26
	30 miles +	9 25%	11 36%	23 39%	43
		36 100%	30 100%	59 100%	N=125 NA= 6

Appendix III
Numerical Data on Divorce from all Gonja

The measures used for the material from the Men's and Women's Marriage Survey[1] are the three ratios discussed by Barnes (1967: 61).

A. The number of marriages ended in divorce expressed as a percentage of all the marriages in the sample.
B. The number of marriages ended in divorce expressed as a percentage of all marriages in the sample that have been completed by death or divorce.
C. The number of marriages ended in divorce expressed as a percentage of all marriages except those that have ended by death.

Barnes notes that ratio C is probably the most satisfactory for comparisons of divorce frequencies in simple societies, as it is less strongly affected by mortality than A, and includes recent marriages, unlike B.

(*a*) DIVORCE RATIOS BY REGION (1966)

The sub-samples of the Men's Marriage Survey covered capitals in eastern, central and western Gonja, and provide an indication of divorce ratios for the three regions. From Table 10 it appears that the incidence of divorce in central Gonja is neither the highest nor the lowest found in the state. The central Gonja sample was from Busunu, for which further data, on women's marriages, is presented below. It is interesting to note that the divorce ratios for Daboya, in north-central Gonja, are very similar to those for Busunu (see Table 11).

Table 10. *Men's Survey: divorce ratios by region*

	Ratio A	Ratio B	Ratio C	Total subjects	Total marriages
Region:					
Eastern					
Gonja	.23	.67	.25	67	115
Central					
Gonja	.29	.61	.36	30	65
Western					
Gonja	.38	.80	.42	78	219

[1] See Appendix II for a description of these samples.

317

(*b*) DIVORCE RATIOS BY ESTATE (1965)

The two sub-samples of the Women's Marriage Survey come from north-central and western Gonja, respectively. Because of the regional differences in divorce ratios the data from each sample is presented separately. However, while the absolute figures for the ratios differ between the two capitals, the same pattern of difference between estates is present in both. In each case the divorce ratios of the women of the ruling estate are substantially higher than those for commoners. Unfortunately only two women of the Muslim estate appear in the Daboya sample.

Table 11. *Women's Survey: divorce ratios for Bole and Daboya*

	Ratio A	Ratio B	Ratio C	Total subjects	Total marriages
Bole* (Western Gonja)	.36	.70	.42	86	115
Daboya* (Northern Gonja)	.25	.55	.32	39	48

* Non-Gonja women, and those whose estate affiliation was unclear, have been omitted from these calculations. As a result the figure for ratio C given here differs slightly from that published in an earlier paper (E. Goody 1969).

Table 12. *Bole Women: divorce ratios by estate*

	Ratio A	Ratio B	Ratio C	Total subjects	Total marriages
Wife's estate:					
Ruling	.51	.83	.57	24	39
Muslim	.23	.50	.29	25	31
Commoner	.31	.67	.37	37	45

Table 13. *Daboya Women: divorce ratios by estate*

	Ratio A	Ratio B	Ratio C	Total subjects	Total marriages
Wife's estate:					
Ruling	.33	.64	.41	15	21
Commoner	.16	.40	.21	22	25
Muslim: too few subjects to calculate divorce ratios. N=2					

(c) CENTRAL GONJA (1957): BUSUNU HEALTH SAMPLE

It proved impossible to use census data for information on the divorce rate because the accuracy necessary for this more complex material cannot be elicited on superficial contact. The censuses were conducted on a single day, so that the replies to the question, "Who slept in this room last night?", would have a uniform meaning and not be complicated by the coming and going of visitors and the regular shifts of co-wives. It has repeatedly been my experience that the number of husbands a woman has had increases directly with the length of one's acquaintance with her. Thus, one of the women I knew best toward the end of my time in the field had told me at length of her various marriages, where they took her and how they came to be dissolved. Yet quite by accident I learned from someone else that she had been married for about two years to still another man. It is true that she had her reasons for not wishing to remember this marriage, but perhaps other women have too.

The following tables are based on records made on all the Busunu women who came to us for medicine. The fact that they had sought us out and wanted something from us made them more patient with detailed questioning than where the reverse was the case. Some comments are in order, however, as to the nature of the sample. Only women of eighteen and above are included, and more than half of these are thirty years of age or under. This does not represent the distribution of this age group in the population as a whole. There are two reasons for this. In the first place, it was our experience in all three villages studied that people were more eager to seek medicine for young children than for themselves. Women under thirty are more likely to have young children than are older women. Secondly, young adults were, not surprisingly, less suspicious of Europeans and their ways, and came to us more frequently than did their elders. There are obvious disadvantages in using a sample heavily weighted in favour of younger women for an analysis of divorce. However, enough older women are included to suggest that the trends continue throughout a woman's life. Information on the marital histories of fifty-five Busunu women is summarized in Tables 14–19.

Table 14. *Percentage of women in each estate and in total sample who have had one and more than one husband*

| | Number of husbands: | | |
	1	2 or more	All
Estate of wife: Ruling	9 64%	5 36%	14 100%
Commoner	27* 66%	14 34%	41 100%
All	36* 65%	19 35%	55 100%

Considering first, in Table 14, women of all ages by estate membership, it is clear that there is no significant difference as to the proportion in each estate who have remarried: about one-third of each group has had more than one husband.

Table 15. *Number of husbands of fifty-five Busunu women by estate and age of wife*

| | | Estate: | | | | | | Number of women |
| | | Ruling | | Commoner | | All | | |
Number husbands:		1	2 or more	1	2 or more	1	2 or more	
	→30	5	1	18*	9	23*	10	33*
Age:	31–40	3	2	6	3	9	5	14
	41+	1	2	3	2	4	4	8
		9	5	27*	14	36*	19	N=55

* Figure includes two women divorced but not yet remarried.

In Table 15 these data are broken down by age and estate. Table 16 retains the age break, but summarizes the data for all estates. As is to be expected, there is a higher proportion who have remarried in the older age groups. While less than one-third of those under thirty had married more than once, half of those over forty had done so.

320

Table 16. *Percentage of women in total sample in each age group who have had one and more than one husband*

		Number of husbands:				
		1		2 or more		
Age of wife:		23*		10		33*
	→30		70%		30%	100%
		9		5		14
	31–40		64%		36%	100%
		4		4		8
	41+		50%		50%	100%

* Figure includes two women divorced but not yet remarried.

Tables 14–16 are concerned with the frequency of remarriage, whether this was occasioned by death or divorce. Information as to how each marriage was dissolved is only available for some of the sample, and the numbers do not allow a breakdown of the data into age groups. Tables 17 and 18 contain the available material.

Table 17. *Manner in which completed marriages ended*

	Number of completed marriages:						
	ONE		TWO		FOUR		
			1 death and		2 deaths and	NA now	
	1 death	1 divorce	1 divorce	2 divorces	2 divorces	ended	Total
Estate of wife:							
Ruling	1	1	0	0	1	2	5
Commoner	4	5	1	1	0	5	16
Both	5	6	1	1	1	7	N=21

Table 17 is based on the twenty-one women in the sample who had completed at least one marriage. They are grouped by estate and by the number of completed marriages. There is no significant difference in the pattern observable for women of the two estates. It is worth noting, however, that multiple remarriages are not necessarily the outcome of a series of divorces. It is impossible to make a general statement on the basis of such low numbers, but observation bears out what the figures at least suggest. That is, women do not fall into two clear groups, one of which tends to form stable unions and the other of which is divorce prone. Table 18 considers the broken marriages recorded in Table 17 by the cause of their dissolution and whether the wife belonged to the ruling or commoner estate. Eleven, or slightly over half of the marriages, were dissolved by divorce. Again there is no significant difference for the women of the two estates.

Table 18. *Manner of termination of nineteen marriages by estate of wife*

| | Marriage ended by: | | |
	Death	Divorce	
Estate:			
Ruling	3	3	6
Commoner	5	8	13
Both estates	8	11	N=19

The last table in this group, Table 19, deals with a problem which is important both for the analysis of the significance of remarriage and for the interpretation of the tables themselves. In this table, the number of husbands reported by the women in the Busunu sample is compared with the number

Table 19. *Number of husbands to whom each woman had borne children, and reported number of husbands*

| | | Reported number of husbands: | | | | |
		1	2	3	4	Total
Number of	0	1	2	1		4
husbands to						
whom living	1	34	2	1		37
children born:						
	2		9		1	10
	3			2		2
Information						
incomplete:		1	1			2
		36	14	4	1	N=55

of husbands to whom they have borne children. There is an incidental finding here worth commenting on. One suggested cause of divorce (Fortes 1949*a*: 87) is barrenness. Of the nineteen women who had remarried, only three had never borne children. Of these, one had been twice widowed and two, once divorced. The latter number represents only about one-tenth of those who have remarried, and it is clear that barrenness is not among the primary causes of divorce in this sample.

As this table shows, there is a close correspondence between the number of husbands women have and the number to whom they bear children. And here it is important to remember that the sample is heavily biased in favour of young women whose child-bearing careers are incomplete. Some who have not yet borne children to their present husbands may still do so, and some will marry and bear children to still further husbands. If we consider all the women in the sample for whom we have information on children born of each marriage, we see that forty-five out of fifty-three, or 85%, have borne children to each husband. If, instead, we consider only those women who have been married at least twice and who have ever borne children, we find that thirteen out of seventeen, or 76%, have borne children to every husband married.

This fact has two important implications. In the first place, it is possible that women are more apt to report marriages in which they have borne children and this is indeed borne out by attempts to obtain detailed marital histories. In several cases additional, childless, marriages were mentioned in later interviews. To the extent that this is the case, the actual frequency of remarriage is higher than indicated by the data here reported. At the same time the figure of 76% of all successive marriages being fertile would be too high. Even so, the figure is high enough to have important implications for the composition of sibling groups. For of the fifty-five women in the sample, twelve or 22% have had children by more than one husband. If we take the figure of 50% for the frequency of remarriage of women over forty (see Table 16), then, assuming that the proportion of fertile marriages to all marriages remains the same, we find that 38% of women over forty may be expected to have borne children to more than one husband. While it is true that fertility declines with age, it is also true that women do not remarry once they have passed the age of child-bearing. The assumption is only partially warranted and the 'true' proportion of women bearing children to more than one husband probably lies somewhere between 27% and 38%.

Appendix IV
Data on Fostering from all Gonja

Additional data on prevalence of fostering throughout Gonja are presented in the following tables. The material from western, northern and eastern Gonja was collected in 1964 and 1965.

Table 20. *Rearing experience of six adult Gonja samples*

	Fostered		Rearing experience: Reared by parents		Total	
	no.	%	no.	%	no.	%
Northern Gonja						
Men	16	(53)	14	(47)	30	(100)
Women	27	(64)	15	(36)	42	(100)
Western Gonja						
Men	41	(53)	36	(47)	77	(100)
Women	50	(56)	39	(44)	89	(100)
Central Gonja						
Men	15	(52)	14	(48)	29	(100)
Eastern Gonja						
Men	6	(15)	33	(85)	39	(100)

Note: The absence of adult women's samples from central and eastern Gonja is unfortunate. However, female fostering is certainly no less prevalent than male fostering in either of these areas. My impression is that girls are fostered slightly more often than boys in Busunu (central Gonja). In eastern Gonja (Kpembe), girls are fostered very much more often than boys.

Table 21. *Distribution of foster children between maternal and paternal kin in five Gonja samples*

	Foster children sent to:					
	Maternal kin no. %	Paternal kin no. %	Others* no. %	Not known no. %	Total no. %	
Northern Gonja						
Boys	6 (38)	9 (56)	1 (6)		16	(100)
Girls	13 (48)	14 (52)			27	(100)
Western Gonja						
Boys	18 (44)	9 (22)	8 (20)	6 (15)	41	(101)
Girls	28 (56)	19 (38)	3 (6)		50	(100)
Eastern Gonja						
Boys	none	5 (83)	1 (17)		6	(100)

* The 'others' category includes those reared by own full siblings, by parents' master or mistress (i.e. children of ex-slaves), by a chief, or by a Koranic teacher.

Table 22. *Crisis and voluntary fostering among men and women of northern and western Gonja*

	Form of fostering:				
	Crisis no. %	Voluntary no. %	Not known no. %	Total no. %	
Northern Gonja					
Men	12 (75)	4 (25)		16	(100)
Women	18 (67)	9 (33)		27	(100)
Western Gonja					
Men*	16 (43)	21 (57)		37	(100)
Women	26 (52)	23 (46)	1 (2)	50	(100)

* These data are taken from a different sample from that used in Tables 20 and 21 (in which there was insufficient information to distinguish between crisis and voluntary fostering).

References

Akenhead, M. (1957), 'Agriculture in Western Dagomba', *The Ghana Farmer*, I, 4.

Barnes, J. A. (1951), *Marriage in a Changing Society*, Rhodes-Livingstone Papers, 20. Cape Town.

(1967), 'The Frequency of Divorce', in *The Craft of Social Anthropology* (ed.) A. L. Epstein. Manchester.

Boateng, E. A. (1959), *A Geography of Ghana*. Cambridge.

Bohannan, P. and L. Bohannan (1953), *The Tiv of Central Nigeria*, International African Institute. London.

Bossard, J. H. S. (1932), 'Residential Propinquity as a Factor in Marriage Selection', *American Journal of Sociology*, 38: 219–24.

Bowdich, T. E. (1824), *A Mission from Cape Coast Castle to Ashantee*. London.

Braimah, J. A. (1970), *The Ashanti and the Gonja at War*. Accra.

Braimah, J. A. and J. R. Goody (1968), *Salaga: The Struggle for Power*. London.

Busia, K. A. (1951), *The Position of the Chief in the Modern Political System of the Ashanti*. London.

Cohen, R. (1971), *Dominance and Defiance*, Anthropological Studies, No. 6. Washington.

Djamour, J. (1959), *Malay Kinship and Marriage in Singapore*, L.S.E. Monographs on Social Anthropology, 40. London.

Dorjahn, V. R. (1958), 'Fertility, Polygyny and their Interrelations in Temne Society', *American Anthropologist*, 60:5.

Finnegan, R. (1965), *Survey of the Limba People of Northern Sierra Leone*. HMSO, London.

Fischer, J. L. (1958), 'The Classification of Residence in Censuses', *American Anthropologist*, 60: 508–17.

Forde, D. (1941), *Marriage and the Family among the Yakö in South-Eastern Nigeria*, L.S.E. Monographs on Social Anthropology, 5. London.

Fortes, M. (1938), *Social and Psychological Aspects of Education in Taleland*, Memorandum XVII, International African Institute, London.

(1945), *The Dynamics of Clanship among the Tallensi*. London.

(1949a), *The Web of Kinship among the Tallensi*. London.

(1949b), 'Time and Social Structure: An Ashanti Case Study', in *Social Structure* (ed.) M. Fortes. London.

(1950), 'Kinship and Marriage among the Ashanti', in *African Systems of Kinship and Marriage* (eds.) A. R. Radcliffe-Brown and D. Forde. London.

References

(1958), Introduction, *The Developmental Cycle in Domestic Groups* (ed.) J. R. Goody. Cambridge.

(1959), *Oedipus and Job in West African Religion.* Cambridge.

Fortes, M. and E. E. Evans-Pritchard (eds.) (1940), *African Political Systems.* London.

Gluckman, M. (1950), 'Kinship and Marriage among the Lozi of Northern Rhodesia and the Zulu of Natal', in (eds.) A. R. Radcliffe-Brown and D. Forde, *African Systems of Kinship and Marriage,* London. For new postscript see *Kinship* (ed.) J. R. Goody, Penguin Modern Sociology Readings, London, 1971.

(1971), 'Marriage Payments and Social Structure among the Lozi and the Zulu, postscript, 1971', in (ed.) J. R. Goody, *Kinship,* London.

The Gold Coast Census of Population 1948: Reports and Tables, 1950. London.

The Population Census of Ghana, 1960. Vol. I. Census Office. Accra.

Goodenough, W. H. (1956), 'Residence Rules', *Southwestern Journal of Anthropology,* 12, 1: 22–37.

Goody, E. N. (1969), 'Kinship Fostering in Gonja' in *Socialization: the Approach from Social Anthropology* (ed.) P. Mayer, ASA Monograph 8. London.

(1970), 'Legitimate and Illegitimate Aggression in a West African State', in *Witchcraft Confessions and Accusations* (ed.) M. Douglas, ASA Monograph 9. London.

(1971), 'Forms of Pro-Parenthood: The Sharing and Substitution of Parental Roles', in *Kinship* (ed.) J. R. Goody, Penguin Modern Sociology Readings. London.

(1972), 'Greeting, Begging and the Presentation of Respect', in *The Interpretation of Ritual* (ed.) J. S. La Fontaine. London.

Goody, E. N. and J. R. Goody (1966), 'Cross-Cousin Marriage in Northern Ghana', in *Man* NS, 1: 343–55.

(1967), 'The Circulation of Women and Children in Northern Ghana', *Man* NS, 2: 226–48.

Goody, J. R. (1954), *The Ethnology of the Northern Territories of the Gold Coast West of the White Volta.* Colonial Office. London.

(1956), *The Social Organisation of the LoWiili.* London.

(1958), (ed.) *The Developmental Cycle in Domestic Groups.* Cambridge.

(1962), *Death, Property and the Ancestors.* Stanford.

(1963), 'Ethnological Notes on the Distribution of the Guang Languages', *Journal of African Languages,* 2: 173–89.

(1966), 'Circulating Succession in Gonja', in (ed.) J. R. Goody, *Succession to High Office.* Cambridge.

(1967), 'The Over-Kingdom of Gonja', in *West African Kingdoms in the Nineteenth Century* (eds.) D. Forde and P. Kaberry. London.

(1969), 'Adoption in Cross-Cultural Perspective', *Comparative Studies in Society and History,* 11: 55–78.

Homans, G. C. (1950), *The Human Group.* New York.

References

Homans, G. C. and D. M. Schneider (1955), *Marriage, Authority and Final Causes*. Glencoe.

Jackson, M. D. (1971), 'The Kuranko. Dimensions of Social Reality in a West African Society'. PhD Thesis, University of Cambridge.

Lewis, I. M. (1962), *Marriage and the Family in Northern Somaliland*, East African Studies 15. Kampala.

Little, K. L. (1951), *The Mende of Sierra Leone*. London.

Lloyd, P. C. (1962), *Yoruba Land Law*. London.

(1968), Divorce among the Yoruba, *American Anthropologist*, 70: 66–81.

Malinowski, B. (1927), 'The Problem of Meaning in Primitive Languages', in *The Meaning of Meaning* (eds.) C. K. Ogden and I. A. Richards. London.

Manoukian, M. (1952), *Tribes of the Northern Territories of the Gold Coast. Ethnographic Survey of Africa*. London.

Marwick, M. G. (1965), *Sorcery in its Social Setting*. Manchester.

Mauss, M. (1954), *The Gift*. Translated by Ian Cunnison. London (originally published 1925).

Mitchell, J. C. and J. A. Barnes (1950), *The Lamba Village: A Report on a Social Survey*. Communication No. 24, School of African Studies. Cape Town.

Nadel, S. F. (1940), 'The Kede: A Riverain State of Northern Nigeria', in (eds.) M. Fortes and E. E. Evans-Pritchard, *African Political Systems*. London.

(1942), *A Black Byzantium*. London.

Oppong, C. (1965), 'Some Sociological Aspects of Education in Dagbon'. (M.A. Thesis) Legon.

(1969), 'A Preliminary Account of the Role and Recruitment of Drummers in Dagbon', *Research Review*, 6:38–51 Institute of African Studies, Legon.

Painter, C. (1970), *Gonja. A Phonological and Grammatical Study*. Bloomington.

Prussin, L. (1969), *Architecture in Northern Ghana*. Berkeley.

Radcliffe-Brown, A. R. (1922), *The Andaman Islanders*. Cambridge.

(1952), *Structure and Function in Primitive Society*. London.

Rattray, R. S. (1923), *Ashanti*. Oxford.

(1927), *Religion and Art in Ashanti*. Oxford.

(1929), *Ashanti Law and Constitution*. Oxford.

(1932), *Tribes of the Ashanti Hinterland*, vol. ii. Oxford.

Schneider, D. M. (1953), 'A Note on Bridewealth and Stability of Marriage', *Man*, 53: 75.

Skinner, E. (1964), *The Mossi of the Upper Volta*. Stanford.

Smith, M. G. (1953), 'Secondary Marriage in Northern Nigeria', *Africa*, 23: 298–323.

(1955), *The Economy of the Hausa Communities of Zaria*. London.

(1960), *Government in Zazzau*. London.

Smith, R. T. (1956), *The Negro Family in British Guiana*. London.

Stenning, D. J. (1959), *Savannah Nomads*. London.

References

Tait, D. (1961), *The Konkomba of Northern Ghana*. London.

Turner, V. W. (1957), *Schism and Continuity in an African Society*. Manchester.

Tutuola, A. (1952), *The Palm-wine Drinkard*. London.

Uchendu, V. C. (1964), 'Kola Hospitality and Igbo Lineage Structure', *Man*, 64:47–50.

Van Gennep, A. (1909), *Les Rites de Passage*. Paris.

Westermann, D. and M. A. Bryan (1952), *Languages of West Africa*. London.

Wilson, M. (1951), *Good Company*. London.

Index

adultery, 73, 74, 76, 113, 159; children born from, 106–7, 307; sanctions against, 75–6, 99, 114, 139–40

affinal relations, 88, 115–20, 214; and marriage, 78, 79; terms of address, 119–20, 140; of wife, 117–19; and witchcraft, 111, 129, 288–9; *see also* parents-in-law

African states, comparison of, 306–8

alliance through marriage, 72, 86, 117, 302

ancestors: danger from, 173, 185, 201–2, 203, 204, 206, 241–8; food given to, 125–6; propitiation of, 99, 105, 168, 234, 243

Ashanti, 5, 7, 9n, 10, 13, 15, 24, 46, 163, 240, 306, 307, 308; attitudes to incest and adultery of, 73; defence against, 32; living in Gonja, 21, 30; and terminal separation, 161

authority, domestic, 59–60, 280–2, 287, 288; final, 57, 195–7, 202, 228–30, 247, 259–60, 268, 281, 287; immediate, 50, 54–9, 178, 224, 228–30, 259–60, 268, 280–1, 283, 285, 286; spheres of, 258–60, 280–5; and women's roles, 161–2

begging behaviour, 2, 168, 184, 187; greeting to beg, 48–9, 50, 68

bilateral system, 306–8

blacksmiths, 21, 46, 217

bridewealth, 94, 141, 153, 303, 307, 308

Buipe division, 28–30, 34, 91; chief of (BuipeWura), 28–9, 91, 274; pattern of chiefship in, 29; three Muslim elements in, 29

Buipe town, 252, 261; change in location of, 29–30; sections of, 39

Busunu sub-division, 30–1, 34; chief of (BusunuWura), 30–1, 38, 91, 117

Busunu town, 37–8

chiefs: competition for office, 8, 14, 48–9, 129, 299; divisional chiefs, 8, 9, 14, 26,

48–9, 72; greeting of, 43, 48; relations with 'subjects', 15–16, 60; residence of, 14–15; Sister's Son chiefs, 9, 29, 37, 38, 51–2, 58, 66, 210; wives of, 115n; and witchcraft, 129; *see also* Yagbum-Wura

chiefship, rules of succession to, 8, 9, 14–15, 31, 87, 165, 218–19, 229

children: after remarriage of mother, 138–9, 178, 223; attitudes towards, 110, 167; born before marriage, 105–7; distribution of on father's death, 154, 165, 197; duties towards parents, 172–6; and grandparents, 179; infant mortality, 123n; residence of, 163–7, 169, 170, 194, 197–9, 223; of siblings, 167, 227–8; *see also* adultery, co-wives, fostering, funerals, parent–child relationship, pawning, witchcraft

circumcision, 123

citizenship, 25, 60, 169, 202, 304

compounds (*langto*), 40–1, 251, 304; composition of, 261, 266–78, 294, 299; co-operation for farm clearing, 53, 54–5, 58, 257; fission of, 58, 260, 269, 295, 299, 300; internal organization of, 50–2, 60, 253, 268, 270, 273, 283–4, 295, 296–7; relations between, 252, 295–6

compound head (*langwura*), 260–1, 296; authority of, 50, 55, 56–9, 61, 280, 285; and farm clearing, 53, 54–5, 296; and house building, 55; and household heads, 263–4, 277–8; succession to office of, 164, 264–6, 301; witchcraft powers of, 128–9

conjugal family: affection and obligation within, 102–3, 259; and estate membership, 302–3; and food production, 52, 53, 225; generation span of, 169; terms of address within, 103, 108

conjugal relationship: affection in, 102, 205; quarrels in, 102; *see also* marital rights and duties

converts to Islam, 10, 11, 97, 298

331

333